Advancing Knowledge and Building Capacity for Early Childhood Research

Edited by

SHARON RYAN, M. ELIZABETH GRAUE,
VIVIAN L. GADSDEN, AND FELICE J. LEVINE

© 2020 American Educational Research Association

Published by the American Educational Research Association
1430 K St., NW, Suite 1200
Washington, DC 20005
Printed in the United States of America

Library of Congress Cataloging-in-Publication Data
Names: Ryan, Sharon, editor. | Graue, M. Elizabeth, 1956- editor. |
    Gadsden, Vivian L., editor. | Levine, Felice J., editor.
Title: Advancing knowledge and building capacity for early childhood
    research / edited by Sharon Ryan, M. Elizabeth Graue, Vivian L. Gadsden,
    Felice J. Levine.
Description: Washington : American Educational Research Association, 2020.
    | Includes bibliographical references and index.
Identifiers: LCCN 2020007397 | ISBN 9780935302820 (paperback) | ISBN
    9780935302837 (epub)
Subjects: LCSH: Early childhood education—Research. | Child
    Development—Research.
Classification: LCC LB1139.225 .A48 2020 | DDC 372.21072—dc23
LC record available at https://lccn.loc.gov/2020007397

Cover Design: Kathleen Dyson

Advancing Knowledge and Building Capacity for Early Childhood Research

Acknowledgments

This volume emanated from a research conference entitled "Advancing Knowledge and Building Capacity for Early Childhood Research: Creating Synergies Among Segregated Scholarly Communities," held in July 2015 by the American Educational Research Association (AERA). The conference was undertaken with core funds of the association and the enthusiastic support of AERA Council, with the aim of advancing research to integrate research traditions in early childhood education and early childhood development.

We are grateful for the opportunity to bring together scholars from a range of perspectives to discuss critical issues about early childhood education. We thank all of the meeting participants and the AERA staff who made it a productive gathering. We also want to thank Kathryn Nakagawa, of Arizona State University, who led the conference with us.

A particular shout-out goes to AERA's Christy Talbot for facilitating communication along the way. The authors who contributed to the volume have been patient beyond belief as the chapters received independent blind review and the book made its way through the publication process. Most important, they have written thoughtful pieces that we believe will catalyze future research on early childhood education and early childhood development. Thanks to the reviewers of individual chapters and of the collection overall, and to the AERA publications staff, who made sure we had a professional product. In particular, we wish to thank John Neikirk, director of publications, and Martha Yager, AERA managing editor, for their standards of high quality and efficiency in moving this work along.

We are also grateful for the chance to work together. It has been a special opportunity to fuse our perspectives and expertise to integrate work and ideas across early childhood development and early education. We are pleased that we are now positioned to share this collection with a wide community of scholars in education research and other related fields and disciplines.

Sharon Ryan
M. Elizabeth Graue
Vivian L. Gadsden
Felice J. Levine

Contents

Chapter 1

Reframing Research in Early Childhood Education: Debates, Challenges, and Opportunities

SHARON RYAN

Rutgers University

M. ELIZABETH GRAUE

University of Wisconsin, Madison

In 2015, the American Educational Research Association (AERA) sponsored a conference designed to bring together scholars who represented different perspectives on the research, methods, and practice of early childhood education. The catalyst for the conference was recognition that while many scholars focus on early childhood, they often work in intellectual siloes, rarely interacting. Here is an excerpt from the invitational letter to scholars engaged in this area of research:

> The boundaries of research communities are particularly stark between those who come from practice in early education (studying teacher education, curriculum, social context), and those who employ disciplinary perspectives to analyze the topic of early education and its effects (child development researchers, economists, and policy researchers). One consequence of these boundaries is a striking lack of symmetry between graduate preparation, research funding, and publication venues that exacerbates the lack of communication among important groups of scholars. Yet early childhood education is an interdisciplinary field requiring that researchers of different communities work together to address complex problems of policy and practice.

A multidisciplinary group met in the summer of 2015, engaging in discussions about the many ways scholars engage in topics related to early childhood education. This volume comes out of that conference. It is designed to reflect how scholarly perspectives shape the contours of knowledge generation. In addition, we hope to illuminate the invisible gaps that prevent productive interchange among scholars who value equity in the opportunities available to young children, their families, and teachers/caregivers.

To do this we include work from people who come at early education from diverse perspectives. But we go beyond the inclusion of different voices to draw attention to the ways that these various perspectives allow us to see certain things and how they obscure others. This is not a subtractive exercise. Instead, we point to limits as opportunities for scholarly attention, as places that researchers from different viewpoints might work together to form a more extensive picture of young children's opportunities, their families' experiences, and their teachers' work.

In the rest of this chapter, we describe some of these opportunities by exploring questions of who and what is researched and how certain kinds of research are used to inform policy. We point to the implications of these patterns—which have produced an early childhood knowledge base with depth in some areas and underdeveloped gaps in others—in the hope that more balanced approaches to early childhood research will be found.

Multiplicity in Early Childhood Education Research and Practice

The care and education of children from birth through age 8 has been a messy space in policy, practice, and research. (Hereinafter, we will use the term *early childhood education* to refer to education for children in this age range.) In efforts to meet wide-ranging societal needs, researchers interested in child care, Head Start, nursery school, kindergarten, and early elementary school reflect many different perspectives on (a) the purposes of early childhood programs (e.g., the "whole child" versus academic instruction); (b) who should have access (targeted or universal access); and (c) who should govern programs (public or private entities). Not surprisingly, the field has developed into a multilayered and fragmented array of program offerings, and its complicated evolution continues (Kagan & Kauerz, 2012).

Despite this fragmentation, early childhood education (ECE, which also stands for early care and education) is in the policy spotlight. The attention has brought needed resources, along with increasing standardization and oversight of services. For example, all 50 states now have early learning standards, many for infants and toddlers as well as for preschool through third grade (Graue, Ryan, Wilinski, Northey, & Nocera, 2018). At the same time, there is growing recognition of the importance of the early childhood workforce, and policy makers are interested in creating more consistency and coherence across the birth-through-third-grade continuum. However, we wonder whether the research base has kept pace with the field's many reforms. Teachers, leaders, and policy makers often lack the information they need to make informed judgements about practices that serve the needs of increasingly diverse students and families.

It is not that research on early childhood is sparse. In fact, there are more publications and ECE-focused research centers generating new research findings than ever. Rather, there are unaddressed tensions surrounding the study of young children and the programs that serve them, which contribute to unevenness in the research base that is used to inform policy and practice. The tensions concern age-old questions: Which disciplines and methods are valued by decision makers for policy and practice? What and who is researched? Whose research perspectives are heard? This chapter considers each of these questions in an effort to highlight the tensions that block conversations and synergies among researchers and programs of inquiry. We worry that the lack of interaction could be a barrier to asking the questions, doing the research, and communicating the findings needed to meet the demands of educating young children in the 21st century. We delve into each of these tensions in more depth to provide a context for the chapters that follow.

What and Who Is Researched?

For much of its history, the field of early childhood education in the United States has used the child as the starting point for practice, learning, and programming. Since the second half of the 20th century, knowledge of young children's development has been used as the primary source for decision making on curriculum and instruction (Silin, 1995). One example is the field's reliance on concepts of *developmentally appropriate practice* (Copple & Bredekamp, 2009) for determining best practices. An understanding of developmentally appropriate practice guides teachers to base instruction on knowledge of children's individual needs and cultures as well as on professional understanding of child development at particular ages and stages. Therefore, much of the research focus in early childhood has been on images of the child and children's learning and development and not necessarily on content and early childhood pedagogy (Genishi, Ryan, Ochsner, & Yarnall, 2001). As a result, with a singular focus on the child, key aspects of curriculum and teaching have been overlooked.

Consider the case of teachers and teaching in the early childhood research literature. Research on teaching has been a line of inquiry in K–12 education since the 1960s, yet it is only in the past 15 years or so that teachers have become a focus in the range of settings comprising the early childhood field. Genishi et al. (2001) traced chapters in Virginia Richardson's (2001) *Handbook of Research on Teaching*, noting that most of them focus on early childhood programs such as Head Start (e.g., Beller, 1973; Stallings & Stipek, 1986) or on research methods for observing teaching (Gordon & Jester, 1973), and not specifically on what teachers *do* or *believe*. To be sure, for some time teacher characteristics such as education and years of experience and other workforce features have been a central variable in analyses of program quality and its impact on child development (e.g., Helburn, 1995; Whitebook, Howes, & Phillips, 1990). However, these studies limit their analyses of teaching young children to a finite set of characteristics and provide little insight into what teachers do with children on a daily basis, what knowledge shapes teachers' decision making, and how context mediates teachers' words and actions.

The in-depth and descriptive research on early childhood teaching that has been conducted over the past decade has come from a handful of qualitative researchers interested mostly in teaching in state-funded preschool programs (e.g., Brown, 2009, 2010; Graue, Rauscher, & Sherfinski, 2009; Graue, Ryan, Nocera, Northey, & Willinsky, 2016; Graue, Ryan, Wilinski, Northey, & Nocera, 2018; Wilinski, 2017). Interviews with teachers and observations of their practice on a regular basis illustrate the complexities of this work and highlight how teachers' work is often mediated by the leadership in the teachers' professional settings and by public policy. In other words, it is not just the teachers' education and experience that shape their work. However, this small volume of research, because of its up-close and in-depth approaches, cannot provide straightforward answers to questions about program effects and the like. The findings are always multiply contingent, which is unsatisfying to those seeking to generalize findings. Unfortunately, few studies combine qualitative portraits of early childhood teaching with quantitative data on program quality and child outcomes. As Ryan and Goffin (2008) have argued, in much of the research base on early childhood, teachers are still "missing in action."

There is still much to be learned about the many roles that support early childhood programs. We do not know much about teaching assistants, program leaders, and others providing the infrastructure (Ryan & Whitebook, 2012) that supports those who work directly with young children, as well as those who work at the policy level. Similarly, little is known empirically about teacher education. While early childhood teacher educators have built up a predominantly qualitative research base on their practices, few larger surveys have been conducted on the content of teacher preparation programs and the knowledge, skills, and dispositions of those who deliver these programs. Yet there is an ever-increasing emphasis on the preparation of qualified and certified teachers of young children.

Researchers have compared the effects of specific curriculum models (e.g., High Scope, Creative Curriculum) on children's learning and development, but we are only now seeing work that examines how subject matter other than literacy is taught in settings serving young children. A window on teaching was provided in the many analyses of the Early Childhood Longitudinal Study (ECLS-B and ECLS-K; e.g., Bassok, Latham, & Rorem, 2016; Engel, Claessens, Watts, & Farkas, 2016), using large-scale representative databases to explore the relations among children's entry skills, instructional practices inferred from survey responses, and children's outcomes. As a result of research investments focused on early math (e.g., DREME [Development and Research in Early Math Education] and the Early Mathematics Collaborative), there is a growing knowledge base related to mathematics teaching *and* learning, with strong efforts to translate knowledge into materials for practice. While some of that work has been curriculum focused, much has explored building teacher knowledge.

Similarly, because most studies of curriculum have been comparisons of the impacts of different models, we know much less about *instruction*—the day-to-day interactions between children and teachers around subject matter. Our knowledge base is very shallow when it comes to how early childhood educators teach key concepts. This kind of information is crucial when young children's education is considered a way to ameliorate the effects of poverty.

In summary, an emphasis on young children's development has channeled research into particular areas. As a consequence, a lot is known about how young children develop cognitively, socially, emotionally, and physically, but much less is known about curriculum and teaching in early childhood settings.

Which Disciplines and Methods Are Valued?

Education is an interdisciplinary field. Yet, for much of the history of early childhood education, psychology has been the primary discipline through which young children's education has been considered (Bloch, 1987). Without this psychologically informed work, we would not have Head Start or the Cost, Quality and Outcomes Study (Peisner-Feinberg et al., 1999). More recently, economic analyses have entered discussions about policy and practice. Cost-benefit analyses (e.g., Barnett & Masse, 2007) that show the long-term savings of a high-quality early education have been used repeatedly by policy makers and advocates to argue for increased investment in programs for young children. Adding to this research are a number of longitudinal evaluations of small-scale experimental preschool programs (e.g., Heckman & Karapakula, 2019; and, specifically about the Perry Preschool Program, Schweinhart et al., 2005) and, more recently, state evaluations of public pre-K (e.g., Barnett, Jung, Youn, & Frede, 2013; Lipsey, Farran, & Durkin, 2018). These evaluations look at programs using various quality measures (e.g., Early Childhood Environment Rating Scale [ECERS], Classroom Assessment Scoring System [CLASS]) in relation to child outcomes, and in the case of longitudinal studies, follow-up surveys and other data to determine the long-term impacts of high-quality programs. We have learned a great deal from these analyses, which have been used to make compelling arguments for the importance of high-quality child care and for public pre-K programs.

However, this work has not given us insight into what early childhood programs look like in action, nor do they provide a sense of how programmatic elements come together to produce a high-quality education for young children. While the predominant question posed has been "Does it work?" we know much less about *how* programs are implemented, or how context and culture mediate program enactment. The K–12 education system has embraced the interpretive work of scholars who seek to understand actor sense-making (e.g., Cynthia Coburn or James Spillane); the early childhood community has been less welcoming of research that examines the tangled path of policy on its way to practice (Graue, Wilinski, & Nocera, 2016). Research like this provides a context for work on student outcomes, so that we are more likely to be able to understand why a policy or a curriculum does not work as expected. There is much we could gain if more resources went into this kind of scholarship.

At the same time, there is an ever-growing research base of examinations of early childhood programs using critical and sociocultural theories that are typically not part of policy and practice debates. Drawing on sociology, anthropology, and philosophy, as well as on insights from linguistics, feminism, and so forth, this research not only focuses on practice and policy-in-practice but also troubles some common assumptions about early childhood education. It has shown how much of our developmental understanding is based on studies of White, middle-class children (e.g., New, 1994), raised awareness of the gendered nature of early childhood programming (e.g., Blaise, 2005), and shown how Western notions of early childhood are colonizing (Grieshaber & Ryan, 2018) and what programming looks like in other countries (Cannella & Viruru, 2007). Adair (2010) made a compelling argument for the power of ethnographic knowledge to inform early childhood policy, suggesting that early childhood policies and programs can have location-contingent outcomes. Though being told, "It depends," is unsettling if you are looking for a clear and simple answer, we think that the questions posed in early education require multiple tools, questions, and perspectives to build a robust foundation for practice.

When we think about the knowledge base and methodological approaches that informed the creation of well-known early childhood programs, it can be challenging to apply their lessons to teaching young children in the 21st century. Children and families have become more culturally and linguistically diverse, and new technologies are making knowledge more available and changing the way children learn. Globalization has made early childhood education more international; program participants and their teachers come from every corner of the globe, as do ideas, curricula, and methods that might be used to inform ECE programming. For example, most countries have signed the U.N. Convention on the Rights of the Child, leading some researchers to research with, not on, children and to seek marginalized children's input into programming (e.g., MacDonald, 2014; Ritchie & Rau, 2013; Smith, 2013). Expanding the disciplinary and methodological lenses used to study and understand early childhood education has the potential to ensure that programs remain responsive to changing demands and that our efforts are inclusive of all children, families, teachers, and communities.

Whose Research Perspectives Are Heard?

As we have noted, the field of early childhood education attracts attention from researchers with diverse interests, perspectives, and tools. These researchers study practice, human development, policy, economics, curriculum, critical perspectives, teacher education, sociology, anthropology, and so on. They work to determine precursors, facilitators, and barriers to learning; to design programs that level the playing field for children with very different opportunities; to determine thresholds for ECE investments; to describe and analyze power relations that marginalize some children and families and normalize others; and to critique the discourses embedded in common ECE practices. This diversity on almost every dimension could predict a robust literature that potentially addresses any problem or issue.

However, a critical stumbling block has been the question of what counts as evidence in building knowledge or advancing policy decision making. Often, quantitative researchers looking for generalizability to a given population are not compelled by the rich accounts of experience created through case studies or interpretive research; qualitative researchers resist the certainty implied by surveys of large numbers of teachers or randomized controlled trials of curriculum effects. As a result, the question of what counts as research—a definition that should be settled in an introductory course—persists and prevents us from fully benefiting from the work and perspectives of peers interested in many of the same things.

This leads to a cascade of effects. We live, think, learn, and communicate in siloed communities, making it unlikely that we will produce synergistic questions or solutions. Our students are educated in programs with little appetite for ventures across different perspectives; they are socialized into a way of seeing the world that can preclude other points of view.

Policy makers and funding agencies are more likely to rely on the expertise of researchers who work with large data sets, hoping that the noisiness of the local will be quieted, increasing the certainty of their decisions. And there is much to be gained from big data. But overemphasizing this approach also makes it likely that policy-oriented researchers will not interact with researchers interested in examining practice more closely, and likely that policy makers and funders will not have access to information that can help with effective program implementation. Implementation science researchers (e.g., Halle, Zaslow,

Martinez-Beck, & Metz, 2013) argue that mixed methods approaches to studying early childhood initiatives can account for contextual factors that may influence implementation. In addition, this work may identify levers that can support early program implementation at all levels, from system-wide to the local level. Limiting analyses of implementation to fidelity to program intentions and protocols ignores the many ways that local actors adopt, adapt, and even reject reforms.

This fragmentation means that the architects of early childhood policies, practices, and programs may not know the full range of possible approaches to better understanding early education. For example, it seems that publications create self-referencing communities that focus on particular types of research and are invisible to other research communities. The standards of evidence and the discourses promoted in *Early Childhood Research Quarterly* are quite different from those in *Contemporary Issues in Early Childhood,* and even more different from *Early Years.* Scholars who present for one of the AERA SIGs related to early childhood, or elsewhere in the association, are not very likely to interact with the Society for Research on Child Development or the American Psychological Association. Knowledge of early education is dispersed across different communities, and much of the research is generated in isolation from different perspectives and methodologies.

One consequence of this fragmentation is that qualitative and practice-based researchers rarely interact with those who do large-scale "policy capturing" studies of programs, and rarely do leaders get to see the possibilities of these conversations for improving programming for young children. At the same time, without efforts to include the voices of those who do the work or those researching from critical perspectives, we may be stuck in the same debates about the purposes of early education, who should participate in its programs, and the key program components. This is a waste of considerable intellectual capital and quite short-sighted when the communities and circumstances in which early education operates continue to become more complex.

Conclusion

In this introduction, we have tried to articulate the social conditions that have fashioned the knowledge production of different research communities and that ultimately shape knowledge use informing policy and programming for young children. We have chosen to take this approach rather than describing authors' contributions to the volume—they more than adequately represent their thinking and we could not do them justice. We hope this context-setting will serve as a window to the field as you read the rest of the book.

As we look back on the conditions that prompted us to propose the conference in 2015, we are both grateful and curious. We are grateful for the opportunity to bring together a group of smart, engaging scholars who are not often in the same room, at the same conference, or in the same journal, for several days of exchange. We are grateful to those who agreed to write chapters and completed them for this book.

But we are also curious about whether we were able to disrupt the social structures that reflect the intellectual separations that prompted our proposal. Let's look at the evidence. The book originally had three sections: (a) children and families, (b) curriculum and teaching, and (c) systems, cultures, and contexts. As the book began to take shape, we found that the chapters did not speak to each other. Rather than add a section to try to knit the conversations together, we opened up the organization of the book. This was our first lesson, in early childhood parlance, that one playdate does not cement a friendship.

Reviewing the chapters, we think that for the most part, authors stayed in their disciplinary lanes, using their considerable expertise to write about their topics. We benefited from this in many ways, as the discussions had coherence and depth. As a result, the volume reflects state(s) of the field rather than discipline-defying acrobatics.

None of this is to say that the experiment was a failure. We see it as a first step in a long process of dissolving whatever it is that impedes cross-fertilization of ideas in early childhood education research. The different perspectives you will see here reflect a field that is complex, messy, and very much alive with ideas.

In presenting these chapters, we hope that new lines of inquiry will be identified that bring different methodologies and disciplines together and encourage partnerships across research paradigms and communities. We hope that in the many ideas presented here we might find ways to think differently about how we conceptualize young children's education and how it is researched.

References

Adair, J. K. (2010). *Ethnographic knowledge for early childhood.* Policy Brief Prepared for the U.S. Department of Education's Office of Early Learning, 1–2.

Barnett, W. S., Jung, K., Youn, M., & Frede, E. (2013). *Abbott Preschool Program Longitudinal Effects Study: Fifth grade follow-up.* New Brunswick, NJ: National Institute for Early Education Research.

Barnett, W. S., & Masse, L. N. (2007). Comparative benefit-cost analysis of the Abercedarian program and its policy implications. *Economics of Education Review, 26*(1), 113–125.

Bassok, D., Latham, S., & Rorem, A. (2016). Is kindergarten the new first grade? *AERA Open, 1*(4), 1–31. Retrieved from https://doi.org/10.1177/2332858415616358

Beller, E. K. (1973). Research on organized programs of early education. In R. M. W. Travers (Ed.), *Second handbook of research on teaching* (pp. 530–600). Chicago: Rand McNally,

Blaise, M. (2005). *Playing it straight: Uncovering gender discourses in the early childhood classroom.* New York, NY: Taylor & Francis.

Bloch, M. N. (1987). Becoming scientific and professional: An historical perspective on the aims and effects of early education. In T. S. Popkewitz (Ed.), *The formation of school subjects: The struggle for creating an American institution* (pp. 25–62). New York, NY: Falmer.

Brown, C. P. (2009). Pivoting a prekindergarten program off the child or the standard? A case study of integrating the practices of early childhood education into elementary school. *Elementary School Journal, 110*(2), 202–227.

Brown, C. P. (2010). Balancing the readiness equation in early childhood education reform. *Journal of Early Childhood Research, 8*(2), 133–160. doi:10.1177/1476718X09345504

Cannella, G., & Viruru, R. (2007). *Childhood and postcolonialization: Power, education and contemporary practice.* New York, NY: Taylor & Francis.

Copple, C., & Bredekamp, S. (2009). *Developmentally appropriate practice in early childhood programs serving children from birth through age 8* (3rd ed.). Washington, DC: National Association for the Education of Young Children.

Engel, M., Claessens, A., Watts, T., & Farkas, G. (2016). Mathematics content coverage and student learning in kindergarten. *Educational Researcher, 45*(5), 293–300. Retrieved from https://doi.org/10.3102/0013189X16656841

Genishi, C., Ryan, S., Ochsner, M., & Yarnall, M. (2001). Teaching in early childhood education: Understanding practices through research and theory. In V. Richardson (Ed.), *Handbook of research on teaching* (4th ed., pp. 1175–1210). Washington, DC: American Educational Research Association.

Gordon, I. J., & Jester, R. E. (1973). Techniques of observing teaching in early childhood education and outcomes of particular procedures. In R. M. Travers (Ed.), *Second handbook of research on teaching* (pp. 184–217). Chicago, IL: Rand Mc Nally.

Graue, M. E., Rauscher, E., & Sherfinski, M. (2009). The synergy of class size reduction and classroom quality. *Elementary School Journal, 110*(2), 178–201. Retrieved from https://doi.org/10.1086/605772

Graue, M. E., Ryan, S., Nocera, A., Northey, K., & Wilinski, B. (2016). Pulling pre-K into a K–12 orbit: The evolution of pre-K in the age of standards. *Early Years, 37*, 108–122.

Graue, M. E., Ryan, S., Wilinski, B., Northey, K., & Nocera, A. (2018). What guides pre-K programs? *Teachers College Record, 120*(8), 1–36.

Graue, M. E., Wilinski, B., & Nocera, A. (2016). Local control in the era of accountability: A case study of Wisconsin preK. *Education Policy Analysis Archives, 24*(60). Retrieved from http://dx.di.org/10.14507/epaa.24.2366

Grieshaber, S., & Ryan, S. (2018). The place of learning in the systematization and standardization of early childhood education. In G. Hall, F. Quinn, & D. Gollnick (Eds.), *Handbook of teaching and learning* (pp. 257–276). New York, NY: Wiley-Blackwell.

Halle, T., Zaslow, M., Martinez-Beck, I., & Metz, A. (2013). Applications of implementation science to early care and education programs and systems: Implications for research, policy, and practice. In T. Halle, A. Metz, & I. Martinez-Beck (Eds.), *Applying implementation science in early childhood programs and systems* (pp. 269–295). Baltimore, MD: Brookes.

Heckman, J., & Karapakula, G. (2019). *The Perry preschoolers at late midlife: A study in design-specific inference.* Cambridge, MA: National Bureau of Economic Research.

Helburn, S. (Ed.). (1995). *Cost, quality, and child outcomes in child care centers* (Technical Report). Denver: University of Colorado, Center for Research in Economic and Social Policy.

Kagan, S. L., & Kauerz, K. (2012). Early childhood systems: Looking deep, wide, and far. In S. L. Kagan & K. Kauerz (Eds.), *Early childhood systems: Transforming early learning* (pp. 3–17). New York, NY: Teachers College Press.

Lipsey, M. W., Farran, D. C., & Durkin, K. (2018). Effects of the Tennessee Prekindergarten Program on children's achievement and behavior through third grade. *Early Childhood Research Quarterly. 45*(4), 155–176. Retrieved from https://doi.org/10.1016/j.ecresq.2018.03.005

MacDonald, A. (2014). Researching with young children: Considering issues of ethics and engagement. *Contemporary Issues in Early Childhood, 14*(3), 255–269.

New, R. (1994). Culture, child development, and developmentally appropriate practices: Teachers as collaborative researchers. In B. Mallory & R. New (Eds.), *Diversity and developmentally appropriate practices: Challenges for early childhood education* (pp. 65–83). New York, NY: Teachers College Press.

Peisner-Feinberg, E. S., Burchinal, M. R., Clifford, R. M., Culkin, M. L., Howes, C., Kagan, S. L., et al. (1999). *The children of the Cost, Quality, and Outcomes Study go to school* (Technical Report). Chapel Hill: University of North Carolina at Chapel Hill, Frank Porter Graham Child Development Center. Retrieved from https://files.eric.ed.gov/fulltext/ED449883.pdf

Richardson, V. (Ed.). (2001). *Handbook of research on teaching* (4th ed.). Washington, DC: American Educational Research Association.

Ritchie, J., & Rau, C. (2013). Renarrativizing indigenous rights-based provision within mainstream early childhood services. In B. Swadener, L. Lundy, J. Habashi, & N. Blanchet-Cohen (Eds.), *Children's rights in education: International perspectives* (pp. 134–149). New York, NY: Peter Lang.

Ryan, S., & Goffin. S. G. (2008). Missing in action: Teaching in early care and education. *Early Education and Development, 19*(3), 385–395.

Ryan, S., & Whitebook, M. (2012). More than teachers: The early care and education workforce. In B. Pianta (Ed.), *Handbook of early education* (pp. 92–110). New York, NY: Guilford Press.

Schweinhart, L. J., Montie, J., Xiang, Z., Barnett, W. S., Belfield, C. R., & Nores, M. (2005). *Lifetime effects: The High/Scope Perry Preschool Study through age 40*. Ypsilanti, MI: High/Scope Educational Research Foundation.

Silin, J. (1995). *Sex, death and the education of our children: Our passion for ignorance in the age of AIDS*. New York, NY: Teachers College Press.

Smith, K. (2103). A rights-based approach to observing and assessing children in the early childhood classroom. In B. B. Swadener, L. Lundy, J. Habashi, & N. Blanchet-Cohen (Eds.), *Children's rights and education: International perspectives* (pp. 99–114). New York, NY: Peter Lang.

Stallings, J. A., & Stipek, D. (1986). Research on early childhood and elementary school teaching programs. In M. C. Wittrock (Ed.), *Handbook of research on teaching* (3rd ed., pp. 727–753). New York, NY: Macmillan.

Whitebook, M., Howes, C., & Phillips, D. A. (1990). *The National Child Care Staffing Study. Final report: Who cares? Child care teachers and the quality of care in America*. Washington, DC: Center for the Child Care Workforce.

Wilinski, B. (2017). *When pre-K comes to school: Policy, partnerships and the early childhood education workforce*. New York, NY: Teachers College Press.

Chapter 2

Fostering Equitable Developmental Opportunities for Dual-Language Learners in Early Education Settings

Bryant Jensen
Brigham Young University

Eugene E. García
Arizona State University

The first language of a quarter of U.S. children is other than English (E. E. García, Jensen, & Scribner, 2009). Research in recent decades confirms that young children have an impressive capacity for acquiring two or more language systems simultaneously (National Academies of Sciences, Engineering, and Medicine [NASEM], 2017). They do so naturally, through regular activities and social interactions (E. E. García, 2017). Some research shows that young bilingual children demonstrate cognitive and communicative advantages over their monolingual peers (e.g., Bialystok, Luk, Peets, & Yang, 2010), which boost their academic development in early education. Yet high levels of linguistic competence in two or more languages, as with young monolingual children, require exposure to rich and diverse lexical, syntactic, and grammatical structures in daily interactions in and out of school (e.g., Hurtado, Marchman, & Fernald, 2008). Thus, language competencies vary among children learning English as a second language—by immigrant generation, socioeconomic status, language ideology, and community resources (NASEM, 2017).

The labels educators assign to young bilingual children have evolved over recent decades (August & Shanahan, 2006), and today we often refer to these children as *dual-language learners* (DLLs). This label is preferred to "English language learners" (ELLs) because it highlights first language practices as a resource that is critical in the process of teaching and learning in early education programs (Barnett, Yarosz, Thomas, Jung, & Blanco, 2007; Castro, Páez, Dickinson, & Frede, 2011). Effective teachers of young DLLs integrate first and second language practices and afford opportunities for children to do the same (Gumperz, 1982; Hakuta & García, 1989). "Translanguaging" (Gort & Sembiante, 2015) affords instructional opportunities (Cazden, Michaels, & Tabors, 1985) and strengthens social relationships in classrooms (E. E. García, 2005, pp. 27–29). Teachers cannot teach in all languages, but they can employ strategies to support the maintenance of the first language and the development of the second language for young DLLs (Espinosa & Magruder, 2015).

We know from meta-analytic studies and research syntheses that bilingual instructional programs[1] in early education and in the elementary grades tend to be better at producing academic development (in English) than English-only programs (e.g., Rolstad, Mahoney, & Glass, 2005). Research syntheses also show that "quality of instruction is more important than the language of instruction" (Cheung & Slavin, 2012, p. 389). Young DLLs benefit from consistent exposure to both their first and second languages in early education settings, but the research on this subject is limited with regard to the specific supports needed for optimal language learning and academic development. We need to know much more about how early education programs can draw on the social-behavioral assets of young DLLs to enhance their academic development (Jensen, Reese, Hall-Kenyon, & Bennett, 2015). The developmental assets of young DLLs include, yet go beyond, language (e.g., Fuller & García Coll, 2010).

One suggestion is for early educators to conduct regular home visits in order to (a) communicate the value of language and literacy development in the first language as a basis for developing English proficiencies (Castro et al., 2011), and (b) acquire "specific information about individual dual language learners' backgrounds, including their early language learning opportunities, family cultural values, and prior knowledge, so [the educators] can individualize instruction and services" (NASEM, 2017, p. 199). Although educators have been encouraged for several years to conduct home visits to integrate the sociocultural/developmental assets of DLLs and other minoritized[2] children into their teaching (González, Moll, & Amanti, 2005; Souto-Manning, 2013), we need more research on how. Specifically, we need studies that (a) specify sociocultural aspects of teaching, (b) demonstrate how activities like home visits develop early educators' cultural knowledge in/for teaching, and (c) examine how sociocultural aspects relate with other teaching qualities that affect young DLLs' learning and development (Jensen, Grajeda, & Haertel, 2018).

In this chapter, we review the sociocultural context of young DLLs' development (Rogoff, 2003) and make practice and research recommendations to enhance equity in early education. We take the case of Mexican American children because it is illustrative and because these children are the largest ethnic subgroup of DLLs (Crosnoe, 2006). We define "equitable developmental opportunities" as the intersection of high-quality and culturally meaningful interactions in classrooms and other early education settings (Jensen, Mejía-Arauz, Grajeda, García, Encinas, & Larsen, 2020). We assert that establishing the body of evidence necessary to foster equitable opportunities for young DLLs at scale requires scholars to move beyond entrenched epistemological and methodological camps (Yoshikawa, Weisner, Kalil, & Way, 2008). It is necessary to develop new measures and to design and test teaching principles that involve examining the cultural assumptions behind dominant practices in early education.

Young Dual-Language Learners

One in four young children in the United States speaks a language in addition to English at home (Child Trends, 2014). This large number is due to increases in immigration flows beginning in the late 1960s, as well as high fertility rates among immigrants relative to the general U.S. population. Hundreds of languages are represented among DLL children; three in four speak Spanish (Capps et al., 2005). Beginning in the 1990s, immigrant families and their DLL children dispersed in large numbers from concentrated enclaves in large cities and in the Southwest to nontraditional communities in Southern states and the Rocky Mountain region, among other places (e.g., Kochhar, Suro, & Tafoya, 2005). It is difficult to find a school, preschool, or early care program today that does not serve a DLL child and her family.

We know from extant research that young children can attain proficiency in more than one language (e.g., Bialystok, 2010; Genesee, 2010; Unsworth, 2016). Dual-language programs in the early years can produce positive outcomes across multiple domains (Barnett et al., 2007; E. E. García & Frede, 2010; Guofang, Edwards, & Gunderson, 2010; Reyes & Kleyn, 2010). In a review of the research literature, Cheung and Slavin (2012) found that English reading outcomes for Spanish-dominant DLLs were stronger (effect size = .21) for those in bilingual programs than for those in English-only programs.

However, language is not the only relevant factor in early developmental contexts of DLLs. These students and their families vary widely in race, ethnicity, socioeconomic status, immigrant generation, religion, country of origin, legal status, integration, social networks, and so on. All of these factors interact with children's development. Although 9 in 10 DLLs are born in the United States, most live in immigrant families where at least one of the parents was born outside the United States. The early development of DLLs is inextricably related to the types of immigrant experiences their families have (Tobin, Adair, & Arzubiaga, 2013). For example, DLLs with an undocumented parent—2 in 5 of all DLLs—face more precarity and institutional hardship than those with two documented parents (Bean, Brown, Leach, Bachmeier, & Tafoya-Estrada, 2013; Jensen & Bachmeier, 2015). Undocumented parental status is associated with greater poverty, lower rates of preschool enrollment, less support from social programs, and higher levels of family uncertainty (Yoshikawa, 2011; Yoshikawa & Kholoptseva, 2013). Maximizing opportunities for DLLs requires an understanding that language development is interdependent with these and an array of other institutional conditions and cultural practices.

Sociocultural Processes in the Development of Young DLLs

Indeed, ecological and cultural processes interact (Weisner, 2002) to shape the development of DLL children. A recent report by the National Research Council (2012) framed children's competencies in terms of three categories: *cognitive, interpersonal,* and *intrapersonal.* Cognitive competencies include thinking skills such as reasoning, problem solving, and memory. Intrapersonal competencies involve affective and conative skills, such as emotional regulation, initiative, interest, and effort. And interpersonal competencies include collaboration, negotiation, flexibility, responsibility, and empathy. Many "21st-century skills" (e.g., complex communication) cross these domains and are mutually reinforcing (Denham, 2006). Some evidence suggests, for example, that self-efficacy (intrapersonal) has a direct effect on student cognition (Pajares, 1996); critical thinking (cognitive) increases positive interpersonal skills (Durlak, Weissberg, Dymnicki,

Taylor, & Schellinger, 2011); and effective communication (interpersonal) is strengthened by rapidly assimilating complex information (cognitive) (Bedwell, Fiore, & Salas, 2011).

Language practices of young children (DLLs and monolinguals alike) transmit sociocultural values (E. E. García & E. H. García, 2012; Schieffelin & Ochs, 1986). These values underlie daily practices at home, at school, and in the community, which afford and constrain development across cognitive, interpersonal, and intrapersonal domains (Cole & Cole, 2010; Rogoff, 2003; Weisner, 2002). Understanding intersections across these developmental domains is critical to understanding DLL development with regard to language and beyond (E. E. García & Markos, 2015).

A *sociocultural* approach to learning and development involves examining the ways that values and practices within social contexts afford and constrain children's opportunities to learn (Tharp & Gallimore, 1988). It recognizes that institutional contexts—such as home, child care center, early education school, and community—interact to socialize, to develop, and to teach children. Without minimizing significant disagreements among sociocultural researchers "who consider . . . 'mediated action' [versus] 'activity' as the basic unit of analysis" (Cole & Engeström, 2007, p. 485), we highlight three principles that cut across sociocultural studies of child development.

First, children's learning and development comprise community practices across various settings. Learning is a social as well as personal process of change (Packer & Goicoechea, 2000; Palincsar, 1998). Cultural values and beliefs are transmitted and adapted across settings in children's daily routines, both in and outside of school settings (Weisner, 2002). Differences in school and everyday "repertoires of practice" (Gutiérrez & Rogoff, 2003) that teachers and children participate in explain, in part, developmental differences among racial and ethnic groups (Boykin & Bailey, 2000; Trueba, 1988; Varelas, Martin, & Kane, 2012). Yet community practices often vary more within than between racial and ethnic groups (Hand, Penuel, & Gutiérrez, 2012), and repertoires themselves are fluid and adapt with new experiences (Lave, 2009). Thus, stereotypic models conflating race or ethnicity with "culture" are problematic. Associations between sociocultural processes and children's development must be addressed contextually rather than through traditional process-product approaches (Cronbach & Snow, 1977; Dunkin & Biddle, 1974; Gage & Needels, 1989).

Second, young DLLs' development builds on prior cultural knowledge and experience. The ways children organize new knowledge is experiential and, thus, cultural. D'Andrade (1995) refers to the mental structures for organizing and making sense of new knowledge as "cultural models," shaped by value systems regarding the importance of some activities (e.g., playtime, domestic labor, leisurely reading) over others (Tharp & Gallimore, 1988). Cultural models inform who participates in activities, the purpose of participation, and rules of interacting (D'Andrade & Strauss, 1992). Children learn and develop through activity participation in informal and formal settings (National Research Council [NRC], 2009; Rogoff, Mejía-Arauz, & Correa-Chávez, 2015). Classroom interactions that draw on the cultural models of DLL children bolster their understanding of, interest in, and appreciation for academic content (Brophy, 2008; González et al., 2005; Jensen, 2014; Tharp, 1989). Early education settings, however, tend to privilege White and upper-middle-class ways of thinking, feeling, and interacting (Adair, 2014; Boutte, 2012; Ladson-Billings, 2014).

Finally, learning constitutes changes in identity and beliefs. Socioculturalists "reject . . . the view that the locus of knowledge is in the individual" (Palincsar, 1998, p. 348). Learning is as much about becoming a member of a community by adopting day-to-day practices as it is about acquiring knowledge and skills that are assessed through a pencil-and-paper test (John-Steiner & Mahn, 1996; Packer & Goicoechea, 2000). Becoming a member of a community means revising how one sees oneself (McCarthey & Moje, 2002). Young DLLs should be afforded ways of connecting their language and cultural identities with their academic sense of self.

Early Education of Mexican American DLLs

Young children of Mexican origin in the United States are illustrative of the ways that language, culture, and developmental opportunity intersect in early education (Crosnoe, 2006). A review of the literature on the development and early education experiences of Mexican American children highlights the critical need for revised frameworks for teaching. One in seven of all U.S. children has a Mexican-born parent or grandparent (Jensen & Sawyer, 2013). Most Mexican American children themselves are U.S.-born, although about two thirds live in immigrant households and speak Spanish as their first language (Giorguli et al., 2014). Most are DLLs and live in homes with close kin networks in which both Spanish and English are used daily (Hernandez, Denton, & Macartney, 2007). Important family differences exist across variables such as immigrant generation, documented status, and socioeconomic status (Giorguli et al., 2014). Children in immigrant households are more likely than their nonimmigrant counterparts to live in poverty and less likely to have a parent with a high school degree (Telles & Ortiz, 2013). On the other hand, those in immigrant homes are more likely than those in nonimmigrant homes to live with both parents and to have strong filial relationships (García Coll & Marks, 2012; Livas Stein, García Coll, & Huq, 2013).

These sociocultural contexts have implications for the development of young Mexican Americans. Mexican American children in immigrant communities tend to demonstrate strong social-behavioral functioning, though relatively weak academic performance (Fuller & García Coll, 2010; Jensen, Reese, et al., 2015). This developmental profile has been characterized as "paradoxical" (Fuller et al., 2009; García Coll & Marks, 2012) because in mainstream U.S. society, children demonstrating stronger academic/cognitive skills also tend to exhibit stronger social-behavioral competencies (Denham, 2006). The paradox is even more pervasive for DLL than for non-DLL Mexican American children because the former group is more likely to be raised by immigrant parents with less formal schooling who value familism, respect for authority, hard work, and group solidarity (Bridges et al., 2012; Livas Stein et al., 2013; Reese, 2013). Mexican immigrant parents often seek to develop children who are *bien educados,* or well brought up (Knight & Carlo, 2012; Reese, Balzano, Gallimore, & Goldenberg, 1995). Respect is a key cultural value for many Mexican immigrant families, exhibited through children's good manners and deferential ways of addressing adults (Valdés, 1996).

Whereas the values and practices associated with a cultural model of *educación* translate into strong intra- and interpersonal functioning of Mexican American children, in many ways they do not correspond with mainstream socialization practices in early education settings. Some have proposed that differences between cultural models of childrearing in home and school settings explain the developmental paradox of young Mexican American children (Bridges et al., 2012; Livas Stein et al., 2013). Jensen, Reese, et al. (2015) found that kindergarten teachers in rural California underappreciated the social competencies of Mexican American DLL children. Differences between parents' and teachers' notions of social competence led to differences in how they perceived and rated children's proficiencies. On average, teachers rated Mexican American DLL children more than a standard deviation lower than parents did, and the differences had implications for children's oral language development: Rater congruence was associated with greater language gains, beyond the effects of parent and teacher ratings alone.

These findings have direct implications for early education settings. Namely, curricula and instructional activities should be designed in ways that recognize and build on the developmental assets of DLLs (Fuller & García Coll, 2010; Galindo & Fuller, 2010). Early educators should, for example, seek to understand how social competence is characterized across homes of young DLL children, and provide ways of activating these competencies during academic activities in the classroom. Programs should help teachers learn to be responsive to the ways many Mexican American children are raised to be *bien educado* at home by allowing them to interact with peers and with the content in culturally familiar ways (Jensen, 2013). Doing so requires educators to confront cultural biases (González et al., 1995) and move beyond "deficit thinking" (Valencia, 1997) about Mexican-origin families—to learn about family routines and practices and find ways to apply what they learn to classrooms and other early education settings.

Some Sociocultural Aspects of Teaching

Cultural practices and values are affirmed for children through their socialization in daily life. Differences in socialization implicate how children learn, view themselves, and engage with others (Mejía-Arauz, Rogoff, Dexter, & Najafi, 2007). Contradictions in socialization practices across settings (e.g., between home and school) can undermine children's learning and development (Rogoff, Callahan, Gutiérrez, & Erickson, 2016; Tharp, 1989). There are many dimensions of socialization that have implications for young DLL children's interpersonal, intrapersonal, and cognitive development. We reference research in cultural psychology, educational anthropology, developmental psychology, social psychology, and multicultural education to highlight five dimensions (not an exhaustive list): *peer collaboration, choice and expression, authenticity of rewards, examining injustice,* and *role flexibility.* We argue that these five aspects of child socialization are (a) detectable to trained observers, (b) commonplace enough to observe within discrete periods, (c) malleable for improvement in early education settings, and (d) associated with the learning and development of young DLLs. These and other relevant dimensions that are manifest in the daily activities of young DLL children across diverse settings have to do with the *content* as well as the *form* of interactions among children and with adults.

Peer Collaboration

"Self-construal" (Kim, 2002) refers to the socialization of self in relation to others—how DLL children, for example, are brought up to identify with group versus individual activity and accomplishment. This concept has been particularly prominent in distinguishing between Eastern and Western forms of interacting (Greenfield, 1994), as well as between indigenous and European-heritage groups in North America (Deyhle & Margonis, 1995; Rogoff, 2003). It is also relevant for children in immigrant families who value solidarity, interdependence, and collaboration, which contrasts with White, middle-class values of efficiency, competition, and individualism, all commonplace in school settings (Maehr & Zusho, 2009).

Peer collaboration is indicative of an interdependent construal (Jensen, 2014). It refers to the extent to which children coordinate and work together toward a shared objective. In collaborative interactions children take turns, encourage one another, seek and offer help, and synchronize their participation in a variety tasks (López, Najafi, Rogoff, & Mejía Arauz, 2012). An array of prosocial skills (e.g., listening, turn taking, assertion) are required to collaborate well. Young DLL children reared in immigrant households tend to demonstrate proficiency in these skills, which often go unrecognized in early education activities. Some research suggests that minoritized children and DLLs benefit more (in terms of academic performance) than their White, non-DLL peers from "cooperative learning" activities (Slavin, 2010; Stevens & Slavin, 1995; Webb & Farivar, 1994).

Choice and Expression

Another cultural dimension of child socialization, fostering "choice and expression," concerns the opportunities children have to exercise autonomy—to make choices about the tasks they engage in, undertake responsibility, and share and monitor their own thinking. In Western thought, autonomy is often conflated with independence. But "autonomy refers not to being independent, detached, or selfish but rather to the feeling of volition that can accompany any act, whether dependent or independent, collectivist or individualist" (R. M. Ryan & Deci, 2000, p. 74).

Drawing on agrarian cultural values (LeVine & White, 1986), many DLL children in low-income immigrant communities are socialized to be autonomous at early ages (Fuller & García Coll, 2010). For children in these settings, transitioning to formal schooling environments—where "questions of how to 'control' classrooms continue to be central in teachers' training" (Rogoff, 2003, p. 211)—can be alienating. Supporting autonomy in classrooms can help young DLLs develop a greater sense of belonging (Adair, 2014). Au and Mason (1981) found that supporting autonomy in reading activities was associated with stronger interest and classroom participation for young native Hawaiian children (Tharp, 1982). Teachers can support child autonomy by providing task options, allowing free movement, asking for help with classroom functions (e.g., a student may serve as a scribe, distribute materials, or collect papers), encouraging unsolicited comments, scaffolding children's own ideas, and encouraging self-monitoring.

Authenticity of Rewards

"Learning by Observing and Pitching In" (LOPI) is a model for child socialization found in many indigenous communities throughout the Americas (Rogoff et al., 2015). LOPI underlies home experiences of many DLLs from low-income communities.[3] It concerns how children participate in everyday activities at home. Under the LOPI model, the learning goal is for children to contribute as active participants to daily tasks, which implies developing several abilities and kinds of knowledge. Children learn through collaborative and flexible social interactions and by listening and observing closely as they try to figure out how to contribute. LOPI contrasts with the ways learning activities are often socialized at school, where children are segregated from adults with decontexualized tasks (Rogoff et al., 1993).

A central component of LOPI is the way adults motivate child learning and participation: through nonmaterial incentives that are inherent rather than external to the purpose of the activity. Rather than by means of stickers or coupons, which are often used in early education settings, participation is motivated in "authentic" ways—the children work with others to complete a difficult task (Alcalá, Rogoff, Mejía-Arauz, Coppens, & Dexter, 2014). This distinction—authentic incentives versus external rewards to organize and motivate activity participation—is especially relevant to classroom management systems (e.g., marbles in the jar) in early education (Jensen, Mejía-Arauz, Grajeda, García, Encinas, & Larsen, 2020). Praising a child in front of her peers or using external rewards can create cultural dissonance and dissuade classroom participation for some young DLLs and others (Guthrie, Coddington, & Wigfield, 2009; Wentzel & Wigfield, 1998).

Examining Injustice

Another dimension of child socialization concerns how issues of personal and societal fairness and bias are addressed with young children. This includes discussing past and present prejudice and discrimination (by race/ethnicity, gender, religion, social class, etc.) to imagine social change (Durden, Escalante, & Blitch, 2015; Hyland, 2010)—examining the issues, exploring resolutions, and identifying their relevance to children's lived experiences. Young children, including DLLs, perceive and internalize messages about difference and power (S. Ryan & Grieshaber, 2004). They demonstrate a keen ability to talk about complex social issues that for many adults can be difficult (Boutte, Lopez-Robertson, & Powers-Costello, 2011). Conversations about injustice in early education settings, though infrequent, usually arise through the curriculum—for example, during a unit on civil rights. Yet such issues can and should also be raised regularly by parents and teachers in the context of children's daily experiences (Aboud et al., 2012; Derman-Sparks, 1989).

Interpretive studies show that examining injustice can build positive intergroup relations in classrooms (Schofield, 1995) and enhance the "social adjustment and academic performance of minority children" (Ogbu, 1987, p. 320). Examining injustice can help young DLLs and others "believe that they are fully rewarded . . . for their education and hard work" (Ogbu & Simons, 1998, p. 171), develop positive identities (Nasir, Snyder, Shah, & Ross, 2012), and "become reflective and active citizens . . . for social change" (Banks & Banks, 1995, p. 152).

Role Flexibility

Finally, role flexibility refers to the fluidity of roles among adults and children in daily activity. Cultural communities differ with regard to the flexibility of roles between experts (e.g., adults) and novices (e.g., children) when completing tasks (Paradise & Rogoff, 2009). In some communities, experts manage the task exclusively. Roles are rigid, divided and assigned by the expert. In other communities, roles are much more fluid: Though with limited experience, the novice attempts a task with some guidance from the expert (Rogoff, 1990). The focus is on activity completion, and roles are fluidly interchanged as a way to improve the task product as well as the quality of learning. Flexible tasks require close listening and observation on the part of the expert and novice alike (Paradise & Haan, 2009). By focusing attention on the task, participants seamlessly swap roles between "observer" and "performer," without "asking or signaling when [participants are] about to 'take over' or [share] 'turn[s]'" (Paradise & Haan, 2009, p. 193).

In early education settings, flexible roles are enacted when the teacher positions herself as a learner by admitting ignorance, demonstrating sustained interest in children's "funds of knowledge" (González et al., 1995), or summarizing an insight from the child. Children are positioned as authorities when they affirm peers, lead an activity, or share an insight. In flexible classrooms, children and the teacher listen to and observe each other closely. They respect one another's response opportunities by pausing, attending, and not interrupting.

Equitable Teaching for DLLs in Early Education Settings

There is ongoing debate about how to teach young DLLs. Socioculturalists argue that curricula and instruction should connect with children's out-of-school experiences, beliefs, and knowledge (Moll, Amanti, Neff, & González, 1992; Souto-Manning & Mitchell, 2010; Vélez-Ibáñez & Greenberg, 1992). Generalists, on the other hand, contend that qualities of teaching are universal, comprised of variables like analytic discussion (Saunders, Goldenberg, & Hamann, 1992) and behavior management (Emmer & Stough, 2001). They cite inferential research demonstrating that generic aspects of teaching quality bolster development for all children (Hamre & Pianta, 2005; Pianta & Hamre, 2009), and for young DLLs in particular (Downer et al., 2012). These generic aspects include the quality of affective interactions (e.g., praise, warmth, sensitivity), organizational interactions (e.g., management, productivity), and instructional interactions (feedback, scaffolding, analytic questioning, language modeling) (La Paro, Pianta, & Stuhlman, 2004).

Our position is pragmatic. We side with Tharp (1989) and others who contend that both generic *and* sociocultural dimensions of teaching quality matter to the development of young DLLs (see Figure 1). In a study of K–2 classrooms in which most children were Latino DLLs, Reese, Jensen, and Ramirez (2014) found that teachers used Spanish to communicate affect—to provide comfort and assistance and to address problems. During a language arts lesson in one classroom, for example, the teacher was reviewing vocabulary words when she noticed that some DLL children could not see the picture cards. She rearranged the seating, then continued in Spanish: "... ¿en qué están?" [What are they in?]. And the children promptly replied: "*En el árbol*" [in the tree]. Overall, teachers in highly

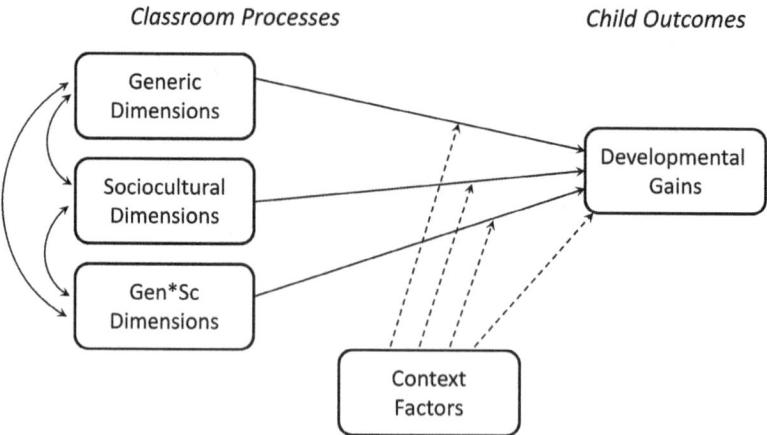

Figure 1. Concept model of the components and effects of equitable teaching. Gen*Sc = interactions between generic and sociocultural aspects of teaching.

emotionally supportive classrooms used Spanish more than six times as often as teachers in less supportive classrooms. Spanish use (a sociocultural dimension) instantiated affective support (a general dimension of classroom quality; Roorda, Koomen, Spilt, & Oort, 2011).

 Thus, we define *equitable teaching* in terms of a combination between generic and sociocultural dimensions (Goldenberg & Gallimore, 1989; Jensen, Mejía-Arauz, Grajeda, García, Encinas, & Larsen, 2020; Tharp, 1989). We submit that cultural dimensions of teacher-child interactions, such as the five discussed above, *instantiate* generic dimensions of quality (Jensen, Grajeda, & Haertel, 2018; Jensen, Pérez Martínez, & Aguilar Escobar, 2016). Figure 1 illustrates this position—how children's development is influenced by generic and sociocultural dimensions of teaching and by the relationships or interactions between them. We suggest that these effects are moderated by contextual factors such as teacher characteristics, child/family background, and other setting variables (e.g., grade level, academic content area). Moderation analyses highlight the situated nature of teaching and learning (Bruner, 1996; Hollins, 2015).

Promising Practices

Our view of equitable teaching as involving a combination of generic and sociocultural dimensions has direct implications for practice with DLLs in early education settings, within and outside of classrooms. Fostering equitable developmental opportunities for young DLLs requires teaching that is both *connected* and *communal*. Teachers enable connected interactions by "actively identifying the relevant knowledge and strengths that students bring to a learning situation" (Bransford, Brown, & Cocking, 2000, p. 78). For connected interactions, teachers learn about and draw regularly on children's out-of-school experiences (routines, relationships, hobbies, interests, traditions, etc.) (Fasheh, 1990; Heath, 1983). Home visits can be a useful way of moving beyond ethnic or socioeconomic stereotypes to learn about what DLL children actually know and do outside of school (González et al., 2005).

Connected interactions incorporate the everyday language practices of young DLLs to build relationships with peers, teachers, and the content (Cazden, 2001; E. E. García, 2005; Jensen & Thompson, 2020). Teachers and children in connected classrooms talk with each other about their out-of-school lives—their routines, hobbies, interests, responsibilities, and family traditions (Weisner, 2002), as well as issues of bias and discrimination (Hyland, 2010). They acknowledge, respect, and appreciate their differences (Cohen & Lotan, 2004), and the teacher often associates out-of-school experiences with the learning objectives of instructional activities. Children "are willing to struggle with . . . abstract notions in science, math, and other content areas when they are motivated by interesting activities they and their families value" (Tharp, Estrada, Dalton, & Yamauchi, 2000, p. 26). Instructional activities in connected classrooms "are situated in problems and issues of students' everyday lives [and] provide vivid opportunities [for] students to stretch their informal understandings to more abstract levels" (p. 26).

Equitable teaching for young DLLs is also communal. Classroom interactions are characterized as interdependent rather than independent and provide children with regular opportunities for exercising choice and for self-expression (Tharp & Gallimore, 1988). Teachers foster collaborative interactions by assigning complementary roles in small group work, encouraging peer assistance and collective problem solving, and scaffolding respectful and analytic peer discussions (López et al., 2012). As mentioned, teachers can allow self-expression and choice by providing children with bona fide task options, allowing them to help with classroom functions, encouraging unsolicited insights, and scaffolding self-direction (Adair, 2014).

Communal classrooms also communicate high expectations of all children in the classroom (Good & Weinstein, 1986). The teacher communicates, through her interactions with children, a firm belief in their capability to succeed. High and equitable expectations are fostered by eliciting participation from all children, providing positive affect to everyone, and by providing adequate time and cues for each child to participate in classroom activities (Jussim, Robustelli, & Cain, 2009). Teachers instill high expectations in all children by praising effort rather than accuracy or ability and grouping children heterogeneously (Ferguson, 2003).

Directions for Future Research

Advocates of *culturally responsive teaching* (CRT) have been making practice recommendations like these in early education for decades (Durden et al., 2015; Gay, 2000; Ladson-Billings, 2014; Mehan, 1998; Souto-Manning & Mitchell, 2010; Souto-Manning et al., 2019; Villegas & Lucas, 2002). Scholars cite affective, sociopolitical, and instructional reasons to enact CRT. Research on CRT demonstrates how cultural concepts (e.g., "funds of knowledge"; González et al., 1995) are associated with instructional quality in particular contexts (Palincsar, 1998). It illustrates how teachers recognize, appreciate, and incorporate the resources of minoritized communities. Studies show how teachers can draw on students' experiences with injustice "to generate knowledge and create new understandings" (Banks & Banks, 1995, p. 153).

Whereas fostering academic performance and other domains of development of minoritized children has been a long-standing aim of CRT (Ladson-Billings, 2014), extant research lacks evidence for educators and policy makers who wish to apply these concepts to enrich the development of young DLLs and others (Gallimore, 2016; Goldenberg, 2008; Jensen, Grajeda, & Haertel, 2018; Lee, 2012; Sleeter, 2012). Most research uses interpretive designs and methods, which elucidate useful constructs and contextual nuance but do not address "the technical problems of bringing [CRT] to scale" (Lee, 2012, p. 353). Indeed, sociocultural and CRT scholarship "have had very little influence on the practices of schooling" (Palincsar, 1998, p. 371) and the learning and development of minoritized children. There is very little empirical information on (a) the ways sociocultural aspects of teaching interact with generic aspects, (b) how these dimensions afford developmental gains for DLLs and other minoritized children, or (c) the ways these effects are moderated by contextual factors (Jensen, 2014).

We recommend three complementary directions for future research. First, there is a need for instruments to measure sociocultural constructs in early education settings (Curenton et al., 2020). These can include observation systems, teacher logs, surveys, or portfolios (Correnti & Martínez, 2012). Measurement work should take as its foundation interpretive research on sociocultural constructs associated with DLL development in situ. The Classroom Assessment of Sociocultural Interactions (CASI) is an example of this—an observation protocol designed to measure ten sociocultural dimensions of classroom interactions, organized into three domains: Life Applications, Self in Group, and Agency (Jensen, Grajeda & Haertel, 2018; Jensen, Mejía-Arauz, Grajeda, García, Encinas, & Larsen, 2020). Scores are assigned at the indicator level; the numerical average among indicator scores comprises dimension scores, and the average of dimension scores comprises domain scores. Life Applications indicators are scored from "disconnected" to "well connected"; Self in Group and Agency are scored from "Not Communal" to "Communal." At the domain level, CASI demonstrates adequate reliability (G coefficients = .75 to .77), although with greater variation in reliability among dimensions. Appropriate CASI uses include research and improvement—preservice and in-service teacher learning and development, complementing (rather than in lieu of) generic measures like the Classroom Assessment Scoring System (CLASS; Pianta & Hamre, 2009). CASI was not designed for summative teacher evaluation or to make decontextualized prescriptions for classroom practice.

Second, there is a need for more intervention development research integrating sociocultural constructs in early education settings with DLLs (Jurich, Iddings, & Clift, 2017). Using design-based research (DBR) methods (Cobb, Confrey, DiSessa, Lehrer, & Schauble, 2003), Valdés, Capitelli, and Alvarez (2011) developed an after-school, volunteer-based program (called One-on-One English) to enrich English development of K–3 Latino DLLs in a small California school district. Gathering assessments on children's oral language (receptive and expressive language, sound blending, and listening comprehension), videotaped interactions, and field notes, the One-on-One team sought to improve young DLLs' oral English by analyzing relationships between theories of second language acquisition (SLA) and SLA pedagogy. Volunteer training, materials use, learning activities, and designed interactions were changed iteratively as data on child performance, field notes, and observations were analyzed. The researchers found that DLLs' English proficiency grew when volunteers provided children with plentiful opportunities to "develop interpersonal, interpretive, and presentational communicative competencies" (p. 192). Greater language growth was attributed to interactions that provided opportunities for rapid turn-taking and spontaneous commenting on topics of interest, even when this entailed "departing from the focus of the interaction planned by the volunteer" (p. 95).

Using DBR allowed Valdés and colleagues (2011) to adapt One-on-One in ways that (a) responded to practitioner demands, (b) enhanced program efficacy, and (c) built theory (diSessa & Cobb, 2004). This approach should be used to develop interventions in classroom spaces as well for young DLLs. DBR projects are intended to solve practical problems with fine-grain research advances (Schoenfeld, 1999). Instead of generalizing practice prescriptions, DBR studies identify principles (Brown & Campione, 1996) that can empower practitioners across settings to respond appropriately to local variability (Bell, 2004). DBR studies can be used to develop and validate formative uses of measures of teaching (Jensen, Haertel, & Gomez, 2020).

Finally, in order to scale interventions that incorporate sociocultural constructs, we recommend that experimental designs examine contextual variations in the effectiveness of these interventions. Smaller "tryouts at carefully chosen sites with less, but still considerable, support" (Brown, 1992, p. 172) are followed by "widespread adoption with minimal support" (p. 172) to determine how intervention components demonstrate impact across settings. Contextual analyses should be incorporated into efficacy work to show how attributes of teachers and children "contribute to variability of treatment effects [because] interventions . . . are mediated through people" (Bryk, 2010). Mixed methods (Yoshikawa et al., 2008) as well as moderated mediation models (Preacher, Rucker, & Hayes, 2007) are useful in this regard.

Conclusion

Policy makers, researchers, and educators alike have a "demographic imperative" (E. E. García et al., 2009) to improve the developmental opportunities of young DLLs. Doing so, we have argued, requires us to think more broadly about the social, linguistic, cultural, and educational milieux in which DLLs learn and develop, in and out of school. More than language differences characterize the experiences of young DLLs and shape their development. We need to examine the cultural assumptions of early education programs and practices, and to implore researchers to use rigorous methods to design and test curricular and instructional innovations. We need to address teaching processes *and* learning outcomes, effectiveness *and* contextual variation, and insights from stories *as well as* numbers (Bryk, 2010).

Educating "is an outrageously complex activity" (Shulman, 1987, p. 11). Palincsar (1998) concluded that it is "hard to imagine a more significant challenge . . . than promoting meaningful learning for children . . . who are culturally and linguistically diverse" (p. 368). To advance early education and foster equitable developmental opportunities for minoritized children like DLLs, our analyses should question entrenched epistemologies (e.g., interpretivism versus positivism) and bridge disciplinary borders (Yoshikawa et al., 2008).

In this chapter, we drew on a large and interdisciplinary body of research to highlight five sociocultural aspects of teaching that have implications for improving early education. Though not a comprehensive list, they reflect two assertions:

- Cultural (e.g., connected, communal) aspects of teaching in early education interact with generic dimensions (e.g., affective, organizational, instructional) to afford equitable developmental opportunities for young DLLs.

- The effects of cultural dimensions of teaching on the developmental gains of DLLs are moderated by contextual differences, especially the attributes of teachers and children.

We do not suggest that early education settings should strive to replicate home settings or vice versa. Culturally responsive teaching is not cultural appropriation. Our primary concern is fostering equitable development for DLLs and other minoritized children through more meaningful activities and social interactions in early education settings. We submit that the recommendations we offer, for practitioners and researchers alike, have implications for a more inclusive, fair, and harmonious educational experience for all young children.

Notes

1. See NASEM (2017, pp. 254–264) for a summary of instructional model types, including research on their effectiveness.

2. Scholars and advocates in recent years use the term *minoritized* instead of *minority* in order to emphasize that DLLs and other children of color do not have access to equitable opportunity even when they comprise the numerical majority in many communities (Sensoy & DiAngelo, 2012, p. 5). They remain excluded and relegated to an underprivileged status. The term refers to any group that is devalued in society, for example by social class, gender, religion, or native language.

3. Comparative studies have found that LOPI practices are associated more with social class (i.e., maternal education) than with country of origin or ethnicity. Rogoff et al. (1993), for example, found that in shared activities, Guatemalan Mayan mothers with more years of formal schooling were much more similar to middle-class European Americans in their parenting practices than to Mayan mothers with little or no schooling, who favored LOPI practices.

References

Aboud, F. E., Tredoux, C., Tropp, L. R., Brown, C. S., Niens, U., & Noor, N. M. (2012). Interventions to reduce prejudice and enhance inclusion and respect for ethnic differences in early childhood: A systematic review. *Developmental Review, 32*(4), 307–336.

Adair, J. K. (2014). Agency and expanding capabilities in early grade classrooms: What it could mean for young children. *Harvard Educational Review, 84*(2), 217–278.

Alcalá, L., Rogoff, B., Mejía-Arauz, R., Coppens, A. D., & Dexter, A. L. (2014). Children's initiative in contributions to family work in indigenous-heritage and cosmopolitan communities in Mexico. *Human Development, 57*(2–3), 96–115.

Au, K. H. P., & Mason, J. M. (1981). Social organizational factors in learning to read: The balance of rights hypothesis. *Reading Research Quarterly, 17*(1), 115–152.

August, D., & Shanahan, T. (Eds.). (2006). *Developing literacy in second-language learners: Report of the National Litearcy Panel on Language-Minority Children and Youth*. New York, NY: Routledge.

Banks, C. A., & Banks, J. A. (1995). Equity pedagogy: An essential component of multicultural education. *Theory Into Practice, 34*(3), 152–158.

Barnett, W. S., Yarosz, D. J., Thomas, J., Jung, K., & Blanco, D. (2007). Two-way and monolingual English immersion in preschool education: An experimental comparison. *Early Childhood Research Quarterly, 22*(3), 277–293.

Bean, F. D., Brown, S. K., Leach, M. A., Bachmeier, J. D., & Tafoya-Estrada, R. (2013). The implications of unauthorized migration for the educational incorporation of Mexican Americans. In B. Jensen & A. Sawyer (Eds.), *Regarding educación: Mexican-American schooling, immigration, and bi-national improvement* (pp. 43–65). New York, NY: Teachers College Press.

Bedwell, W. L., Fiore, S. M., & Salas, E. (2011). *Developing the 21st century (and beyond) workforce: A review of interpersonal skills and measurement strategies.* Paper prepared for the NRC Workshop on Assessing 21st Century Skills, Washington, DC.

Bell, P. (2004). On the theoretical breadth of design-based research in education. *Educational Psychologist, 39,* 243–253.

Bialystok, E. (2010). Global-local and trail-making tasks by monolingual and bilingual children: Beyond inhibition. *Developmental Psychology, 46*(1), 93–105.

Bialystok, E., Luk, G., Peets, K. F., & Yang, S. (2010). Receptive vocabulary differences in monolingual and bilingual children. *Bilingualism: Language and Cognition, 13*(4), 525–531.

Boutte, G. S. (2012). Urban schools: Challenges and possibilities for early childhood and elementary education. *Urban Education, 47*(2), 515–550.

Boutte, G. S., Lopez-Robertson, J., & Powers-Costello, E. (2011). Moving beyond color-blindness in early childhood classrooms. *Early Childhood Education Journal, 39*(5), 335.

Boykin, W. A., & Bailey, C. T. (2000). *The role of cultural factors in school relevant cognitive functioning: Description of home environmental factors, cultural orientations, and learning preferences.* Baltimore, MD: Center for Research on the Education of Students Placed At Risk.

Bransford, J. D., Brown, A. L., & Cocking, R. R. (Eds.). (2000). *How people learn: Brain, mind, experience, and school.* Washington, DC: National Academies Press.

Bridges, M., Cohen, S. R., McGuire, L. W., Yamada, H., Fuller, B., Mireles, L., & Scott, L. (2012). Measuring the social behavior of Mexican American children. *Early Childhood Research Quarterly, 27,* 555–567.

Brophy, J. (2008). Developing students' appreciation for what is taught in school. *Educational Psychologist, 43*(3), 132–141.

Brown, A. L. (1992). Design experiments: Theoretical and methodological challenges in creating complex interventions in classroom settings. *Journal of the Learning Sciences, 2*(2), 141–178.

Brown, A. L., & Campione, J. (1996). Psychological theory and the design of innovative learning environments: On procedures, principles, and systems. In L. Schauble & R. Glaser (Eds.), *Innovations in learning: New environments for education.* Mahwah, NJ: Lawrence Erlbaum.

Bruner, J. (1996). *The culture of education.* Cambridge, MA: Harvard University Press.

Bryk, A. (2010). *Systematic naturalistic inquiry: Toward a science of performance improvement.* Plenary address given at the annual meeting of the Society for Research on Educational Effectiveness, Washington, DC.

Capps, R., Fix, M., Murray, J., Ost, J., Passel, J. S., & Herwantoro, S. (2005). *The new demography of America's schools: Immigration and the No Child Left Behind Act.* Washington, DC: Urban Institute.

Castro, D. C., Páez, M., Dickinson, D. K., & Frede, E. (2011). Promoting language and literatcy in young dual language learners: Research, practice, and policy. *Child Development Perspectives, 5*(1), 15–21.

Cazden, C. B. (2001). *Classroom discourse: The language of teaching and learning.* Portsmith, NH: Heinemann.

Cazden, C. B., Michaels, S., & Tabors, P. (1985). Spontaneous repairs in sharing time narratives: The intersection of metalinguistic awareness, speech event and narrative style. In S. Freedman (Ed.), *The acquisition of written language: Revision and response* (pp. 51–64). Norwood, NJ: Ablex.

Cheung, A. C., & Slavin, R. E. (2012). Effective reading programs for Spanish-dominant English language learners (ELLs) in the elementary grades: A synthesis of research. *Review of Educational Research, 82*(4), 351–395.

Child Trends. (2014). *Racial and ethnic composition of the child population.* Bethesda, MD: Author.

Cobb, P., Confrey, J., DiSessa, A., Lehrer, R., & Schauble, L. (2003). Design experiments in educational research. *Educational Researcher, 32*(1), 9–13.

Cohen, E. G., & Lotan, R. A. (2004). Equity in heterogeneous classrooms. In J. Banks & C. A. M. Banks (Eds.), *Handbook of research on multicultural education* (2nd ed., pp. 736–750). San Francisco, CA: Jossey-Bass.

Cole, M., & Cole, S. R. (2010). *The development of children.* New York, NY: Worth.

Cole, M., & Engeström, Y. (2007). Cultural-historical approaches to designing for development. In J. Valsiner & A. Rosa (Eds.), *The Cambridge handbook of sociocultural psychology* (pp. 484–507). New York, NY: Cambridge University Press.

Correnti, R., & Martínez, J. F. (2012). Conceptual, methodological, and policy issues in the study of teaching: Implications for improving instructional practice at scale. *Educational Assessment, 17*(2–3), 51–61.

Cronbach, L. J., & Snow, R. E. (1977). *Aptitudes and instructional methods: A handbook for research on interactions.* New York, NY: Irvington.

Crosnoe, R. (2006). *Mexican roots, American schools: Helping Mexican immigrant children succeed.* New York, NY: Teachers College Press.

Curenton, S. M., Iruka, I. U., Humphries, M., Jensen, B., Durden, T., Rochester, S. E., et al. (2020). Validity for the Assessing Classroom Sociocultural Equity Scale (ACSES) in early childhood classrooms. *Early Education and Development, 31*(2), 269–288.

D'Andrade, R. (1995). *The development of cognitive anthropology.* Cambridge, UK: Cambridge University Press.

D'Andrade, R., & Strauss, C. (Eds.). (1992). *Human motives and cultural models.* New York, NY: Cambridge University Press.

Denham, S. (2006). Social-emotional competence as support for school readiness: What is it and how do we assess it? *Early Education and Development, 17*(1), 57–89.

Derman-Sparks, L. (1989). *Anti-bias curriculum: Tools for empowering young children.* Washington, DC: National Association for the Education of Young Children.

Deyhle, D., & Margonis, F. (1995). Navajo mothers and daughters: Schools, jobs, and the family. *Anthropology & Education Quarterly, 26*(2), 135–167.

DiSessa, A. A., & Cobb, P. (2004). Ontological innovation and the role of theory in design experiments. *Journal of the Learning Sciences, 13*(1), 77–103.

Downer, J. T., López, M. L., Grimm, K. J., Hamagami, A., Pianta, R. C., & Howes, C. (2012). Observations of teacher-child interactions in classrooms serving Latinos and dual language learners: Applicability of the Classroom Assessment Scoring System in diverse settings. *Early Childhood Research Quarterly, 27*(1), 21–32.

Dunkin, M. J., & Biddle, B. J. (1974). *The study of teaching.* New York, NY: Holt, Rinehart & Winston.

Durden, T. R., Escalante, E., & Blitch, K. (2015). Start with us! Culturally relevant pedagogy in the preschool classroom. *Early Childhood Education Journal, 43*(3), 223–232.

Durlak, J. A., Weissberg, R. P., Dymnicki, A. B., Taylor, R. D., & Schellinger, K. B. (2011). The impact of enhancing students' social and emotional learning: A meta-analysis of school-based universal interventions. *Child Development, 82*(1), 405–432.

Emmer, E., & Stough, L. (2001). Classroom management: A critical part of educational psychology, with implications for teacher education. *Educational Psychologist, 36*(2), 103–112.

Espinosa, L., & Magruder, E. S. (2015). Practical and proven strategies for teaching young dual language learners. In L. Espinosa (Ed.), *Getting it right for young children from diverse backgrounds: Applying research to improve practice* (pp. 76–113). Upper Saddle River, NJ: Prentice Hall.

Fasheh, M. (1990). Community education: To reclaim and transform what has been made invisible. *Harvard Educational Review, 60*, 19–35.

Ferguson, R. F. (2003). Teachers' perceptions and expectations and the Black-White test score gap. *Urban Education, 38*(4), 460–507.

Fuller, B., Bridges, M., Bein, E., Jang, H., Jung, S., Rabe-Hesketh, S., et al. (2009). The health and cognitive growth of Latino toddlers: At risk or immigrant paradox? *Maternal and Child Health Journal, 13*(6), 755–768.

Fuller, B., & García Coll, C. (2010). Learning from Latinos: Contexts, families, and child development in motion. *Developmental Psychology, 46*(3), 559–565.

Gage, N. L., & Needels, M. C. (1989). Process-product research on teaching: A review of the criticisms. *Elementary School Journal, 89*(3), 253–300.

Galindo, C., & Fuller, B. (2010). The social competence of Latino kindergartners and growth in mathematical understanding. *Developmental Psychology, 46*(3), 579–592.

Gallimore, R. (2016). It depends: The first law of education research and development. In M. C. Hay (Ed.), *Methods that matter: Integrating mixed methods for more effective social science research* (pp. 64–78). Chicago, IL: University of Chicago Press.

García, E. E. (2005). *Student cultural diversity: Understanding and meeting the challenge* (3rd ed.). Boston, MA: Houghton Mifflin.

García, E. E. (2017). A conceptual framework for educational success of dual language learners: Reducing the achievement gap. In S. Wepner & D. Gomes (Eds.), *Giving credence to changing suburban schools* (pp. 148–162). New York, NY: Rowman & Littlefield.

García, E. E., & Frede, E. C. (2010). *Young English language learners: Current research and emerging directions for practice and policy.* New York, NY: Teachers College Press.

García, E. E., & García, E. H. (2012). *Understanding the language development and early education of Hispanic children.* New York, NY: Teachers College Press.

García, E. E., Jensen, B., & Scribner, K. (2009). The demographic imperative. *Educational Leadership, 66*(1), 8–13.

García, E. E., & Markos, A. (2015). Early childhood education and dual language learners. In W. E. Wright, S. Boun, & O. García (Eds.), *The handbook of bilingual and multilingual education* (pp. 301–381). Malden, MA: John Wiley & Sons.

García Coll, C., & Marks, A. K. E. (2012). *The immigrant paradox in children and adolescents: Is becoming American a developmental risk?* Washington, DC: American Psychological Association.

Gay, G. (2000). *Culturally responsive teaching: Theory, research, and practice.* New York, NY: Teachers College Press.

Genesee, F. (2010). Dual language development in preschool children. In E. E. García & E. C. Frede (Eds.), *Young English language learners: Current research and emerging directions for practice and policy* (pp. 59–79). New York, NY: Teachers College Press.

Giorguli, S., Jensen, B., Bean, F., Brown, S., Sawyer, A., & Zuniga, V. (2014). *El bienestar educativo de niños de inmigrantes Mexicanos en los Estados Unidos y en México* [The educational well-being of

Mexican immigrants in the United States and in Mexico]. In A. Escobar, L. Lowell, & S. Martin (Eds.), *Diálogo binacional sobre migrantes Mexicanos en Estados Unidos y México* [Binational dialogue about Mexican migrants in the United States and in Mexico]. Guadalajara, México: Centro de Investigaciones y Estudios Superiores en Antropología Social.

Goldenberg, C. (2008). Teaching English language learners: What the research does—and does not—say. *American Educator, 32*(2), 8–44.

Goldenberg, C., & Gallimore, R. (1989). Teaching California's diverse student population: The common ground between educational and cultural research. *California Public Schools Forum, 3,* 41–56.

González, N., Moll, L., & Amanti, C. (2005). *Funds of knowledge: Theorizing practices, households, communities, and classrooms.* Mahwah, NJ: Lawrence Erlbaum.

González, N., Moll, L., Tenery, M., Rivera, A., Rendon, P., Gonzales, R., & Amanti, C. (1995). Funds of knowledge for teaching in Latino households. *Urban Education, 29*(4), 444–471.

Good, T. L., & Weinstein, R. (1986). Teacher expectations: A framework for exploring classrooms. In K. Zumwalt (Ed.), *Improving teaching.* Alexandria, VA: ASCD.

Gort, M., & Sembiante, S. F. (2015). Navigating hybridized language learning spaces through translanguaging pedagogy: Dual language preschool teachers' languaging practices in support of emergent bilingual children's performance of academic discourse. *International Multilingual Research Journal, 9*(1), 7–25.

Greenfield, P. M. (1994). Independence and interdependence as developmental scripts: Implications for theory, research, and practice. In P. M. Greenfield & R. R. Cocking (Eds.), *Cross-cultural roots of minority child development* (pp. 1–37). Hillsdale, NJ: Lawrence Erlbaum.

Gumperz, J. J. (1982). *Discourse strategies.* Cambridge, UK: Cambridge University Press.

Guofang, L., Edwards, P. A., & Gunderson, L. (2010). *Best practices in ELL instruction.* New York, NY: Guilford Press.

Guthrie, J. T., Coddington, C., & Wigfield, A. (2009). Profiles of reading motivation among African American and Caucasian students. *Journal of Literacy Research, 41*(3), 317–353.

Gutiérrez, K. D., & Rogoff, B. (2003). Cultural ways of learning: Individual traits or repertoires of practice. *Educational Researcher, 32*(5), 19–25.

Hakuta, K., & García, E. E. (1989). Bilingualism and education. *American Psychologist, 44*(2), 374–379.

Hamre, B. K., & Pianta, R. C. (2005). Can instructional and emotional support in the first-grade classroom make a difference for children at risk of school failure? *Child Development, 76*(5), 949–967.

Hand, V., Penuel, W. R., & Gutiérrez, K. D. (2012). (Re)framing educational possibility: Attending to power and equity in shaping access to and within learning opportunities. *Human Development, 55,* 250–268.

Heath, S. B. (1983). *Ways with words: Language, life, and work in communities and classrooms.* New York, NY: Cambridge University Press.

Hernandez, D. J., Denton, N. A., & Macartney, S. E. (2007). Young Hispanic children in the 21st century. *Journal of Latinos and Education, 6*(3), 209–228.

Hollins, E. R. (2015). *Culture in school learning: Revealing the deep meaning.* New York, NY: Routledge.

Hurtado, N., Marchman, V. A., & Fernald, A. (2008). Does input influence uptake? Links between maternal talk, processing speed and vocabulary size in Spanish-learning children. *Developmental Science, 11*(6), F31–F39.

Hyland, N. E. (2010). Social justice in early childhood classrooms: What the research tells us. *Young Children, 65*(1), 82–90.

Jensen, B. (2013). Finding synergy to improve learning opportunities for Mexican-origin children and youth. In B. Jensen & A. Sawyer (Eds.), *Regarding* educación: *Mexican-American schooling, immigration, and bi-national improvement* (pp. 299–324). New York, NY: Teachers College Press.

Jensen, B. (2014). Framing sociocultural interactions to design equitable learning environments. In J. L. Polman, E. A. Kyza, D. K. O'Neill, I. Tabak, W. R. Penuel, A. S. Jurow, et al. (Eds.), *Learning and becoming in practice: The International Conference of the Learning Sciences (ICLS)* (Vol. 2., pp. 903–910). Boulder, CO: International Society of the Learning Sciences.

Jensen, B., & Bachmeier, J. (2015). *A portrait of U.S. children of Central American origins and their educational opportunity.* Washington, DC: MacArthur Foundation.

Jensen, B., Grajeda, S., & Haertel, E. (2018). Measuring cultural dimensions of classroom interactions. *Educational Assessment, 23*(4), 250–276.

Jensen, B., Haertel, E., & Gomez, L. (2020). *Validating formative uses of measures of teaching for school improvement.* Manuscript under review.

Jensen, B., Mejía-Arauz, R., Grajeda, S., García, S. T., Encinas, J., & Larsen, R. (2020). Measuring cultural aspects of teacher-child interactions to foster equitable developmental opportunities for young Latino children. *Early Childhood Research Quarterly*

Jensen, B., Pérez Martínez, G. M., & Aguilar Escobar, A. (2016). Framing and assessing classroom opportunity to learn: The case of Mexico. *Assessment in Education: Principles, Policy & Practice, 23*(1), 149–172.

Jensen, B., Reese, L., Hall-Kenyon, K., & Bennett, C. (2015). Social competencies and oral language development for young Latino children of immigrants. *Early Education & Development, 26*(7), 933–955.

Jensen, B., & Sawyer, A. (2013). Regarding *educación*: A vision for school improvement. In B. Jensen & A. Sawyer (Eds.), *Regarding* educación: *Mexican-American schooling, immigration, and bi-national improvement* (pp. 1–26). New York, NY: Teachers College Press.

Jensen, B., & Thompson, G. (2020). Equity in teaching academic language—An interdisciplinary approach. *Theory Into Practice, 59*(1), 1–7.

John-Steiner, V., & Mahn, H. (1996). Sociocultural approaches to learning and development: A Vygotskian framework. *Educational Psychologist, 31*(3/4), 191–206.

Jurich, D., Iddings, A. C. D., & Clift, R. T. (2017). Using a design-based research approach: Educating early childhood teachers to understand, engage, and teach the culturally and linguistically diverse child. In A. C. D. Iddings (Ed.), *Re-designing teacher education for culturally and linguistically diverse students* (pp. 33–51). New York, NY: Routledge.

Jussim, L., Robustelli, S. L., & Cain, T. R. (2009). Teacher expectations and self-fulfilling prophecy. In K. R. Wentzel & A. Wigfield (Eds.), *Handbook of motivation at school* (pp. 349–380). New York, NY: Routledge.

Kim, M. S. (2002). *Non-Western perspectives on human communication: Implications for theory and practice.* Thousand Oaks, CA: Sage.

Knight, G. P., & Carlo, G. (2012). Prosocial development among Mexican American youth. *Child Development Perspectives, 6*(3), 258–263.

Kochhar, R., Suro, R., & Tafoya, S. M. (2005). *The new Latino South: The context and consequences of rapid population growth.* Washington, DC: Pew Hispanic.

Ladson-Billings, G. (2014). Culturally relevant pedagogy 2.0: a.k.a. the remix. *Harvard Educational Review, 84*(1), 74–84.

La Paro, K. M., Pianta, R. C., & Stuhlman, M. (2004). Classroom Assessment Scoring System (CLASS): Findings from the pre-K year. *Elementary School Journal, 104*(5), 409–426.

Lave, J. (2009). The practice of learning. In K. Illeris (Ed.), *Contemporary theories of learning: Learning theorists . . . in their own words* (pp. 200–208). New York, NY: Routledge.

Lee, C. D. (2012). Conceptualizing cultural and racialized process in learning. *Human Development, 55*(5–6), 348–355.

LeVine, R. A., & White, M. I. (1986). *Human conditions: The cultural basis of educational development.* New York, NY: Routledge & Kegan Paul.

Livas Stein, G., García Coll, C., & Huq, N. (2013). Fostering resilience in Mexican American youth through cultural and family assets. In B. Jensen & A. Sawyer (Eds.), *Regarding educación: Mexican-American schooling, immigration, and bi-national improvement* (pp. 234–254). New York, NY: Teachers College Press.

López, A., Najafi, B., Rogoff, B., & Mejía-Arauz, R. (2012). Collaboration and helping as cultural practices. In J. Valsiner (Ed.), *The Oxford Handbook of Culture and Psychology* (pp. 869–884). New York, NY: Oxford University Press.

Maehr, M. L., & Zusho, A. (2009). Achievement goal theory: The past, present, and future. In K. R. Wentzel & A. Wigfield (Eds.), *Handbook of motivation at school* (pp. 77–104). New York, NY: Routledge.

McCarthey, S., & Moje, E. B. (2002). Identity matters. *Reading Research Quarterly, 37,* 228–237.

Mehan, H. (1998). The study of social interaction in educational settings: Accomplishments and unresolved issues. *Human Development, 41,* 245–269.

Mejía-Arauz, R., Rogoff, B., Dexter, A., & Najafi, B. (2007). Cultural variation in children's social organization. *Child Development, 78*(3), 1001–1014.

Moll, L., Amanti, C., Neff, D., & González, N. (1992). Funds of knowledge for teaching: Using a qualitative approach to connect homes and schools. *Theory Into Practice, 21,* 132–142.

Nasir, N. S., Snyder, C. R., Shah, N., & Ross, K. M. (2012). Racial storylines and implications for learning. *Human Development, 55,* 285–301.

National Academies of Sciences, Engineering, and Medicine. (2017). *Promoting the educational success of children and youth learning English: Promising futures.* Washington, DC: National Academies Press.

National Research Council. (2009). *Learning science in informal environments: People, places, and pursuits.* Board on Science Education, Center for Education, Division of Behavioral and Social Sciences and Education. Washington, DC: National Academies Press.

National Research Council. (2012). *Education for life and work: Developing transferrable knowledge and skills in the 21st century.* Washington, DC: National Academies Press.

Ogbu, J. (1987), Variability in minority school performance: A problem in search of an explanation. *Anthropology & Education Quarterly, 18*(4), 312–334.

Ogbu, J., & Simons, H. (1998). Voluntary and involuntary minorities: A cultural-ecological theory of school performance with some implications for education. *Anthropology & Education Quarterly, 29*(2), 155–188.

Packer, M. J., & Goicoechea, J. (2000). Sociocultural and constructivist theories of learning: Ontology, not just epistemology. *Educational Psychologist, 35*(4), 227–241.

Pajares, F. (1996). Self-efficacy beliefs in academic settings. *Review of Educational Research, 66*(4), 543–578.

Palincsar, A. (1998). Social constructivist perspectives on teaching and learning. *Annual Review of Psychology, 49,* 345–375.

Paradise, R., & Haan, M. D. (2009). Responsibility and reciprocity: Social organization of Mazahua learning practices. *Anthropology and Education Quarterly, 40*(2), 187–204.

Paradise, R., & Rogoff, B. (2009). Side by side: Learning by observing and pitching it. *Ethos, 37*(1), 102–138.

Pianta, R. C., & Hamre, B. (2009). Conceptualization, measurement, and improvement of classroom processes: Standardized observation can leverage capacity. *Educational Researcher, 38*(2), 109–119.

Preacher, K. J., Rucker, D. D., & Hayes, A. F. (2007). Addressing moderated mediation hypotheses: Theory, methods, and prescriptions. *Multivariate Behavioral Research, 42*(1), 185–227.

Reese, L. (2013). Cultural change and continuity in US and Mexican settings. In B. Jensen & A. Sawyer (Eds.), *Regarding* educación: *Mexican American schooling, immigration, bi-national improvement* (pp. 213–233). New York, NY: Teachers College Press.

Reese, L., Balzano, S., Gallimore, R., & Goldenberg, C. (1995). The concept of "*educación*": Latino family values and American schooling. *International Journal of Education Research, 23*(1), 57–81.

Reese, L., Jensen, B., & Ramirez, D. (2014). Emotionally supportive classroom contexts for young Latino children in rural California. *Elementary School Journal, 114*(4), 501–526.

Reyes, S. A., & Kleyn, T. (2010). *Teaching in two languages: A guide for K–12 bilingual educators.* Thousand Oaks, CA: Corwin.

Rogoff, B. (1990). *Apprenticeship in thinking: Cognitive development in social context.* New York, NY: Oxford University Press.

Rogoff, B. (2003). *The cultural nature of human development.* New York, NY: Oxford University Press.

Rogoff, B., Callahan, M., Gutiérrez, K. D., & Erickson, F. (2016). The organization of informal learning. *Review of Research in Education, 40*(1), 356–401.

Rogoff, B., Mejía-Arauz, R., & Correa-Chávez, M. (2015). A cultural paradigm—Learning by observing and pitching in. *Advances in Child Development and Behavior, 49*, 1–22.

Rogoff, B., Mistry, J., Göncü, A., Mosier, C., Chavajay, P., & Heath, S. B. (1993). Guided participation in cultural activity by toddlers and caregivers. *Monographs of the Society for Research in Child Development*, 1–179.

Rolstad, K., Mahoney, K., & Glass, G. V. (2005). The big picture: A meta-analysis of program effectiveness research on English language learners. *Educational Policy, 19*(4), 572–594.

Roorda, D. L., Koomen, H. M. Y., Spilt, J. L., & Oort, F. J. (2011). The influence of affective teacher-student relationships on students' school engagement and achievement: A meta-analytic approach. *Review of Educational Research, 81*(4), 493–529.

Ryan, R. M., & Deci, E. L. (2000). Self-determination theory and the facilitation of intrinsic motivation, social development, and well-being. *American Psychologist, 55*, 68–78.

Ryan, S., & Grieshaber, S. (2004). It's more than child development: Critical theories, research, and teaching young children. *Young Children, 59*(6), 44–52.

Saunders, W., Goldenberg, C., & Hamann, J. (1992). Instructional conversations beget instructional conversations. *Teaching and Teacher Education, 8*(2), 199–218.

Schieffelin, B. B., & Ochs, E. (1986). *Language socialization across cultures.* Cambridge, UK: Cambridge University Press.

Schoenfeld, A. (1999). Looking toward the 21st century: Challenges of educational theory and practice. *Educational Researcher, 28*(7), 4–14.

Schofield, J. W. (1995). Promoting positive intergroup relations in school settings. In W. D. Hawley & A. W. Jackson (Eds.), *Toward a common destiny: Improving race and ethnic relations in America* (pp. 257–290). San Francisco, CA: Jossey-Bass.

Sensoy, O., & DiAngelo, R. (2012). *Is everyone really equal? An introduction to key concepts in social justice education.* New York, NY: Teachers College Press.

Shulman, L. (1987). Knowledge and teaching: Foundations of the new reform. *Harvard Educational Review, 57*(1), 1–23.

Slavin, R. E. (2010). Instruction based on cooperative learning. In R. E. Mayer & P. A. Alexander (Eds.), *Handbook of research on learning and instruction* (pp. 358–374). New York, NY: Routledge.

Sleeter, C. (2012). Confronting the marginalization of culturally responsive pedagogy. *Urban Education, 47*(3), 562–584.

Souto-Manning, M., Falk, B., López, D., Barros Cruz, L., Bradt, N., Cardwell, N., et al. (2019). A transdisciplinary approach to equitable teaching in early childhood education. *Review of Research in Education, 43*(1), 249–276.

Souto-Manning, M. (2013). *Multicultural teaching in the early education classroom: Approaches, strategies, and tools.* New York, NY: Teachers College Press.

Souto-Manning, M., & Mitchell, C. H. (2010). The role of action research in fostering culturally responsive practices in a preschool classroom. *Early Childhood Education Journal, 37*(4), 269–277.

Stevens, R. J., & Slavin, R. E. (1995). The cooperative elementary school: Effects on students' achievement, attitudes, and social relations. *American Educational Research Journal, 32*(2), 321–351.

Telles, E., & Ortíz, V. (2013). Intergenerational assimilation patterns of Mexican American students. In B. Jensen & A. Sawyer (Eds.), *Regarding educación: Mexican-American schooling, immigration, and bi-national improvement* (pp. 27–42). New York, NY: Teachers College Press.

Tharp, R. (1982). The effective instruction of comprehension: Results and descriptions of the Kamehameha Early Education Program. *Reading Research Quarterly, 17*, 503–527.

Tharp, R. (1989). Psychocultural variables and constants: Effects on teaching and learning in schools. *American Psychologist, 44*(2), 349–359.

Tharp, R., Estrada, P., Dalton, S., & Yamauchi, L. A. (2000). *Teaching transformed: Achieving excellence, fairness, inclusion, and harmony.* Boulder, CO: Westview.

Tharp. R., & Gallimore, R. (1988). *Rousing minds to life: Teaching, learning, and schooling in social context.* New York, NY: Cambridge University Press.

Tobin, J., Adair, J. K., & Arzubiaga, A. (2013). *Children crossing borders: Immigrant parent and teacher perspectives on preschool for children of immigrants.* New York, NY: Russell Sage Foundation.

Trueba, H. T. (1988). Culturally based explanations for minority students' academic achievement. *Anthropology & Education Quarterly, 19*(3), 270–287.

Unsworth, S. (2016). Quantity and quality of language input in bilingual language development. In E. Nicoladis & S. Montanari (Eds.), *Lifespan perspectives on bilingualism* (pp. 136–196). Berlin, Germany: De Gruyter Mouton /American Psychological Association.

Valdés, G. (1996). *Con respeto: Bridging the differences between culturally diverse families and schools.* New York, NY: Teachers College Press.

Valdés, G., Capitelli, S., & Alvarez, L. (2011). *Latino children learning English: Steps in the journey.* New York, NY: Teachers College Press.

Valencia, R. R. (Ed.). (1997). *The evolution of deficit thinking: Educational thought and practice.* New York, NY: Routledge.

Varelas., M., Martin, D. B., & Kane, J. M. (2012). Content learning and identity construction: A framework to strengthen African American students' mathematics and science learning in urban elementary schools. *Human Development, 55*, 319–339.

Vélez-Ibáñez, C., & Greenberg, J. (1992). Formation and transformation of funds of knowledge among U.S.-Mexican households. *Anthropology & Education Quarterly*, 313–335.

Villegas, A. M., & Lucas, T. (2002). Preparing culturally responsive teachers: Rethinking the curriculum. *Journal of Teacher Education, 53*(1), 20–32.

Webb, N. M., & Farivar, S. (1994). Promoting helping behavior in cooperative small groups in middle school mathematics. *American Educational Research Journal, 31*(2), 369–395.

Weisner, T. (2002). Ecocultural understanding of children's developmental pathways. *Human Development, 45*, 275–281.

Wentzel, K., & Wigfield, A. (1998). Academic and social motivational influences on students' academic performance. *Educational Psychology Review, 10*, 155–175.

Yoshikawa, H. (2011). *Immigrants raising citizens: Undocumented parents and their children.* New York, NY: Russell Sage Foundation.

Yoshikawa, H., & Kholoptseva, J. (2013). *Unauthorized immigrant parents and their children's development.* Washington, DC: Migration Policy Institute.

Yoshikawa, H., Weisner, T. S., Kalil, A., & Way, N. (2008). Mixing qualitative and quantitative research in developmental science: Uses and methodological choices. *Developmental Psychology, 44*(2), 344–354.

Chapter 3

Developmentally Appropriate Practice in Early Childhood Education Redefined: The Case of Math

DEBORAH J. STIPEK
Stanford University

NICHOLAS C. JOHNSON
San Diego State University

For decades, early childhood educators have subscribed to the canons of developmentally appropriate education (DAP). A perusal of the National Association for the Education of Young Children (NAEYC) guidelines, however, shows that DAP is a set of dynamic standards that have changed over time. The first NAEYC position statement on DAP in 1987 maintained that early childhood instruction should take place during child-initiated, child-directed play activities. The teacher's primary role was to "prepare the environment for children to learn through active exploration and interaction with adults, other children, and materials" (Bredekamp, 1987, p. 3). In 1997 the guidelines recommend an "optimal balance between children's self-initiated learning and adult guidance" (Bredekamp & Copple, 1997, p. 11). The most recent guidelines (Copple & Bredekamp, 2009) maintain an emphasis on child-initiated activities, play, and teacher responsiveness to individual children's needs and interests, in combination with a teacher-planned, comprehensive curriculum that helps children attain key goals in academic domains such as literacy and mathematics. These recent guidelines also include a substantial section of recommendations for specific teaching practices. In brief, over the last three decades, NAEYC guidelines and general views in the field of early childhood education have increasingly endorsed teacher-planned, academic instruction. We see additional evidence of increased interest in academic skill development in states' adoption of academic standards for preschool.

The shift toward a greater emphasis on academic development in children's early years has been driven by K–12 accountability pressures, concerns about significant achievement disparities that exist before children begin school (which has long-term implications for their learning and success in school), and research demonstrating that children can develop academic skills and enjoy doing so before they enter kindergarten. The reformulation of the role of the teacher and of academic learning in early childhood suggests the importance of research on how children develop academic skills, as well as on effective strategies for supporting children's learning. This chapter reviews research focused on effective teaching that is responsive to individual children's interests and developmental needs.

Why Study Early Math Learning?

Until recently, practitioners and researchers in early childhood education have given much less attention to mathematics teaching and learning than to language and literacy. Greater attention to math has been stimulated by recent evidence indicating that early mathematics proficiency is associated with later proficiency in both mathematics and reading and may even be linked to higher rates of high school graduation and college attendance (Duncan et al., 2007; Duncan & Magnuson, 2011; Pagani, Fitzpatrick, Archambault, & Janosz, 2010; Romano, Kohen, Babchishin, & Pagani, 2010). Although the mechanisms underlying such associations are not yet understood, the evidence for the importance of ensuring that all students have access to early mathematics instruction is compelling.

Attention to math skills in early childhood is also critical to reducing achievement disparities. Children who have low math scores in the fall of their kindergarten year—and who continue to lag behind their better prepared peers—are disproportionately children of color and from low-income families. In an analysis of ECLS-K data, Duncan and Magnuson (2011) found that students in the bottom SES quintile (with average family income of about $15,500) had math scores well over one standard deviation below children in the top SES quintile (average family income of $100,000; see also Reardon, 2011). Each move up a socioeconomic quintile in the SES distribution was associated with approximately a quarter of a standard deviation of improvement in math scores (Garcia, 2015). These findings make it clear that closing the achievement gap requires closing the opportunity gap and devoting attention and resources to children before school entry.

Connections between math learning and the development of executive functions (EF), which are highly predictive of the development of both academic and social skills (Obradovic, Portilla, & Boyce, 2012), further suggest the importance of math in early childhood. Early EF competencies predict later mathematics achievement (e.g., Clements & Sarama, 2015; Mazzocco & Kover, 2007; Stipek & Valentino, 2015; see Clements, Sarama, & Germeroth, 2016, for a review), and students who excel at mathematics tend to excel on EF skills also (Clements et al., 2016; Desco et al., 2011; Stipek & Valentino, 2015). Given the strong correlations, it is not surprising that the same SES-related achievement differences found for math skills also exist for executive functions (Garcia, 2015). Although a causal connection has not been demonstrated, the strong association suggests that efforts to improve either EF or math skills may strengthen both.

What Kinds of Math Learning Experiences Do Young Children Have?

Young Children's Math Learning Experiences at Home

Parents tend to engage in early math activities far less frequently than in literacy activities (Anders et al., 2012; Blevins-Knabe, Austin, Musun, Eddy, & Jones, 2000; Blevins-Knabe & Musun-Miller, 1996; Cannon & Ginsburg, 2008; Skwarchuk, 2009). Moreover, several studies have shown that parents generally focus on a narrow and basic set of math skills when they engage their children in math activities at home, primarily counting and writing numbers and basic operations. Little attention is given to other facets of early math such as geometry, measurement, spatial awareness, and algebra (Blevins-Knabe & Musun-Miller, 1996; Missall, Hojnoski, Caskie, & Repasky, 2015).

The few studies that have examined differences related to race, ethnicity, or social class have reported conflicting results (Tudge & Doucet, 2004; Vandermaas-Peeler, Nelson, Bumpass, & Sassine, 2009). Saxe, Guberman, and Gearhart (1987) reported that frequency of math activities did not differ between low- and middle-SES families, but the complexity of parent-child math interactions did, with middle-SES parents likely to engage their children in more advanced math concepts than low-SES parents in the sample.

We know that the amount of parent engagement in math activities with young children is associated with a variety of beliefs and views related to math, but we do not know which of the various beliefs that have been studied best explain parents' practices. Extant evidence suggests that the relatively low frequency of math activities at home may be explained by parents' greater anxiety related to math (Maloney, Ramirez, Gunderson, Levine, & Beilock, 2015), negative views of their own experience with math or a preference for literacy over math (Cannon & Ginsburg, 2008; Missall et al., 2015), a belief that math skills are less important for kindergarten readiness than are literacy skills (Cannon & Ginsburg, 2008; Skwarchuk, 2009), a belief that the school environment is a more important contributor to math skill development than the home environment (Starkey & Klein, 2008), and a lack of knowledge about what math young children can learn or what activities parents can offer to support their children's math development (Cannon & Ginsburg, 2008; DeFlorio & Beliakoff, 2015). Future research would be useful to identify key beliefs that interventions might seek to influence.

Young Children's Math Learning Experiences at School

Extant research indicates that the more time children spend in math instruction, the more gains they make in math achievement (Fuhs, Farran, Meador, & Norvell, 2012; Guarino, Hamilton, Lockwood, & Rathbun, 2006). But typically, little time is devoted to math in either preschool or kindergarten. In the preschool classrooms that they observed, Fuhs et al. (2012) found that only 3% of children's time was focused on math, compared to 11% on reading readiness. In a 2009 study, nearly 500 Head Start teachers reported counting out loud and working with geometric manipulatives as their most common math activities, followed by activities with shapes and patterns and calendar-related activities (National Center on Quality Teaching and Learning, 2015). Teachers reported conducting all of these activities at least 3 to 4 times a week, on average.

Using ECLS-K data to analyze kindergarten instruction, Bassok, Latham, and Rorem (2016) found the amount of time teachers reported spending on reading and language arts rose from about 328 minutes per week (a little over an hour a day) in 1998 to 414 minutes per week in 2010—an increase of about 25%. In contrast, teachers reported allocating far less time to math activities, with no increase from 1998 to 2010 (200 and 198 minutes, respectively).

There is not a great deal of information on time spent in math activities in the early elementary grades, but the ECLS-K study, which included a nationally representative sample of kindergartens, provides some information (Guarino et al., 2006). Teachers indicated how often they engaged in particular kinds of math activities: 1 (never), 2 (once a month or less), 3 (two or three times a month), 4 (once or twice a week), 5 (three or four times a week), and 6 (daily). The average scores for different math activities were as shown in Table 1.

Table 1. Frequency of Engaging in Math Activities Reported by Kindergarten Teachers

Skill Areas Taught	Examples of Skills Taught	Mean Scores
Numbers and geometry	Counting out loud, understanding correspondence between number and quantity, writing numbers between 1 and 10, recognizing and naming geometric shapes, ordering objects by size or other properties	$M = 4.47$ (between 1–2 and 3–4 times per week)
Advanced numbers and operations	Counting by 2s, 5s, and 10s, counting beyond 100, reading three-digit numbers	$M = 3.48$ (between 3–4 times per month and 1–2 times per week)
Traditional practices and computation	Completing math worksheets, solving math problems from textbooks, writing numbers between 1 and 100, adding and subtracting single-digit numbers	$M = 3.19$ (2–3 times per month)
Measurement and advanced topics	Working with measuring instruments, reading simple graphs, telling time, estimating probability	$M = 2.72$ (2–3 times per month)

Math instruction was less frequent than literacy instruction in kindergarten, as has also been found for preschool. Three of the literacy activities (phonics, $M = 5.53$; reading and writing, $M = 4.36$; and comprehension, $M = 4.69$) were reported to be taught more than 1–2 times a week; in comparison, only one math activity was taught with that frequency. It is possible that math instruction has increased since this study was conducted, however.

What Kinds of Experiences Support Children's Math Learning?

Young children are remarkably capable of engaging with powerful mathematical ideas. As they participate and make sense of the world around them, children display rich and varied informal understandings that are mathematical in nature. For example, in running out of blocks of a particular size, a child may see that he or she can create a larger block using two smaller blocks. Another child may attempt to extend a number sequence by counting "28, 29, twenty-ten, twenty-eleven," and so on. These children reveal emerging understandings of geometric equivalence and the patterns in the base-ten number system. Their intuitive strategies and discoveries can serve as a basis for continued development, as they begin to connect and make explicit their emerging conceptions with regard to knowing and doing mathematics.

A large body of research documents the development of young children's mathematical learning and its basis in their intuitive strategies and sense-making capabilities. Children's understanding of counting and quantity develop long before they enter school

(Clements & Sarama, 2007; Fuson, 1988; Gelman & Gallistel, 1986), and they can solve a wide range of story problems prior to receiving formal instruction in mathematical operations (Carpenter, 1985; Riley & Greeno, 1988). Given opportunities to make sense of problem situations related to their own experience, children as young as kindergarten or first grade can solve a variety of problems related to multiplication, division, and even fractions by representing the action or relationships in story situations (Carpenter, Ansell, Franke, Fennema, & Weisbeck, 1993; Empson, 1999; Kouba, 1989; Mack, 1993). For example, to share five cookies between two friends, a child might draw five circles, distribute two cookies to each friend, and then partition the final cookie by drawing a line down the middle, "breaking the cookie in half."

Teachers and parents can create opportunities for young children's rich mathematical ideas to emerge though planned instructional activities, like those included in many early childhood mathematics curricula. Play, too, can provide opportunities to surface and support children's mathematical orientation to their surroundings (e.g., van Oers, 2010; Wager & Parks, 2016). A critical goal is to provide learning opportunities that elicit children's informal mathematical ideas across a variety of settings, and to support children in "mathematizing" these experiences by attending and responding to the mathematics embedded within their natural interests and discoveries across a range of contexts. For example, in lining up wooden blocks, a child may use two triangles to construct a shape similar to a square. Noticing this, a teacher can draw the child's attention to what they have done to highlight the mathematics, "I see you used two triangles to create one square." The teacher could continue by inviting the child (or other children) to build on this idea of equivalent shapes: "Are there any other shapes you can use to make a rectangle the same size as this one?" (Parks & Blom, 2013). Over time, connecting children's natural sense-making with important mathematical concepts will provide a foundation for their continued success (NAEYC & National Council of Teachers of Mathematics [NCTM], 2010). We turn now to research on effective strategies for helping children progress in their mathematical understanding.

Strategies at Home for Helping Children Progress in Mathematical Understanding

Studies of math experiences have demonstrated that the frequency and quality of parents' math engagement with their children prior to school entry predict children's math achievement. Engagement in both formal math activities (e.g., recognizing numbers, counting, comparing quantities, practicing simple sums) and informal math activities (e.g., playing numeracy-related games, measuring while cooking) predict children's knowledge of the symbolic number system, counting skills, number recognition abilities, number comparisons, and speed and efficiency when performing math tasks (Anders et al., 2012; Casey et al., 2018; Kleemans, Peeters, Segers, & Verhoeven, 2012; LeFevre, Clarke, & Stringer, 2002; LeFevre et al., 2009; Lukie, Skwarchuk, LeFevre, & Sowinski, 2014; Niklas & Schneider, 2014; Skwarchuk, Sowinski, & LeFevre, 2014).

Parental number talk in the home, in particular, has been shown to be a significant predictor of young children's math learning, especially children's cardinal number knowledge (Gunderson & Levine, 2011; Levine, Suriyakham, Rowe, Huttenlocher, & Gunderson, 2010). Levine and colleagues (2010) conducted the first study on parent number talk, observing parents and children ages 14–30 months at home during typical daily activities. Their findings showed that the frequency of number talk predicted children's cardinal number knowledge at 46 months. Gunderson and Levine (2011) reported, more specifically, that number talk in the context of counting or labeling sets of objects predicted cardinal number knowledge, but other types of number talk did not. Parents' spatial language has also been shown to predict children's spatial knowledge (Pruden, Levine, & Huttenlocher, 2011).

Only a few parent intervention studies have been published, but they demonstrate that it is possible to promote parents' math interactions with preschool children and children's math learning (Borriello & Liben, 2017; Niklas, Cohrssen, & Tayler, 2015; Starkey & Klein, 2000; Van Voorhis, 2011). There is, nevertheless, much to be learned about how best to promote collaborative partnerships among practitioners, parents, and families to support children's mathematical learning. For example, could parent interventions affect beliefs, mentioned above, which have been shown to correlate with the frequency and quality of parents' efforts to engage their young children in math activities? Would simply providing parents with ideas for math activities to engage in with their children be sufficient? Could parent interventions be efficiently and effectively implemented by their children's teachers? Research addressing these kinds of questions could be used to guide efforts to enhance parents' involvement in their children's learning of mathematics.

Strategies at School for Helping Children Progress in Mathematical Understanding

Culture and Relationships. While powerful, young children's intuitive mathematical ideas can also be quite fragile. Perry and Dockett (2008) call attention to the situated nature of children's competence. They point out that children are often able to do more in familiar settings or with family members than in unfamiliar situations or with unfamiliar adults. Perry and Dockett's recognition that children often demonstrate "multiple competencies in contexts that are familiar and significant for them" (p. 77) was a major shift from other researchers' focus on perceptual and conceptual limitations in children's thinking.

Drawing upon and connecting children's mathematical experiences with their family, linguistic, cultural, and community knowledge and practices is thus viewed by experts as a central feature of providing high-quality learning opportunities (Graue, Whyte, & Delaney, 2014; NAEYC & NCTM, 2010; Wager & Carpenter, 2012). Relationships are also believed to be central to young children's learning (Shonkoff & Phillips, 2000), and nurturing children's emerging competence and confidence requires establishing and maintaining positive relationships with teachers and peers.

Focusing on the Big Mathematical Ideas of Early Childhood. What mathematics should be emphasized in early childhood? There has long been a focus on number and operations as critical foundations for mathematical understanding. For example, NCTM's *Principles and Standards for School Mathematics* identified number and operations as the major emphasis of prekindergarten through Grade 2, and the *Common Core State Standards for Mathematics* (CCSSM) identify the domains related to number as the "major work" of K–2 (National Governors Association [NGA] & Council of Chief State School Officers [CCSSO], 2010; Student Achievement Partners, 2012).

There is mounting empirical support for this emphasis. Recent research highlights the importance of early number and arithmetic for later mathematics achievement (Bailey, Siegler, & Geary, 2014; Jordan, Kaplan, Ramineni, & Locuniak, 2009). Guarino et al. (2006) found children's performance on advanced numbers and operations in kindergarten to be positively associated with achievement gains. Nguyen et al. (2016) reported similar findings, connecting children's use of more advanced counting and problem-solving strategies with future mathematics achievement.

Rittle-Johnson, Fyfe, Hofer, and Farran (2016) demonstrated the importance of considering learning trajectories when investigating links between children's performance and later achievement. They found that different skills predicted later math achievement at different points in children's schooling. In preschool, for example, nonsymbolic quantity, counting, and patterning knowledge predicted fifth-grade mathematics achievement, but by the end of first grade, symbolic mapping, calculation, and patterning knowledge were the most powerful predictors (Rittle-Johnson et al., 2016). Given evidence that kindergarten teachers report spending a great deal of instructional time on concepts already learned by most children during preschool (Engel, Claessens, Watts, & Farkas, 2016), important questions remain as to how to shift instructional emphases away from activities with little mathematical substance (e.g., rote counting, calendar work) toward approaches that leverage children's early number skills in the service of more advanced content regarding number and operations.

A strong foundation in number and operations is a necessary but insufficient foundation for continued mathematical success. Recent consensus documents contend that mathematics in early childhood should also emphasize geometry, measurement, and spatial relations (Clements, Sarama, & DiBiase, 2004; National Research Council & Committee on Early Childhood Mathematics, 2009); measurement and data are also included among the major clusters of standards for first and second grades in the Common Core State Standards (NGA & CCSSO, 2010). While the longitudinal effects of young children's geometric and spatial knowledge have received less emphasis in the research community, there is evidence that spatial skills in preschool predict later skills related to geometry (Verdine, Golinkoff, Hirsh-Pasek, & Newcombe, 2017), and a growing number of researchers argue for continued research in this domain (e.g., Moss, Bruce, & Bobis, 2016).

In addition, mathematics educators have increasingly focused on supporting students to engage effectively in mathematical practices, such as making sense of problems, communicating ideas, and making connections between mathematical concepts and representations (Clements et al., 2004). Policy documents reflect this shift, emphasizing the need for teachers and curriculum designers to attend to the learning and doing of mathematics in relation to one another (NCTM, 2000; NGA & CCSSO, 2010; NRC, 2001). The consensus document from NAEYC and NCTM (2010) explains:

> While content represents the what of early childhood mathematics education, the processes—problem solving, reasoning, communication, connections, and representation—make it possible for children to acquire content knowledge. These processes develop over time and when supported by well designed opportunities to learn. (p. 6)

Opportunities for students to engage in these disciplinary practices can occur across varied contexts, including intended, seeded, and child-initiated activities (Wager, 2013). Substantive research has provided compelling examples of what student engagement in practices (such as communication) looks and sounds like, and has connected the details of these practices to student achievement (Lampert & Cobb, 2003; Webb et al., 2009). However, fewer large-scale studies have examined links between student achievement outcomes in early childhood settings and students' engagement in mathematical practices. Vivid illustrations of the ways in which students engage in mathematical practices, coupled with short- and long-term impacts on students' content learning, will be helpful in moving the field forward.

Early Childhood Mathematics Curricula. A growing number of early childhood curricula aim to support educators in implementing high-quality mathematics instructional programs, many of which have been developed by researchers with explicit goals of engaging students in the core mathematical ideas described above. For example, Building Blocks preschool curriculum incorporates both software and teacher-led activities such as circle time, story time, and designated math activities. The design of Building Blocks is based on children's learning trajectories in number and geometry, with the overall goal of helping children to connect their informal math knowledge to more formal mathematical concepts (Clements & Sarama, 2009). Building Blocks has been extensively researched and has demonstrated significant impacts on student achievement in randomized trials (Clements & Sarama, 2008; Clements, Sarama, Wolfe, & Spitler, 2013). Big Math for Little Kids (BMLK) is a preschool and kindergarten curriculum designed to build on young children's spontaneous engagement in mathematics. It offers a sequence of intentional activities designed to mathematize play by repeating activities over time while gradually increasing the challenge of the mathematics. A recent cluster-randomized controlled trial found that students in classrooms that used the BMLK curriculum outperformed peers in "business-as-usual" classrooms (Presser, Clements, Ginsburg, & Ertle, 2015). Math Shelf is a preschool and kindergarten intervention program that uses tablet computers to present a sequence of games, puzzles, and manipulatives to build students' basic number sense. Low-income preschool children who played Math Shelf outperformed those who played other popular math apps, and kindergarteners who used Math Shelf outperformed peers who participated in their regular classroom mathematics activities (Schacter & Jo, 2016; Schacter et al., 2016). Early Learning in Mathematics (ELM) is a comprehensive kindergarten curriculum that employs a direct instructional approach with goals of developing conceptual understanding and procedural fluency. A randomized block study found that students in classrooms that used the ELM curriculum outperformed their control group peers (Clarke et al., 2011). The findings were particularly strong for students deemed at risk. In a study comparing the impact of 14 preschool curricula, only one—Pre-K Mathematics, supplemented with DLM Early Childhood Express Math Software—was found to have stronger effects on math skills than the "business-as-usual" instruction it was compared to (Preschool Curriculum Evaluation Research Consortium, 2008). However, it was also the only curriculum in the study that was specifically focused on math instruction. Collectively, the curricula noted here employ a range of instructional approaches and technologies. All, however, incorporate sequenced activities based on children's learning progressions with number, and all incorporate (in some way) intentional teaching. For a recent review of early math curricula, see National Center on Quality Teaching and Learning (2015).

Research investigating the effects of the above curricula on student achievement has taken place in preschool or kindergarten settings (or sometimes both). Our review did not uncover any research investigating mathematics curricula that spanned the entirety of early childhood.[1] The research on elementary school curricula is decidedly mixed. For example, an independent study commissioned by IES investigated the effects of four elementary curricula that spanned a range of designs and instructional approaches: Investigations in Number, Data, and Space (hereinafter "Investigations"); Math Expressions; Saxon Math ("Saxon"); and Scott Foresman–Addison Wesley Mathematics (SFAW). The study characterized the Investigations curriculum as employing a student-centered approach, Saxon and SFAW as teacher-directed, and Math Expressions as a blend of teacher-directed and student-centered. Results of the study showed that in terms of spring first-grade mathematics achievement, students receiving instruction via Math Expressions and Saxon outperformed those in classrooms using Investigations and SFAW (Agodini & Harris, 2010). On the other hand, in a comparison of curricula across two urban school districts, Stein and Kaufman (2010) found that teachers implementing the Investigations curriculum were more successful in maintaining cognitive demand than those using Everyday Mathematics, and that Investigations provided more effective supports for teachers' understanding of mathematical goals.

The range of findings on the effectiveness of various curricula illustrate the difficulties in disentangling effects of instructional materials themselves from their implementation. As Stein, Remillard, and Smith (2007) state in their review of research on the effects of mathematics curricula on student learning, "a substantial difference exists between the curriculum as represented in instructional materials and the curriculum as enacted in the classroom by teachers and students" (p. 321). Of the studies Stein and colleagues (2007) reviewed, only a handful examined curricular materials in relation to their implementation (e.g., Boaler & Staples, 2008; Hiebert et al., 2005; Stein, Grover, & Henningsen, 1996), and these studies involved older students. Accordingly, we turn next to the topic of teachers' implementation of math instruction.

Teachers' Classroom Practice. Recommendations for "effective" classroom practices inevitably bring with them debates between the proponents of various approaches: student-centered (or child-initiated) versus teacher-directed; traditional versus reformist; problem solving versus basic skills, and so on. Some very early research comparing preschool and early elementary instructional approaches showed advantages of direct instruction (e.g., Stebbins, St. Pierre, Proper, Anderson, & Cerva, 1977). But critics claimed that the rote methods used prepared children only for success on tests of very basic skills and did not develop conceptual understanding (House, Glass, McLean, & Walker, 1978). These early studies nevertheless suggest the value of purposeful and somewhat structured instruction, which differed from most instruction that focused on child-initiated activities at the time.

While many scholars advocate a move away from a simple dichotomy between student-centered and teacher-directed instruction (U.S. Department of Education, 2008), there are genuine philosophical and theoretical differences among various positions, even if the positions do not accurately describe how teachers actually teach (Chiatovich & Stipek, 2016). A more productive characterization of approaches for research is offered by Baroody, Purpura, and Reid (2012). They propose a continuum between direct instruction and unguided discovery learning that takes into account differences not only between the extreme positions, but also in what is given prominence in blended approaches. For example, how do teachers surface multiple strategies? Do they first ask students to generate their own strategies, or do they introduce multiple procedures and then allow students to choose among them? These are subtle but potentially important differences, and little research has attempted to contrast particular approaches in ways that capture the nuances of students' and teachers' roles. In Purpura, Baroody, Eiland, and Reid's (2016) examination of differences between the effects of fully guided, minimally guided, and highly guided discovery approaches to supporting first-graders' learning of basic addition facts, only the highly guided discovery learning condition supported both students' learning of specific number facts and their ability to apply those ideas to unpracticed number combinations. Fisher, Hirsh-Pasek, Newcombe, and Golinkoff (2013) contrasted the effects of didactic instruction, guided play, and free play on preschoolers' learning of geometry, finding that students in the guided play condition outperformed the other groups. These early findings suggest that blended approaches that foreground children's agency and sense-making in the context of intentionally designed learning opportunities are a promising line of future inquiry.

Despite continued questions about the utility of particular approaches, there is an emerging consensus on the kinds of experiences in schools that support young children's opportunities to learn meaningful mathematics. The list below synthesizes recommendations from recent documents published by several national organizations: *Early Childhood Mathematics,* a joint position statement from NAEYC and NCTM (2010); *Mathematics Learning in Early Childhood,* from the National Research Council and the Committee on Early Childhood Mathematics (2009); and *Teaching Math to Young Children,* from the Institute of Education Sciences (Frye et al., 2013; IES).

- Recognize and build from children's informal mathematical knowledge and their linguistic, cultural, family, and community resources.

- Help children to focus on, describe, and extend the mathematical opportunities present in everyday activities.

- Intentionally devote time to engaging children in mathematics through planned mathematical activities and by capitalizing on mathematical opportunities in play.

- Integrate mathematics with other activities and other activities with mathematics.

- Ground mathematics curriculum and teaching practices in research-based knowledge that details developmental progressions in number and operations, geometry, and measurement.

- Ensure that learning opportunities build on children's existing understanding by thoughtfully and continually assessing their mathematical knowledge, skills, and strategies.

Attempting to parse these recommendations for specific insights related to teachers' classroom practice once again highlights the interconnected nature of what is taught, how it is experienced and taken up by students, and what mathematics is learned (Cohen, Raudenbush, & Ball, 2003). There are, however, many parallels among these documents. They all agree that early childhood teachers should intentionally devote instructional time toward the learning of mathematics, support students to "mathematize" their experiences and environment, build from students' prior knowledge and experiences, ground instruction in research-based knowledge on the development of student thinking, and adjust instruction in relation to what teachers learn about students' understanding.

The Disconnect Between Preschool and Elementary School Math Instruction

Much of the research discussed heretofore includes children *either* in preschool or in the early elementary grades. Similarly, most state standards, curricula, and assessment instruments apply either to preschool or elementary school. The math instruction children receive in preschool is, accordingly, typically disconnected from the instruction they receive in kindergarten and later grades.

This discontinuity may explain in part the frequently observed diminishing ("fadeout") of the effects of high-quality preschool over the early elementary grades (Graves, 2006; Kauerz, 2006; Takanishi, 2016). The quality of instruction is clearly important, but presumably so are coherence and continuity in instruction across grades. If instruction in the early elementary grades does not build on the gains made in preschool, the preschool advantage may be lost.

We know something about the qualities of coherent instruction. Researchers in cognitive science and school reform suggest the importance of ensuring that topics in each grade build on those covered in previous grades, and that instruction becomes increasingly complex in accordance with the discipline, is targeted just above each student's skill level, and is aligned with typical learning trajectories (see Stipek, Clements, Coburn, Franke, & Farran, 2017, for a review). Stipek et al. (2017) also suggest the value of making connections between constructs and topics and giving students opportunities to broaden and deepen their skills by applying them in novel contexts.

The scant evidence available suggests that what children typically experience does not follow these recommendations. Engel, Claessens, and Finch (2013) found in a nationally representative sample of kindergarteners that before they entered kindergarten, children had already mastered most of the mathematics skills kindergarten teachers reported teaching. A later study by Engel and colleagues (Engel et al., 2016) revealed, not surprisingly, that instruction on the basic content that most children had already mastered was negatively associated with learning gains made in kindergarten.

Similar problems may exist at the preschool level. A study comparing children who had two years of Head Start (ages 3–5 years) with children who had one year of Head Start (ages 3–4) followed by a year of Oklahoma's state preschool (age 4–5) found that the latter children made significantly greater academic gains than the former (Jenkins, Farkas, Duncan, Burchinal, & Vandell, 2016). The authors speculate that because Head Start typically combines 3- and 4-year-olds into one class, children's second year may not have extended what they learned the first year.

Coherence and continuity in instruction between preschool and the early elementary grades requires continuity in standards, assessments, and curriculum, which some evidence suggests have not been achieved in the United States (Kagan, Carroll, Comer, & Scott-Little, 2006). States and districts and schools throughout the country, however, have launched efforts to create greater continuity in children's instructional experience by promoting continuity between preschool and K–12 standards (NGA, 2012), by developing continuous assessment instruments and curricula (Marietta & Marietta, 2013), and by providing opportunities for preschool and elementary-grade teachers to collaborate and participate in the same professional development activities (Sadowski, 2006; Valentino & Stipek, 2016).

Early childhood educators worry that efforts to create continuity between the early elementary grades and preschool will result in "pushing down" an emphasis on a narrow set of academic skills and reducing time and attention to social-emotional development and play (Miller & Almon, 2009). But continuity can be achieved without undermining developmentally appropriate practice in preschool. Indeed, a few states, such as Ohio (Ohio Department of Education, 2015) have begun to include social skills in elementary-grade standards. We are not suggesting either pushing down or pushing up standards, but we are suggesting the need for alignment between preschool and kindergarten standards, which in some states may involve more attention to academic skills in preschool and to social-emotional development in kindergarten.

Research is needed to document the effects of various state and district strategies for improving coherence and continuity to determine which strategies impact classroom instruction and under what conditions. Assessment instruments and curricula also need to be developed. The task of creating greater continuity is hampered by the dearth of instruments and curricula that extend from preschool through the elementary grades. We therefore also strongly recommend efforts to develop such instruments and to study their effects on children's classroom experience in both elementary and preschool.

Conclusion

Policy makers, researchers, and practitioners view the preschool years as fertile and important ground for developing the foundation of academic skills. A great deal of research has been conducted on strategies for developing early literacy skills, and preschool teachers are making literacy skills a priority. Math teaching and learning are no less important, but we have some catching up to do. This chapter reviews the knowledge base to date and makes recommendations for specific areas of research needed to guide future policies and practices. While we learn more about supporting young children's math skill development, we also need to pay attention to connections between preschool and the early elementary grades to ensure a seamless learning experience.

Acknowledgment

The preparation of this manuscript was supported in part by a grant from the Heising-Simons Foundation. The opinions expressed are those of the authors and do not reflect those of the funding agency.

Note

1. In our review, Everyday Mathematics was the only curriculum that spanned preschool through Grade 3. However, the only study design that met the group design standards of What Works Clearing House involved students in Grades 3–5 (U.S. Department of Education, 2015).

References

Agodini, R., & Harris, B. (2010). An experimental evaluation of four elementary school math curricula. *Journal of Research on Educational Effectiveness, 3*(3), 199–253. Retrieved from https://doi.org/10.1080/19345741003770693

Anders, Y., Rossbach, H.-G., Weinert, S., Ebert, S., Kuger, S., Lehrl, S., et al. (2012). Home and preschool learning environments and their relations to the development of early numeracy skills. *Early Childhood Research Quarterly, 27*(2), 231–244.

Bailey, D. H., Siegler, R. S., & Geary, D. C. (2014). Early predictors of middle school fraction knowledge. *Developmental Science, 17*(5), 775–785. Retrieved from https://doi.org/10.1111/desc.12155

Baroody, A. J., Purpura, D. J., & Reid, E. E. (2012). Comments on learning and teaching early and elementary mathematics. In J. S. Carlson & J. R. Levin (Eds.), *Instructional strategies for improving students' learning: Focus on early reading and mathematics* (pp. 163–175). Charlotte, NC: Information Age.

Bassok, D., Latham, S., & Rorem, A. (2016). Is kindergarten the new first grade? *AERA Open, 1*(4), 1–31.

Blevins-Knabe, B., Austin, A. B., Musun, L., Eddy, A., & Jones, R. M. (2000). Family home care providers' and parents' beliefs and practices concerning mathematics with young children. *Early Child Development and Care, 165*(1), 41–58.

Blevins-Knabe, B., & Musun-Miller, L. (1996). Number use at home by children and their parents and its relationship to early mathematical performance. *Early Development and Parenting, 5*(1), 35–45.

Boaler, J., & Staples, M. (2008). Creating mathematical futures through an equitable teaching approach: The case of Railside School. *Teachers College Record, 110*(3), 608–645.

Borriello, G. A., & Liben, L. S. (2017), Encouraging maternal guidance of preschoolers' spatial thinking during block play. *Child Development, 89*(4), 1209–1222. doi:10.1111/cdev.12779

Bredekamp, S. (Ed.). (1987). *Developmentally appropriate practice in early childhood programs serving children from birth through age 8.* Washington, DC: National Association for the Education of Young Children.

Bredekamp, S., & Copple, C. (Eds.). (1997). *Developmentally appropriate practice in early childhood programs serving children from birth through age 8* (2nd ed.). Washington, DC: National Association for the Education of Young Children.

Cannon, J., & Ginsburg, H. P. (2008). "Doing the math": Maternal beliefs about early mathematics versus language learning. *Early Education and Development, 19*(2), 238–260.

Carpenter, T. P. (1985). Learning to add and subtract: An exercise in problem solving. In E. A. Silver (Ed.), *Teaching and learning mathematical problem solving: Multiple research perspectives* (pp. 17–40). Hillsdale, NJ: Lawrence Erlbaum.

Carpenter, T. P., Ansell, E., Franke, M. L., Fennema, E., & Weisbeck, L. (1993). Models of problem solving: A study of kindergarten children's problem-solving processes. *Journal for Research in Mathematics Education, 24*(5), 428–441. Retrieved from https://doi.org/10.2307/749152

Casey, B. M., Lombardi, C. M., Thomson, D., Nguyen, H. N., Paz, M., Theriault, C. A., & Dearing, E. (2018). Maternal support of children's early numerical concept learning predicts preschool and first-grade math achievement. *Child Development, 89*(1), 156–173. doi:10.1111/cdev.12676

Chiatovich, T., & Stipek, D. J. (2016). Instructional approaches in kindergarten: What works for whom? *Elementary School Journal, 117*(1), 1–29. Retrieved from https://doi.org/10.1086/687751

Clarke, B., Smolkowski, K., Baker, S. K., Fien, H., Doabler, C. T., & Chard, D. J. (2011). The impact of a comprehensive tier I core kindergarten program on the achievement of students at risk in mathematics. *Elementary School Journal, 111*(4), 561–584. Retrieved from https://doi.org/10.1086/659033

Clements, D. H., & Sarama, J. (2007). Early childhood mathematics learning. In F. K. Lester (Ed.), *Second handbook of research on mathematics teaching and learning* (Vol. 1, pp. 461–555). Charlotte, NC: Information Age.

Clements, D. H., & Sarama, J. (2008). Experimental evaluation of the effects of a research-based preschool mathematics curriculum. *American Educational Research Journal, 45*(2), 443–494. Retrieved from https://doi.org/10.3102/0002831207312908

Clements, D. H., & Sarama, J. (2009). *Learning and teaching early math: The learning trajectories approach* (1st ed.). New York, NY: Routledge.

Clements, D. H., & Sarama, J. (2015). Learning executive function and early mathematics. In C. Kurose & N. Albert (Eds.), *Mathematical instruction for perseverance collected papers.* Chicago, IL: Spencer Foundation.

Clements, D. H., Sarama, J., & DiBiase, A.-M. (Eds.). (2004). *Engaging young children in mathematics: Standards for early childhood mathematics education.* New York, NY: Routledge.

Clements, D. H., Sarama, J., & Germeroth, C. (2016). Learning executive function and early mathematics: Directions of causal relations. *Early Childhood Research Quarterly, 36,* 79–90.

Clements, D. H., Sarama, J., Wolfe, C. B., & Spitler, M. E. (2013). Longitudinal evaluation of a scale-up model for teaching mathematics with trajectories and technologies: Persistence of effects in the third year. *American Educational Research Journal, 50*(4), 812–850. Retrieved from https://doi.org/10.3102/0002831212469270

Cohen, D. K., Raudenbush, S. W., & Ball, D. L. (2003). Resources, instruction, and research. *Educational Evaluation and Policy Analysis, 25*(2), 119–142. Retrieved from https://doi.org/10.3102/01623737025002119

Copple, C., & Bredekamp, S. (Eds.). (2009). *Developmentally appropriate practice in early childhood programs serving children from birth through age 8* (3rd ed.). Washington, DC: National Association for the Education of Young Children.

DeFlorio, L., & Beliakoff, A. (2015). Socioeconomic status and preschoolers' mathematical knowledge: The contribution of home activities and parent beliefs. *Early Education and Development, 26*(3), 319–341.

Desco, M., Navas-Sanchez, F. J., Sanchez-Gonzalez, J., Reig, S., Robles, O., Franco, C., et al. (2011). Mathematically gifted adolescents use more extensive and more bilateral areas of the fronto-parietal network than controls during executive functioning and fluid reasoning tasks. *NeuroImage, 57,* 281–292.

Duncan, G. J., Dowsett, C. J., Claessens, A., Magnuson, K., Huston, A. C., Klebanov, P., et al. (2007). School readiness and later achievement. *Developmental Psychology, 43*(6), 1428–1446.

Duncan, G., & Magnuson, K. (2011). The nature and impact of early achievement skills, attention skills, and behavior problems. In G. Duncan & R. J. Murnane (Eds.), *Whither opportunity: Rising inequality, schools, and children's life chances* (pp. 47–69). New York, NY: Russell Sage.

Empson, S. B. (1999). Equal sharing and shared meaning: The development of fraction concepts in a first-grade classroom. *Cognition and Instruction, 17*(3), 283–342.

Engel, M., Claessens, A., & Finch, M. (2013). Teaching students what they already know? The (mis)alignment between mathematics instructional content and student knowledge in kindergarten. *Educational Evaluation and Policy Analysis, 35*(2), 157–178.

Engel, M., Claessens, A., Watts, T., & Farkas, G. (2016). Mathematics content coverage and student learning in kindergarten. *Educational Researcher, 45*(5) 293–300.

Fisher, K. R., Hirsh-Pasek, K., Newcombe, N., & Golinkoff, R. M. (2013). Taking shape: Supporting preschoolers' acquisition of geometric knowledge through guided play. *Child Development, 84*(6), 1872–1878. Retrieved from https://doi.org/10.1111/cdev.12091

Frye, D., Baroody, A. J., Burchinal, M., Carver, S. M., Jordan, N. C., & McDowell, J. (2013). *Teaching math to young children: A practice guide.* Washington, DC: Institute of Education Sciences. Retrieved from https://ies.ed.gov/ncee/wwc/Docs/PracticeGuide/early_math_pg_111313.pdf

Fuhs, M., Farran, D. C., Meador, D., & Norvell, J. (2012, June). Classroom activities and organization: Comparing tools of the mind to control classrooms. In D. C. Farran (Chair), *Developing self-regulation in preschool classrooms: Results from research on the Tools of the Mind prekindergarten curriculum.* Symposium presented at the biennial meeting of the Head Start Research Conference, Washington, DC.

Fuson, K. C. (1988). *Children's counting and concepts of number.* New York, NY: Springer.

Garcia, E. (2015). *Inequalities at the starting gate: Cognitive and noncognitive skills gaps between 2010–2011 kindergarten classmates.* Washington, DC: Economic Policy Institute.

Gelman, R., & Gallistel, C. R. (1986). *The child's understanding of number* (2nd ed.). Cambridge, MA: Harvard University Press.

Graue, E., Whyte, K., & Delaney, K. K. (2014). Fostering culturally and developmentally responsive teaching through improvisational practice. *Journal of Early Childhood Teacher Education, 35*(4), 297–317. Retrieved from https://doi.org/10.1080/10901027.2014.968296

Graves, B. (2006). *PK–3: What is it and how do we know it works?* New York, NY: Foundation for Child Development.

Guarino, C. M., Hamilton, L. S., Lockwood, J. R., & Rathbun, A. H. (2006). *Teacher qualifications, instructional practices, and reading and mathematics gains of kindergartners* (NCES 2006–031). Washington, DC: National Center for Education Statistics.

Gunderson, E., & Levine, S. C. (2011). Some types of parent number talk count more than others: Relations between parents' input and children's cardinal-number knowledge. *Developmental Science, 14*(5), 1021–1032.

Hiebert, J., Stigler, J. W., Jacobs, J. K., Givvin, K. B., Garnier, H., Smith, M., et al. (2005). Mathematics teaching in the United States today (and tomorrow): Results from the TIMSS 1999 Video Study. *Educational Evaluation and Policy Analysis, 27*(2), 111–132.

House, E. R., Glass, G. V., McLean, L. D., & Walker, D. F. (1978). No simple answer: Critique of the Follow Through evaluation. *Harvard Educational Review, 48*, 128–160.

Jenkins, J. M., Farkas, G., Duncan, G. J., Burchinal, M., & Vandell, D. L. (2016). Head Start at ages 3 and 4 versus Head Start followed by state pre-K: Which is more effective? *Educational Evaluation and Policy Analysis, 38*(1), 88–112.

Jordan, N. C., Kaplan, D., Ramineni, C., & Locuniak, M. N. (2009). Early math matters: Kindergarten number competence and later mathematics outcomes. *Developmental Psychology, 45*(3), 850–867. Retrieved from https://doi.org/10.1037/a0014939

Kagan, S. L., Carroll, J., Comer, J. P., & Scott-Little, C. (2006). Alignment: A missing link in early childhood transitions. *Young Children, 61*(5), 26–30, 32.

Kauerz, K. (2006). *Ladders of learning: Fighting fade-out by advancing PK–3 alignment.* (Issue Brief No. 2). Washington, DC: New America Foundation.

Kleemans, T., Peeters, M., Segers, E., & Verhoeven, L. (2012). Child and home predictors of early numeracy skills in kindergarten. *Early Childhood Research Quarterly, 27*(3), 471–477.

Kouba, V. L. (1989). Children's solution strategies for equivalent set multiplication and division word problems. *Journal for Research in Mathematics Education, 20*(2), 147–158. Retrieved from https://doi.org/10.2307/749279

Lampert, M., & Cobb, P. (2003). Communication and language. In J. Kilpatrick, W. G. Martin, & D. Schifter (Eds.), *A research companion to principles and standards for school mathematics* (pp. 237–249). Reston, VA: National Council of Teachers of Mathematics.

LeFevre, J., Clarke, T., & Stringer, A. P. (2002). Influences of language and parental involvement on the development of counting skills: Comparisons of French- and English-speaking Canadian children. *Early Child Development and Care, 172*, 283–300.

LeFevre, J.-A., Skwarchuk, S.-L., Smith-Chant, B. L., Fast, L., Kamawar, D., & Bisanz, J. (2009). Home numeracy experiences and children's math performance in the early school years. *Canadian Journal of Behavioural Science/Revue Canadienne Des Sciences Du Comportement, 41*(2), 55–66. Retrieved from http://doi.org/10.1037/a0014532

Levine, S. C., Suriyakham, L. W., Rowe, M. L., Huttenlocher, J., & Gunderson, E. A. (2010). What counts in the development of young children's number knowledge? *Developmental Psychology, 46*(5), 1309–1319.

Lukie, I., Skwarchuk, S., LeFevre, J., & Sowinski, C. (2014). The role of child interests and collaborative parent-child interactions in fostering numeracy and literature development in Canadian homes. *Early Childhood Education Journal, 42*(4), 251–259.

Mack, N. K. (1993). Learning rational numbers with understanding: The case of informal knowledge. In T. P. Carpenter, E. Fennema, & T. A. Romberg (Eds.), *Rational numbers: An integration of research* (pp. 85–105). Mahwah, NJ: Lawrence Erlbaum.

Maloney, E., Ramirez, G., Gunderson, E., Levine, S. C., & Beilock, S. (2015). Intergenerational effects of parents' math anxiety on children's math achievement and anxiety. *Psychological Science, 26*(9), 1480–1488.

Marietta, G., & Marietta, S. (2013). *PreK–3rd's lasting architecture: Successfully serving linguistically and culturally diverse students in Union City, New Jersey.* New York, NY: Foundation for Child Development.

Mazzocco, M. M., & Kover, S. T. (2007). A longitudinal assessment of executive function skills and their association with math performance. *Child Neuropsychology, 13*, 18–45.

Miller, E., & Almon, J. (2009). *Crisis in the kindergarten: Why children need to play in school.* College Park, MD: Alliance for Childhood.

Missall, K., Hojnoski, R. L., Caskie, G. I. L., & Repasky, P. (2015). Home numeracy environments of preschoolers: Examining relations among mathematical activities, parent mathematical beliefs, and early mathematical skills. *Early Education and Development, 26*(3), 356–376.

Moss, J., Bruce, C. D., & Bobis, J. (2016). Young children's access to powerful mathematics ideas: A review of current challenges and developments in the early years. In L. D. English & D. Kirshner (Eds.), *Handbook of international research in mathematics education* (3rd ed., pp. 153–190). New York, NY: Routledge.

National Association for the Education of Young Children & National Council of Teachers of Mathematics. (2010). *Early childhood mathematics: Promoting good beginnings.* Washington, DC. Retrieved from https://www.naeyc.org/files/naeyc/file/positions/psmath.pdf

National Center on Quality Teaching and Learning. (2015). *Mathematics preschool curriculum consumer report.* Washington, DC: U.S. Department of Health and Human Services, Administration for Children and Families, Office of Head Start.

National Council of Teachers of Mathematics. (2000). *Principles and standards for school mathematics.* Reston, VA: Author.

National Governors Association. (2012). Governor's role in aligning early education and K–12 reforms: Challenges, opportunities, and benefits for children. Washington, DC: Author.

National Governors Association & Council of Chief State School Officers. (2010). *Common core state standards for mathematics.* Washington, DC: Authors. Retrieved from corestandards.org

National Research Council. (2001). *Adding it up: Helping children learn mathematics* (J. Kilpatrick, J. Swafford, & B. Findell, Eds.). Washington, DC: National Academies Press.

National Research Council & Committee on Early Childhood Mathematics. (2009). *Mathematics learning in early childhood: Paths toward excellence and equity* (C. T. Cross, T. A. Woods, & H. A. Schweingruber, Eds.). Washington, DC: National Academies Press.

Nguyen, T., Watts, T. W., Duncan, G. J., Clements, D. H., Sarama, J. S., Wolfe, C., et al. (2016). Which preschool mathematics competencies are most predictive of fifth grade achievement? *Early Childhood Research Quarterly, 36,* 550–560. Retrieved from https://doi.org/10.1016/j.ecresq.2016.02.003

Niklas, F., Cohrssen, C., & Tayler, C. (2015). Improving preschoolers' numerical abilities by enhancing the home numeracy environment. *Early Education and Development, 27*(3), 372–383. doi:10.1080/10409289.2015.1076676

Niklas, F., & Schneider, W. (2014). Casting the die before the die is cast: The importance of the home numeracy environment for preschool children. *European Journal of Psychology of Education, 29*(3), 327–345.

Obradovic, J., Portilla, X., & Boyce, T. (2012). Executive functioning and developmental neuroscience. In R. Pianta (Ed.), *Handbook of early childhood education* (pp. 324–351). New York, NY: Guilford.

Ohio Department of Education. (2015). *Ohio's new learning standards: Kindergarten through Grade 3.* Columbus, OH: Author.

Pagani, L., Fitzpatrick, C., Archambault, I., & Janosz, M. (2010). School readiness and later achievement: A French Canadian replication and extension. *Developmental Psychology, 46*(5), 984–994.

Parks, A. N., & Blom, D. C. (2013). Helping young children see math in play. *Teaching Children Mathematics, 20*(5), 310–317.

Perry, B., & Dockett, S. (2008). Young children's access to powerful mathematical ideas. In L. D. English & D. Kirshner (Eds.), *Handbook of international research in mathematics education* (2nd ed., pp. 75–108). New York, NY: Routledge.

Preschool Curriculum Evaluation Research Consortium. (2008). *Effects of preschool curriculum programs on school readiness* (NCER 2008–2009). Washington, DC: National Center for Education Research, Institute of Education Sciences.

Presser, A. L., Clements, M., Ginsburg, H., & Ertle, B. (2015). Big Math for Little Kids: The effectiveness of a preschool and kindergarten mathematics curriculum. *Early Education and Development, 26*(3), 399–426. Retrieved from https://doi.org/10.1080/10409289.2015.994451

Pruden, S. M., Levine, S. C., & Huttenlocher, J. (2011). Children's spatial thinking: Does talk about the spatial world matter? *Developmental Science, 14,* 1417–1430.

Purpura, D. J., Baroody, A. J., Eiland, M. D., & Reid, E. E. (2016). Fostering first graders' reasoning strategies with basic sums: The value of guided instruction. *Elementary School Journal, 117*(1), 72–100. Retrieved from https://doi.org/10.1086/687809

Reardon, S. (2011). The widening academic achievement gap between the rich and the poor: New evidence and possible explanations. In G. Duncan & R. Murnane (Eds), *Whither opportunity? Rising inequality, schools, and children's life chances* (pp. 91–116). New York, NY: Russell Sage Foundation.

Riley, M. S., & Greeno, J. G. (1988). Developmental analysis of understanding language about quantities and of solving problems. *Cognition and Instruction, 5*(1), 49–101. Retrieved from https://doi.org/10.1207/s1532690xci0501_2

Rittle-Johnson, B., Fyfe, E. R., Hofer, K. G., & Farran, D. C. (2016). Early math trajectories: Low-income children's mathematics knowledge from ages 4 to 11. *Child Development, 88*(5), 1727–1742. Retrieved from https://doi.org/10.1111/cdev.12662

Romano, E., Kohen, D., Babchishin, L., & Pagani, L. S. (2010). School readiness and later achievement: Replication and extension study using a nation-wide Canadian survey. *Developmental Psychology, 46*, 995–1007.

Sadowski, M. (2006). *Core knowledge for PK–3 teaching: Ten components of effective instruction* (PreK–3rd Action Brief No. 5). New York, NY: Foundation for Child Development.

Saxe, G. B., Guberman, S. R., & Gearhart, M. (1987). Social processes in early number development. *Monographs of the Society for Research in Child Development, 52*(2). Retrieved from https://www.culturecognition.com/sites/default/files/Saxe%2CGuberman%2CGearhart_Monograph.pdf

Schacter, J., & Jo, B. (2016). Improving low-income preschoolers' mathematics achievement with Math Shelf, a preschool tablet computer curriculum. *Computers in Human Behavior, 55*(Part A), 223–229. Retrieved from https://doi.org/10.1016/j.chb.2015.09.013

Schacter, J., Shih, J., Allen, C. M., DeVaul, L., Adkins, A. B., Ito, T., et al. (2016). Math Shelf: A randomized trial of a prekindergarten tablet number sense curriculum. *Early Education and Development, 27*(1), 74–88. Retrieved from https://doi.org/10.1080/10409289.2015.1057462

Shonkoff, J., & Phillips, D. (2000). *From neurons to neighborhoods: The science of early childhood development.* Washington, DC: National Academies Press.

Skwarchuk, S.-L. (2009). How do parents support preschoolers' numeracy learning experiences at home? *Early Childhood Education Journal, 37*(3), 189–197.

Skwarchuk, S.-L., Sowinski, C., & LeFevre, J.-A. (2014). Formal and informal home learning activities in relation to children's early numeracy and literacy skills: The development of a home numeracy model. *Journal of Experimental Child Psychology, 121*, 63–84.

Starkey, P., & Klein, A. (2000). Fostering parental support for children's mathematical development: An intervention with Head Start families. *Early Education & Development, 11*(5), 659–680.

Starkey, P., & Klein, A. (2008). Sociocultural influences on young children's mathematical knowledge. In O. N. Saracho & B. Spodek (Eds.), *Contemporary perspectives on mathematics in early childhood education* (pp. 253–276). Charlotte, NC: Information Age.

Stebbins, L. B., St. Pierre, R. G., Proper, E. C., Anderson, R. B., & Cerva, T. R. (1977). *Education as experimentation: A planned variation model* (Vol. 4-A). Cambridge, MA: Abt Associates.

Stein, M. K., Grover, B. W., & Henningsen, M. (1996). Building student capacity for mathematical thinking and reasoning: An analysis of mathematical tasks used in reform classrooms. *American Educational Research Journal, 33*(2), 455–488. Retrieved from https://doi.org/10.3102/00028312033002455

Stein, M. K., & Kaufman, J. H. (2010). Selecting and supporting the use of mathematics curricula at scale. *American Educational Research Journal, 47*(3), 663–693. Retrieved from https://doi.org/10.3102/0002831209361210

Stein, M. K., Remillard, J., & Smith, M. S. (2007). How curriculum influences student learning. In F. K. Lester (Ed.), *Second handbook of research on mathematics teaching and learning* (Vol. 1, pp. 319–369). Charlotte, NC: Information Age.

Stipek, D. J., Clements, D., Coburn, C., Franke, M., & Farran, D. (2017). PK–3: What does it mean for instruction? *SRCD Social Policy Report, 30*(2), 1–23.

Stipek, D. J., & Valentino, R. (2015). Early childhood memory and attention as predictors of academic growth trajectories. *Journal of Educational Psychology, 107*(3), 771–778.

Student Achievement Partners. (2012). *Mathematics: Focus by grade level.* New York, NY: Author. Retrieved from http://achievethecore.org/category/774/mathematics-focus-by-grade-level

Takanishi, R. (2016). *First things first! Creating the new American primary school.* New York, NY: Teachers College Press.

Tudge, J., & Doucet, F. (2004). Early mathematical experiences: Observing young Black and White children's everyday activities. *Early Childhood Research Quarterly, 19,* 21–39.

U.S. Department of Education. (2008). *Foundations for success: The final report of the National Mathematics Advisory Panel.* Washington, DC: Author.

U.S. Department of Education. (2015). *Primary mathematics intervention report: Everyday mathematics.* Washington, DC: Institute of Education Sciences, What Works Clearinghouse. Retrieved from http://whatworks.ed.gov

Valentino, R., & Stipek, D. J. (2016). *PreK–3 alignment in California's education system: Obstacles and opportunities.* Stanford, CA: Stanford University Policy Analysis for California Education.

Vandermaas-Peeler, M., Nelson, J., Bumpass, C., & Sassine, B. (2009). Numeracy-related exchanges in joint storybook reading and play. *International Journal of Early Years Education, 17*(1), 67–84.

Van Oers, B. (2010). Emergent mathematical thinking in the context of play. *Educational Studies in Mathematics, 74*(1), 23–37. Retrieved from https://doi.org/10.1007/s10649-009-9225-x

Van Voorhis, F. L. (2011). Adding families to the homework equation: A longitudinal study of mathematics achievement. *Education and Urban Society, 43*(3), 313–338.

Verdine, B. N., Golinkoff, R. M., Hirsh-Pasek, K., & Newcombe, N. S. (2017). Links between spatial and mathematical skills across the preschool years. *Monographs of the Society for Research in Child Development, 82*(1), 7–30. Retrieved from https://doi.org/10.1111/mono.12280

Wager, A. A. (2013). Practices that support mathematics learning in a play-based classroom. In L. D. English & J. T. Mulligan (Eds.), Reconceptualizing early mathematics learning (pp. 163–181). Dordrecht, Netherlands: Springer Netherlands. Retrieved from http://link.springer.com/chapter/10.1007/978-94-007-6440-8_9

Wager, A. A., & Carpenter, T. P. (2012). Learning trajectories through a sociocultural lens. In J. S. Carlson & J. R. Levin (Eds.), Instructional strategies for improving students' learning: Focus on early reading and mathematics (pp. 197–204). Charlotte, NC: Information Age.

Wager, A. A., & Parks, A. N. (2016). Assessing early number learning in play. ZDM, 48(7), 991–1002. Retrieved from https://doi.org/10.1007/s11858-016-0806-8

Webb, N. M., Franke, M. L., De, T., Chan, A. G., Freund, D., Shein, P., et al. (2009). "Explain to your partner": Teachers' instructional practices and students' dialogue in small groups. Cambridge Journal of Education, 39(1), 49–70. Retrieved from https://doi.org/10.1080/03057640802701986

Chapter 4

Connecting Research on Children's Mathematical Thinking With Assessment: Toward Capturing More of What Children Know and Can Do

MEGAN FRANKE
University of California, Los Angeles

BRANDON MCMILLAN
Brigham Young University

NICHOLAS C. JOHNSON
San Diego State University

ANGELA CHAN TURROU
University of California, Los Angeles

Researchers in the United States and around the world have accumulated robust findings about the development of young children's mathematical thinking (e.g., Baroody & Purpura, 2017; Clements & Sarama, 2007; Moss, Bruce, & Bobis, 2016; National Research Council [NRC], 2001, 2009). The research is full of detail and nuance about young children's mathematical ideas, and it consistently reveals that young children know more than we might expect. For instance, children can model and solve story problems without prior instruction (Carpenter & Moser, 1984). Research-based knowledge about the development of young children's thinking also has been widely influential in the design of curricula, standards, and professional development (e.g., Clements, Sarama, Wolfe, & Spitler, 2013; National Governors Association Center for Best Practices & Council of Chief State School Officers, 2010; Schifter, Bastable, & Russell, 1998; Sowder, 2007; TERC (Firm), Pearson Education, & Scott Foresman, 2008). The results from these studies point to the importance of learning about and attending to the details of children's mathematical thinking in order to help teachers learn from their ongoing practice and make instructional decisions that recognize and build from children's existing understanding (Franke, Carpenter, Levi, & Fennema, 2001; Jacobs, Lamb, & Philipp, 2010). This extensive body of research has further potential to inform policy that aims to expand early learning opportunities that attend specifically to the importance of early mathematics learning.

The goal of this chapter is to describe what we have learned from research on young children's mathematical thinking and suggest how the field might better leverage the details of children's mathematical thinking in research that attempts to document what young children know and what matters for future learning. To address these issues, we call attention to the limitations of current assessment practices, make explicit the various theoretical stances toward learning, and argue for broader considerations of what understanding mathematics can look and sound like. We echo other scholars (e.g., Turiel, Chung, & Carr, 2016) in challenging the binary of "you either know it or you don't" and argue for a renewed focus on the details of understanding, particularly *partial understanding*, revealed by children's responses in assessment settings. By partial understandings, we refer to the aspects of understanding that students draw on in their work that are mathematically productive and relevant to their overall understanding. We suggest that greater attention to children's partial understandings could reveal different constellations of knowledge, offering multiple productive pathways to learning.

Attention to partial understanding has been central in prior research on children's mathematical thinking. As early as the work of Piaget, researchers have argued for attention to the range of processes underlying students' correct and incorrect answers. Much of the research documenting children's mathematical thinking continued in this tradition and attempted to capture the nuance, the different boundaries of students' ideas, and the processes underlying their thinking. These detailed studies proved highly useful in mapping the complex and interconnected terrain of early mathematics learning, providing a view of development that highlighted young children's sense-making (e.g., Baroody, Lai, & Mix, 2006).

Over time, however, much of the nuance and variability has been ignored and only particular details have been chosen as consequential indicators of knowledge. For example, to identify causal mechanisms for later learning or discrete components of a linear learning trajectory, many studies consider only correct versus incorrect responses or a single aspect (such as the ability to quickly verbalize "three" when shown a card with 3 dots) of a complex construct (demonstrating a cardinal understanding of number) as markers of knowledge. Our concern is that these approaches tend to overlook what the nuances of children's responses or processes might reveal about their understanding. These decisions—while often practical, expedient, and cost effective—have serious consequences for which child is deemed to be mathematically knowledgeable, and how policy and practice might support learning.

In this chapter we highlight what we know about children's mathematical thinking. We then examine how current assessment practices often limit what educators learn about an individual child's thinking, the body of children's thinking overall, and the content of mathematics. We argue for the importance of detailing children's partial understandings, accounting for all of the knowledge that students bring and how such ideas are related to one another. Attending to the breadth, depth, and nuance of children's partial understandings is critical to better informing the consequential decisions we make about children in mathematics.

What We Know About Young Children's Mathematical Understanding

Young children possess mathematical understandings that are complex and sophisticated (Baroody, 2004; Ginsburg, 1977; Hughes, 1986; Steffe, 2004; Van de Rijt, Van Luit, & Pennings, 1999). They can count, problem-solve, and reason about spatial relations. Children can explain and represent their mathematical ideas from an early age (for reviews of the literature, see Clarke, Cheeseman, & Clarke, 2006; Clements & Sarama, 2007; Perry & Dockett, 2008). This research documents young children's mathematical ideas and consistently finds that young children know more than we expect. The nature of young children's mathematical knowledge has significant implications for creating learning opportunities that draw on and extend children's varied and wide-ranging capabilities. In the following section we present a selective summary of young children's mathematics. We focus on research in whole number counting and problem solving and spatial relations to highlight the wealth of research knowledge and its implications for assessment.

What Young Children Know: Counting

Children come to school knowing something about how to count. Most children (94%) come to kindergarten counting to at least 10, and 68% can count to 20 or higher (Child Trends Data Bank, 2015). Yet saying the counting words in a correct sequence to 20 is only one aspect of counting. Extensive research has investigated the principled ideas that give counting meaning (e.g., Baroody et al., 2006). These principles include the stable order of the counting sequence (1, 2, 3 . . .), the one-to-one principle (one number word corresponds to one object), and the cardinal principle (the last number word stated in counting a collection represents the number of items in the collection).[1]

Early research suggested that counting principles were learned in sequence: children first learned the counting sequence, then moved to one-to-one correspondence before applying the cardinal principle (Gelman & Gallistel, 1978). However, researchers subsequently found that some children demonstrated understanding "out of order"; that is, they could use one-to-one correspondence without having perfected the counting sequence (e.g., Fuson, 1988). These findings raised questions about the robustness of a fixed developmental sequence in counting. Variation in children's use of counting principles led researchers to consider the relationship between student response and measurement. The kinds of understanding that children demonstrated were heavily influenced by the assessment tasks themselves—e.g., how the tasks were posed and the size of the collection the children were asked to count (Fuson, 1988; Sarnecka & Carey, 2008; Wynn, 1990).

In addition, cognitive and brain research documents the development of the counting principles and the processes that underlie them. There remains much to be learned here, but studies show that the size of the sets, the ways the cardinal principle is defined and measured, and the underlying mechanisms of cardinal understanding (such as finger gnosia—mentally representing one's fingers) are consequential for young children's counting (Dehaene, Spelke, & Feigenson, 2004; Noël, 2005; McCrink & Wynn, 2008).[2] While there is growing evidence that counting principles are learned in relation to one another, there remains disagreement about what young children know and understand about the relationships between the principles, and differences in how researchers operationalize particular skills and understandings (Baroody, 1992, 2017; Clements & Sarama, 2007; Mix, Sandhofer, Moore, & Russell, 2012). The important evolution of understanding in children's counting points to the need to consistently reconsider how particular construct definitions are related to conceptions of skills and understanding and how these definitions shape the ways that understanding is assessed and the claims that follow.

What Young Children Know: Solving Story Problems

Children build on their understanding of counting to solve problems. In large national studies, few children are seen as being able to solve problems before kindergarten (e.g., 4%; National Center for Education Statistics [NCES], 2001). Yet in other research studies, often where students are interviewed, researchers find that students as young as 3 and 4 can solve addition and subtraction problems when provided concrete materials (Clements & Sarama, 2007; Hughes, 1986; Huttenlocher, Jordan, & Levine, 1994). Carpenter and his colleagues found that 88% of kindergartners could provide a correct strategy for solving common addition problems by using concrete materials to model the action in the problem (Carpenter, Ansell, Franke, Fennema, & Weisbeck, 1993).

Children come to school with the ability to model the action in story contexts (Carpenter, Hiebert, & Moser, 1981, 1983). For example, when presented with a story about having 7 cookies and then eating 3, children naturally count out 7 blocks, remove 3, and count to figure out how many are left. The ability to model the action in a story context supports children in solving a range of addition, subtraction, multiplication, and division problems; solving problems that are not as readily modeled leads to difficulty (Carpenter, 1985; Kouba, 1989; Riley & Greeno, 1988).

The research on the development of children's mathematical thinking in relation to the operations is quite robust, indicating that children's intuitive strategies elegantly build upon one another as they become more mathematically sophisticated (Empson, Levi, & Carpenter, 2011; NRC, 2001). As children model the relationships in problems, over time they come to see that they do not necessarily need to represent every item in the problem while still modeling what is happening to the quantities (for example, in the cookie story, the child begins by saying "7," then counts back until she has raised 3 fingers: "6, 5, 4"). These early strategies provide the base understanding for future strategies and thus can be leveraged to support learning (Carpenter, Fennema, & Franke, 1996).

To be clear, while we can map a trajectory of strategies that children are likely to use in ways that are helpful for teachers, this is not a prescription for what students will do when they solve a given problem. In earlier studies of the development of children's strategies, and in practice, we see variability in the strategies children choose to use, sometimes because of the type of problem or specific numbers involved, and other times because they have more than one strategy they can use and choose the one that serves them well in that context (Carpenter & Moser, 1984; Siegler, 1994; Steffe, von Glasersfeld, Richards, & Cobb, 1983).

In addition, young children's ability to make use of their informal knowledge requires that they can relate to a story's context so that they understand what the quantities represent and the action that can be modeled. Thus, assessments of young children's problem solving are often contingent on their interest in or understanding of the story context, not just their understanding of the mathematics. Their ability to successfully navigate the assessment also requires that they balance their nonschool knowledge and their understanding of what "school" wants them to do. Children quickly pick up that the *school way* to solve problems is to use number facts and symbols ("I know it's supposed to be 7 minus 3, so can I remember that the answer is 4?"), and often abandon their nonschool based strategies to solve problems the way they think others want them to.[3]

What Young Children Know: Spatial Reasoning

Spatial reasoning in young children has gained significant attention in recent years as it has been found to be a predictor not only of future mathematical understanding but also of success in reading and high school graduation (Duncan et al., 2007). However, researchers know less about children's knowledge of spatial reasoning. Although historically considered an innate ability, a meta-analysis of research validates that spatial reasoning is in fact malleable (Uttal et al., 2013). Research demonstrates that spatial reasoning has a crucial relationship with mathematical thinking (Mix & Cheng, 2012) and is a reliable predictor of students' knowledge of number (Verdine, Irwin, Golinkoff, & Hirsh-Pasek, 2014). Spatial instruction has been linked to benefits not only in the spatial domain but also in number skills, such as improved calculation and basic magnitude and counting skills (Cheng & Mix, 2014; Thompson, Nuerk, Moeller, & Cohen Kadosh, 2013; Verdine, Golinkoff, Hirsh-Pasek, & Newcombe, 2014).

Research in geometric and spatial thinking has identified a progression of children's thinking within these content domains (Clements & Battista, 1992; Clements & Sarama, 2007; Piaget & Inhelder, 1967; Van Hiele, 1986). Similar to counting and problem solving, children come to school with geometric and spatial abilities (Clements & Battista, 1992; Clements & Sarama, 2007; Clements, Swaminathan, Hannibal, & Sarama, 1999; NRC, 2009). In particular, infants and toddlers have demonstrated the ability to locate objects in space using landmark cues (Newcombe & Huttenlocher, 2000), to form spatial categories (Quinn, 1994, 2004), and to perform better than would be expected by chance on mental transformations including rotations and translations (Levine, Huttenlocher, A. Taylor, & Langrock, 1999). Clements et al. (1999) reported that more than 90% of children from ages 3 years, 5 months, to 4 years, 4 months, could correctly identify a circle, and 82% could point out a square. Sixty percent of children ages 4 to 6 pointed out triangles, and 50% pointed out rectangles.

Young students are capable of more than simply identifying and sorting shapes; they can reason about distinguishing characteristics at an early age (Clements & Sarama, 2007; Clements et al., 1999; Lehrer, Jenkins, & Osana, 1998). However, attempting to assess geometric and spatial reasoning is often complicated by measures that rely on students' verbal explanations (Clements et al., 1999; Lehrer, Jenkins, & Osana, 1998), tying the development of spatial reasoning with language development (Bowerman, 1996; Clements & Sarama, 2007). Future research concerning the role of language needs to account for broader ways of communicating about geometric and spatial ideas, such as gesturing (Radford, 2009), and needs to consider measures that allow students to explain in ways that make sense to them.[4]

Conceptualizing Learning in the Context of Mathematical Thinking

Research on children's mathematical thinking draws on different theories of learning, leading to different methodological approaches and illuminating different aspects of knowing. As researchers consider how the outcomes of particular approaches to assessment are used to make consequential policy and practice decisions, it is important to be clear about which aspects of knowing are being prioritized. We argue that such decisions would benefit from greater attention to the richness of understandings and the varied ways those understandings are demonstrated. This requires a theory of learning that enables researchers to see how history, context, and interaction shape what they learn about what students know.

We consider learning to be situated where cultural histories and experiences shape how one engages in any setting and where one's experiences and histories have been shaped by political, economic, and social structures (Gutiérrez, 2002, 2013; Lave, 1988; Nasir, Hand, & E. V. Taylor, 2008; Rogoff, 1990). Research that takes knowing and coming to know as inseparable focuses on the relationships between individuals and the roles, positions, and patterns of activity that are made available to them as they participate in the practices of various communities (Brown & Campione, 1996; Lave, 1993; Lave & Wenger, 1991). So, in making claims about what individuals know, it is necessary to attend to how they respond in relation to a given context, how that context is driven by how schools and classrooms work, how mathematics is defined and by whom, how the tasks that are used influence sense-making and take up students' cultural resources, and so on. Rather than seeing differences in student responses across contexts as indicative of lack of knowledge—the inability to abstract, generalize or transfer—we see them as evidence of situationally specific knowledge and choices. Researchers documenting children's mathematical thinking have long considered the contextual and interpersonal nature of children's sense-making (e.g., Steffe et al., 1983); in this chapter we build on these ideas and extend them to center the relations among ideas, tasks, and people, and to examine how those relations may be driven by existing ways of doing things.

Reconciling Research on Children's Mathematical Thinking and Assessment

Despite the extensive body of literature documenting young children's rich and varied capabilities, the current discourse around mathematical knowledge or readiness tends to focus on what some children do not know rather than on what they know. For example, reports regularly show that low-income students of color do not perform at the same level as their White, middle- and upper-class counterparts. (e.g., NRC, 2009). The 2015 Child Trends Data Bank reported that in 2007, 67% of young children ages 3–6 living above poverty levels were able to count out loud to 20 or higher, while only 49% of young children living in poverty could do so. When compared to White or Black children, Hispanic children were less likely to count to 20 or higher before they started kindergarten. The Child Trends data are not unusual for large-scale examinations of groups of students (see NCES, 2001). Despite recent evidence showing that the "academic readiness gap" in mathematics between low-income and higher income groups narrowed by 10% between 1998 and 2010 (Reardon &

Portilla, 2016), some groups of children continue to be seen as coming to school with rich mathematical knowledge while others are seen as lacking such knowledge. Yet a different study (Seo & Ginsburg, 2004), which assessed students in an informal setting, found no differences across socioeconomic groups. Reconciling research that focuses on children's lack of knowledge with research that highlights children's remarkable sense-making capabilities leads us to wonder whether we are maximizing and marshalling the learnings from research on children's mathematical thinking in the most effective ways. It may be that assessments that rely on narrow tasks and measure only correct/incorrect responses are underestimating what students know, perhaps in ways that differentially affect particular groups of students. Considering the details of students' thinking and how we assess students may enable us to create better ways to more completely document students' knowledge.

How Might the Nature, Administration, and Scoring of Tasks Influence What Assessments Reveal?

We argue that greater attention to methodological decisions about what is captured related to children's mathematical knowledge could further enrich research efforts in early childhood education. Specifically, we call for increased attention to three aspects of assessment:

- The characteristics of the tasks that are posed can open or close opportunities for students to show what they know.

- The administration of the assessment can invite or close off participation.

- The scoring of assessments can broaden or limit what is seen as known.

Taken together, the tasks, administration, and scoring of assessments can narrow how children demonstrate understanding. Addressing these methodological issues as they relate to determining what a child knows would allow the field to move beyond a discourse that too often focuses on what children lack. This could provide new data and possibilities for understanding performance disparities and why the effects of interventions that produce early gains quickly fade out.

Three Examples From Preschool Interviews

To illustrate these methodological issues, we present three examples drawn from our recent work interviewing 476 preschool students ages 3 to 4 (Johnson, Turrou, McMillan, Raygoza, & Franke, 2019). We provide these examples not to make broad claims about our data, but rather to ground the discussion of assessment tasks, administration, and scoring in specific, concrete cases that highlight the details of children's thinking and participation.

Example 1: Hazel Counts 30 Pennies. We videotaped 3-year-old Hazel counting an unorganized pile of 30 pennies. She counted confidently, sliding each penny across the table from its original pile into a new one as she counted, "1, 2, 3, 4, 5, 6, 7, 8, 9, 10, 11, 12, 14, 16, 17, 18, 19, 11, 12, 14, 16, 17, 18, 19, 11, 12, 14, 16, 17, 18, 19, 11, 12." When she had finished counting the entire collection and was asked how many pennies there were, she confidently announced: "12."

Clearly, Hazel did not "correctly" count this large set of pennies. However, focusing only on the outcome of her count rather than on the details of *how* she counted overlooks that Hazel demonstrated a great deal of understanding about counting. For example, though she skipped 13 and 15, she otherwise used an accurate counting sequence from 1 to 19. Furthermore, her move to extend the counting sequence beyond 19 by returning to 11 shows an emerging awareness of the patterns of the base-ten number system.[5] The careful reader will also notice that Hazel recited 33 numbers for a collection of 30 items (she in fact double-counted the 4th, 5th, and 13th pennies). Despite this, her application of one-to-one correspondence was quite consistent overall (90%) and became more consistent the farther she counted (she did not double-count after the 13th penny). Finally, when asked how many pennies were in her collection, she stated "12," the last number used in her counting sequence; this is consistent with the cardinal principle that the last number used when counting names the total quantity of the set.

In this example, a novel assessment task of counting 30 pennies was administered in a manner that allowed Hazel to count and organize the collection any way she wanted. The task and administration enabled her to show her partial understanding, and scoring beyond correct/incorrect captured her emergent use of the counting principles.

Example 2: Mia Counts 15 Bears. Often when assessing children's counting, researchers line up objects for the children and ask them to count. Mia, who was almost 4 years old, was asked to count a set of 8 blue bears that had been placed in a line for her. She counted "1, 2, 3, 5 . . ." and then used four more number words out of sequence. As she counted she touched each bear in correspondence with each number word. When asked how many bears she had, she did not give a response.

A few minutes later Mia was given an unorganized pile of 15 bears of various colors and asked how many bears were in the collection. Mia began by removing 3 yellow bears from the pile, standing the bears up as she counted "1, 2, 3," and declared, "This is 3." Rather than continuing from the 3, Mia counted out another 3 blue bears and stated, "This is 3," then followed the same process again for the next set of 3 red bears. When asked how many bears she had in her collection, she said, "3."

Mia demonstrated much understanding of counting across these two tasks, but not necessarily the understandings the tasks were designed to capture. On the first task, she showed a limited understanding of the conventional counting sequence, but showed that she understood each bear was to be assigned exactly one number word when counting. On the second task she demonstrated cardinal understanding: She was able to generate sets of 3. This might be viewed as surprising—in the first task Mia did not apply the cardinal principle to her count, and generating a set of a given number is typically viewed as a more sophisticated understanding of cardinality (e.g., National Research Council, 2009).[6]

Despite not being able to provide "correct" responses, across these two tasks, Mia demonstrated understanding of both one-to-one correspondence and cardinality. The larger set size, objects of different colors, the opportunity to count them the way she wanted to, and the scoring of the details of her count would provide potentially useful information about what Mia knew.

Example 3: Kevin Finds the Triangles. A common task used to assess children's understanding of geometry and spatial relations involves identifying triangles on a page filled with drawings of different shapes. Often there are triangles of different orientations and side lengths and many nontriangle examples. Children are provided with counters, and asked to place counters on all of the triangles. When Kevin was presented with this task, he began by placing counters on the isosceles triangle, the right triangle, and then the "upside down" equilateral triangle (see Figure 1). He then paused, noticing that many counters were still available, and continued by placing counters over the other shapes until eventually all shapes had been assigned a counter.

One interpretation of Kevin's response is that he does not know what a triangle is. Another is that he is able to recognize some shapes as triangles, but that his knowledge is fragile and the presence of additional counters suggested that he was not finished with matching shapes and counters. Kevin's process on this task was not an anomaly; often when we administered this task, children began by correctly identifying at least some of the triangles on the page. However, once identified, children often continued to mark shapes until they had marked every single shape on the page.

Children's comments also revealed understanding of, for instance, shape composition or possible transformations. For example, some children used two counters to indicate that both parts of the lower-left figure were triangles (one on the big one, one on the little one), or placed a counter over the lower-right figure and stated that it *would* be a triangle if you connected the lines. These "incorrect" performances reflect significant mathematical understanding.

While this task created opportunities to learn about children's knowledge of the characteristics of triangles, it also made us wonder if children equally understood what the task was asking and felt confident to stop without some acknowledgement. Attending to the sequence in which children applied their counters and to their comments about their choices rather than only to the results suggests that children's participation reflects their efforts to negotiate pleasing the assessor and making meaning of the task.

Our goal with these three examples has been to highlight how the characteristics of tasks, their administration, and their scoring determine what is captured in an assessment and can broaden or limit opportunities for children to demonstrate competence. We recognize that many experimental studies attempt to account for variability in their design. However,

Figure 1. The identifying triangles task and the sequence in which Kevin identified the triangles.

the data derived from approaches that, for example, randomize students, average across responses, and control for a host of mediating variables are limited in several ways. First, it is difficult to understand the nature of the differential responses to assessments within and across groups (so it is not clear what the averages mean for whom, and in which group). Second, averaging student responses may be masking student understanding (consider a case of three item scores averaged to yield .67 versus knowing the student used three valid direct modeling strategies but miscounted on one item). Third, underestimating what students know always positions them as behind or lacking in knowledge. Rather than attempting to explain learning in terms of a single indicator, methodological approaches that embrace and investigate variability could provide specific, actionable data for practitioners and policy makers alike.

Capturing the Details of What Children Know

Capturing details may enable more learning about the different constellations of understandings that are fruitful for children and a deeper representation of the mathematics itself. We see possibilities in placing greater attention on the partial ideas that emerge in the context of assessments. Recall that while Mia did not engage in the task as the assessor intended, her performance demonstrated that she did know something about cardinality—she could create a set of three, label it as "three," and continue to count in that way until she had completed counting the set of bears. Capturing Mia's performance in this way not only identifies the counting knowledge Mia did have but also details her knowledge in a way that allows for capturing subtleties in her knowledge, enabling a more complete and accurate capturing of growth. We see the same possibilities of moving beyond all-or-nothing characterizations of children's performances when considering Hazel's knowledge of one-to-one correspondence. An all-or-nothing approach toward assessing one-to-one correspondence only would result in a claim that Hazel did not demonstrate this principle for even a quantity as small as five objects. But acknowledging where she successfully used one-to-one correspondence would enrich assessors' ability to show what she knows and capture her growth over time.[7] To be clear, we do not want to "over"-claim what children can do; rather we are calling for a broader recognition of the knowledge children do have and for assessment practices that better capture the ways children coordinate all of the knowledge it takes to count.

In addition, how a child's response is scored often determines whether the child is offered opportunities to engage in more challenging tasks. Taking up rigid views of developmental trajectories that privilege mastery shape what counts as knowing. If Hazel's double-count of the fourth penny is interpreted as not having mastered the discrete skill of counting small quantities, not only would we learn less about Hazel, but the assessor would skip, say, an addition word problem task with the assumption that she could not solve it given that she did not demonstrate the prerequisite skill of counting. Yet, if we consider broader understandings that may be reflected in a child's performance, there are many aspects of solving a problem that Hazel may demonstrate even if she does not show consistent use of one-to-one correspondence. How we capture knowledge within a task not only impacts what we learn about a child's understanding within that task, but also shapes the future opportunities we provide to continue to probe that child's understanding.

Broadening Opportunities for Children to Show What They Know

In considering how we capture what it is that children are to know mathematically, it is imperative to attend to *the situations we construct* to determine what children know. Mathematics is a cultural practice, a practice that emerges in communities as people attempt to solve problems in their daily lives (Bishop, 1988; Diversity in Mathematics Education Center for Learning and Teaching, 2007; Lerman, 1994; Presmeg, 2007; Stigler & Hiebert, 1999). Children's histories, cultural practices, languages, knowledge, and sense of themselves shape who they are, what they know, and how they participate. Considering mathematics as a cultural practice, and viewing children as agents in the process, complicates how we make sense of what students know and understand (Christensen, 2004; Cook-Sather, 2002; Dockett & Perry, 2007).

Given that children are sense-makers who bring with them not just mathematical knowledge but their own personal experiences from in and out of school (National Association for the Education of Young Children [NAEYC], 2009; NAEYC & National Council of Teachers of Mathematics [NCTM], 2010), assessments may not be capturing the ways that children share what they know. In assessments, particularly large-scale studies, we put children in situations where they are asked to respond to tasks that are quite unnatural—and potentially more unnatural for some than others. We have evidence that children are more likely to utilize their mathematical knowledge when the task is natural and meaningful to them (Wager, Graue, & Harrigan, 2015). For instance, children's experience with counting might involve grabbing a big handful of items from a tub and figuring out how many they have, but in an assessment the child sits as the items are placed in a line by the assessor. What is intended to serve as a scaffold may implicitly communicate that the child's job is to count (but not to move) the objects. In other situations we score children who do not respond quickly enough as incorrect, when their hesitation may not be at all related to their mathematical knowledge (such as when they are expected to show knowledge of subitizing). We ask children to use tools that they have never seen before and score their inability to use them as not knowing. We ask children to talk with people they do not know; yet we have evidence that who they are talking to influences what they share. As the examples of Mia and Kevin illustrate, children's responses and participation in assessment situations reflect efforts to demonstrate competence in unfamiliar situations— situations that for low-income children of color are further complicated by power differentials between the children and primarily European American adult researchers and assessors (Parks & Schmeichel, 2014).

Reconceptualizing What It Means to Capture What Children Know

A number of researchers have called for rethinking what it means to assess young children in mathematics (see, for example, Anderson & Gold, 2006; Carr & Claxton, 2002; Cook-Sather, 2002; Wager & Parks, 2016). This scholarship has provided a number of alternative approaches and insights into what needs to change in how we assess and interpret what we learn from assessments. Central to these arguments is that the context in which children are assessed and the language used, as well as the tasks posed and how they are coded, shape children's participation and responses.

We recognize that we cannot address all of these concerns in most large-scale assessment situations. However, we can improve them as we build into assessments and trainings a set of guidelines for how to structure interactions to make students comfortable in an otherwise unfamiliar situation and give us our best chance of capturing all that they know. Assessors can watch for signals that a child feels comfortable participating in the assessment and feels able to share ideas in any way that makes sense. We can prepare assessors to monitor closely the body language of the child and respond in situationally specific ways (e.g., shifting from being seated up in a chair to sitting on the ground next to a particularly hesitant child; offering opportunities for the child to tell a story or step away for a moment). We can allow the child to engage with the materials prior to using them to do the mathematics. We can consider whether the assessment occurs in a space where the child feels comfortable and can see a known adult.

We can also improve assessments by allowing children to drive the language choice. Multilingual assessors who make clear the languages they speak can support children to feel more free to speak in their native language or speak a mixture of languages. It can be difficult for children who are learning mathematics in school in English and speak another language at home to manage what they know in which language in the context of an assessment. We can encourage children to talk in whatever way makes sense to them, on occasion posing the task or asking a follow-up question in another language to provide continued language support throughout the assessment.

In addition, we can be sensitive to the fact that the mathematical tasks posed and the details of the coding will drive what is learned and the claims made in our studies. The objects that students count matter; asking students about what they did matters. From our examples of Hazel and Mia, counting bears versus pennies leads to some variation in results, as does counting 8 bears of the same color lined up versus counting 15 bears of different colors poured from a bag onto a table. When children stand the bears up as they count, we often see better one-to-one correspondence and more accurate counts. Larger collections are not an impediment but an opportunity to gain more knowledge of children's mathematical understanding. When counting a larger quantity we saw greater detail in a breakdown of the counting principles used (Johnson et al., 2019). Documenting these differences requires coding for more than an all-or-nothing performance, as nuance in the children's responses provides additional information.

We understand that these recommendations require more resources (more time, more skilled assessors, etc.), and we anticipate great resistance due to concerns about variability in the design and administration of assessments influencing results. However, the use of uniform administrative protocols already creates variability, a variability that favors particular children at the expense of others.

Extending Current Research

While research currently investigates the relationship between mathematical assessments and a range of student outcomes, this research area would benefit from the participation of those studying young children's mathematical thinking. Research partnerships could be built on the rich understandings of the nuances of children's thinking to redesign and study features of task, administration, and scoring and the resulting claims about student knowledge. In particular, this joint research could investigate (a) how particular tasks, administration, and scoring influence children's responses and the claims made about what children know; (b) how a prompt from the assessor influences student responses; (c) how different ways of coding a child's response influence outcome claims; or (d) how different tasks can enrich what we learn about children's mathematical thinking.

In addition, we argue that continued attention to the nuances of children's thinking could lead to a better understanding of their mathematical thinking itself, and of the content of mathematics. We are left with many researchable questions. How do different constellations of understanding emerge as students take on more sophisticated mathematical tasks? Does Hazel's understanding of the number system show us where to look for a meaningful way to document what children understand? Does Mia's situationally specific use (and nonuse) of the cardinal principle push us to enrich how we define understanding of cardinality? Are her partial understandings helpful for her sense-making of other mathematical ideas, such as producing an initial quantity to solve a story problem?

Implications for Policy and Practice

Supporting high-quality early childhood learning experiences is widely recognized as important for student learning, and expanding access to early childhood education is increasingly seen by researchers and policy makers as a potential lever to address economic and racial inequality in America's cities. Given increased attention to relationships between students' performance on measures of early childhood mathematical knowledge and later outcomes, this chapter has focused on mathematics.

We concur that supporting young children to help them learn mathematics in meaningful ways is a critical goal for early childhood educators, researchers, and policy makers. If we are to better understand what it is that young children know, and uncover the supposed critical role of mathematics in later success, we need to continue to press for nuanced data about what children know. Current large-scale measures present too narrow a view of what counts as mathematics, and they are administered in ways that may systematically underestimate the mathematics knowledge of students in particular communities. Research in early childhood needs to move beyond what Turiel and colleagues (2016) call the "more or less syndrome," where the tendency is to identify a single trait or aspect of knowledge and then to measure whether individuals possess more or less of this trait and its relation to overall performance. Knowledge or school success then becomes a consequence of how much of a given trait children possess. The danger is that we focus too much on having "it" or not having "it" and miss out on the larger constellation of what children do know, their underlying sense-making processes, and the conditions that support them.

We also recognize that changing how we measure and make claims about children's mathematical knowledge and understanding will not address the long-standing inequalities that determine outcomes unless these efforts are accompanied by policies to disrupt the history of disinvestment in urban schools and neighborhoods and address the ways in which these communities are nested within larger sociopolitical structures (Anyon, 2014; Ladson-Billings, 2006). However, beginning to examine the assumptions underlying our claims about what children understand, and capturing a wider constellation of knowing, can change how researchers, teachers, and policy makers see young people as knowers and doers of mathematics, and can influence the decisions we make about their opportunities for future learning.

Acknowledgment

The research reported in this manuscript was supported in part by grants from the Heising-Simons Foundation. The opinions expressed are those of the authors and do not reflect those of the funding organization.

Notes

1. We limit our focus here to the three "how to count" principles identified by Gelman and Gallistel (1978, 1986), as those aspects of counting are the most extensively researched and most relevant for practitioners.

2. Significant findings are emerging from brain research. Much of this work focuses on the underlying mechanisms of counting. We have been selective in order to highlight issues emerging in relation to existing research findings in other fields.

3. This phenomenon has been well documented with respect to older children (e.g., Carraher, Carraher, & Schliemann, 1985; Kazemi, 2002; Lave, 1988; Nasir, Hand, & E. V. Taylor, 2008; Saxe, 1988) but has received less attention in early childhood studies.

4. We have focused this brief review on young children's counting, problem solving, and spatial relations. Research has also documented young children's abilities across a wide variety of content, such as algebraic reasoning (Carpenter & Levi, 2000; Jacobs, Franke, Carpenter, Levi, & Battey, 2007) and fractions knowledge (Empson, 1999; Mix, Levine, & Huttenlocher, 1999; Streefland, 1993).

5. Extending the counting sequence involves developing an understanding that the names of larger numbers are formed by naming each successive decade in combination with the single-digit sequence (e.g., NRC, 2009). It is our contention that "rule-governed errors" (Ginsburg, 1989) reveal an emergent understanding of the patterns in the base-ten number system.

6. An alternative explanation is that Mia first subitized (nonverbally) and then counted out loud up to 3 to produce the set. However, on a previous subitizing task Mia did not provide a correct response when shown a card with 3 dots.

7. Hazel is not an anomaly; in our interviews with more than 450 preschoolers, 41% of students who demonstrated no one-to-one correspondence when counting 8 bears showed some one-to-one while counting 31 pennies (Johnson et al., 2019).

References

Anderson, D., & Gold, E. (2006). Home to school: Numeracy practices and mathematical identities. *Mathematical Thinking and Learning, 8*(3), 261–286. doi:10.1207/s15327833mtl0803_4

Anyon, J. (2014). *Radical possibilities: Public policy, urban education, and a new social movement.* New York, NY: Routledge.

Baroody, A. J. (1992). The development of preschoolers' counting skills and principles. In J. Bideaud, C. Meljac, & J.-P. Fischer (Eds.), *Pathways to number: Children's developing numerical abilities* (pp. 99–126). Hillsdale, NJ: Lawrence Erlbaum.

Baroody, A. J. (2004). The developmental bases for early childhood number and operations standards. In D. H. Clements, J. Sarama, & A.-M. DiBiase (Eds.), *Engaging young children in mathematics: Standards for early childhood mathematics education* (pp. 173–219). Mahwah, NJ: Lawrence Erlbaum.

Baroody, A. J. (2017). The use of concrete experiences in early childhood mathematics instruction. In J. Sarama, D. Clements, C. Germeroth, & C. Day-Hess (Eds.), *Advances in child development and behavior* (Vol. 53, pp. 43–94). Amsterdam, Netherlands: Elsevier.

Baroody, A. J., Lai, M., & Mix, K. S. (2006). The development of young children's early number and operation sense and its implications for early childhood education. In B. Spodek & O. Saracho (Eds.), *Handbook of research on the education of young children* (Vol. 2, pp. 187–221). Mahwah, NJ: Lawrence Erlbaum.

Baroody, A. J., & Purpura, D. J. (2017). Early number and operations: Whole numbers. In J. Cai (Ed.), *Compendium for research in mathematics education* (pp. 308–354). Reston, VA: National Council of Teachers of Mathematics.

Bishop, A. J. (1988). Mathematics education in its cultural context. *Educational Studies in Mathematics*, *19*(2), 179–191.

Bowerman, M. (1996). The origins of children's spatial semantic categories: Cognitive versus linguistic determinants. In J. J. Gumperz & S. C. Levinson (Eds.), *Studies in the social and cultural foundations of language, No. 17. Rethinking linguistic relativity* (pp. 145–176). New York, NY: Cambridge University Press.

Brown, A. L., & Campione, J. C. (1996). Psychological theory and the design of innovative learning environments: On procedures, principles, and systems. In L. Schauble & R. Glaser (Eds.), *Innovations in learning* (pp. 289–326). Hillsdale, NJ: Lawrence Erlbaum.

Carpenter, T. P. (1985). Learning to add and subtract: An exercise in problem solving. In E. A. Silver (Ed.), *Teaching and learning mathematical problem solving: Multiple research perspectives* (pp. 17–40). Hillsdale, NJ: Lawrence Erlbaum.

Carpenter, T. P., Ansell, E., Franke, M. L., Fennema, E., & Weisbeck, L. (1993). Models of problem solving: A study of kindergarten children's problem-solving processes. *Journal for Research in Mathematics Education*, *24*(5), 428–441. doi.org/10.2307/749152

Carpenter, T. P., Fennema, E., & Franke, M. L. (1996). Cognitively guided instruction: A knowledge base for reform in primary mathematics instruction. *Elementary School Journal*, *97*(1), 3–20. Retrieved from https://doi.org/10.2307/1001789

Carpenter, T. P., Hiebert, J., & Moser, J. M. (1981). Problem structure and first-grade children's initial solution processes for simple addition and subtraction problems. *Journal for Research in Mathematics Education*, *12*(1), 27–39.

Carpenter, T. P., Hiebert, J., & Moser, J. M. (1983). The effect of instruction on children's solutions of addition and subtraction word problems. *Educational Studies in Mathematics*, *14*(1), 55–72.

Carpenter, T. P., & Levi, L. (2000). *Developing conceptions of algebraic reasoning in the primary grades* (No. 00-2). Madison, WI: National Center for Improving Student Learning and Achievement in Mathematics and Science.

Carpenter, T. P., & Moser, J. M. (1984). The acquisition of addition and subtraction concepts in grades one through three. *Journal for Research in Mathematics Education*, *15*(3), 179–202.

Carr, M., & Claxton, G. (2002). Tracking the development of learning dispositions. *Assessment in Education: Principles, Policy & Practice*, *9*(1), 9–37.

Carraher, T. N., Carraher, D., & Schliemann, A. (1985). Mathematics in the streets and in schools. *British Journal of Developmental Psychology*, *3*, 21–29. doi:10.1111/j.2044-835X.1985.tb00951.x

Cheng, Y. L., & Mix, K. S. (2014). Spatial training improves children's mathematics ability. *Journal of Cognition and Development*, *15*(1), 2–11.

Child Trends Data Bank. (2015). *Early school readiness: Indicators of child and youth well-being.* Retrieved from http://www.childtrends.org/wp-content/uploads/2015/07/07_School_Readiness.pdf

Christensen, P. H. (2004). Children's participation in ethnographic research: Issues of power and representation. *Children & Society, 18*(2), 165–176.

Clarke, B., Cheeseman, J., & Clarke, D. (2006). The mathematical knowledge and understanding young children bring to school. *Mathematics Education Research Journal, 18*(1), 78–102.

Clements, D. H., & Battista, M. T. (1992). Geometry and spatial reasoning. In D. A. Grouws (Ed.), *Handbook of research on mathematics teaching and learning* (pp. 420–464). New York, NY: Macmillan.

Clements, D. H., & Sarama, J. (2007). Early childhood mathematics learning. In F. K. Lester (Ed.), *Second handbook of research on mathematics teaching and learning* (Vol. 1, pp. 461–555). Charlotte, NC: Information Age.

Clements, D. H., Sarama, J., Wolfe, C. B., & Spitler, M. E. (2013). Longitudinal evaluation of a scale-up model for teaching mathematics with trajectories and technologies: Persistence of effects in the third year. *American Educational Research Journal, 50*(4), 812–850.

Clements, D. H., Swaminathan, S., Hannibal, M. A. Z., & Sarama, J. (1999). Young children's concepts of shape. *Journal for Research in Mathematics Education, 30*(2), 192–212.

Cook-Sather, A. (2002). Authorizing students' perspectives: Toward trust, dialogue, and change in education. *Educational Researcher, 31*(4), 3–14.

Dehaene, S., Spelke, E. & Feigenson, L. (2004). Core systems of number. *Trends in Cognitive Sciences, 8*(7), 307–314.

Diversity in Mathematics Education Center for Learning and Teaching. (2007). Culture, race, power, and mathematics education. In F. K. Lester (Ed.), *Second handbook of research on mathematics teaching and learning* (pp. 405–433). Charlotte, NC: Information Age.

Dockett, S., & Perry, B. (2007). Trusting children's accounts in research. *Journal of Early Childhood Research, 5*(1), 47–63.

Duncan, G. J., Dowsett, C. J., Claessens, A., Magnuson, K., Huston, A. C., Klebanov, P., et al. (2007). School readiness and later achievement. *Developmental Psychology, 43*(6), 1428–1446.

Empson, S. B. (1999). Equal sharing and shared meaning: The development of fraction concepts in a first-grade classroom. *Cognition and Instruction, 17*(3), 283–342.

Empson, S. B., Levi, L., & Carpenter, T. P. (2011). The algebraic nature of fractions: Developing relational thinking in elementary school. In J. Cai & E. Knuth (Eds.), *Early algebraization* (pp. 409–428). Berlin, Germany: Springer.

Franke, M. L., Carpenter, T. P., Levi, L., & Fennema, E. (2001). Capturing teachers' generative change: A follow-up study of professional development in mathematics. *American Educational Research Journal, 38*(3), 653–689.

Fuson, K. C. (1988). *Children's counting and concepts of number.* New York, NY: Springer.

Gelman, R., & Gallistel, C. R. (1978). *The young child's understanding of number: A window on early cognitive development.* Cambridge, MA: Harvard University Press.

Gelman, R., & Gallistel, C. R. (1986). *The child's understanding of number* (2nd ed.). Cambridge, MA: Harvard University Press.

Ginsburg, H. P. (1977). *Children's arithmetic: The learning process.* New York, NY: Van Nostrand.

Ginsburg, H. P. (1989). *Children's arithmetic: How they learn it and how you teach it* (2nd ed.). Austin, TX: Pro-Ed.

Gutiérrez, R. (2002). Enabling the practice of mathematics teachers in context: Toward a new equity research agenda. *Mathematical Thinking and Learning, 4*(2–3), 145–187.

Gutiérrez, R. (2013). The sociopolitical turn in mathematics education. *Journal for Research in Mathematics Education, 44*(1), 37–68.

Hughes, M. (1986). *Children and number difficulties in learning mathematics.* Oxford, UK: Blackwell.

Huttenlocher, J., Jordan, N. C., & Levine, S. C. (1994). A mental model for early arithmetic. *Journal of Experimental Psychology: General, 123*(3), 284–296.

Jacobs, V. R., Franke, M. L., Carpenter, T. P., Levi, L., & Battey, D. (2007). Professional development focused on children's algebraic reasoning in elementary school. *Journal for Research in Mathematics Education, 38*(3), 258–288.

Jacobs, V. R., Lamb, L. L., & Philipp, R. A. (2010). Professional noticing of children's mathematical thinking. *Journal for Research in Mathematics Education,* 169–202.

Johnson, N. C., Turrou, A. C., McMillan, B. G., Raygoza, M. C., & Franke, M. L. (2019). "Can you help me count these pennies?" Surfacing preschoolers' understandings of counting. *Mathematical Thinking and Learning, 21*(4), 237–264. doi.org/10.1080/10986065.2019.1588206

Kazemi, E. (2002). Exploring test performance in mathematics: The questions children's answers raise. *Journal of Mathematical Behavior, 21*(2), 203–224.

Kouba, V. L. (1989). Children's solution strategies for equivalent set multiplication and division word problems. *Journal for Research in Mathematics Education, 20*(2), 147–158.

Ladson-Billings, G. (2006). From the achievement gap to the education debt: Understanding achievement in U.S. schools. *Educational Researcher, 35*(7), 3–12.

Lave, J. (1988). *Cognition in practice: Mind, mathematics and culture in everyday life.* New York, NY: Cambridge University Press.

Lave, J. (1993). The practice of learning. In S. Chaiklin & J. Lave (Eds.), *Understanding practice: Perspectives on activity and context* (pp. 3–32). New York, NY: Cambridge University Press.

Lave, J., & Wenger, E. (1991). *Situated learning: Legitimate peripheral participation.* Cambridge, UK: Cambridge University Press.

Lehrer, R., Jenkins, M., & Osana, H. (1998). Longitudinal study of children's reasoning about space and geometry. In R. Lehrer & D. Chazan (Eds.), *Designing learning environments for developing understanding of geometry and space* (pp. 137–167). Mahwah, NJ: Lawrence Erlbaum.

Lerman, S. (Ed.). (1994). *Cultural perspectives on the mathematics classroom.* Dordrecht, Netherlands: Springer Science & Business Media.

Levine, S. C., Huttenlocher, J., Taylor, A., & Langrock, A. (1999). Early sex differences in spatial skill. *Developmental Psychology, 35*(4), 940–949.

McCrink, K., & Wynn, K. (2008). Mathematical reasoning. In *Encyclopedia of infant and early childhood development* (Vol. 2, pp. 280–289). San Diego, CA: Academic Press.

Mix, K. S., & Cheng, Y. (2012). The relation between space and math: Developmental and educational implications. In J. B. Benson (Ed.), *Advances in child development and behavior* (Vol. 42, pp. 197–243). Amsterdam, Netherlands: Academic Press, Elsevier.

Mix, K. S., Levine, S. C., & Huttenlocher, J. (1999). Early fraction calculation ability. *Developmental Psychology, 35*(1), 164–174.

Mix, K. S., Sandhofer, C. M., Moore, J. M., & Russell, C. (2012). Acquisition of the cardinal word principle: The role of input. *Early Childhood Research Quarterly, 27,* 274–283.

Moss, J., Bruce, C. D., & Bobis, J. (2016). Young children's access to powerful mathematics ideas: A review of current challenges and developments in the early years. In L. D. English & D. Kirshner (Eds.), *Handbook of international research in mathematics education* (3rd ed., pp. 153–190). New York, NY: Routledge.

Nasir, N. S., Hand, V., & Taylor, E. V. (2008). Culture and mathematics in school: Boundaries between "cultural" and "domain" knowledge in the mathematics classroom and beyond. *Review of Research in Education, 32*(1), 187–240.

National Association for the Education of Young Children. (2009). *Developmentally appropriate practice in early childhood programs serving children from birth through age 8* [Position statement].

Washington, DC: Author. Retrieved from https://www.naeyc.org/files/naeyc/file/positions/PSDAP.pdf

National Association for the Education of Young Children & National Council of Teachers of Mathematics. (2010). *Early childhood mathematics: Promoting good beginnings* [Joint position statement]. Washington, DC: National Association for the Education of Young Children. Retrieved from https://www.naeyc.org/files/naeyc/file/positions/psmath.pdf

National Center for Education Statistics. (2001). *Entering kindergarten: A portrait of American children when they begin school: Findings from The Condition of Education 2000,* Nicholas Zill and Jerry West, NCES 2001–035. Washington, DC: U.S. Government Printing Office.

National Governors Association Center for Best Practices & Council of Chief State School Officers. (2010). *Common Core State Standards Mathematics.* Washington, DC: Authors.

National Research Council. (2001). *Adding it up: Helping children learn mathematics* (J. Kilpatrick, J. Swafford, & B. Findell, Eds.). Washington, DC: National Academy Press.

National Research Council. (2009). *Mathematics learning in early childhood paths toward excellence and equity* (C. T. Cross, T. A. Woods, & H. A. Schweingruber, Eds.). Washington, DC: National Academies Press.

Newcombe, N. S., & Huttenlocher, J. (2000). *Making space: The development of spatial representation and reasoning.* Cambridge, MA: MIT Press.

Noël, M. E. (2005). Finger gnosia: A predictor of numerical abilities in children? *Child Neuropsychology, 11,* 413–430.

Parks, A. N., & Schmeichel, M. (2014). Children, mathematics, and videotape: Using multimodal analysis to bring bodies into early childhood assessment interviews. *American Educational Research Journal, 51*(3), 505–537.

Perry, B., & Dockett, S. (2008). Young children's access to powerful mathematical ideas. In L. D. English & D. Kirshner (Eds.), *Handbook of international research in mathematics education* (2nd ed., pp. 75–108). New York, NY: Routledge.

Piaget, J., & Inhelder, B. (1967). *The child's conception of space* (F. J. Langdon & J. L. Lunzer, Trans.). New York, NY: Norton. (Original work published 1948)

Presmeg, N. (2007). The role of culture in teaching and learning mathematics. In F. K. Lester (Ed.), *Second handbook of research on mathematics teaching and learning* (pp. 435–458). Charlotte, NC: Information Age.

Quinn, P. C. (1994). The categorization of above and below spatial relations by young infants. *Child Development, 65*(1), 58–69.

Quinn, P. C. (2004). Spatial representation by young infants: Categorization of spatial relations or sensitivity to a crossing primitive? *Memory & Cognition, 32*(5), 852–861.

Radford, L. (2009). Why do gestures matter? Sensuous cognition and the palpability of mathematical meanings. *Educational Studies in Mathematics, 70*(2), 111–126.

Reardon, S. F., & Portilla, X. A. (2016). Recent trends in income, racial, and ethnic school readiness gaps at kindergarten entry. *AERA Open, 2*(3), 1–18.

Riley, M. S., & Greeno, J. G. (1988). Developmental analysis of understanding language about quantities and of solving problems. *Cognition and Instruction, 5*(1), 49–101. doi.org/10.1207/s1532690xci0501_2

Rogoff, B. (1990). *Apprenticeship in thinking: Cognitive development in social context.* New York, NY: Oxford University Press.

Sarnecka, B. W., & Carey, S. (2008). How counting represents number: What children must learn and when they learn it. *Cognition, 108*(3), 662–674.

Saxe, G. B. (1988). Candy selling and math learning. *Educational Researcher, 17*(6), 14–21.

Schifter, D., Bastable, V., & Russell, S. J. (1998). *Developing mathematical ideas: Building a system of tens.* Parsippany, NJ: Dale Seymour.

Seo, K. H., & Ginsburg, H. P. (2004). What is developmentally appropriate in early childhood mathematics education? Lessons from new research. In D. H. Clements & J. Sarma (Eds.), *Engaging young children in mathematics: Standards for early childhood mathematics education* (pp. 91–104). New York, NY: Routledge.

Siegler, R. S. (1994). Cognitive variability: A key to understanding cognitive development. *Current Directions in Psychological Science, 3*(1), 1–5.

Sowder, J. T. (2007). The mathematical education and development of teachers. In F. K. Lester (Ed.), *Second handbook of research on mathematics teaching and learning* (pp. 157–223). Charlotte, NC: Information Age.

Steffe, L. P. (2004). PSSM from a constructivist perspective. In D. H. Clements & J. Sarama (Eds.), *Engaging young children in mathematics* (pp. 221–252). Mahwah, NJ: Lawrence Erlbaum.

Steffe, L. P., von Glasersfeld, E., Richards, J., & Cobb, P. (1983). *Children's counting types: Philosophy, theory, and applications.* New York, NY: Praeger.

Stigler, J. W., & Hiebert, J. (1999). *The teaching gap: Best ideas from the world's teachers for improving education in the classroom.* New York, NY: Simon and Schuster.

Streefland, L. (1993). Fractions: A realistic approach. In T. P. Carpenter, E. Fennema, & T. A. Romberg (Eds.), *Rational numbers: An integration of research* (pp. 289–325). Mahwah, NJ: Lawrence Erlbaum.

TERC (Firm), Pearson Education, & Scott Foresman. (2008). *Investigations in number, data, and space.* Glenview, IL: Pearson Scott Foresman.

Thompson, J. M., Nuerk, H. C., Moeller, K., & Cohen Kadosh, R. C. (2013). The link between mental rotation ability and basic numerical representations. *Acta Psychologica, 144*(2), 324–331.

Turiel, E., Chung, E., & Carr, J. A. (2016). Struggles for equal rights and social justice as unrepresented and represented in psychological research. In S. S. Horn, M. D. Ruck, & L. S. Liben (Eds.), *Equity and justice in developmental science: Theoretical and methodological issues* (Vol. 50, pp. 1–29). doi.org/10.1016/bs.acdb.2015.11.004

Uttal, D. H., Meadow, N. G., Tipton, E., Hand, L. L., Alden, A. R., Warren, C., et al. (2013). The malleability of spatial skills: A meta-analysis of training studies. *Psychological Bulletin, 139,* 352–402. doi:10.1037/a0028446

Van de Rijt, B. A. M., Van Luit, J. E. H., & Pennings, A. H. (1999). The construction of the Utrecht early mathematical competence scales. *Educational and Psychological Measurement, 59*(2), 289–309.

Van Hiele, P. M. (1986). *Structure and insight: A theory of mathematics education.* Orlando, FL: Academic Press.

Verdine, B. N., Golinkoff, R. M., Hirsh-Pasek, K., & Newcombe, N. S. (2014). Finding the missing piece: Blocks, puzzles, and shapes fuel school readiness. *Trends in Neuroscience and Education, 3*(1), 7–13.

Verdine, B. N., Irwin, C. M., Golinkoff, R. M., & Hirsh-Pasek, K. (2014). Contributions of executive function and spatial skills to preschool mathematics achievement. *Journal of Experimental Child Psychology, 126,* 37–51.

Wager, A. A., Graue, M. E., & Harrigan, K. (2015). Swimming upstream in a torrent of assessment. In B. Perry, A. MacDonald, & A. Gervasoni (Eds.), *Mathematics and transition to school* (pp. 15–30). Singapore: Springer. doi.org/10.1007/978-981-287-215-9_2

Wager, A. A., & Parks, A. N. (2016). Assessing early number learning in play. *ZDM, 48*(7), 991–1002.

Wynn, K. (1990). Children's understanding of counting. *Cognition, 36*(2), 155–193.

Chapter 5

When Is a Child Not a Child Outcome? Humanizing Research in Early Childhood Education

Amy Noelle Parks
Michigan State University

Anita A. Wager
Vanderbilt University

In arguing for his ecological model for understanding human interactions, Bronfenbrenner (1977, p. 517) called developmental psychology "the science of the strange behavior of children in strange situations with strange adults for the briefest possible periods of time." An apt description, given that much of what we know about young children's learning, growth, and development comes from experimental or assessment interviews of children in schools or laboratories where investigators spend just minutes with each child in conditions designed to minimize variations in context. Given these constraints, perhaps what is most surprising about the field of developmental psychology is just how much we have been able to learn.

One of the strengths of research that relies on clinical or assessment interviews to assess outcomes is that it strips away much of the complexity that exists in the everyday world and allows social scientists to explore relationships between qualities, characteristics, practices, and outcomes that might otherwise go unnoticed. For example, a growing cluster of research has demonstrated the critical role of executive function and other noncognitive factors in children's long-term success, pushing the field of early childhood to maintain its focus on socio-emotional factors (e.g., Denham, Bassett, Zinsser, & Wyatt, 2014; O'Toole, Monks, & Tsermentseli, 2017). This line of research has shown that children's abilities to tap pencils as directed by researchers, walk balance beams at a variety of speeds, delay eating snacks, and recognize emotions from pictures show relationships with both academic and nonacademic outcomes (such as measures of aggression).

In relationship to content area learning, research using clinical and assessment interviews has helped to identify particular pedagogical practices that are likely to pay off in terms of children's learning. For example, in mathematics, Siegler and Ramani (2008, 2009) have shown that relatively short episodes of play with linear board games can improve children's abilities to estimate, count, and make comparisons. In literacy, research that draws on measures of oral language and decoding has demonstrated the importance of attending to children's talk in addition to their engagement with print in prekindergarten and kindergarten classrooms (e.g., Kelley, Goldstein, Spencer, & Sherman, 2015; Kendeou, Van den Broek, White, & Lynch, 2009).

In addition, over the last decade, an increasingly large body of research has sought to link measures executed in individual assessment interviews to measures of classroom quality performed with observational protocols (e.g., Clements, Sarama, Spitler, Lange, & Wolfe, 2011; Jerome, Hamre, & Pianta, 2009; Neuman, Pinkham, & Kaefer, 2015; Stipek & Byler, 2004). These protocol studies, frequently done with large numbers of children, have generally shown that the indicators of classroom quality as measured by the instruments have a positive relationship with academic and socio-emotional outcomes as measured in assessment interviews. Given these findings, these protocols have allowed both researchers and program evaluators to make relatively quick assessments of the quality of instruction in large numbers of classrooms.

In addition to experimental and observational studies, the field of early childhood education has been substantially informed by large-scale, quantitative studies that, rather than focusing on children's behavior for short periods of time, examine children in large numbers over long periods of time. Like clinical interview and protocol studies, these "big picture" studies have also been quite successful in finding ways to simplify complex environments and experiences so that we can understand the relationships between early experiences in childhood and outcomes later in life. For example, longitudinal studies have demonstrated that well-known preschool programs, like the Perry Preschool Project and the Abecedarian Project, which both used curricula that could be described as child-centered and included many components for parent outreach, have consistently had positive long-term outcomes (Berrueta-Clement, Schweinhart, Barnett, Epstein, & Weikart, 1984; Campbell & Ramey, 1994). Similarly, large-scale studies have shown that the impact of prekindergarten varies with children's family income and racial identification (Magnuson, Meyers, Ruhm, & Waldfogel, 2004), with the type of curriculum and instruction provided (Miller & Bizzell, 1983; Schweinhart & Weikart, 1997; Weiland & Yoshikawa, 2013), and with the amount of preparation teachers received (Phillipsen, Burchinal, Howes, & Cryer, 1997).

Broadly, we have a host of interview measures, observation protocols, study designs, and statistical methods that have done a remarkable job identifying relationships between well-defined inputs and outputs. However, when we turn our attention from the orderly work of designing studies toward the messy work of designing learning environments—which includes building relationships with children and families, juggling the needs of multiple children and the demands of diverse content, and, most importantly, guiding the young of our species toward knowledgeable and ethical adulthood—it becomes a challenge to preserve clean lines between experimental and control groups, between independent and dependent variables, and between learning and development. In fact, stripping away the messy complexity of classroom contexts to do experimental studies can produce interventions that are not robust enough to survive integration back into messy classrooms. Or it can produce interventions that ultimately are not culturally relevant to the children with whom the interventions interact. There is a need for more research that begins in the messy spaces where teachers and children spend their days.

We do think there is much to learn from well-designed, large-scale quasi-experimental research projects and clinical interview studies, but we also urge a turn toward research informed by the perspectives of those who have worked as teachers in early childhood education. Often, lines drawn between researchers in human development or educational psychology and those in early childhood education emphasize differences in theories, methodologies, and disciplinary content; however, we want to center another area of difference. Researchers who have worked as practitioners are likely to use their experiences to shape their research programs (e.g., Ballinger, 1992; Cowhey, 2006; Dyson, 2013). Often, this means that rather than trying to simplify the complexity of classrooms to make relationships clear, their work tends to embrace noise and confusion and often seeks to illuminate the ways in which particular teaching practices, curricula, or standards create varying experiences for different children, teachers, and classroom contexts. To portray this complexity, their work often relies on close descriptions of human interactions in classrooms and schools based on ethnographic (e.g., Falchi, Axelrod, & Genishi, 2014; Graue, 1993; Yoon, 2014), phenomenological (e.g., Greve, 2009; Parnell, 2011), or post-structural traditions (e.g., Blaise, 2012; Davies, 2003).

Unfortunately, it is not enough to simply call for diverse methodological approaches in early childhood education. Growing out of the National Research Council's (2002) report on educational research, which called for "scientifically-based" research based on five key principles, including working toward findings that generalize across populations and settings, the research community in early childhood has for some time privileged large-scale, experimental designs that seek to generalize findings and practices across contexts (Feuer, Towne, & Shavelson, 2002). Given this methodological emphasis—which dovetails with the theoretical and methodological commitments of other fields that produce early childhood research (e.g., economics, child development) —it is critical to push for other kinds of research. In particular, we want to call for research that seeks to preserve an emphasis on children as dynamic, complicated, and contradictory human beings, rather than as data points on a variety of measures. This focus is not just about being child-centered but also about recognizing that serving the needs of racially, economically, and linguistically diverse children requires research methods that deal well with nuance and context.

A move toward embracing the complexity of early childhood education might be described as working toward humanizing research. It would involve "dialogic consciousness raising and the building of relationships of care and dignity for both researchers and participants" (Paris, 2011, p. 140). This stance makes care for and responsiveness to participants a key criterion in evaluating the quality of all research. Paris goes on to argue that while such a stance is important in all educational research, it is particularly important when working with people who are marginalized by social categories, such as race, class, and language. We would also argue that a humanizing stance that seeks to build relationships of care and dignity is particularly important in work with young children, who may be even less able than older participants to protect their own interests.

We see a humanizing stance as particularly relevant in the current era, when increased funding and interest in early childhood is drawing scholars from a variety of disciplines into the field, even though these scholars may not have deep knowledge of the practices, ethical commitments, and history of early childhood education. In addition to the ethical reasons for a turn toward humanizing research, we see it as potentially powerful for producing more relevant, field-shaping research. Because research that is humanizing necessarily considers the complexity of real human beings in early childhood classrooms and all of their entanglements with each other and with broader, societal power structures, it is more likely to produce findings that will form teaching practice.

In the rest of this chapter, we discuss areas of research in early childhood that we would like to move away from and areas we would like to move toward. Our goal in describing both is to push the field toward thinking about children and classroom contexts in holistic ways that attend to the complexity of diverse classroom contexts, recognizing, as Erickson (2014, p. 4) has written, that "educational treatments as instantiated on the ground are the enactment of daily life in classrooms—ways of life lived in real time and place, not static models of life in a social world of nowhere and no when." In thinking about this work, we are informed by previous scholarship that has sought to demonstrate the social complexity of early childhood classrooms by illuminating ways that young children navigate complex discourses of race, language, gender, and class through their engagements in a variety of academic practices (e.g., Comber & Simpson, 2001; Dyson, 1997; Souto-Manning, 2009; Vasquez, 2014).

Substantive Research Directions

To understand the need for a turn toward humanizing research, we explore where the field is today to identify what counts as foundational research on early childhood. In order to unpack what the field values as "knowledge"—defined here as ideas that in their repeating are taken as true (Davies, 2003; Foucault, 1980)—we look to what is widely considered to be the most prominent journal in the field, *Early Childhood Research Quarterly (ECRQ)*. We did a preliminary review of the 25 most cited articles published in *ECRQ* since 2012 to provide a broad indication of what counts as the research foundation for the field. The review included open coding of the research questions and data sources to identify commonalities. From these broad codes we narrowed and combined codes, then identified relationships between codes—the associations the studies endeavored to reveal. Following the overview of the types of research, findings, and implications in the 25 most frequently cited articles, we explore the methodological approaches, research questions posed, and assumptions in the top three most cited articles, then offer our ideas about what other methodological approaches might reveal. This process is not intended to disparage these articles or scholars, but to highlight for the field how the emphasis on this type of research—how using this as our research foundation—makes invisible the individual nature of a child, and how the child will remain invisible without a turn in direction.

First, we identified the most frequent themes and combined the codes to arrive at those most shared: *learning environments, family and child background, academic outcomes,* and *behavioral outcomes.* The learning environment, which may have an impact on learning both at home and in school, included literacy- and math-related activities, home organization, parental stress, parenting styles, school quality, teacher responsivity, and curriculum. Family and child background generally included gender, native language, maternal education, socioeconomic status, and race/ethnicity. Academic outcomes included measures of mathematics and/or literacy skills. Behavioral measures included attention span, self-control, executive function, and engagement. We recognize that we are taking a broad view of the studies and combining some categories and omitting several others, but found this approach provided a way of describing the field. These codes were representative of the questions and data sources in 20 of the 25 studies. For the most part, the studies explored the associations and measured the significance of relationships between these codes. Figure 1 reveals the relationships and number of studies for each.

The idea that the relationships represented in Figure 1 provide the research foundation of the field supports our notion that the outcomes revealed in much of the research on early childhood do not provide an understanding of the child in ways that contribute to understandings of how they might best be taught. In fact, only 2 of the 25 studies reviewed attended explicitly to learning environments in school in ways that would inform early childhood teaching. Further, the three most cited articles highlighted on the *ECRQ* website and discussed more fully below, provide little more than general guidance for classroom practices.

The three most frequently cited articles tell us that (a) 4-year-olds' attention spans, as rated by parents, contribute to later academic outcomes, including college completion (McClelland, Acock, Piccinin, Rhea, & Stallings, 2013); (b) home and school factors, such as child-parent interactions around "numeracy stimulation," other family background factors, and quality preschool, work together to influence later numeracy outcomes (Anders et al., 2012); and (c) school outreach to families is associated with family involvement, which is in turn associated with children's mathematics and reading gains (Anders et al., 2012). All three studies endeavor to identify factors that "predict" later learning outcomes based on analysis of data from large-scale studies and do not provide sufficient descriptions of context to inform the work of practitioners in other places.

In a study of data of 430 children from the Colorado Adoption Project and the Nature and Nurture in Social Demography study, McClelland and colleagues (2013) found that

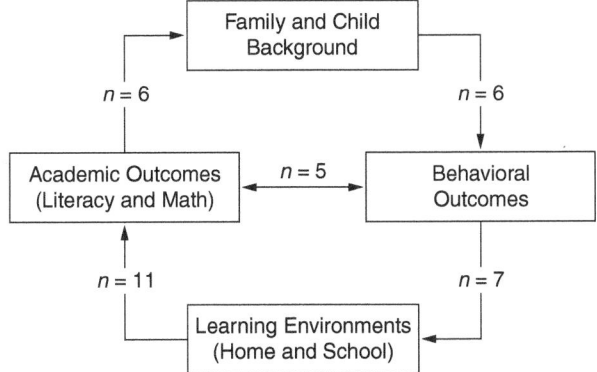

Figure 1. Landscape of early childhood research.

attention span–persistence at age 4 contributes to achievement throughout schooling and to college completion, and that early attention span–persistence has more direct effects on later achievement. The authors suggest that one implication for teaching is to incorporate "early childhood curricula that include engaging and fun activities that help children pay attention and persist on tasks" (p. 322). This idea is hardly foreign to early childhood teachers and educators. Since 1986, the National Association for the Education of Young Children has recommended that young children have opportunities to learn through play, with engaging materials, and through inquiry (Bredekamp & Copple, 1986). Yet we caution that another implication and unintended consequence of studies such as this one might be to focus more attention on what counts as being a "well behaved" child. This focus might result in sorting children in ways that contribute further to referrals of particular populations of children to special education for behavioral problems (Lee, 2008; Swadener & Lubeck, 1995).

Anders and colleagues' (2012) study of 532 children in 97 German preschools was premised on the idea that "the quality of the home learning environment is related to the availability of educational resources, such as books, and the nature of parenting activities, such as reading to the child, using complex language, playing with numbers, counting, and taking the child to the library" (p. 232). They found that family background factors such as parents' native language, maternal education, and socioeconomic status were associated with children's initial numeracy levels and growth, and they suggested that preschool might be particularly beneficial for children whose parents' first language was other than German. In addition, they found that both school and home environments were important for literacy and numeracy development and that the effects of the two learning environments are not "simply additive" (p. 242). Although important, these ideas do not provide any specific suggestions for working with children in schools. Further, these outcomes describe populations broadly and often blame child and family characteristics that are not aligned with the norm (Souto-Manning & Swick, 2006; Swadener & Lubeck, 1995).

Galindo and Sheldon's (2012) study of data from the Early Childhood Longitudinal Study Kindergarten Class of 1998–1999 found associations between (a) school outreach and family involvement, (b) family involvement and math and reading achievement gains, and (c) school outreach and students' reading and math achievement gains. One recommendation was for schools to "implement practices to engage, involve, and inform students' families and create opportunities for family involvement in reading-related and math-related activities at school and at home" (pp. 100–101). Because of the nature of the study, we don't have a sense of what that looks like in practice, what kinds of activities are more effective, or how schools and teachers might better engage families.

We found four key themes in looking across these three articles. In each article, the authors (a) provided statistics, which described populations but not individuals; (b) demonstrated statistical, but not actual, significance when we looked for ways to apply the statistical findings to teaching; (c) funneled our attention toward proficiency rather than growth; and (d) failed to acknowledge the interconnectedness of learning as a whole child.

All four of these themes contribute to a disconnect between the research base and the work of teaching. Because teaching is about engaging with individuals, it is hard for practitioners to draw from a research base that is about populations and focuses on impacts measurable only with sophisticated statistical techniques. As such, we want to move away from studies that attend to problems in measurement, methodology, and data. These types of studies normalize a "standard child" rather than recognizing and exploring naturally occurring diversity in children's lives and experiences (Viruru, 2001). For example, instruments commonly used to measure classroom quality in early childhood contexts, such as the CLASS (Pianta, La Paro, & Hamre, 2008), focus observers' attention on the "experiences of the typical or average student" (p. 11), which allows classroom life to be represented efficiently with just a few numbers. However, these summaries of average experiences do not offer insight into the experiences of children who are routinely marginalized in classrooms, nor do they provide guidance on teaching *particular* children. This is not intended to be a critique of individuals but of research traditions that are disconnected from teachers, teacher educators, and children. We worry that traditions that focus on outcomes, rather than human beings, can perpetuate ideas about deficiencies in children and families and teachers (Souto-Manning & Swick, 2006).

In general, the research we reviewed failed to embody concern for educating children as people with rich social and emotional (as well as cognitive) lives or for taking asset-based views of children and families. While we do not expect these themes to be dominant in studies of large-scale data sets, we hope they will influence the kinds of research questions and analyses pursued in future research in early childhood environments. Those conducting research in early childhood contexts would benefit from attending to the ways that the instructional practices and treatment of children in their studies align, or do not align, with broader conceptions of children in the early childhood community.

Making Room for Other Kinds of Research

In addition to suggesting that we enrich the bird's-eye view of large-scale studies with close-up descriptions of people and places, we also want to suggest moves toward particular kinds of studies that have potential for helping us to understand the complexity of work with young children.

Studies That Center Children's Perspectives. For good reasons, much of the work in early childhood education has focused on the teacher—questions asked, curricula used, quality of interactions, and so forth—and less has focused on understanding how children experience schooling. Even in studies that focus on children through clinical interviews, interest has been much more in children's scores on particular measures than on making sense of their experiences of the world. Observational studies that center children's experiences in classrooms can do the classic ethnographic work of "making the familiar strange" (Erickson, 1986, p. 121). For example, through ethnographic observations of kindergarteners, Yoon (2014) documented how young children used opportunities to write to build or to shut down relationships with peers and to explore bigger issues, such as what it meant to dress like a girl. The children Yoon observed did not see writing primarily in terms of adult goals—developing skills with alphabetic print, for example—but as another opportunity to pursue their own agendas. Studies that center the perspectives of children also help to remind adults who do research with children that we are forever outsiders to their experiences. Cosaro (2003, 2005), a sociologist who studies children from an ethnographic perspective, stresses the importance of adults seeking to understand the "joy, wonder, and complexity" (Cosaro, 2003, p. 205) of childhood. We would like to see more research that embraces this call.

One promising method for doing this work is participatory research with children, which has grown in popularity in recent years, with researchers asking young children to engage in the work of posing questions, collecting data, and doing analysis (e.g., Alderson & Morrow, 2011; Bradbury-Jones & Taylor, 2015). For example, Gray and Winter (2011), in working with prekindergarteners with identified disabilities, used a doll to launch conversations with children about what they would like to investigate about their school and to help them engage in methods to answer their questions. Over the course of the project, children actively disagreed with school staff about both the subject of the investigation (for example, rejecting a focus on the writing table, which the children dismissed as boring). The study demonstrated both that children are capable of engaging in such work and that even the adults who work most closely with children do not always have clear insight into their thinking.

New technologies also present some interesting possibilities for making children's experiences more central. For example, Green (2016) provided prekindergarteners with small, wearable cameras that the children could turn off and on to document their engagements with the natural world during outdoor explorations. In addition to giving the children control over data collection, this method allowed Green to analyze the nature walk from the viewpoint of the children wearing the cameras. The ever-increasing flexibility of video cameras and their ease of use will offer rich opportunities for documenting children's perspectives of their schooling experiences in the coming years.

Broadly, we believe that theories and methods drawn from the field of childhood studies (A. James & Prout, 2015; A. L. James, 2010) could help us to understand more about how children experience their school days, because that field tends to view children not only as students but also as people with their own interests, rights, and agendas. Taking the children's lives seriously ought to inform many aspects of our work as researchers (Lundy, McEvoy, & Byrne, 2011). First, ethically, we would need to consider the ways in which we seek assent from children to participate in studies and to manage that participation. If children's perspectives were taken as seriously as adults' perspectives, then when children said they wanted to go back to the classroom during assessment interviews, we would take them back rather than coax them to finish with stickers or stretch breaks. Second, in designing interventions to produce cognitive outcomes, taking children's perspectives seriously would require that we seek to understand whether these interventions produce experiences of excitement or boredom, joy or pain, along with gains on cognitive measures. Finally, in analyzing policies related to teachers, we would also consider the impact on children. For example, we might ask whether encouraging adults to profit from the labor of children—as in policies that that link teacher pay to children's performance on tests—is socially acceptable.

Broadly, work that focuses on children's perspectives shakes our adult-centered view of the world.

Studies That Account for the Role of Context. In his essay on future directions for educational research, Erickson (2014, p. 4) calls for abandoning our search for "best practices," in favor of "pretty good practices" that could be "described in specific enough detail by qualitative researchers, including teachers themselves, so that other teachers could understand what those practices felt like, and could try them out in their own classrooms." We would like to see studies like this—studies that rely on close descriptions of classroom life informed by ethnographic methods—take a more prominent place in the research on early childhood education.

For example, Hatt's (2012) close description of the way smartness was constructed in a kindergarten classroom, relying on interviews, artifacts, and a year of observations, allowed readers to see how common classroom practices like public behavior charts, choosing children for jobs, and celebrating developmental milestones like shoe tying position some students as smart and others as lacking. The analysis also demonstrated the ways in which these practices were shaped by racial categories in the classroom and the ways that the particular children in the room experienced the practices (e.g., crying and saying they hated school). Because of the close description provided, the article made it possible for readers to think about the ways that other classrooms were similar to and different from the site of study, creating opportunities to make conjectures about what might happen in classrooms with different racial or ethnic makeups or instructional routines. This sort of drawing of conclusions is quite different from thinking about the "average" impact of practices. As Erickson (2014, p. 3) says, "a teacher does not teach children in general, but particular children in particular circumstances of learning and teaching in classrooms and in community life."

Studies That Make Connections. In their book on case study research, Bartlett and Varvus (2017) recommended that researchers reconceptualize the boundaries of case studies beyond borders of geographical place and limited time periods to highlight broader relationships. This kind of work can allow us to understand how the local contexts in which we work are situated in the national and global communities and can make clear any points of contrast that allow us to see the constraints in our own settings as more permeable. For example, to write the case studies for her book on early childhood education, Wilinski (2017) spent significant time in prekindergarten classrooms in Wisconsin, which allowed her to provide close descriptions of the work of teaching, including the tensions teachers faced related to curriculum, salary, and instructional practices; she also connected these close descriptions of classroom life to state and federal policies about early childhood education, demonstrating the ways that policy decisions about the location of public prekindergartens (e.g., in private centers or public schools) impact the daily lives of teachers and children in classrooms. By not dwelling exclusively in either the world of policy or that of classroom interactions, Wilinski made it possible to evaluate policies in relation to the ways they impact actual human beings, rather than focusing solely on measures of outcome.

Similarly, Hayashi and Tobin (2015) made connections across a great expanse of time in their study of teaching in Japanese preschools. Drawing on video data taken in sessions separated by a decade, Hayashi and Tobin looked at how teachers used their bodies in different ways as they became more experienced as early childhood practitioners. Their analysis showed how expertise in teaching was intimately related to the ways teachers use their bodies to do things like mediate conflicts between children or draw attention to instruction. Again, the rich descriptions created opportunities for other researchers and practitioners to think about the ways teachers use their bodies in other early childhood settings. The growing number of studies in education broadly that are bringing the body into analysis help to make clear the complexity of the work of teaching, which is shaped not merely by the words we say, but by the facial expressions we use, our gestures, our posture, and our proximity to children. In addition, the longitudinal aspect of the study framed the work of teaching in a way that moves beyond summaries of practice, such as scores on observation protocols or assessments of teacher or student knowledge. We believe the field would benefit from more studies that seek to draw connections between context-rich descriptions of early childhood settings and other important features of early childhood education, including assessment data from clinical interviews, changes in policies and standards, adoption of curricula, and political and cultural geographies.

Relating Research to Policy and Practice

The proliferation of research demonstrating the benefits of prekindergarten for children's academic performance in kindergarten and beyond has contributed to an increase in policies and funding that support prekindergarten and research in early childhood. Although the increased attention to prekindergarten is welcome, we worry that policy and funding decisions based on decontextualized and dehumanized studies will reify the conditions these studies reveal.

There is a great need for fine-grained studies that could help us specify the factors that shape children's preschool experiences in sufficient detail that we can confidently make recommendations about teacher preparation, curricula, and program structures. For example, one large-scale evaluation of preschool curricula found only small effects on students (Preschool Curriculum Evaluation Research Consortium, 2008), demonstrating a need for analysis that goes beyond the level of curriculum (and beyond factors such as class size, program length, and teacher degree), toward looking at teacher practices. Fine-grained analyses are also important in terms of building a body of knowledge to shape prekindergarten teacher preparation. Relationships among variables do little to help novice practitioners learn how to enact teaching that is both responsive to children and ambitious in relation to disciplinary content. However, close-up studies of skilled teachers' practices—particularly if done with video—provide models that teachers can come to understand and appropriate.

As we have stated in previous work, "one thing we find particularly concerning is that, while there is a research base available, very little of it is useful in terms of practice" (Parks & Wager, 2015, p. 137). To address this concern and those previously stated, we have three recommendations for policy, research, and practice. First, researchers need to break down the barriers between disciplinary fields—we envision this happening with multiple constituents, including funding agencies, research journals, and researcher preparation programs. If funding agencies required (or, at a minimum, strongly encouraged) multidisciplinary teams much the way they require studies using qualitative methods to add a quantitative component, researchers could provide contextual evidence through deep studies of classrooms to support or refute findings from large-scale studies. Working in teams would bring the strength of multiple research traditions to better understand the nuanced experiences of children at home, in school, and in between.

Second, working collaboratively across multiple contexts to conduct some of the studies we recommend would provide a foundation for understanding how children learn and how to teach them. Again, if funding agencies were to recommend multisite research, the results would be much more useful than those of single-site studies, as researchers and practitioners could examine and compare experiences in multiple contexts.

Third, we ask both journal editors and funding agencies to value observational studies in natural contexts as well as large-scale, quasi-experimental studies. Observational studies can provide the context and nuance—missing from the large-scale studies—that we find necessary to inform practice and better understand children's lives and learning opportunities.

In addition to rethinking barriers produced by expectations from funding agencies, early childhood journals should broaden their criteria to recognize the legitimacy and importance of research that goes beyond large-scale studies to attend to the rich understanding provided by in-depth studies of a single child or classroom.

Conclusion

As we prepared to submit this chapter, another study was published—featured in *Educational Researcher*—using large data sets to identify factors that contributed to changes in kindergarteners' academic achievement from 1998 to 2010 (Bassock & Latham, 2017). The study documented that in 2010 children in kindergarten scored higher on measures of academic proficiency; demonstrated fewer differences in academic outcomes based on race; and nevertheless were rated *less* favorably on measures of approaches to learning and self-control. The authors of the study highlighted the importance of understanding the causes of this change and reminded readers of the many unanswered questions about the "impact of kindergarten curricula and pedagogy on children's development" (p. 15). The kinds of humanizing studies we suggest have the potential to provide evidence that is currently invisible in large-scale reports, by helping us see how differences in context shape children's experiences and how various practices in early childhood education either lift up or diminish the children in our care. We are concerned about the field's tendency to privilege studies that describe and evaluate early childhood education through future-oriented lenses that assess early childhood experiences primarily in terms of what those experiences provide in terms of later schooling and life outcomes. We want to move toward research programs that keep the lives of actual children and teachers in focus.

Our hope is that the suggestions we have made here with respect to multidisciplinary and ethnographic research will help researchers understand and value childhood as a unique stage in life, not merely a preparatory experience for adulthood, and honor the experiences of individual children.

References

Alderson, P., & Morrow, V. (2011). *The ethics of research with children and young people: A practical handbook.* Thousand Oaks, CA: Sage.

Anders, Y., Rossbach, H. G., Weinert, S., Ebert, S., Kuger, S., Lehrl, S., et al. (2012). Home and preschool learning environments and their relations to the development of early numeracy skills. *Early Childhood Research Quarterly, 27*(2), 231–244.

Ballinger, C. (1992). Because you like us: The language of control. *Harvard Educational Review, 62*(2), 199–208.

Bartlett, L., & Varvus, F. (2017). Rethinking case study research: A comparative approach. New York: Routledge.

Bassok, D., & Latham, S. (2017). Kids today: The rise in children's academic skills at kindergarten entry. *Educational Researcher, 46*(1), 7–20.

Berrueta-Clement, J. R., Schweinhart, L. J., Barnett, W. S., Epstein, A. S., & Weikart, D. P. (1984). *Changed lives: The effects of the Perry Preschool Program on youths through age 19* (Monographs of the High/Scope Educational Research Foundation, No.8). Ypsilanti, MI: High/Scope Foundation.

Blaise, M. (2012). *Playing it straight: Uncovering gender discourse in the early childhood classroom.* New York, NY: Routledge.

Bradbury-Jones, C., & Taylor, J. (2015). Engaging with children as co-researchers: Challenges, counter-challenges and solutions. *International Journal of Social Research Methodology, 18*(2), 161–173.

Bredekamp, S., & Copple, C. (1986). *Developmentally appropriate practice in early childhood programs.* Washington, DC: National Association for the Education of Young Children.

Bronfenbrenner, U. (1977). Toward an experimental ecology of human development. *American Psychologist, 32*(7), 513.

Campbell, F. A., & Ramey, C. T. (1994). Effects of early intervention on intellectual and academic achievement: A follow-up study of children from low-income families. *Child Development, 65*(2), 684–698.

Clements, D. H., Sarama, J., Spitler, M. E., Lange, A. A., & Wolfe, C. B. (2011). Mathematics learned by young children in an intervention based on learning trajectories: A large-scale cluster randomized trial. *Journal for Research in Mathematics Education, 42*(2), 127–166.

Comber, B., & Simpson, A. (Eds.). (2001). *Negotiating critical literacies in classrooms.* Mahwah, NJ: Lawrence Erlbaum.

Cosaro, W. A. (2003). *We're friends right? Inside kids' culture.* Washington, DC: Joseph Henry.

Cosaro, W. A. (2005). *The sociology of childhood.* London, UK: Pine Forge.

Cowhey, M. (2006). *Black ants and Buddhists: Thinking critically and teaching differently in the primary grades.* Portsmouth, NH: Stenhouse.

Davies, B. (2003). *Frogs and snails and feminist tales.* Cresskill, NJ: Hampton.

Denham, S. A., Bassett, H. H., Zinsser, K., & Wyatt, T. M. (2014). How preschoolers' social–emotional learning predicts their early school success: Developing theory-promoting, competency-based assessments. *Infant and Child Development, 23*(4), 426–454.

Dyson, A. H. (1997). *Writing superheroes: Contemporary childhood, popular culture, and classroom literacy.* New York, NY: Teachers College Press.

Dyson, A. H. (2013). *Rewriting the basics: Literacy learning in children's cultures.* New York, NY: Teachers College Press.

Erickson, F. (1986). Qualitative methods in research on teaching. In M. C. Wittrock (Ed.), *Handbook of research on teaching* (pp. 119–161). New York, NY: Macmillan.

Erickson, F. (2014). Scaling down: A modest proposal for practice-based policy research in teaching. *Education Policy Analysis Archives, 22*(9), 1–11.

Falchi, L. T., Axelrod, Y., & Genishi, C. (2014). "Miguel es un artista"—and Luisa is an excellent student: Seeking time and space for children's multimodal practices. *Journal of Early Childhood Literacy, 14*(3), 345–366.

Feuer, M. J., Towne, L., & Shavelson, R. J. (2002). Scientific culture and educational research. *Educational Researcher, 31*(8), 4–14.

Foucault, M. (1980). *Power/knowledge: Selected interviews and other writings 1972–1977.* New York, NY: Pantheon.

Galindo, C., & Sheldon, S. B. (2012). School and home connections and children's kindergarten achievement gains: The mediating role of family involvement. *Early Childhood Research Quarterly, 27*(1), 90–103.

Graue, M. E. (1993). *Ready for what? Constructing meanings of readiness for kindergarten.* Albany, NY: SUNY Press.

Gray, C., & Winter, E. (2011). Hearing voices: Participatory research with preschool children with and without disabilities. *European Early Childhood Education Research Journal, 19*(3), 309–320.

Green, C. (2016). Sensory tours as a method for engaging children as active researchers: exploring the use of wearable cameras in early childhood research. *International Journal of Early Childhood, 48*(3), 277–294.

Greve, A. (2009). Friendships and participation among young children in a Norwegian kindergarten. *Participatory Learning in the Early Years: Research and Pedagogy, 78*–92.

Hatt, B. (2012). Smartness as a cultural practice in schools. *American Educational Research Journal, 49*(3), 438–460.

Hayashi, A., & Tobin, J. (2015). *Teaching embodied: Cultural practice in Japan.* Chicago, IL: University of Chicago Press.

James, A., & Prout, A. (Eds.). (2015). *Constructing and reconstructing childhood: Contemporary issues in the sociological study of childhood.* New York, NY: Routledge.

James, A. L. (2010). Competition or integration? The next step in childhood studies? *Childhood, 17*(4), 485–499.

Jerome, E. M., Hamre, B. K., & Pianta, R. C. (2009). Teacher–child relationships from kindergarten to sixth grade: Early childhood predictors of teacher-perceived conflict and closeness. *Social Development, 18*(4), 915–945.

Kelley, E. S., Goldstein, H., Spencer, T. D., & Sherman, A. (2015). Effects of automated Tier 2 storybook intervention on vocabulary and comprehension learning in preschool children with limited oral language skills. *Early Childhood Research Quarterly, 31*, 47–61.

Kendeou, P., Van den Broek, P., White, M. J., & Lynch, J. S. (2009). Predicting reading comprehension in early elementary school: The independent contributions of oral language and decoding skills. *Journal of Educational Psychology, 101*(4), 765–778.

Lee, K. (2008). ADHD in American early schooling: From a cultural psychological perspective. *Early Child Development and Care, 178*(4), 415–439.

Lundy, L., McEvoy, L., & Byrne, B. (2011). Working with young children as co-researchers: An approach informed by the United Nations Convention on the Rights of the Child. *Early Education and Development, 22*(5), 714–736.

Magnuson, K. A., Meyers, M. K., Ruhm, C. J., & Waldfogel, J. (2004). Inequality in preschool education and school readiness. *American Educational Research Journal, 41*(1), 115–157.

McClelland, M. M., Acock, A. C., Piccinin, A., Rhea, S. A., & Stallings, M. C. (2013). Relations between preschool attention span–persistence and age 25 educational outcomes. *Early Childhood Research Quarterly, 28*(2), 314–324.

Miller, L. B., & Bizzell, R. P. (1983). The Louisville Experiment: A comparison of four programs. In Consortium for Longitudinal Studies (Ed.), *As the twig is bent: Lasting effects of preschool programs* (pp. 171–199). Hillsdale, NJ: Lawrence Erlbaum.

National Research Council. (2002). *Scientific research in education.* (R. J. Shavelson & L. Towne, Eds.). Committee on Scientific Principles for Educational Research. Washington, DC: National Academies Press.

Neuman, S. B., Pinkham, A., & Kaefer, T. (2015). Supporting vocabulary teaching and learning in prekindergarten: The role of educative curriculum materials. *Early Education and Development, 26*(7), 988–1011.

O'Toole, S. E., Monks, C. P., & Tsermentseli, S. (2017). Executive function and theory of mind as predictors of aggressive and prosocial behavior and peer acceptance in early childhood. *Social Development, 26,* 907–920.

Paris, D. (2011). "A friend who understand fully": Notes on humanizing research in a multiethnic youth community. *International Journal of Qualitative Studies in Education, 24*(2), 137–149.

Parks, A. N., & Wager, A. A. (2015). What knowledge is shaping teacher preparation in early childhood mathematics? *Journal of Early Childhood Teacher Education, 36*(2), 124–141.

Parnell, W. (2011). Revealing the experience of children and teachers even in their absence: Documenting in the early childhood studio. *Journal of Early Childhood Research, 9*(3), 291–309.

Phillipsen, L. C., Burchinal, M. R., Howes, C., & Cryer, D. (1997). The prediction of process quality from structural features of child care. *Early Childhood Research Quarterly, 12*(3), 281–303.

Pianta, R. C., La Paro, K. M., & Hamre, B. K. (2008). *Classroom Assessment Scoring System™. Manual K–3.* Baltimore, MD: Brookes.

Preschool Curriculum Evaluation Research Consortium. (2008). Effects of preschool curriculum programs on school readiness (NCER 2008–2009). Washington, DC: National Center for Education Research, Institute of Education Sciences.

Schweinhart, L. J., & Weikart, D. P. (1997). The High/Scope Preschool Curriculum Comparison Study Through Age 23. *Early Childhood Research Quarterly, 12*(2), 117–143.

Siegler, R. S., & Ramani, G. B. (2008). Playing linear numerical board games promotes low-income children's numerical development. *Developmental Science, 11*(5), 655–661.

Siegler, R. S., & Ramani, G. B. (2009). Playing linear number board games—but not circular ones—improves low-income preschoolers' numerical understanding. *Journal of Educational Psychology, 101*(3), 545–560.

Souto-Manning, M. (2009). Negotiating culturally responsive pedagogy through multicultural children's literature: Towards critical democratic literacy practices in a first grade classroom. *Journal of Early Childhood Literacy, 9*(1), 50–74.

Souto-Manning, M., & Swick, K. J. (2006). Teachers' beliefs about parent and family involvement: Rethinking our family involvement paradigm. *Early Childhood Education Journal, 34*(2), 187–193.

Stipek, D., & Byler, P. (2004). The early childhood classroom observation measure. *Early Childhood Research Quarterly, 19*(3), 375–397.

Swadener, B. B., & Lubeck, S. (1995). *Children and families "at promise": Deconstructing the discourse of risk.* New York: SUNY Press.

Vasquez, V. (2014). *Negotiating critical literacies with young children.* New York, NY: Routledge.

Viruru, R. (2001). Colonized through language: The case of early childhood education. *Contemporary Issues in Early Childhood, 2*(1), 31–47.

Weiland, C., & Yoshikawa, H. (2013). Impacts of a prekindergarten program on children's mathematics, language, literacy, executive function, and emotional skills. *Child Development, 84*(6), 2112–2130.

Wilinski, B. (2017). *When pre-K comes to school: Policy, partnerships, and the early childhood education workforce.* New York, NY: Teachers College Press.

Yoon, H. S. (2014). Can I play with you? The intersection of play and writing in a kindergarten classroom. *Contemporary Issues in Early Childhood, 15*(2), 109–121.

Chapter 6

Parents, Their Children, and Their Children's Early Childhood Education Teachers

ROBERT CROSNOE

University of Texas at Austin

The interplay between parents and early childhood educators—or, for simplicity's sake, teachers—has implications for children's learning and development, and it is affected by interpersonal processes, institutional and cultural practices, and larger social structures (e.g., racial/ethnic stratification, migration streams) that bring parents and teachers together or push them apart (Lareau, 2000; Souto-Manning & Swick, 2006; Tobin, Adair, & Arzubiaga, 2013). Consequently, this interplay has long been a focus of both educational research and the policy and practice that the research informs (see Sheridan & Moorman, 2015). Scholars and stakeholders use many terms to describe and discuss the interplay, some emphasizing the parents (e.g., parental engagement), some emphasizing the educators (e.g., school outreach), some emphasizing both in positive ways (e.g., family-school partnerships), and some emphasizing both in negative ways (e.g., family-school conflict). In this chapter, I am going with a more generic term—*parent-teacher relations*—that connects *both* actors but without any assumptions about the valence of this connection. It encompasses the tone, level of coordination, and balance of connections (or lack thereof) between home and school.

Because of the academic and developmental significance of parent-teacher relations, efforts to facilitate closer relations and reduce barriers between home and school have great potential value. After all, parent-teacher relations are central to two of the dominant philosophical forces of early childhood education policy and practice: (a) the traditional philosophy of developmentally appropriate practices in early childhood education, which emphasizes multidimensional learning ecologies that connect school to community; and (b) the standards and accountability movement, which has called for a more active role by families in schools (Graue, 2008; Ryan & Grieshaber, 2005). These forces need to be contextualized within the racially, ethnically, socioeconomically, and linguistically diversifying population of U.S. children, who have disparate rates of early childhood education enrollment (Karoly & Gonzalez, 2011). As one example, the enrollment of Latino/a children lags behind that of other racial/ethnic groups, including other minority groups (see Figure 1). In this context, policy and programmatic efforts to influence parent-teacher relations need to reflect the lessons learned from research in this area, which has a rich history and also much promise for the future.

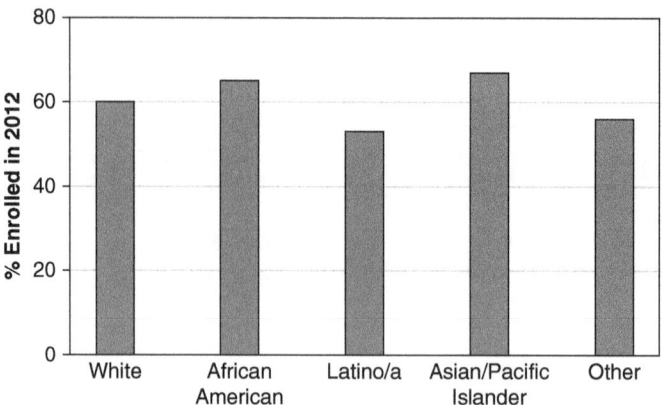

Figure 1. Enrollment of 4- and 5-year-olds in center-based early care and education arrangements before the start of kindergarten, by race/ethnicity. The statistics in this figure are from the National Household Education Survey of 2012 (Rathbun & Zhang, 2016).

The purpose of this chapter, therefore, is to discuss research on parent-teacher relations in early childhood education, as well as the degree to which this literature is reflected in policy efforts to promote such connections as a means of increasing educational attainment across diverse segments of the population. I lay out some of the knowns and unknowns in this field, integrating how researchers think about these issues in ways that are and are not aligned with policy and practice. My general goal is to help us, as researchers, to think of ways to get scholars, policy makers, and practitioners on the same page. My specific goal is to advance a three-point argument:

- Policy can benefit from high-quality research insights about parent-teacher relations as reciprocal arrangements, which can take multiple and complex forms and are vulnerable to issues of differential status and power.

- Research can better fulfill this role when it demonstrates impact and speaks in personal and relatable ways to the needs of teachers, parents, and children.

- The partnership between research and policy is evident in efforts to help parents and teachers form relationships on a more even playing field.

This argument is about parent-teacher relations and the intergenerational transmission of inequality. In other words, parents from disadvantaged groups are less likely than other parents to have positive relations with their children's early education teachers. These unsatisfactory relations disrupt children's learning during a critical period; this undermines their prospects as they move through the educational system, increasing the odds of continued disadvantage in adulthood. However, my argument is also about breaking this transmission. In other words, building positive relations between parents and their children's teachers can facilitate smoother transitions into the K–12 system in ways that support social mobility into adulthood.

Before getting into the heart of this three-point argument, I should make clear that I approach the topic from the standpoint of someone who has conducted a great deal of mixed-methods research on early childhood education. A particular focus of this line of my research program has been the experiences of children from low-income and/or Mexican immigrant families, the ways in which they come to be enrolled in early childhood education, and how they—and their parents—fare in it (Crosnoe, Bonazzo, & Wu, 2015). Although I conduct this research at the meeting point of sociology of education, demography, and developmental science, I will bring in perspectives from other disciplines (e.g., anthropology, education sciences) in this chapter to provide a more well-rounded view of the issues at hand.

The Current State of Knowledge

The first point of my argument—about parent-teacher relations being reciprocal arrangements that take many forms and have many vulnerabilities—reflects the shift in relevant educational research from a more one-sided focus on parental involvement in education to the two-sided concept of family-school partnerships. This shift has occurred for secondary and elementary education as well as early childhood education (Epstein, 2016). Based on the multidisciplinary and multimethod literature, we can be fairly sure about a few things.

First, positive parent-teacher relations help to scaffold and support children's school readiness and early achievement. The apparent benefits likely arise when teachers and parents are able to join forces to promote the interests of children. I say "apparent" because the portion of associations between parent-teacher relations and child outcomes that is causal still needs to be better established. At the heart of these relations are parents sharing with teachers while teachers share with parents—maximizing available information, reinforcing each other's inputs, and mutually developing plans for action. My own qualitative research has shown a more complicated interplay for many Latino/a immigrant families. Specifically, some parents' visible involvement behaviors can signal to teachers that they are "good" parents with the "right" values, encouraging more investment of teachers in their children over peers with parents who are not following the desired script even if they are equally committed to their children's education (Crosnoe et al., 2015). Similarly, qualitative research on Haitian immigrant families has elucidated the ways that parents can enforce boundaries between home and school as a means of protecting family privacy and resisting the Americanizing influence of schools, with children potentially losing out on teachers' investment as a result (Doucet, 2011). In such cases, parent-teacher relations may not be building valuable resources but instead reflecting some inequalities in the system (more on this below). When parents and teachers genuinely work together, their partnership can help children both realize and exceed their potential early, to get a better start in an educational system that is highly cumulative (Crosnoe, 2015).

Second, positive parent-teacher relations can take many forms. Often, these relations involve direct interactions between parents and early childhood educators, and the interactions enable the sharing of information as well as a mutual form of socialization. For example, parents can talk to teachers about their children's needs, worries, and special talents, as well as their own values, beliefs, and circumstances. Doing so helps teachers better personalize the early childhood education experience for individual children. At the same time, teachers can describe to parents their own teaching philosophies and goals and their own assessments of children, and they can demystify the inner workings of schools for parents. Doing so gives parents a better understanding of how they can support their children and make sure that they get the most out of their early educational experiences. Parent-teacher relations can also take more indirect or parallel forms. For example, parents may construct stimulating learning activities for their children at home that either mirror, supplement, or complement what is going on in the children's early childhood education programs, either as a result of explicit coordination or more organically. Alternatively, teachers may engage in practices or lessons in their programs that reinforce parents' own views and values about education and their children—again, either through some degree of planning or not (McWayne, Melzi, Schick, Kennedy, & Mundt, 2013; Fantuzzo, Tighe, & Childs, 2000).

Third, parent-teacher relations are situated within broad systems of stratification in our diversifying society that may disrupt the development and/or interfere with the benefits of positive relations. In some (certainly not all) situations, for example, there are socioeconomic differences—as when the children of low-income parents are taught by middle-class teachers—that create and exacerbate power differentials between home and school and/or the perception that power is imbalanced. The strong role of socioeconomic background in socialization into approaches to education and parental involvement may also mean that teachers and parents have divergent perspectives on what the role of each is. Similarly, racial/ethnic differences between parents and teachers can create feelings of real or perceived mistrust, and associated cultural differences may result in parents and teachers misunderstanding each other. Immigrant parents may have similar trouble connecting with teachers—and teachers with immigrant parents—because of the mixture of racial/ethnic, socioeconomic, and language factors that characterize the majority of immigrant families in the United States. These factors sometimes create barriers between them and their children's early childhood education programs and schools. At worst, relations across socioeconomic and demographic lines may involve stereotyping, shortchanging, and scapegoating and lead to conflict or alienation (Lareau, 2000; Souto-Manning & Swick, 2006; Tobin, Adair, Arzubiaga, 2013).

In a classic example of such complex dynamics, ethnographic research in California from the 1980s and 1990s revealed how low-income Latino/a parents often felt alienated or devalued by early childhood education programs that required culturally specific knowledge and that did not seem to recognize the many resources and insights that such parents could bring to the table (Delgado-Gaitan, 1991). In a more recent example, experimental evidence has suggested that the implicit biases of White early childhood educators about African American boys' behaviors worsened when teachers had some understanding of children's parents and family life, a pattern that was reversed among African American educators (Gilliam, Maupin, Reyes, Accavitti, & Shic, 2016).

Bringing together these three themes, one cannot help but see the connection to inequality. *If* multiple forms of positive parent-teacher relations are associated with better educational outcomes for young children *and* the tone, coordination, and balance of these parent-teacher relations are affected by socioeconomic, racial/ethnic, and related dimensions of stratification, then parent-teacher relations during early childhood *may* be a channel in the intergenerational transmission of inequality in the United States.

These themes of research on parent-teacher relations in the context of early childhood programs and elementary schools are certainly aligned with the spirit of policy highlighting the value of engaging parents in their children's education and the role of this engagement in reducing educational disparities among diverse groups of young people. Yet, in my observation, some of the main traditions of policy often seem out of step with these themes, particularly the need to see parent-teacher relations as an important but complicated two-way street.

For example, policies and programs often emphasize the incorporation of parents into programs and schools rather than more mutual engagement. I distinctly recall, in my own qualitative research in early childhood education programs in Texas, how immigrant parents would speak about being partners with their children's teachers ("Me and her, we're a team," said one Mexican immigrant to me about her child's pre-K teacher, in a fairly representative comment; Crosnoe, 2020, p. xx). Further conversation would usually reveal that this team was one-sided. In particular, well-meaning teachers often gave directives to parents about how they could support them without much dialogue. Indeed, many mothers focused on teachers' assignments of home activities as the best way to be part of the team. "Like send homework, so you can have something to do with them," said one mother when asked about how she expected teachers to engage parents. I think, therefore, that the policy tendency toward school-directed interactions and engagement is grounded in reality, but it is also potentially counterproductive to the real goal of using parent-teacher relations to help children.

Another example is the assumption of much policy that parents and teachers meet on an even playing field, in similarly valued and mutually recognized positions. Most researchers studying low-income and/or racial/ethnic minority communities, including me, will surely find that assumption problematic. Consider the seminal "funds of knowledge" research showing how parents from marginalized populations can feel devalued in educational programs that see them as lacking anything to add to children's learning experiences. Such parents may lack conventionally valued educational credentials or occupational prestige, but their experiences in work, home, and community nevertheless offer ways for teachers to reach children—by, for example, leveraging parental work skills (e.g., building) to teach spatial lessons or using culturally grounded family scenarios to teach math (Civil, 2016; Moll, 1992). Thus, efforts to bring parents and teachers together without interrogating the assumption of a level playing field are likely to be undermined.

Finally, many policies and programs create significant expectations of "work" for both parents and teachers that may come to seem like a burden to both. Again, conducting community- or school-based research with parents with young children and early childhood educators certainly drives home the point that additional work is exactly what both sets of adults do not need.

Fortunately, there are new directions that research can take that may be able to improve this alignment. I turn to those next.

Salient Issues to Be Considered

The second point of my argument—concerning how new strands of research can better support policy efforts based on more nuanced understandings of parent-teacher relations—highlights several conceptual and practical gaps in the field that need to be filled. One gap, to which I alluded earlier, concerns the extent to which the apparent short- and long-term benefits of parent-teacher relations—educational (e.g., achievement) and socioemotional (e.g., attachment to school)—reflect cause and effect. To what extent do these benefits represent the effects of parent-teacher relations on children's outcomes, and to what extent are they simply a function of unknown or unmeasured factors that influence parent-teacher relations and children's outcomes at the same time. This question is particularly important to consider for low-income, racial/ethnic minority, and immigrant families, who encounter many experiences and circumstances (e.g., economic stress) that can simultaneously shape parenting and child development. Some researchers have even argued that the apparent benefits are so suspect that they should not be given much attention in the policy world (Domina, 2005; Robinson & Harris, 2014). This criticism has been voiced more often in sociological and economic subfields of education research. The causally informed methods and models of these disciplinary subfields could be leveraged more effectively and broadly to establish the degree to which parent-teacher relations really matter.

A related gap concerns whether and how the extensive current knowledge about parent-teacher relations and children's K–12 progress, adjustment, and functioning transfers down to the early childhood education period. Both parenting and teaching follow a developmental gradient as children grow older (Sheridan & Moorman, 2015); therefore, researchers need to ask, and answer, the question of whether our conceptualizations of parent-teacher relations based on elementary school (or later) should be rethought for the early childhood period. Doing so will require more comparative and longitudinal studies, which are difficult to fund and execute. Worth stressing here is that comparative and longitudinal do not simply equate with quantitative. They are approaches that can be leveraged for various types of data collection.

A third gap concerns the mechanisms through which parents and teachers in early childhood education programs form positive relations with each other. Such mechanisms are often assumed or discussed but without extensive direct empirical inquiry, so the need to carefully elucidate them is great. Also warranting greater attention are the mechanisms by which positive parent-teacher relations facilitate learning and skill development among children over time. Qualitative studies of families and early childhood education programs often provide foundational knowledge of such mechanisms that is useful for theory building in its own right and also can organize subsequent quantitative work (Adair, Tobin, & Arzubiaga, 2012; Crosnoe et al., 2015). Unfortunately, qualitative work on early education is too often disconnected from the related quantitative literature, when the two should be speaking to each other. For example, measurement of parent-child relations is dominated by scales that can be easily quantified (such as by counts of how often parents talk to teachers) but that do not get into the substance of interactions, such as what parents and teachers talk about (see the frequencies for one battery of items in the Early Childhood Longitudinal Study–Birth Cohort, in Figure 2). In addition, these scales are often overly school-focused and do not deeply tap into what parents do on their own. More dialogue between qualitative and quantitative researchers can deepen this area of measurement.

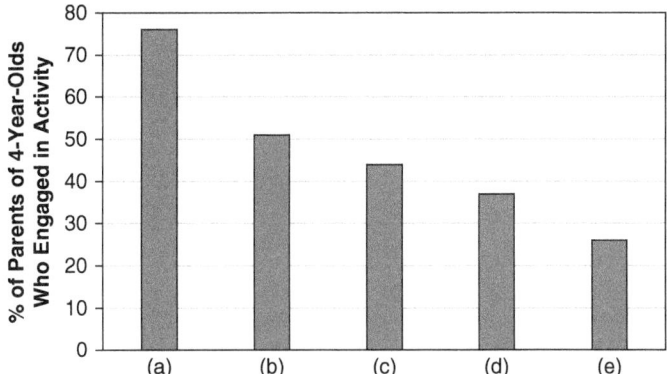

Figure 2. Distribution of five questionnaire items on parents' involvement in their children's early childhood education programs. The participants answered the following questions: Since your child began going to the current program, have you (a) attended a school/center meeting? (b) gone to a conference with the teacher? (c) attended a school/center event? (d) volunteered or served on a committee? (e) attended/chaperoned a field trip? Data are from Early Childhood Longitudinal Study–Birth Cohort.

A fourth gap concerns diversity. Just as the field has made great strides in recognizing the important role of the increasing diversification of the population of children and parents in the United States and many other developed countries, the increasing diversification of the population of teachers also deserves attention. Although the workforce of early childhood educators is significantly less diverse than the children enrolled in their programs (and the population as a whole), about a quarter of early childhood educators are racial/ethnic minorities (National Center for Education Statistics, 2016; U.S. Department of Education, 2016). The ways in which parents of different socioeconomic and demographic backgrounds interact with, perceive, and feel about their children's schools and early childhood education programs have been studied for some time. A more holistic consideration of parent-teacher relations takes in the backgrounds of teachers at the same time, such as by exploring the implications and challenges of sociodemographic matches and mismatches (e.g., by race/ethnicity, socioeconomic status, language use) between parents and teachers. Doing so requires careful attention to sampling in both quantitative and qualitative data collections, which may increase effort and cost.

Filling these gaps involves important steps in creating a well-rounded understanding of parent-teacher relations during early childhood and what they mean for children's futures. However, these steps can better help to inform policy by speaking to factors that are valued in the policy arena. For example, improving causal inference in our research is aligned with the policy need for demonstration of valid impacts. The search for mechanisms in general and the use of qualitative research in particular helps to capture "real world" experiences and voices that personalize research for policy makers and stakeholders.

Promising Directions for Future Research

Notably, research is already starting to fill these gaps and inform the alignment between research and policy. Consider the quantitative research conducted by developmental scientists elucidating the paths through which parents from socially and economically disadvantaged segments of the population end up enrolling their children in early childhood education. This research demonstrates that the under-enrollment of the children of low-income parents in early childhood education is often rooted in the fact that such programs do not meet parents' changing and often unpredictable child care needs. Research has also largely debunked ideas that the underenrollment of the children of Latino/a immigrants reflects cultural differences (i.e., preferences for keeping children at home) rather than the same socioeconomic difficulties that many nonimmigrant parents face (Coley, Votruba-Drzal, Collins, & Cook, 2014). Such research is creating a more integrated view of children's early ecology and what parents bring into their interactions with teachers, while also providing information about patterns of children's selection into early childhood education that may be useful in efforts to improve causal inference.

Similarly, qualitative research by anthropologists is shedding light on how parents' views of their children's early childhood education providers may differ from how those providers view them, especially when differences in culture and language are involved. This research also illuminates important dilemmas that can arise even when parents and teachers are from the same minority population. For example, teachers who are immigrants themselves are in a unique position to connect with immigrant parents, but they are often held back by feelings of being torn between the cultural knowledge that they developed in their home countries and the pedagogical traditions they have learned in the new country (Adair et al., 2012). For example, Adair and colleagues relayed the story of a teacher named Rosa who had come to the United States from Mexico and eventually trained to be an early childhood education teacher. Rosa struggled with the tension between the play-based approach to learning in her program and the ideas about more formalized academic learning she had brought with her to the United States. As Adair and colleagues explained, Rosa's narrative suggested "a process of becoming a professional that required her to give up one set of beliefs and replace them with another." Such insights capture the lived experiences of teachers (and parents) in ways that increase understanding of how to provide culturally sensitive training for early childhood educators and that discourage "one size fits all" approaches to building parent-teacher relations.

One point I want to make is that, although some of these new policy-relevant directions for research call for new data collections, the models for these data collections already exist. The NICHD Study of Early Child Care and Youth Development, for example, includes linked home, school, and child care observations that allow researchers to study parallels in what is going on in different settings and see how influences from different settings interact with each other. Notably, the Fragile Families study fielded several waves of quantitative data collections on parents and children (and child care providers) and embedded a focused qualitative study for a subset of families within the overall study design. That strategy allows researchers to go back and forth between quantitative and qualitative data, unpacking the former with the latter and then using the latter to revise measurements in the former. Sometimes, *new* ways forward can be found in *old* things.

Relating Research to Policy and Practice

The third point of my argument—concerning the need for better alignment between research and policy—shines a light on some current translational activities dealing with parent-teacher relations. Here, I discuss two evidence-based efforts to address thorny issues of status and power in parent-teacher relations.

One method for addressing these issues is to help parents and teachers come to the table with greater understanding of each other's expectations, assumptions, and goals. Programs that demystify the educational system (i.e., that communicate the importance of school readiness skills and norms of visible parental involvement) can help parents gain a sense of how to interact with teachers and other personnel and how to structure home activities that fit well with what their children are doing in their early childhood education programs and schools. These programs are especially effective when they include a socialization component for teachers too, allowing teachers to get a better sense of the parents and communities that they are serving and how what is self-evident to the teachers themselves may not be for those served (Goldenberg & Light, 2009; Moore, Caal, Lawner, Rojas, & Walker, 2014). Such programs can also increase effectiveness by empowering parents to participate in schools' agenda-setting and helping teachers to make connections between what children do in school and what is happening in their homes (Delgado-Gaitan, 1991).

Another method for addressing these issues to is to empower the parents of children in early childhood programs by investing in the human capital of parents. Such investments— which can take the form of educational supports and vocational training for parents when children are enrolled in Head Start or another early childhood program—can reduce some socioeconomic and related barriers between parents and teachers or other school personnel. Greater knowledge of what helps children succeed in the educational system, enhanced personal efficacy and other "noncognitive" skills, and greater stability in work and economic circumstances can result from educational investments in parents. These results, in turn, can enable parents to develop more agency in their interaction with teachers and their construction of complementary home environments (Chase-Lansdale & Brooks-Gunn, 2014; Sabol et al., 2015).

These approaches help parents and teachers to reduce any socioeconomic and demographic barriers getting in the way of strong and positive relations, allow parents and teachers to better see each other even when such barriers persist, and provide resources to connect home and school even when such barriers do not exist. Research has shown that this mutual understanding and respect between parents and teachers is key to helping children succeed, and evidence-based programs are acting on that knowledge.

Conclusion

To recap the basic points laid out at the beginning of the chapter: First, policy can benefit from the insights of high-quality research about parent-teacher relations as two-way streets that take multiple and complex forms and are vulnerable to issues of differential status and power. Second, research can better fulfill this role when it demonstrates impact and speaks in personal and relatable ways to the needs of teachers, parents, and children. Third, this partnership between research and policy is evident in efforts to help parents and teachers form relationships on a more even playing field. This three-point argument is focused on (a) helping individual children get the most out of early childhood education, and (b) reducing systematic disparities across groups in early childhood education before the disparities can contribute to the intergenerational transmission of inequality.

To close, I would like to add that, whenever I survey the research in the area of parent-teacher relations in early childhood education programs, elementary school, and beyond, I am impressed by the breadth and depth of the literature. This research has much to offer policy makers and practitioners aiming to improve the future prospects of young children. There are clear strategies we can take to better inform policy and practice, just as there are changes in policy and practice that could be made to better reflect what is known. Some mixture of continuing what we have done well while addressing our limitations is the way forward.

Acknowledgments

Support for this research came from the Institute of Education Sciences (Award R305A150027; Robert Crosnoe, PI) and from the Eunice Kennedy Shriver National Institute of Child Health and Human Development, which awarded grants to the Population Research Center at the University of Texas at Austin (Grant P2CHD04284; Debra Umberson, PI).

Note

The author can be contacted at Population Research Center, University of Texas at Austin, 305 East 23rd Street, Austin, TX 78712.

References

Adair, J. K., Tobin, J., & Arzubiaga, A. E. (2012). The dilemma of cultural responsiveness and professionalization. *Teachers College Record, 114*(12). Retrieved from https://www.tcrecord.org/content.asp?contentid=16719

Chase-Lansdale, P. L., & Brooks-Gunn, J. (2014). Two-generation programs in the twenty-first century. *Future of Children, 24,* 13–39.

Civil, M. (2016). STEM learning research through a funds of knowledge lens. *Cultural Studies of Science Education, 11*(1), 41–59.

Coley, R. L., Votruba-Drzal, E., Collins, M., & Cook, K. D. (2014). Comparing public, private, and informal preschool programs in a national sample of low-income children. *Early Childhood Research Quarterly, 36,* 91–105.

Crosnoe, R. (2015). Continuities and consistencies across home and school systems. In S. Sheridan & E. Moorman (Eds.), *Processes and pathways of family-school partnerships across development* (pp. 61–80). New York, NY: Springer International.

Crosnoe, R., Bonazzo, C., & Wu, N. (2015). *Healthy learners: A whole child approach to reducing disparities in early education.* New York, NY: Teachers College Press.

Delgado-Gaitan, C. (1991). Involving parents in the schools: A process of empowerment. *American Journal of Education, 100*(1), 20–46.

Domina, T. (2005). Leveling the home advantage: Assessing the effectiveness of parental involvement in elementary school. *Sociology of Education, 78*, 233–249.

Doucet, F. (2011). (Re)Constructing home and school: Immigrant parents, agency, and the (un)desirability of bridging multiple worlds. *Teachers College Record, 113*(12), 2705–2738.

Epstein, J. L. (2016). *School, family, and community partnerships: Preparing educators and improving schools.* Boulder, CO: Westview.

Fantuzzo, J., Tighe, E., & Childs, S. (2000). Family Involvement Questionnaire: A multivariate assessment of family participation in early childhood education. *Journal of Educational Psychology, 92*, 367–376.

Gilliam, W. S., Maupin, A. N., Reyes, C. R., Accavitti, M., & Shic, F. (2016). *Do early educators' implicit biases regarding sex and race relate to behavior expectations and recommendations of preschool expulsions and suspensions?* New Haven, CT: Yale Child Study Center.

Goldenberg, L., & Light, D. (2009). *Lee y Seras: Evaluation report.* New York, NY: Education Development Center.

Graue, E. (2008). Teaching and learning in a post-DAP world. *Early Education and Development, 19*, 441–447.

Karoly, L. A., & Gonzalez, G. C. (2011). Early care and education for children in immigrant families. *Future of Children, 21*, 71–101.

Lareau, A. (2000). *Home advantage: Social class and parental intervention in elementary education.* Lanham, MD: Rowman & Littlefield.

McWayne, C. M., Melzi, G., Schick, A. R., Kennedy, J. L., & Mundt, K. (2013). Defining family engagement among Latino Head Start parents: A mixed-methods measurement development study. *Early Childhood Research Quarterly, 28*, 593–607.

Moll, L. (1992). Funds of knowledge for teaching: Using a qualitative approach to connect homes and classrooms. *Theory Into Practice, 31*(2), 132–141.

Moore, K. A., Caal, S., Lawner, E. K., Rojas, A., & Walker, K. (2014). *Abriendo Puertas/Opening Doors parenting program: Summary report of program implementation and impacts.* Washington, DC: Child Trends.

National Center for Education Statistics. (2016). *Preschool and kindergarten enrollment.* Washington, DC: Author.

Rathbun, A., & Zhang, A. (2016). *Primary early care and education arrangements and achievement at kindergarten entry* (NCES 2016-070). Washington, DC: National Center for Education Statistics, U.S. Department of Education.

Robinson, K., & Harris, A. (2014). *The broken compass.* Cambridge, MA: Harvard University Press.

Ryan, S., & Grieshaber, S. (2005). Shifting from developmental to postmodern practices in early childhood teacher education. *Journal of Teacher Education, 56*, 34–45.

Sabol, T. J., Sommer, T. E., Chase-Lansdale, P. L., Brooks-Gunn, J., Yoshikawa, H., King, C. T., & Ross, E. C. (2015). Parents' persistence and certification in a two-generation education and training program. *Children and Youth Services Review, 58*, 1–10.

Sheridan, S., & Moorman, E. (Eds.). (2015). *Processes and pathways of family-school partnerships across development.* New York, NY: Springer International.

Souto-Manning, M., & Swick, K. J. (2006). Teachers' beliefs about parent and family involvement: Rethinking our family involvement paradigm. *Early Childhood Education Journal, 34*, 187–193.

Tobin, J., Adair, J. K., & Arzubiaga, A. (2013). *Children crossing borders: Immigrant parent and teacher perspectives on preschool for children of immigrants.* New York, NY: Russell Sage Foundation.

U.S. Department of Education. (2016). *The state of racial diversity in the educator workforce.* Washington, DC: Author.

Chapter 7

Conversations in Early Childhood Classrooms: Preliminary Findings From a Professional Development Intervention

STEPHANIE M. CURENTON
Boston University

SHANA E. ROCHESTER
Boston University

YUSRA M. SYED
Emory Healthcare

SHARI L. GARDNER
SRI International

Seminal research studies using large longitudinal data sets have consistently shown that oral language skills during early childhood are important predictors of reading skills in elementary school (Kendeou, Van den Broek, White, & Lynch, 2009; NICHD Early Child Care Research Network, 2005). Recent work continues to demonstrate the important role that oral language skills play in later reading (see Lervåg, Hulme, & Melby-Lervåg, 2018). These studies have focused primarily on vocabulary and listening comprehension. However, comparatively few studies in early childhood development and early schooling have examined children's conversational discourse skills. In this chapter, we focus on young children's oral language discourse skills (i.e., classroom conversations) and their importance both for preschoolers' concomitant language development and for their future educational success.

We begin by examining why and how conversations within classrooms contribute to children's early literacy. Then, we review empirical research related to conversation-based professional development (PD) interventions for teachers. Findings from this body of work (see Cabell et al., 2011; Girolametto, Weitzman, & Greenberg, 2003; Pence, Justice, & Wiggins, 2008; Piasta, Justice, Cabell, Wiggins, Turnbull, & Curenton, 2012) show that targeted conversation-based PD has a positive influence on teachers' conversational practice and children's language outcomes. We discuss two limitations of the research to date: low uptake of empirically tested strategies from past work, and the lack of attention in existing approaches to the unique needs of culturally and linguistically diverse learners.

We then offer the Conversation Compass approach (Curenton, 2016) as a supplement or alternative to existing conversation-based PD interventions. Conversation Compass is aimed at addressing the language diversity of ethnic and racial minority children and improving teacher uptake of empirically tested strategies. We provide preliminary findings from classroom case studies comparing teachers who were trained in the Conversation Compass approach with their co-teachers who were not. Last, we summarize the implications of conversation-based strategies for educational practice with young children and for education policy on curricula and education standards.

Early Childhood Classrooms and Young Children's Language Development: The Importance of Classroom Conversations

During the prekindergarten period (birth to age 4), environmental input explains 60%–70% of the variance in typically developing children's oral language abilities, specifically their vocabulary and grammar abilities (Spinath, Price, Dale, & Plomin, 2004). Environmental inputs come from interactions in the home and also in early childhood education programs. Nearly 70% of all 4-year-olds are enrolled in a preprimary program before Grade 1 (McFarland et al., 2017), making the classroom environments of early childhood programs a major source of environmental language input for young children.

Early education classrooms are particularly important to the language development of children from low-income homes. National research shows low-income preschoolers enter early childhood programs with less developed oral language skills than their higher-income peers (National Center for Education Statistics, 2012). Hart and Risley (1995) found that home environments of children whose parents received public assistance during the 1980s were relatively lower in terms of quality and quantity of language input (i.e., number of vocabulary words) compared to the home environments of highly educated higher-income families. However, other researchers, drawing primarily on ethnographic methods, do not report lower quality language interactions in lower-income homes. For example, Sperry, Sperry, and Miller (2018) report that children living in low-income and working-class families from five geographic regions, spanning the 1970s through the 1990s, had home language environments that were comparable to those of their middle-income peers. Furthermore, Heath's (1983) seminal work from the 1980s found that, at home, working-class African American parents engaged in complex patterns of conversational discourse, though different from those their children encountered in school. She explained that the African American parents asked their children "real questions," meaning open-ended questions to which there was no predetermined answer, and that parents and children as young as toddlers were engaged in sophisticated oral storytelling. This body of work examining socioeconomic differences in young children's home language environments points to the complexity and diversity of those environments. The findings also highlight the potential value of classroom environments for supplementing language input from the home and capitalizing on the skills that low-income children bring to the classroom.

The question that remains is *how* the classroom environment can facilitate such important language input. Justice, Jiang, and Strasser (2018) identify three dimensions of what they call the "language-learning" environment of the classroom. One dimension is linguistic responsivity (e.g., how the teacher engages children in conversations). A second is "data-providing" features of teachers' talk (e.g., mean length of utterance [MLU], syntax, vocabulary). A third is system-level general environment (e.g., global ratings of classroom quality related to language practices). The authors found that the systems-level dimension was only moderately correlated with the other two dimensions and was unrelated to children's language outcomes. They suggest that in order to understand the language-learning environment of early childhood classrooms, it is best to examine the specific linguistic features of teachers' talk (Dimension 2) and their linguistic responsivity (Dimension 1). More specifically, they found that it was only teachers' linguistic responsivity (i.e., how well teachers facilitated children's conversation skills) that predicted children's vocabulary growth throughout the school year. The authors' factor analysis led them to conclude that linguistic responsivity is comprised of several communication-facilitation strategies, all of which loaded onto a significant factor called Communication-Facilitation Strategies. The strategies are

- looking expectantly and being warm and receptive to encourage children's interaction,

- using a slow pace of conversation to allow children to participate,

- using open-ended questions to stimulate conversation, and

- facilitating peer-to-peer communication.

Having prior empirical support for the association between children's outcomes and how teachers facilitate classroom conversations is particularly compelling during this time, given that the Common Core Standards focus on speaking and listening skills. The Common Core Standards require that, by the end of kindergarten, children be able to respond audibly to express thoughts, feelings, and ideas (National Governors Association & Council of Chief State School Officers, 2010).[1] Children are also expected to engage in collaborative discussion around instructional topics/texts, and such discussions should have multiple turn-taking exchanges and follow the pragmatic rules for turn-taking during conversation. As it relates to questioning, students are expected to be able to ask and/or answer questions and, if need be, clarify what they have said. The mastery of all these skills occurs in the context of classroom conversations, with both peers and teachers. Given these standards, coupled with what we know about the importance of communication-facilitation strategies, there may be rich opportunities to build children's communication skills in the years before formal schooling.

Research that investigates classroom conversations during the early childhood years prior to kindergarten entry shows that many early education teachers seldom expose children to high-level classroom conversations (Dickinson, 2001; Foorman, Anthony, Seals, & Mouzaki, 2002; Girolametto & Weitzman, 2002). Goh, Yamauchi, and Ratliffe (2012) found that preschool children have limited opportunities to practice their conversational skills due to restrictions on teachers' time. Unfortunately, many low-income children bear the brunt of these workforce constraints at greater rates than their higher income peers. Research suggests that classrooms vary dramatically in the quality of their language-learning environments, particularly classrooms where the majority of children are living in poverty (Connor, Morrison, & Slominski, 2006; Farran, Aydogan, Kang, & Lipsey, 2006; Pianta et al., 2005; Sylva et al., 2006). Observational studies that examine the language-learning environment of low-income classrooms report that teachers' classroom talk relies too heavily on behavioral directives, closed-ended questions, and talk that is not cognitively challenging (Durden & Dangel, 2008; Gest, Holland-Coviello, Welsh, Eicher-Catt, & Gill, 2006; Massey, Pence, Justice, & Bowles, 2008). These descriptions of talk are a stark contrast to the communication-facilitation strategies reported to have positive outcomes for children's vocabulary.

Not only is the quality of conversations problematic for classrooms serving children living in poverty, but some evidence also indicates that conversations are constrained when children are culturally and linguistically diverse (CALD).[2] Teachers report being uncertain about the strategies needed to support CALD learners' language and literacy skills (Diamond & Powell, 2011) because many teachers lack knowledge about the cultural traditions and communication styles of these children (Buysse, Castro, West, & Skinner, 2005; Curenton, 2006; Gándara, Maxwell-Jolly, & Driscoll, 2005; Zepeda, Castro, & Cronin, 2011). Goldberg (2013) explains that, for all children, high-quality conversations around academic texts and topics are important for facilitating language skills. However, CALD learners may need additional support during classroom conversations because they face the challenge of learning both the social and the academic language of English concurrently during preschool (Aukerman, 2007) and later elementary grades (Goldenberg, 1992; Zhang & Stahl, 2011). Fortunately, there is a compelling body of evidence demonstrating the effectiveness of high-quality conversations in fostering children's language skills and successful teacher PD efforts.

Empirical Research Related to Professional Development for Classroom Conversations

There is a wide body of rigorous evidence that PD trainings that focus on oral language (i.e., conversations) during children's early school years provide the foundation for later school success because they enable teachers to build young students' language abilities. Girolametto et al. (2003) found that when daycare professionals in Canada were trained to enhance the quality of their language input by asking children more open-ended questions and using follow-up comments, toddlers improved in their expressive language skills (namely, their number of utterances and MLU). Wasik and colleagues also demonstrated positive effects for children's vocabulary following professional development that taught Head Start teachers how to ask open-ended questions during storybook reading and dramatic play (Wasik & Bond, 2001; Wasik, Bond, & Hindman, 2006). Other studies found that when teachers received training to increase their communication-facilitation strategies, there were positive effects on children's vocabulary, MLU, and early literacy skills (Cabell et al., 2011; Piasta et al., 2012). Furthermore, when teachers received training to use communication-facilitation strategies, they engaged their students in more multi-turn conversations (e.g., four or more back-and-forth turn-taking exchanges) and more spontaneous child-initiated conversations, which can have a positive impact on children's vocabulary growth throughout the year.

Despite the benefits of these oral language professional development trainings, implementation fidelity is consistently low (e.g., Cabell et al., 2011; Pence et al., 2008; Piasta et al., 2012). Justice, Mashburn, Pence, & Wiggins (2008) suggested that implementation, or the extent to which teachers incorporate strategies into their practice, may be low because classroom conversation training requires teachers to learn how to engage in dynamic spoken exchanges in which they follow the child's lead (often child initiated). Such exchanges cannot be scripted. Bond and Wasik's (2009) work incorporated the "conversation station" into the classroom, a designated place in the classroom facilitated by one of the teachers and designed to engage children in one-on-one teacher-child conversation. However, even though their approach provided a routine time and place for conversations throughout the day, it did not involve training teachers specifically on any of the communication-facilitating strategies that Justice and her colleagues found to be related to positive language outcomes.

A limitation of existing professional development approaches related to classroom conversations is that they do not explicitly address the cultural and linguistic diversity of the children who participate in these interventions even though the children are ethnically and racially diverse. Bilingual children whose home language is English need additional language support in the classroom, above and beyond what is generally provided to children who are monolingual English speakers. Another limitation is that nearly all of the documented professional development interventions around conversations comprised samples of teachers who were mostly White. In addition, questions remain as to whether conversation interactions in classrooms might be different if the workforce were racially, ethnically, and linguistically diverse. Some research has found that CALD children have more active voices in the classroom when teachers value bilingualism and/or children's home language (Baker, 2019; Phillips Galloway & Lesaux, 2017; Strickland & Marinak, 2016). A third limitation is that the model for classroom conversation interventions relies heavily on the modality of one-on-one teacher-child interactions, even though as Goh and colleagues (2012) explained, there is little time for such conversations throughout the day. Early and colleagues' (2010) breakdown of the early childhood day shows that children actually spend most of their day interacting with each other and talking in groups (e.g., circle time, small groups). These limitations in implementing and addressing classroom conversations suggest a need for a classroom conversation approach that explicitly applies principles of communication facilitation where both the teachers and children are culturally, racially, and linguistically diverse.

Extending Communication-Facilitation Strategies: The Conversation Compass Approach

Developed by Curenton (2016), Conversation Compass is a conversation-based professional development approach in which teachers learn how to routinely and systematically use three strategies. First, they learn the importance of organizing peer groups of young children around age-appropriate learning activities to generate *instructional conversations*. Research on instructional conversations focuses both on elementary school students (Goldenberg, 1992; Zhang & Stahl, 2011) and early childhood students (Goh et al., 2012). Goh and her colleagues (2012) describe instructional conversations not as spontaneous casual conversations but, rather, intentional conversations that facilitate children's learning around a topic or theme. The authors implemented their instructional conversation intervention in preschool settings where small-group discussions between teachers and children took place. These discussions allowed the young learners to share their previous experiences and knowledge and integrate new information to broaden their understanding of different concepts. One of the many results of this intervention indicated that teachers had already been teaching through dialogue in their classrooms, but they gained a sense of value and appreciation for meaningful conversations around academic content after focusing on instructional conversations.

Conversation Compass expands Goh and her colleagues' (2012) research on instructional conversations by focusing on *instructional peer conversations* that revolve around planned thematic discussions with small groups of children. The teacher's role during these discussions is to facilitate students' collaborative reasoning with peers by using challenging open-ended questions. Research shows students learn better when group size is small and when students are collaborating with their peers (e.g., Blumenfeld, Marx, Soloway, & Krajcik, 1996; Cohen, 1994).

Second, in Conversation Compass, teachers learn how to engage in feedback loops and how to ask a range of open-ended questions that vary in their level of cognitive challenge. The ideas for this feedback loop are based on the communication-facilitating strategies and language-modeling strategies that undergird the prior body of work in this area (Cabell et al., 2011; Girolametto et al., 2003; Pence, Justice, & Wiggins, 2008; Piasta et al., 2012). These strategies are broken down in a simplified circular mnemonic with the anchors of "Ask Open-Ended Questions," "Actively Listen," and "Mirror to Expand or Clarify." Consistent with Justice, Jiang, and Strasser's work (2018), such anchors in this feedback loop would mainly correspond to Dimension 1 (linguistic responsivity that fosters children's communication, such as asking open-ended questions and actively listening), but aspects of Dimension 2 (data-driven features of teachers talk) would be represented in the "Mirror to Expand or Clarify" anchor that focuses specifically on the grammar and vocabulary of teachers' talk. There is empirical justification for including these anchors in the feedback loop. Justice and her colleagues (2018) found a positive relationship between the complexity of teachers' talk and teacher responsiveness during a conversational exchange. Thus, the feedback loop is a parsimonious and simplified way to train teachers in linguistic responsivity and "data-driven" language modeling, as described by Justice, Jiang, and Strasser.

Conversation Compass's feedback loop also presents teachers with a mnemonic for how to scaffold between less challenging and more challenging open-ended questions. A "Question Trail" is another visual mnemonic that attempts to simplify and expand prior empirical work related to open-ended questions (Peterson & McCabe, 1994; Wasik & Bond, 2001). It provides a visual guide for moving from *wh-* questions (who, what, when, where) to *how* and *why* questions and on to hypothesis-generating questions, such as *what if*

The cognitive challenge of these questions spans widely as they fall along different points of Blank, Rose, and Berlin's (1978) continuum of *literal* (concrete) to *inferential* (abstract) reasoning. For instance, to answer *wh-* questions, children can rely on their knowledge of concrete, observable information, but to answer *how, why,* or *what if* questions requires children to make inferences about their knowledge and to speculate about possibilities. Massey, Pence, Justice, and Bowles (2008) detail how *wh-* questions predominate in teachers' talk. However, the hope is that visually presenting this range of questions in a sequence that goes from less challenging to more challenging will remind teachers' to use a range of questions.

Third, in the Conversation Compass approach, teachers learn the importance of systematically observing children's conversations skills. To observe children's conversations with their peers, teachers can use the Tracking Conversations sheet, specifically designed to facilitate naturalistic observations of children's conversations. The Tracking Conversations sheet can be used as a progress-monitoring tool; teachers can modify their interactions with children or better facilitate peer conversations based on the results. To assess children's overall classroom conversation skills, teachers can complete the Conversation Compass Communication Screener (CCCS), which has proved to be highly correlated with other teacher-reported child outcome measures used in preschool classrooms (Curenton, Sims, Rochester, & Gardner, 2019; Gardner & Curenton, 2017). The CCCS is used to assess individual children's communication abilities, and it provides a benchmark for how children are using conversational discourse in the classroom. A revised version, the CCCS-R, comprises four subscales ("Decontextualized Language/Pre-Academic Talk," "Social Communication," "Negative Communication Behaviors," and "Narrative and Vocabulary Knowledge"). It has both concurrent and predictive validity with standardized assessments of children's language and literacy skills (Curenton, Sims, Rochester, & Gardner, 2019).

Fourth, the Conversation Compass explicitly focuses on the importance of building children's academic language skills (Snow, 2010). Academic language is the type of discourse valued at school because it supports children's ability to read, comprehend, and write academic texts. Academic language skills include skills such as abstract reasoning, comprehension of technical vocabulary (e.g., words used in math, science, or literary analysis), and discussions and composition of written texts (O'Connor & Michaels, 2019). In the preschool years, children are developing academic language skills through read alouds and classroom conversations that allow them to ask and answer questions and describe their inquiry process (Michael Luna, 2017). In the Conversation Compass approach, teachers are guided in how to foster academic language skills by using conversations to facilitate children's abstract reasoning, vocabulary, and discussions about stories.

Finally, the Conversation Compass approach focuses explicitly on how culture and home language traditions may influence children's classroom conversation skills. A literature review by Vernon-Feagans, Hammer, Miccio, and Manlove (2001) details how the language and literacy development of African American and Latinx children is distinct from that of their White peers and suggests how they may face unique challenges given the quantity and quality of language input in their homes. Nevertheless, research has shown that Latinx (Melzi, Schick, & Kennedy, 2011), as well as Head Start children from a variety of ethnic backgrounds, responded positively to a conversation-based home language intervention focused on reminiscing about past experiences (Reese, Leyva, Sparks, & Grolnick, 2010). Evidence from prior work demonstrates that Black and Latinx children are also responsive to conversation-based interactions at school. The majority of child participants in prior studies were Black and Latinx children,[3] and those studies demonstrated positive changes in children's language and early literacy outcomes after teachers were trained in conversation-based PD (Cabell et al., 2011; Justice, Jiang, & Strasser, 2018; Piasta et al., 2012).

Overall, the Conversation Compass approach builds on the empirical findings from the literature on conversation-based PD in three ways: (a) by adding aspects of real-world classroom practice, such as a focus on academic language; (b) by explicitly focusing on diversity (i.e., both the challenges and strengths of Black and Latinx home language traditions); and (c) by simplifying the body of literature in a teacher-friendly manner by means of a workbook for early childhood educators.

Conversation Compass in Action: PD Training With a Head Start Program

In October 2011, Curenton was approached by the education supervisor of a Head Start program in the northeastern United States and was asked to conduct an in-service workshop on oral language skills. All of the teachers working at the program were required to participate in the program-wide training, which was designed to enhance classroom conversations. This was a six-hour on-site training developed and led solely by Curenton. The training consisted of (a) a PowerPoint presentation explaining key concepts of the instructional strategy (e.g., back-and-forth exchanges, questioning, and engaging in decontextualized discourse); (b) video examples of teachers from the program engaging in small-group conversations; (c) small-group breakout discussions and planning sessions around using the lesson planning tools; and (d) instructions on how to conduct classroom assessments about children's conversational skills. At the end of this training, each teacher received a printed manual that explained the strategy and contained copies of the lesson planning tools. The education supervisor encouraged teachers to use the lesson planning tools in their daily activities, but there was no formal requirement to do so. Also, at the end of the training workshop, teachers were asked to complete an evaluation (written survey) of the in-service. The mean response rate for completion was 79%, and the response was overwhelmingly positive, with the majority of participants indicating that they highly valued the in-service workshop. The specific responses for the three teachers (Rachel, Stacey, and Eileen)[4] who were selected for follow-up are presented in Table 1. Also, during an interview follow-up with Rachel and Eileen in May 2011, both teachers indicated that they were applying the strategies they had learned in the training to their classroom practices. Rachel noted that she regularly reread the training manual.

Follow-Up Observations

The following year, beginning in October 2012, both the program staff and Curenton were interested in observing whether the teachers were using the Conversation Compass

Table 1. Teachers' Individual Feedback Regarding the In-Service Workshop on Conversation Compass (on a Scale of 1 to 5)

Items	Rachel	Stacey	Eileen
The Conversation Compass . . .			
Provides me with new information about how to talk with children	5	2	5
Can help build children's language skills	5	5	5
Can be used with children who are bilingual (or children who speak a dialect of English, Creole, or Patios)	5	5	5
The learning modules/activities in the training . . .			
Provided me with concrete information about how to use the conversation strategies	5	3	5
Helped me develop a deeper understanding of the Conversation Compass	5	3	5
The trainer was . . .			
Knowledgeable about early childhood language	5	4	5
In the future . . .			
I plan to use these conversation suggestions in my classroom	5	5	5

Note. 1 = strongly disagree; 2 = mildly disagree; 3 = not sure; 4 = mildly agree; 5 = strongly agree.

approach. The education supervisor selected three classrooms in the same center to participate in follow-up observations.[5] Each classroom contained a teacher who had received the PD in the prior year (the "PD teachers" were Rachel, Stacey, and Eileen) and a teacher who had not (the "non-PD teachers" were Madge, Miriam, and Mary). The teachers worked in pairs in the classrooms, and the PD teachers had been intentionally paired with co-teachers who had not received the Conversation Compass PD in the prior year. All teachers had received training in the HighScope Curriculum before the start of the school year.

Our goal was to observe how language was used in the classrooms and to discover how teachers who had received the PD compared to their co-teachers who had not. Specifically, we were interested in (a) whether PD teachers engaged in more linguistic responsive strategies (i.e., turn-taking, questioning) than the comparison teachers; (b) whether PD teachers used more complex language (i.e., MLU and mean length of turn-taking exchange [MLT]); and (c) whether the children's talk was different when they were engaged in conversations with PD teachers versus non-PD teachers (i.e., did they use more casual language or "internal state talk" such as talk about thoughts and feelings?).

Participants

After selection, teachers and families were introduced to the study in a welcome letter explaining the purpose of the observation study. Informed consent was obtained from teachers and children. Teachers and families received gift cards as incentives for their participation.

The teachers were racially and ethnically diverse female preschool teachers, half of whom were born outside of the United States (from Jamaica, Philippines, and Central America [country unspecified]). These six teachers taught a total of 54 preschoolers. The children came from a variety of ethnic, racial, and national backgrounds (e.g., Latinx, Black/African American, Asian). Rachel and Madge worked in Classroom 1; Stacey and Miriam worked in Classroom 2; Eileen and Mary worked in Classroom 3. The program staff and/or teachers described the children as being 35% dual language learners (DLLs), based on their families' reports of home languages spoken. However, none of the teachers were certified to teach children with limited English proficiency or to teach English as a second language. Table 2 provides descriptive and demographic information for the teachers and children across the three classrooms.

Data Collection

Three trained undergraduate research assistants observed in the three classrooms for eight weeks, from October to December 2012. In Weeks 1–2, the research asssistants only observed and took notes, with the goal of allowing the teachers and the children to become acclimated to their presence. In Week 3, the research assistants began videotaping natural-istic conversations and interactions that occurred in the classrooms between the teachers and the children. For example, they videotaped teacher-student interactions taking place during small-group, teacher-directed instruction (e.g., recall or planning time) or during free-choice time when students worked and played in a center of their choosing (e.g., block area, house area, table activities). The data used included the videotapes and transcripts of these interactions.

Throughout November and December of 2012, the Head Start staff conducted CLASS (Pianta, LaParo, & Hamre, 2008) observations of each classroom as part of their ongoing program monitoring. These observations were conducted separately and inde-pendently of the study, and the study team was made aware of the scores only after follow-up observations were complete. CLASS scores range from 1 (*lowest*) to 7 (*highest*); the scores are a reflection of the entire classroom experience and are not tied to a specific teacher.

In Classroom 1, taught by Rachel and Madge, CLASS scores were in the moderate range: Emotional Climate = 6.19, Classroom Organization = 5.84, Instructional Support = 4.84. In Classroom 3, taught by Eileen and Mary, scores also were moderate: Emotional Climate = 5.69, Classroom Organization = 5.09, Instructional Support = 4.17. In Classroom 2, taught by Stacey and Miriam, observational scores were not calculated, because for half of the fall semester there was a temporary substitute working in the room and the program staff chose to wait until a permanent teacher was in place. The permanent teacher was not hired until after our study observations were complete.

Descriptive Analysis

All teachers were taped for 10–20 minutes. A total of 47 observations were recorded, but some teachers had more observations than others. Because some teachers had more video-taped observations, only the longest videotaped interaction was transcribed and manually reviewed for questions for each teacher. To manually code for questions, the third and

Table 2. Teacher and Student Demographics Across Classrooms

	Classroom Teacher Characteristics					Classroom Student Characteristics			
Classroom	Name	Position	Degree (Field of Study)	Race/Ethnicity	Years of Teaching Experience	Number of Girls/ Boys	Number of Students by Race/Ethnicity	DLLs	IEPs
1	Rachel (PD)	Assistant	AA (management)	Black/African American	1.5	9/9	8 Black/African American 10 Hispanic/Latinx	10	2
	Madge (non-PD)	Lead	BA (ECE)	Black/African American	21				
2	Stacey (PD)	Lead	BA (ECE)	White/Caucasian	2	9/9	5 Black/African American 10 Hispanic/Latinx 2 Asian 1 Multiracial	5	1
	Miriam (non-PD)	Temporary assistant	n/a	White/Latina	n/a				
3	Eileen (PD)	Assistant	HS (CD)	Black/Jamaican American	12	10/8	4 Black/African American 14 Hispanic/Latino	4	1
	Mary (non-PD)	Lead	BA (applied mathematics)	Asian/ Filipino	5				

Note. DLLs = number of students who are dual language learners; IEPs = number of students who have an Individualized Education Plan; PD = received professional development training; AA = two-year associate of arts degree; non-PD = did not receive professional development training; BA = four-year bachelor of arts degree; ECE = early childhood education; HS = high school diploma; CD = child development. All teachers' names have been changed to a pseudonym in order to protect their confidentiality.

fourth authors counted for the numbers of *how/why* versus *wh-* questions within the transcript. The longest videotaped interactions were determined by length of video.

Videos were transcribed in the summer and fall of 2014 by the third author, a multilingual (English, Spanish, Hindi, and Urdu) undergraduate research assistant who served as the primary transcriber for the study. Across the sample, the teacher utterances per video ranged from 88 to 324, and children's utterances ranged from 54 to 212. Due to the variance in transcript length, the *proportion* and *ratio* were calculated to control for variation in transcription length; they were calculated by dividing the linguistic feature (e.g., internal state words, conjunctions, questions, mean length of turn [MLT], and mean length of utterance [MLU]) by the total number of utterances in the transcript. Videos were transcribed and analyzed using the Child Language Data Exchange System (CHILDES; MacWhinney, 2000). All video observations were transcribed by two people, one as the primary transcriber (i.e., the transcriber who created the initial transcription) and one as secondary transcriber (i.e., the transcriber who checked the initial transcription by watching the videotapes and verifying the transcription). Any discrepancies were discussed by the transcribers until they reached a consensus. After transcriptions, CHILDES' computerized language analysis (CLAN) program was used to analyze the descriptive outcomes of the conversations.

Patterns of the data from the PD versus non-PD teachers were analyzed. On average, as depicted in descriptive means (and standard deviations) from Table 3, teachers who participated in Conversation Compass PD engaged their students in longer conversations that included more turn-taking exchanges than did their co-teachers working in the same classroom. In addition, the PD teachers asked more *how/why* and *wh-* questions. The third author's notes from watching all the videotapes and counting the types of questions confirmed that the language interactions were different across teachers, particularly as they related to open-ended *how/why* and *wh-* questions. The PD teachers also

Table 3. Conversation Features Comparing PD With Non-PD

Conversation Features	Conversation Compass PD *(SD)*	Non-PD *(SD)*
Total number of turn-taking exchanges (utterances between teachers and children)	108.67 (38.55)	84.00 (36.50)
Children's conversational language		
Proportion of internal state words	.05 (.04)	.02 (.01)
Proportion of coordinating conjunctions	.07 (.02)	.01 (.00)
Teachers' conversational language		
Proportion of *how/why* questions	.31 (.11)	.17 (.12)
Proportion of *wh-* questions	.75 (.05)	.39 (.26)
Ratio of words per speaking turn (MLT)	11.01 (3.68)	8.91 (4.35)
Ratio of words per utterance (MLU)	4.20 (0.27)	3.53 (0.95)

Note. PD = received professional development training; non-PD = did not receive professional development training. The *proportion* and *ratio* were calculated to control for variation in transcription length; they were calculated by dividing the linguistic feature (e.g., internal state words, conjunctions, questions, mean length of turn [MLT], and mean length of utterance [MLU]) by the total number of utterances in the transcript.

used more words per utterance (MLU), and they used more words at each conversational turn-taking exchange (MLT). Many of the same children were engaged in conversations throughout the day with both teachers; therefore, the element that consistently changed in the conversation was the teacher, not necessarily the child. During conversations with the PD teachers, children used more causal language (i.e., coordinating conjunctions such as *but, and, yet, so*) and more internal state language (i.e., talk about thoughts and/or emotions), as opposed to conversations with the non-PD teachers. These results align with prior work of Justice, Jiang, and Strasser (2018), who found that in their conversation-based PD intervention, the intervention teachers were more linguistically responsive than comparison teachers and the intervention was positively related to child outcomes.

Another source of descriptive data comes from comparing a PD teacher (Rachel) with her non-PD co-teacher (Madge) working in the same classroom (Table 4). The conversation took place during "planning time," which is the part of the HighScope Curriculum where children have to articulate where they want to play during work time (free-choice play). The example illustrates how the Conversation Compass PD teachers asked more questions and had more turn-taking exchanges; in addition, Rachel engaged the children in a joint conversation about letter recognition and phonemes. In contrast, the comparison teacher used the same classroom routine in a perfunctory manner that only required the children to provide a predetermined response (e.g., stating with one word or pointing to the area where they wanted to go); she did not encourage children to engage in joint conversations with their peers or to do any critical thinking.

These descriptive results are intriguing, but additional trials of the approach are needed. A recent iteration of the Conversation Compass approach includes an online training course that has been completed by several teachers working in a Head Start program in the Northeast, and the approach has been modified to train infant/toddler teachers and family child care providers in Ohio (Curenton & Granda, 2019). Future research with this approach needs to increase the sample size and include standardized measures of children's language and literacy skills in addition to measures from the classroom language sample. In addition, robust experimental or quasi-experimental designs testing the approach need to be conducted.

Policy Considerations for Supporting Classroom Conversations in Preschool

The convergence of several policy drivers highlights the importance of addressing classroom conversations—namely, requirements in the Common Core State Standards coupled with the limitations in early childhood teachers' practice and knowledge related to CALD learners' oral language needs—and demonstrates a critical need for PD efforts (both preservice and in-service) focused on communication-facilitation strategies to promote preschool children's language development. It is imperative to consider the racial, ethnic, and linguistic diversities of children when investing in PD because these children have unique language, curricular, and instructional practice needs, especially those who

Table 4. Examples of Conversations From the Same Classroom of a PD and Non-PD Teacher

	Conversation Compass PD Teacher		Non-PD Teacher
Rachel:	Can we help Isabel out to see what letter she has?	Madge:	Who has the pink rectangle?
Child 1:	A "E"!	Child 1:	Sam [child points and teacher looks at another child who shouted].
Rachel:	A "E"!	Madge:	Where would you like to go?
Rachel:	A letter E	Child 2:	The blocks [child points].
Rachel:	Do we know what some words are that start with the letter E? What are some words that start with the letter E?	Madge:	Okay.
		Madge:	Who has the [teacher takes away child's card] purple square?
Child 2:	Eric!	Child 3:	Me [child raises hand]!
Rachel:	Eric. E—ric [teacher makes the short e sound].	Madge:	Where would you like to go?
Child 3:	Elephant.	Child 3:	Umm. block area [child points].
Rachel:	E—lephant [teacher makes the short e sound]. And who else?	Madge:	That's toy area.
		Child 3:	Toy area.
Child 4:	Daddy!	Madge:	Okay. No guns. If you make a gun today you are going to be sitting.
Rachel:	What's your daddy's name?		
Child 4:	Eduardo.		
Rachel:	Eduardo [teacher points to child in acknowledgment].		
Child 5:	xxx. [unintelligible].		
Rachel:	Egg [teacher makes the short e sound]. Right. An(d) also with the letter E. E—egg [teacher makes the short e sound].		
Rachel:	What would you like to do for work time?		
Child 5:	Paint.		
Rachel:	A who?		
Child 5:	My cat.		
Rachel:	Your cat? What is your cat's name?		
Child 5:	Bachi.		
Rachel:	Bachi? Let's see, B—achi [teacher makes the sound of the letter B]. What letter is that?		
Child 5:	xxx [unintelligible].		
Rachel:	A "B". Bachi starts with the letter B [teacher makes the /bbb/ sound.]		

Note. PD = received professional development training; non-PD = did not receive professional development training. The transcripts were edited for ease of comprehension and transcribed as spoken.

come from low-income households with few resources. Both the National Association for the Education of Young Children (NAEYC) and the National Association of Early Childhood Specialists in State Departments of Education (NAECS-SDE) characterize high-quality instruction as "thoughtfully planned, challenging, engaging, developmentally appropriate, culturally and linguistically responsive, comprehensive, and likely to promote positive outcomes for all young children" (p. 2, NAEYC & NAECS-SDE, 2003). Teachers facilitate children's learning and development when they engage in culturally responsive practices, create lessons that reflect the cultural heritage of their students, and plan activities that encourage ethnic and language minority children to take active roles (Castro et al., 2017). Designing PD efforts that equip teachers with the appropriate and effective skills to engage children from *all* backgrounds in meaningful conversations will enhance young children's ability to be ready for school and to achieve long-term overall academic success.

Conclusion

Our goal for this chapter was to demonstrate that classroom conversations are an important aspect of high-quality instruction in the classroom. The preschool classroom setting is a key environmental context for fostering children's oral language development because so many young children attend early education programs. Several early childhood scholars have demonstrated that classroom conversations during the early school years provide the foundation for later school success (see Bond & Wasik, 2009; Cabell et al., 2011; Girolametto, Weitzman, & Greenberg, 2003; Piasta et al., 2012). Classroom conversations serve as the vehicle through which children receive knowledge about the use and meaning of sociocultural linguistic artifacts and/or symbols, such as stories, letters, or numbers. As Dickinson (2006) points out, the most powerful predictor in the preschool classroom accounting for children's later literacy skills is use of teacher instructional strategies that support extended conversations. Thus, classroom discourse is at the core of pedagogy and practice and is worth the educational policy investment.

Acknowledgments

We thank the teachers and families who made this work possible and the Head Start program for collaborating with us on this work. We also thank Dakota Cintron, Wilfredo Benitez, and Jevonna Morrison, the undergraduate research assistants who collected the classroom observations. And we thank the W. K. Kellogg Foundation for funding the Conversation Compass professional development work.

Notes

1. The American Speech and Hearing Association provides guidance as to how these standards can be modified for children with hearing loss (https://www.asha.org/aud/Common-Core-State-Standards-and-Students-With-Hearing-Loss/).

2. Children who are racially and/or ethnically diverse and whose households are linguistically diverse are referred to as culturally and linguistically diverse (CALD) learners; they represent numerous racial and ethnic backgrounds and nationalities, including but not limited to Afro-Caribbean immigrants, Korean Americans, Chicanos, African Americans, and Puerto Ricans.

3. These prior studies did not involve separate analyses by child ethnicity.

4. All names are pseudonyms.

5. Therefore, this was a sample of convenience that was selected by the program, not the researcher.

References

Aukerman, M. (2007). A culpable CALP: Rethinking the conversational/academic language proficiency distinction in early literacy instruction. *The Reading Teacher, 60*(7), 626–636. doi:10.1598/RT.60.7.3

Baker, M. (2019). Playing, talking, co-constructing: Exemplary teaching for young dual language learners across program types. *Early Childhood Education Journal, 47*(1), 115–130. doi:10.1007/s10643-018-0903-0

Blank, M., Rose, S. A., Berlin, L. J. (1978). *The language of learning: The preschool years.* New York, NY: Grune & Stratton.

Blumenfeld, P. C., Marx, R. W., Soloway, E., & Krajcik, J. (1996). Learning with peers: From small group cooperation to collaborative communities. *Educational Researcher, 25*(8), 37–39. doi:10.2307/1176492

Bond, M. A., & Wasik, B. A. (2009). Conversation stations: Promoting language development in young children. *Early Childhood Education Journal, 36*(6), 467–473. doi:10.1007/s10643-009-0310-7

Buysse, V., Castro, D. C., West, T., & Skinner, M. (2005). Addressing the needs of Latino children: A national survey of the state administrators of early childhood programs. *Early Childhood Research Quarterly, 20*(2), 146–163. doi:10.1016/j.ecresq.2005.04.005

Cabell, S. Q., Justice, L. M., Piasta, S. B., Curenton, S. M., Wiggins, A., Turnbull, K. P., et al. (2011). The impact of teacher responsivity education on preschoolers' language and literacy skills. *American Journal of Speech-Language Pathology, 20*(4), 315–330. doi:10.1044/1058-0360(2011/10-0104)

Castro, D. C., Gillanders, C., Franco, X., Bryant, D. M., Zepeda, M., Willoughby, M. T., et al. (2017). Early education of dual language learners: An efficacy study of the Nuestros Niños School Readiness professional development program. *Early Childhood Research Quarterly, 40*, 188–203. doi:10.1016/j.ecresq.2017.03.002

Cohen, E. G. (1994). Restructuring the classroom: Conditions for productive small groups. *Review of Educational Research, 64*(1), 1–35. doi:10.3102/00346543064001001

Connor, C. M., Morrison, F. J., & Slominski, L. (2006). Preschool instruction and children's emergent literacy growth. *Journal of Educational Psychology, 98*(4), 665–689. doi:10.1037/0022-0663.98.4.665

Curenton, S. M. (2006). Oral storytelling: A cultural art that promotes school readiness. *Young Children, 61*(5), 78–89. Retrieved from https://www.naeyc.org/resources/pubs/yc

Curenton, S. M. (2016). *Conversation compass: A teacher's guide to high-quality language learning in young children.* St. Paul, MN: Readleaf.

Curenton, S. M., & Granda, C. (2019). Building blocks of infant-toddler conversation skills: Using the Conversation Compass© to drive innovation in Early Head Start classroom conversations. *Early Child Development and Care*, 1–11. doi.org/10.1080/03004430.2019.1647190

Curenton, S. M., Sims, J., Rochester, S. E., & Gardner, S. L. (2019). The Conversation Compass Communication Screener–Revised. *Early Childhood Research Quarterly, 47*, 182–193. doi.org/10.1016/j.ecresq.2018.10.013

Diamond, K. E., & Powell, D. R. (2011). An iterative approach to the development of a professional intervention for Head Start teachers. *Journal of Early Intervention, 33*(1), 75–93. doi:10.1177/1053815111400416

Dickinson, D. K. (2001). Putting the pieces together: Impact of preschool on children's language and literacy development in kindergarten. In D. K. Dickinson & P. O. Tabors (Eds.), *Beginning literacy with language* (pp. 223–255). Baltimore, MD: Brookes.

Dickinson, D. K. (2006). Toward a toolkit approach to describing classroom quality. *Early Education and Development, 17*(1), 177–202. doi:10.1207/s15566935eed1701_8

Durden, T. R., & Dangel, J. R. (2008). Teacher-involved conversations with young children during small group activity. *Early Years, 28*(3), 251–266. doi:10.1080/09575140802393793

Early, D. M., Iruka, I. U., Ritchie, S., Barbarin, O. A., Winn, D. M. C., Crawford, G. M., et al. (2010). How do pre-kindergarteners spend their time? Gender, ethnicity, and income as predictors of experiences in pre-kindergarten classrooms. *Early Childhood Research Quarterly, 25*(2), 177–193. doi:10.1016/j.ecresq.2009.10.003

Farran, D., Aydogan, C., Kang, S., & Lipsey, M. (2006). Preschool classroom environments and the quantity and quality of children's literacy and language behaviors. In D. K. Dickinson & S. B. Neuman (Eds.), *Handbook of early literacy research* (Vol. 2, pp. 257–268). New York, NY: Guilford.

Foorman, B. R., Anthony, J., Seals, L., & Mouzaki, A. (2002). Language development and emergent literacy in preschool. *Seminars in Pediatric Neurology, 9*(3), 173–184. doi:10.1053/spen.2002.35497

Gándara, R., Maxwell-Jolly, J., & Driscoll, A. (2005). *Listening to teachers of English language learners: A survey of California teachers' challenges, experiences, and professional development needs.* Santa Cruz, CA: Center for the Future of Teaching and Learning.

Gardner, S. L., & Curenton, S. M. (2017). Conversation Compass Communication Screener: A conversation screener for teachers. *Early Child Development and Care, 187*(3–4), 487–497. doi:10.1080/03004430.2016.1246443

Gest, S. D., Holland-Coviello, R., Welsh, J. A., Eicher-Catt, D. L., & Gill, S. (2006). Language development subcontexts in Head Start classrooms: Distinctive patterns of teacher talk during free play, mealtime, and book reading. *Early Education and Development, 17*(2), 293–315. doi:10.1207/s15566935eed1702_5

Girolametto, L., & Weitzman, E. (2002). Responsiveness of child care providers in interactions with toddlers and preschoolers. *Language, Speech, and Hearing Services in Schools, 33*(4), 268–281. doi:10.1044/0161-1461(2002/022)

Girolametto, L., Weitzman, E., & Greenberg, J. (2003). Training day care staff to facilitate children's language. *American Journal of Speech-Language Pathology, 12*, 299–311. doi:10.1044/1058-0360(2003/076)

Goh, S. S., Yamauchi, L. A., & Ratliffe, K. T. (2012). Educators' perspectives on instructional conversations in preschool settings. *Early Childhood Education Journal, 40*(5), 305–314. doi:10.1007/s10643-012-0518-9

Goldberg, C. (2013). Unlocking the research on English learners: What we know—and don't yet know—about effective instruction. *American Educator, 37*(2), 4–11. Retrieved from https://www.aft.org/ae

Goldenberg, C. (1992). Instructional conversations: Promoting comprehension through discussion. *The Reading Teacher, 46*(4), 316–326. Retrieved from https://ila.onlinelibrary.wiley.com/journal/19362714

Hart, B., & Risley, T. R. (1995). *Meaningful differences in the everyday experience of young American children.* Baltimore, MD: Brookes.

Heath, S. B. (1983). *Ways with words: Language, life and work in communities and classrooms.* Cambridge, MA: Cambridge University Press.

Justice, L. M., Jiang, H., & Strasser, K. (2018). Linguistic environment of preschool classrooms: What dimensions support children's language growth? *Early Childhood Research Quarterly, 42*(1), 79–92. doi:10.1016/j.ecresq.2017.09.003

Justice, L. M., Mashburn, A. J., Pence, K., & Wiggins, A. (2008). Experimental evaluation of a preschool language curriculum: Influence on children's expressive language skills. *Journal of Speech, Language, and Hearing Research, 51*(4), 983–1001. doi:10.1044/1092-4388(2008/072)

Kendeou, P., Van den Broek, P., White, M. J., & Lynch, J. S. (2009). Predicting reading comprehension in early elementary school: The independent contributions of oral language and decoding skills. *Journal of Educational Psychology, 101*(4), 765–778. doi:10.1037/a0015956

Lervåg, A., Hulme, C., & Melby-Lervåg, M. (2018). Unpicking the developmental relationship between oral language skills and reading comprehension: It's simple, but complex. *Child Development, 89*(5), 1821–1838. doi:10.1111/cdev.12861

MacWhinney, B. (2000). *The CHILDES project: Tools for analyzing talk: Vol. 1. Transcription format and programs* (3rd ed.). Mahwah, NJ: Lawrence Erlbaum.

Massey, S. L., Pence, K. L., Justice, L. M., & Bowles, R. P. (2008). Educators' use of cognitively challenging questions in economically disadvantaged preschool classroom contexts. *Early Education and Development, 19*(2), 340–360. doi:10.1080/10409280801964119

McFarland, J., Hussar, B., de Brey, C., Snyder, T., Wang, X., Wilkinson-Flicker, S., et al. (2017). *The condition of education: 2017* (NCES 2017-144). Washington, DC: National Center for Education Statistics.

Melzi, G., Schick, A. R., & Kennedy, J. L. (2011). Narrative elaboration and participation: Two dimensions of maternal elicitation style. *Child Development, 82*(4), 1282–1296. doi:10.1111/j.1467-8624.2011.01600.x

Michael Luna, S. M. (2017). Academic language in preschool: Research and context. *The Reading Teacher, 71*(1), 89–93. doi:10.1002/trtr.1582

National Association for Education of Young Children & National Association of Early Childhood Specialists in State Departments of Education. (2003). *Early childhood curriculum, assessment, and program evaluation: Building an effective, accountable system in programs for children birth through age 8: Joint position statement.* Retrieved from www.naeyc.org/about/positions/pdf/CAPEexpand.pdf

National Center for Education Statistics. (2012). *The condition of education: 2012.* Washington, DC: U.S. Department of Education.

National Governors Association & Council of Chief State School Officers. (2010). *Common Core State Standards for English language arts and literacy in history/social studies, science, and technical subjects.* Washington, DC: Authors.

NICHD Early Child Care Research Network. (2005). Pathways to reading: The role of oral language in the transition to reading. *Developmental Psychology, 41*(2), 428–442. doi:10.1037/0012-1649.41.2.428

O'Connor, C., & Michaels, S. (2019). Supporting teachers in taking up productive talk moves: The long road to professional learning at scale. *International Journal of Educational Research, 97*, 166–175. doi:org/10.1016/j.ijer.2017.11.003

Pence, K. L., Justice, L. M., & Wiggins, A. K. (2008). Preschooler teachers' fidelity in implementing a comprehensive language-rich curriculum. *Language, Speech, and Hearing Services in Schools, 39*(3), 329–341. doi:10.1044/0161-1461(2008/031)

Peterson, C., & McCabe, A. (1994). A social interactionist account of developing decontextualized narrative skill. *Developmental Psychology, 30*(6), 937–948. doi:10.1037/0012-1649.30.6.937

Phillips Galloway, E., & Lesaux, N. (2017). A matter of opportunity: Language and reading development during early childhood for dual-language learners. In N. Kucirkova, C. E. Snow, V. Grøver, & C. McBride (Eds.), *The Routledge international handbook of early literacy education: A contemporary guide to literacy teaching and interventions in a global context* (pp. 26–49). London, England: Routledge.

Pianta, R. C., Howes, C., Burchinal, M., Bryant, D., Clifford, R., Early, D., et al. (2005). Features of pre-kindergarten programs, classrooms, and teachers: Do they predict observed classroom quality and child-teacher interactions? *Applied Developmental Science, 9,* 144–159. doi:10.1207/s1532480xads0903_2

Pianta, R. C., La Paro, K. M., & Hamre, B. K. (2008). *Classroom Assessment Scoring System (CLASS) preschool version.* Baltimore, MD: Brookes.

Piasta, S. B., Justice, L. M., Cabell, S. Q., Wiggins, A. K., Turnbull, K. P., & Curenton, S. M. (2012). Impact of professional development on preschool teachers' conversational responsivity and children's linguistic productivity and complexity. *Early Childhood Research Quarterly, 27*(3), 387–400. doi:10.1016/j.ecresq.2012.01.001

Reese, E., Leyva, D., Sparks, A., & Grolnick, W. (2010). Maternal elaborative reminiscing increases low-income children's narrative skills relative to dialogic reading. *Early Education and Development, 21*(3), 318–342. doi:10.1080/10409289.2010.481552

Snow, C. E. (2010). Academic language and the challenge of reading for learning about science. *Science, 328*(5977), 450–452. doi:10.1126/science.1182597

Sperry, D., Sperry, L., & Miller, P. (2019). Reexamining the verbal environments of children from different socioeconomic backgrounds. *Child Development, 90*(4), 1303–1318. doi:10.1111/cdev.13125

Spinath, F. M., Price, T. S., Dale, P. S., & Plomin, R. (2004). The genetic and environmental origins of language disability and ability. *Child Development, 75*(2), 445–454. doi:10.1111/j.1467-8624.2004.00685.x

Strickland, M. J., & Marinak, B. A. (2016). Not just talk, but a "dance"! How kindergarten teachers opened and closed spaces for teacher–child authentic dialogue. *Early Childhood Education Journal, 44*(6), 613–621. doi:10.1007/s10643-015-0750-1

Sylva, K., Siraj-Blatchford, I., Taggart, B., Sammons, P., Melhuish, E., Elliot, K., et al. (2006). Capturing quality in early childhood through environmental rating scales. *Early Childhood Research Quarterly, 21*(1), 76–92. doi:10.1016/j.ecresq.2006.01.003

Vernon-Feagans, L., Hammer, C. S., Miccio, A., & Manlove, E. (2001). Early language and literacy skills in low-income African American and Hispanic children. In S. B. Neuman, & D. K. Dickinson (Eds.), *Handbook of early literacy research* (Vol. 1, pp. 192–210). New York, NY: Guilford Press.

Wasik, B. A., & Bond, M. A. (2001). Beyond the pages of a book: Interactive book reading and language development in preschool classrooms. *Journal of Educational Psychology, 93,* 243–250. doi:10.1037/0022-0663.93.2.243

Wasik, B. A., Bond, M. A., & Hindman, A. (2006). The effects of a language and literacy intervention on Head Start children and teachers. *Journal of Educational Psychology, 98*(1), 63–74. doi:10.1037/0022-0663.98.1.63

Zepeda, M., Castro, D. C., & Cronin, S. (2011). Preparing early childhood teachers to work with young dual language learners. *Child Development Perspectives, 5*(1), 10–14. http://doi.org/10.1111/j.1750-8606.2010.00141.x

Zhang, J., & Stahl, K. A. D. (2011). Collaborative reasoning: Language-rich discussions for English learners. *The Reading Teacher, 65*(4), 257–260. doi:10.1002/TRTR.01040

Chapter 8

Understanding Long-Term Preschool "Fadeout" Effects—Be Careful What You Ask For: Magical Thinking Revisited

ADAM WINSLER AND KAITLYN MUMMA

George Mason University

Interest in publicly funded pre-K programs has never been higher among researchers, policy makers, teachers, and parents. In 2015, 70% of four-year-olds and 42% of three-year-olds attended preschool (Phillips et al., 2017). Most U.S. states (46) now offer publicly funded preschool to young children (Barnett, Friedman-Krauss, & Jung, 2016). The Every Student Succeeds Act (ESSA) includes federal funding for early intervention and supports state-funded preschool programs (ESSA, 2015). During his term in office, President Barack Obama implemented the Preschool Development Grants program in 2014 to improve and increase the number of high-quality public pre-K programs. Eighteen states were awarded $226 million to build/enhance preschool programs. In total, about $37 billion dollars are spent each year by federal and state governments on early childhood programs (Phillips et al., 2017).

A common stipulation for continued receipt of federal funds for early childhood education (ECE) is that recipients be able to show evidence that ECE programs are beneficial for children. Increasingly, the expectation is that pre-K programs should be able to show significant, positive, long-lasting "impacts" on children (Duncan & Magnuson, 2013). The typical expectation is that children who attended the target pre-K program not only enter kindergarten with a notable advantage over similar children who did not attend the program (a fine and reasonable goal) but also continue to perform better in school many years later (in third, fifth, and eighth grades) on all outcome measures, compared to children who either went to a different type of pre-K program at age 4 or no program at all. This is despite the fact that all the children (regardless of ECE program attended) go on to attend the same K–12 public school education system, which is, by design, committed to helping all children, to bringing up the rear, and to reducing achievement gaps. If children who went to the target pre-K program are not still outperforming those who did not by a large margin at, say, third grade, then "fadeout" is said to have occurred, indicating no "long-term impact." Policy makers and researchers might conclude from such results that the pre-K program did not work, that it is not worth public investment, and the program's funding might be cut (Bailey, Duncan, Odgers, & Yu, 2016a; J. L. Garcia, Heckman, Leaf, & Prados, 2016; Whitehurst, 2016).

In this time of heightened funding for the development of effective state pre-K programs at scale, policy makers, funders, researchers, and the public are once again (as they did in 1965 with Head Start) expecting one or two years of attending a relatively high-quality publicly funded pre-K program to inoculate children living in deep poverty against all of the world's ills, evils, and inequalities over the course of their lives. Seventeen years ago, Brooks-Gunn (2003) wrote an influential piece entitled "Do You Believe in Magic? What We Can Expect From Early Childhood Intervention Programs." She argued then (and we need a reminder now) that it is magical thinking and not helpful for science, policy, or practice to expect that attending one or two years of even an excellent, high-quality pre-K program at age 3 or 4 is going to protect children from the conditions of poverty, and keep them for years to come on an even playing field with the rest of the country's children who have more resources (Love et al., 2002). In this chapter, we critically examine the concept of preschool fadeout effects, the assumptions and metrics involved in studying them, and conclusions that are made about long-term, sustained effects. In addition, we review factors that affect fadeout which, in our assessment, have little or nothing to do with pre-K programs. Finally, we make recommendations for future research and policy.

Understanding Fadeout

Understanding the concept of preschool fadeout effects is critically important today. Long-term evaluations of a variety of modern, publicly funded, center-based pre-K or Head Start programs at large scale—in an entire city or state (e.g., Tulsa, Boston, Tennessee, Chicago, Miami)—are appearing with third-, fifth-, and eighth-grade outcomes (Anderson, Kitchens, & Phillips, 2016; Ansari et al., 2016; Barnett, Friedman-Krauss, & Jung, 2016; Lipsey, Farran, & Hofer, 2015; Peisner-Feinberg & Burchinal, 2016; Phillips, Gormley, & Anderson, 2016; Pressler, Raver, & Friedman-Krauss, 2016; Reynolds et al., 2014; Weiland et al., 2017). Further, many states are implementing and evaluating their own pre-K programs, for example, Georgia, New Mexico, Maryland, Virginia, and Arkansas (Ackerman & Coley, 2012; Hudstedt, Barnett, Jung, & Goetze, 2009; SRI Education, 2016; Sunderman & Titan, 2014).

Some programs find "sustained effects" for at least some outcomes and/or for some groups of children. For example, Ansari et al. (2016) examined differences in third-grade outcomes for Latino children from the Miami School Readiness Project ($N = 11,902$) and found sustained effects on math and reading scores and GPA in third grade for public school pre-K programs (compared to center-based child care). In other words, children who attended pre-K programs were *still* outperforming children who had attended center-based care as they had done in kindergarten (Ansari & Winsler, 2016), controlling for a variety of selection effects (Ansari et al., 2016). Similarly, Hill, Gormley, and Adelstein (2015) found persisting effects for third-grade math and reading for pre-K programs in Tulsa, Okla. Sustained effects are also sometimes observed through eighth grade. Children who attended Tulsa's CAP Head Start program showed higher math scores and lower retention and absenteeism rates in eighth grade compared to those who did not attend a Head Start program or Tulsa's pre-K program (Phillips et al., 2016). It is worth noting, however, that no differences were found (thus fadeout was present) on other outcomes, such as eighth-grade GPA, advanced course or gifted enrollment, special education status, and school suspension.

Other studies have found longer term effects observed in adulthood for some preschool intervention programs (Ramey & Campbell, 1991; Schweinhart, Berruta-Clement, Barnett, Epstein, & Weikart, 1985). The Chicago Longitudinal Study reports that children who participated in their programs reached higher levels of education as adults (ages 18, 20, 22) than children who did not (Ou & Reynolds, 2006; Ou, Reynolds, & Topitzes, 2004). However, it is important to point out two issues in this regard: (a) There was fadeout on other outcomes; and (b) even when the long-term effects were observed on various adult-hood outcomes, fadeout was sometimes observed in elementary school, when differences in the cognitive or IQ measures given during the school years became smaller or disappeared altogether (Ramey et al., 1976).

The above are examples of sustained effects that are sometimes found. However, it is also fairly common to find fadeout or convergence effects where the difference in achievement at school entry favoring the group that experienced the target pre-K program relative to a comparison group gets smaller and disappears over time (e.g., by first or third grade; Lipsey et al., 2015; Love et al., 2002). Fadeout can take several different forms (described and illustrated in more detail in the next section), but typically, children who did not receive the early intervention catch up with the children who received it (thus the alternative term, *convergence*). In some cases, a comparison group actually starts to outperform the pre-K group years later (Lipsey et al., 2015), and in still other cases, there are "sleeper effects," where full fadeout is observed but, later, the pre-K/intervention group starts excelling again relative to the comparison group (Clements, Sarama, Wolfe, & Spitler, 2013; Magnuson, Ruhm, & Waldfogel, 2007). It is also important to note that subgroup differences in fadeout are often found, where sustained effects are seen for only certain types of children (i.e., Black, male, Latino, or ELL students) (Anderson et al., 2016; Bassok, 2010; Phillips et al., 2016).

The Shape of Fadeout (a.k.a., Know Your Initial Status, Final Status, and Rate of Change)

Fadeout may take a variety of shapes and forms, depending on where children in the two groups start and finish. Each pattern has a different interpretation. The six panels in Figure 1 reflect a variety of hypothetical shapes that fadeout can take. Each of the panels starts with large differences at the end of pre-K between the children who went to the target pre-K program and those who did not; by fifth grade, there is no difference (i.e., fadeout or convergence has occurred). In Panels A ("Stability and Catch-Up") and B ("Differential Growth"), we see the classic pattern of the comparison group catching up with the experimental group. In Panel A, an experimental group remains relatively stable over time (see "Different Metrics for Fadeout/Convergence," below), and the comparison group catches up with the advanced level at which the pre-K children are functioning. In Panel B, both groups improve over time, but the comparison group (which starts out very much behind) has more room for improvement and its slope is steeper, eventually catching up with the pre-K children, who are also improving over time but at a slower rate.

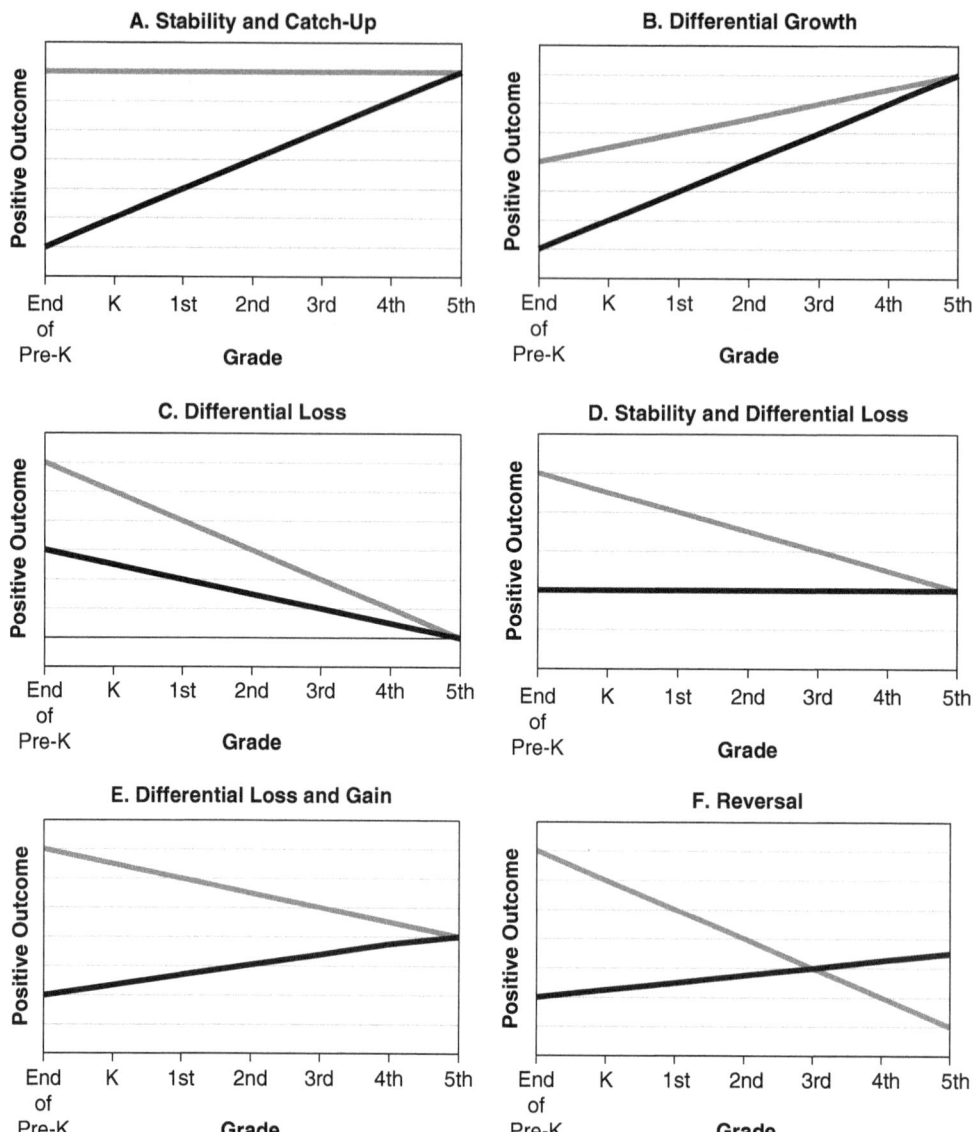

Figure 1. Possible shapes of fadeout. The gray lines represent the pre-K group; the black lines, the comparison group.

Panel C ("Differential Loss") shows another possibility, where both groups lose ground over time but at different rates: The preschool group catches up to the comparison group by fifth grade. Panel D ("Stability and Differential Loss") shows yet another possibility, where the comparison group shows stability in absolute and/or relative standing (see "Different Metrics for Fadeout/Convergence," below), and the pre-K children lose their advantage and meet the other children by fifth grade. Panel E ("Differential Loss and Gain") is theoretically possible as well: The comparison group gains over time, the pre-K group loses ground, and they meet in the middle by fifth grade. Finally, in Panel F ("Reversal"), the comparison group not only catches up but actually starts to perform better than the pre-K group. This pattern was seen in the Tennessee pre-K study (Lipsey et al., 2015), where children who attended Tennessee preschool programs out-performed children in the comparison group after the program; however, the scores converged in first and second grades, and by third grade the comparison group out-performed the pre-K group on some outcomes.

These graphs suggest that if one simply compared the performance of the two groups at one point in time, say, in third grade (as most researchers do), the mean difference between the groups (the effect size d) would look the same across all graphs (except for panel F)—that is, the difference would be zero and the two groups would appear identical in third grade. Given the various possibilities in panels A–F, very different things may be occurring over time. Hence, it is critical for researchers examining sustained effects of pre-K to conduct longitudinal analyses (preferably growth curves, if possible) to determine students' initial status, their final status at the last time point, and the shape of change over time for children in both groups.

Different Metrics for Fadeout/Convergence

The term *fadeout* itself comes with some unfortunate connotations that can be misleading for researchers and policy makers. It is important to be clear on its meaning, the metric(s) used, and the type of analysis conducted in research on long-term sustained effects of pre-K programs. An implicit assumption that comes with the term fadeout is that a longitudinal study is involved with individual children and skills being followed over time. One of the problems with the term is that it implies that individual children are losing skills over time. That is, they started off after the pre-K program in great shape, well ahead of their peers, and then, over time, their skills declined or they lost their advantage. Typically, however, this is not the case. A longitudinal analysis of change over time within the child is usually not conducted, and instead the contrast is simply made at one point in time (i.e., third or eighth grade), the question being, What is the difference between the academic performance of the treated group compared to that of the comparison group at X point in time? That is very different from longitudinal analyses that look at gains over time in the skills or abilities of individual children and whether those are increasing or decreasing.

The Y axis in the graphs in Figures 1 and 2 can represent at least three different things:

1. *Change in children's absolute skill levels* (very rare). This is the only situation where it is appropriate to use the words "gains" or "losses," because those words mean that children are increasing or losing skills over time, compared to where the same children were previously. Barring conditions such as serious disorder, biological insult, or extreme neglect, all children in reasonable environments are likely to grow in whatever cognitive/academic skills are assessed (i.e., language, cognition, math). However, positive growth in social-emotional skills and approaches to learning and school engagement are not guaranteed over time, especially in the context of poverty, underresourced schools, and toxic stress (Attar, Guerra, & Tolan, 1994). Although discussions of fadeout do not typically involve actual loss of academic skills by individual children, such loss is indeed possible and perhaps should be explored. Important here is for researchers and policy

makers to be aware that fadeout most likely does *not* mean individual children losing skills over time compared to prior skill levels. Thus, we should avoid using terms like "gains" and "losses" unless we are measuring change over time within children.

2. *Raw mean differences* (very common). To determine raw mean differences, a raw performance indicator of some sort is calculated at one point in time (such as third or fifth grade) and the two groups are compared to each other. This comparison ignores where the child's level of skill was earlier in time (says nothing about whether children's skills have increased or been lost) but simply shows how different the groups are from each other on average at one time point. Both groups could be doing well, above benchmarks, or both groups could be doing terribly, below standard. It is also possible for one group to be above and the other below an important benchmark. There is a large difference in interpretation for a scenario where the pre-K group is close to being at national averages but the comparison group is far below, and a scenario where both groups are well above national averages. The effect size of the difference between the two groups' means may be exactly the same in both scenarios even when the meaning is quite different. Thus, we suggest that studies examining fadeout in this way add interpretations of how well both groups of children are doing relative to a practical standard.

3. *Differential relative standing (i.e., nationwide percentile) at one point in time* (common). The third metric for the Y axis occurs when values represent average performance of the children in the two groups relative to nationally standardized scores, such as national percentiles. If there are multiple time points measured, a reduction in such a score indicates that the child is losing ground relatively speaking, compared to other children nationwide at the same age. Here, the use of the word "gain" or "loss" may be appropriate if it is clear that the gain or loss is relative to some standard and is not interpreted as regression or loss of the child's individual absolute skills over time. Our earlier point regarding the importance of interpreting how well the pre-K and comparison groups are doing relative to a performance benchmark is helpful in this context as well. The main takeaway is that it is important to know what is being measured: the metric being used and what it does and does not mean. Current scholarship on the sustained effects of pre-K programs has not generally considered these issues.

What Sustained Effects Look Like

In the previous section, we focused on the various shapes that fadeout/convergence can take and the meanings that might be attached to the effects, depending on the metric used. In this section, we focus on possible shapes of sustained effects and ask, What do sustained effects really look like and what do they mean? Figure 2 shows a variety of shapes that sustained effects can take.

In each panel, the difference between the pre-K group and the comparison group remains the same at fifth grade as it was at the end of pre-K (or larger). As is clear from the graphs, there are many possible patterns, each with a different interpretation and meaning.

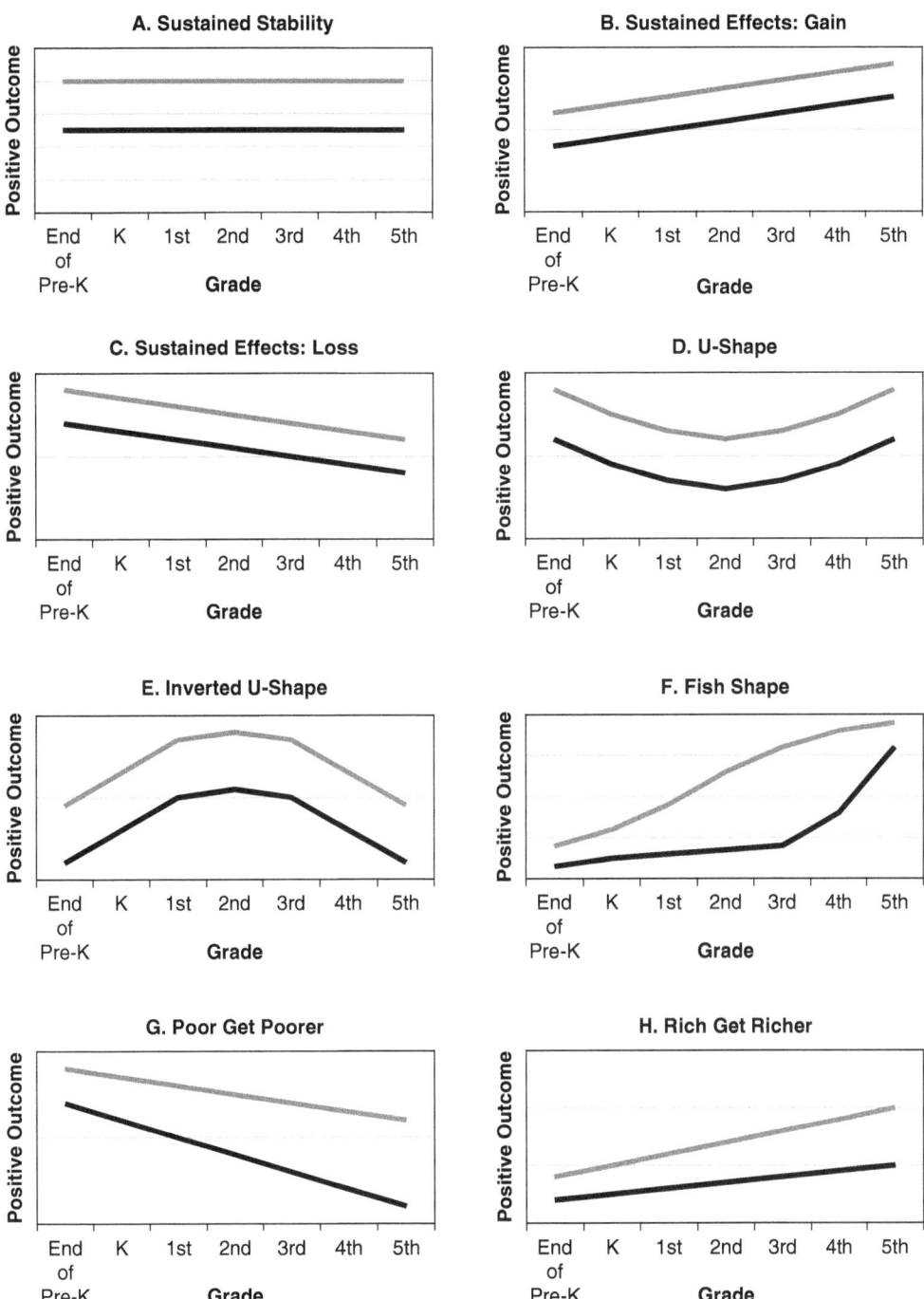

Figure 2. Possible shapes of sustained effects (no fadeout). The gray lines represent the pre-K group; the black lines, the comparison group.

However, all lead to the same simple conclusion in fifth grade—that the group that experienced the target pre-K program is *still* doing better, many years later, than the group that did not get the program. Panel A ("Sustained Stability") describes a situation where there is stability, likely measured in terms of some kind of standardized comparison or percentile score; the children leave fifth grade with the same skills advantage over comparison children that they had at kindergarten entry. Panel B ("Sustained Effects: Gain") depicts a scenario where all children are making gains over time (in either absolute or relative terms) but those who went to the target pre-K program continue to perform better in fifth grade, on whatever outcome is measured. This is presumably what policy makers and researchers hope to see for all outcomes measured and for as long as possible: all children making gains but those who got the high-quality deluxe version of the pre-K experience continuing to outperform their less fortunate peers who did not get the high-quality preschool experience. Panel C ("Sustained Effects: Loss") depicts another possibility, especially in high-poverty neighborhoods: In this scenario, all children are losing ground over time, likely relative to a standardized benchmark rather than with actual loss of skills (although this is possible too), but those who went to the pre-K program maintain their advantaged position in relation to the comparison group (even though both groups are losing ground).

Panels D through F show potential nonlinear trajectories over time in which both groups may show peaks or valleys in their performance, but they do so in parallel, with the pre-K group always doing better than the comparison. In Panel F, the difference between the two groups widens during middle elementary school but then goes back to about the same differential in fifth grade, still favoring the pre-K group. Panels G and H plot other distinct possibilities, where the gap between those who did and did not receive the pre-K program not only is sustained but widens over time. Panel G ("Poor Get Poorer") shows the pattern where loss of skills over time occurs for both groups but the decline is steeper for those who did not get the pre-K experience in question. This was the pattern observed in the early Abecedarian studies showing declines in child IQ scores measured at multiple time points for both groups (to be expected given continued exposure to the toxic stress of deep poverty), but the decline in IQ was not as steep for the treatment group (Ramey & Campbell, 1991).

Finally, Panel H presents a "Rich Get Richer" scenario in which the pre-K group takes off and not only maintains an advantage relative to the reference group but continues to pull ahead. This "Matthew effect" has been observed in a variety of domains, including early literacy instruction (Duff, Tomblin, & Catts, 2015) and IQ (Shaywitz et al., 1995). This pattern could have something to do with the child (an intrinsic quality or a change in the child resulting from exposure to the pre-K program) or with the environment (e.g., the later school climate) (Duff et al., 2015; Shaywitz et al., 1995), as is discussed in detail below. Matthew effects can also be seen in the opposite direction. That is, students who start out performing low may continue to perform low and even perform worse over time (Morgan, Farkas, & Hibel, 2008; Scarborough & Parker, 2003), as in Figure 2, Panel C, but with the downward slope becoming steeper for the comparison group). Once a student is behind, it is difficult to catch up within the confines of the school day.

Figure 3 shows a few other possible shapes of change for the pre-K and comparison groups. Panel A shows "Fadeout With Resurrection," where differences between pre-K groups converge over time but, a year or two later, the pre-K group starts to pull ahead

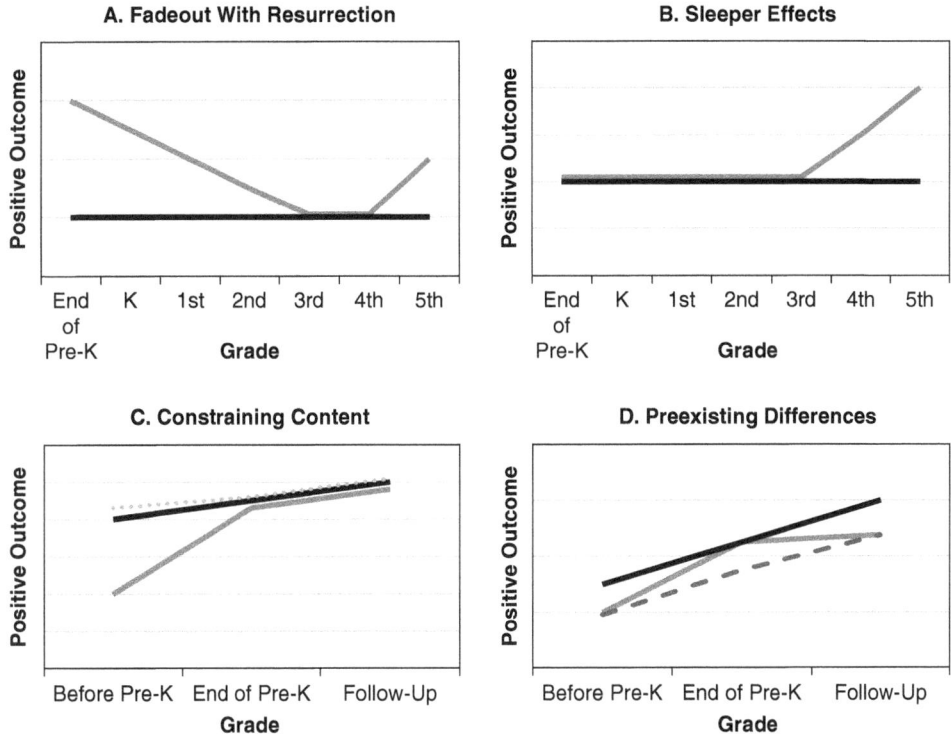

Figure 3. Other possibilities. In Panels A and B, the gray lines represent the pre-K group; the black lines, the comparison group. In Panel C the dotted line represents the hypothetical ceiling; the black line, high-functioning non-attenders; the gray line, pre-K attenders. In Panel D, the dashed line represents the comparison group in poverty; the black line, high-functioning non-attenders; the gray line, pre-K attenders.

again. This pattern has been seen in ECE math interventions (Clements et al., 2013) and was seen (in a loose sense) in some of the older boutique programs like Abecedarian and Perry Preschool, where convergence was seen for some measured outcomes in elementary school but, later on, large differences in other outcomes (graduation rates, health, pregnancy) were found (Ramey et al., 1976; Schweinhart et al., 1985). Panel B ("Sleeper Effects") shows the pattern characterized by no sustained effects for several years, followed much later by the target pre-K group starting to outperform the comparison group (again), a pattern which has also been observed (Barnett, 2011; Magnuson et al., 2007; van Aar, Leijten, de Castro, & Overbeek, 2016).

The Central Problem: Is This What We Want?

We wish to pose here a critical question to the research, education, philanthropic, philo-sophic, and policy communities. As explained above and shown in the various patterns seen in Figure 2, what "sustained effects" means is that we (as researchers, funders, and policy makers) fully expect and desire for it to be the case that what children bring with them to kindergarten (based on early childhood experiences, including family, neighbor-hood, and preschool) is the same as what they leave school with. To demand that we see "sustained effects" of ECE programs (measured by mean differences between preschool groups at a later time point) means that the inequalities seen in children's school entry skills—the gap at the kindergarten door between those who did and did not go to a certain pre-K program—will always be present throughout schooling for the children. Hence, what children come to school with is what will be at the end of their schooling, and there is little progression, change, improvement, or reduction in achievement gaps or chances for teachers to make a difference in students' trajectories.

Our question: Is this really what we want? Are any of the potential shapes of sustained effects of pre-K depicted in Figure 2 acceptable from an ethical, political, social justice, moral, or public educational system perspective? Is this what we want from our public educational system? Do we want it to function in a way that maintains the disparities observed upon entry into the system? This is what complete sustained effects of pre-K programs would mean. Is it not a foundational principle for public education in the United States to be "the great equalizer" (Bernardi & Ballarino, 2016; Harper & Davis, 2012)—to reduce disparities and level the playing field, to give all children a chance to do well and a chance to catch up to those children with more resources (and better pre-K experiences)? Should the gaps and inequalities that exist between children with different ECE and early home experiences at school entry persist to the end of time? Our provocative answer is no. The problem is that funders, researchers, and policy makers say yes when they insist that "sustained effects" must be present. Too often, they are happy with one of the no-fadeout graphs in Figure 2, and programs are at risk of losing funding if they show another pattern. We will come back to this later, but we now turn to a variety of other factors that contribute to fadeout or sustained effects that have nothing to do with the quality or merit of the pre-K programs in question.

Factors Affecting Fadeout/Convergence That Have Little to Do With the Pre-K Program

Unclear, Minimally Different Comparison Conditions (a.k.a., Know Your Counterfactual!)

As pointed out by others (Barnett, Friedman-Krauss, Gomez, et al., 2016; Feller, Grindal, Miratrix, & Page, 2016), in the 1970s when the well-known pre-K programs began, the contrast made was between children who received an intense experimental pre-K program and children who stayed at home and never experienced formal child care. However, these days, attending some kind of center-based or formal preschool is normative, with 70% of four-year-olds and 42% of three-year-olds attending preschool (Phillips et al., 2017). It is currently not possible to find a comparison group of children without any type of child care experience to test for the effects of pre-K programs. That is, the large effect sizes observed in those early studies are unlikely to replicate in the modern day because the counterfactual has changed. Today, the comparison is between those who have received some kind of "special" pre-K program (the one being evaluated) and those who attended some *other* type of center-based "business as usual" pre-K or child care program (or Head Start) that is likely also doing several of the good things known to help children get ready for school that are happening at the targeted pre-K program. The difference in performance between the two groups of children assessed at any time point (the effect size, *d*) is likely to be smaller than in the past because the programs being compared are much more similar to one another, and average quality of ECE everywhere is increasing over time as we learn more about what is good for children.

Given these shifts in access and participation of young children in early education programs, it is critical for researchers to collect good data on the type, quantity, and quality of the child care experiences that children in the comparison group receive and to keep track of what the comparison group actually is for the different studies. Comparison groups often include children who went to Head Start or some other subsidized preschool program, and sometimes it is unclear what kind of child care/preschool (i.e., Head Start, center-based care, family child care, home-based) was in place for the comparison group. As discussed later in this chapter, the extent of fadeout observed depends on the counterfactual/comparison being made—pre-K versus center-based care, or center-based care versus family child care (Mumma et al., 2020). Again, it is critical to "know your counterfactual."

A related problem is that even in large random assignment experimental studies, large numbers of children in the comparison group actually have received the very same pre-K program to which they are compared! For example, in the Head Start Impact Study, about 16% of the control group went to a Head Start program (and 44% went to some other kind of center-based care) (Love, Chazan-Cohen, Raikes, & Brooks-Gunn, 2013). In the Tennessee evaluation, 27% of the comparison group attended Head Start or private center–based child care (Lipsey, Hofer, Dong, Farran, & Bilbrey, 2013). How can one expect sustained effects when so many of the comparison group experienced either the same or a very similar pre-K program? The challenge of defining the modern pre-K evaluation counterfactual is also illustrated in the case of the Boston Public Schools pre-K program evaluation (Weiland et al., 2017). The lottery system used by the school district to assign eligible families to their high-quality public-school-based pre-K program, for a variety of logistical and practical reasons, did not create a clear group of similar children/families who wanted, but did not receive, the pre-K program. Many of the children in the counterfactual did actually experience the pre-K program, and there were critical demographic differences in the schools and families participating in the experimental and counterfactual conditions (Weiland et al., 2017).

Finally, it is important to clarify when a counterfactual should perhaps no longer be considered a counterfactual. Bailey and colleagues (2016a) point out that fadeout effects are practically guaranteed when rapid development of academic skills occurs in the "counterfactual condition," that is, the comparison group who did not get the pre-K program, once they get to elementary school. The authors suggest that perhaps early childhood interventionists should turn their attention to boosting and assessing other skills, such as executive functioning, for which this does not happen. However, once the children previously in the counterfactual pre-K condition arrive at the same elementary schools that are attended by the children who experienced the special pre-K program, *there is no longer a counterfactual condition!* It is not reasonable to expect, then, when all children now experience the same condition of elementary school public education, that the differences observed before school are going to remain. It might make sense to expect sustained effects if the counterfactual/comparison children were educated in a completely different environment throughout elementary school, but they are not. We propose that once all the children get to the same elementary schools, there is no counterfactual condition anymore, and it is unreasonable to expect that the children in one group will maintain the advantages with which they entered. We have to find other ways of assessing the long-term impacts of ECE programs.

Elementary School or Teacher Approach

Clearly, what happens in kindergarten and early public school is going to affect not only children's outcomes in general but gaps between children who attended different types of ECE. It is well documented that children are already extremely variable in the skills that they bring to kindergarten, and kindergarten teachers have to deal with a great diversity of skill levels (E. Garcia & Weiss, 2015). Some children have been reading books to themselves for years and others may have never seen a book. Some children can count to 1,000, and some cannot reliably count to 10. Some children have serious trouble following directions, cooperating with others, and sitting still, whereas others excel in these social-behavioral skills. How kindergarten teachers, and elementary schools more generally, react to this breadth of skills and experiences is likely going to influence whether researchers will see preschool fadeout effects.

A variety of philosophical or ideological possibilities are present for how teachers respond to the diversity of child skills. First, teachers often choose to focus their time on children who have the lowest skill sets to bring them up to the levels of the higher-functioning children in the classroom (a "catch-up" or "bring up the rear" strategy). If children who did not go to a high-quality pre-K program arrive at school with fewer skills than those who did (a finding confirmed by many studies (Ansari & Winsler, 2016; Currie & Thomas, 2000; Lipsey et al., 2013; Weiland & Yoshikawa, 2013), then a teacher or school that follows this strategy will clearly contribute to fadeout effects being seen over time—the big differences in skills between children who attended pre-K and those who did not will get smaller over time, as the lower-functioning children catch up. Indeed, a central, long-held ideal in American public education is for public education to be "the great equalizer" (Growe & Montgomery, 2003; Mather & Jarosz, 2014). This focus of public schools clearly contributes to convergence/fadeout effects over time—effects that are *supposed* to occur, according to this widely held philosophy (Magnuson et al., 2007).

Alternatively, another possibility is that teachers and schools focus on the children who come into kindergarten with strong skills and make sure they keep advancing (a "Rich Get Richer" strategy; Figure 2, Panel H). This approach takes children with higher skills and increases their skills differentially, increasing the gap between the children who had the initial skills (i.e., those who went to the high-quality pre-K) and those who did not, thus leading to increasing and sustained effects of pre-K over time. Finally, a third possibility is for teachers to try to reach all the children at whatever level they are and bring all children up at the same rate (a "raise all boats" strategy). Such a philosophy will presumably lead to sustained effects of pre-K as well—children maintain their relative rank compared to other children over time, and they leave with the same advantage or disadvantage with which they came. That pattern remains throughout schooling (Figure 2, Panel A).

The field needs studies to test the above possibilities, with measures at the teacher and classroom levels to discover teachers' philosophies, strategies, and behaviors and determine which are associated with children's greatest gains over time. However, such studies have not been done in relation to sustained effects of pre-K programs. There are suggestions from other literatures to suggest that teacher expectations/beliefs affect the way teachers interact with and stimulate or discourage different groups of children. Researchers have studied various factors in this "Pygmalion effect" (Austin, Tang, & Howard, 2015; Rosenthal & Jacobson, 1968), such as philosophy of teaching (Fergus, Noguera, & Martin, 2014); attitude/bias about certain groups of children, such as negative views about those in poverty (Hauser-Cram, Sirin, & Stipek, 2003); lower expectations for Black students (Rowley et al., 2014); and gender differences in teacher math language (Mizala, Martínez, & Martínez, 2015). Such differential treatment affects student learning and later trajectories (Allen et al., 2013). It is likely that teachers make conscious and unconscious decisions about which children to invest in. Such decisions should affect the results of research on pre-K program fadeout, especially if teachers have knowledge of their students' ECE experiences and ideas about how ECE leads to differential school readiness (Baker, Tichovolsky, Kupersmidt, Voegler-Lee, & Arnold, 2015).

Elementary School Quality

Research on elementary school contributions to differential preschool fadeout has focused on the more global construct of elementary school *quality,* typically poorly and vaguely measured as either the "grade" given to the school by the state department of education based on the school's average high-stakes test scores (Mumma et al., 2020; Zhai, Raver, & Jones, 2012), or something like the amount of reading instruction, or class size (Magnuson et al., 2007). It is unclear what to hypothesize about how the previously discussed philosophies might play out in schools of varying quality. Is it the best, high-quality schools, or teachers, or kindergarten classrooms, that focus on helping the children who are behind to catch up, or is that something that happens primarily at lower quality schools? Do the best, or do the worst schools/teachers tend to implement either a "lift all boats" or "rich get richer" philosophy? These are important questions for future research. For now, we can only describe the research with mixed results that has examined whether school *quality* is associated with sustained effects of pre-K.

A recent line of research has been showing that characteristics of the public elementary school attended by children who went to different types of ECE programs can moderate the long-term effects of preschool, albeit in different ways with mixed effects. It is especially critical to study how school quality can influence preschool fadeout, since research shows that some students who attend preschool programs targeted for low-income families are more likely to later enroll in schools of poorer quality. Currie and Thomas (2000) examined the quality of schools that Black and White Head Start attendees enrolled in after they had completed Head Start. Black children who attended Head Start later attended schools of significantly worse quality than Black children who did not attend Head Start.

However, this finding did not hold true for White children, suggesting that Black children who attend Head Start are particularly disadvantaged, and that White children who attend Head Start end up attending schools of similar quality compared to other White children who did not attend Head Start. Similarly, Lee and Loeb (1995) identified the type of schools Head Start attendees were likely to attend as eighth graders. Former Head Start students attended middle schools of significantly lower socioeconomic status (SES), lower average achievement, lower quality, and lower perceived safety compared to students who had not attended Head Start but attended a similar preschool program (Lee & Loeb, 1995). In sum, if students who attend publicly funded ECE programs later attend worse schools than their peers who attended other programs, then the children's later elementary school experiences are confounded with pre-K type. It is no wonder that the initial relative advantages seen for such students might fade out over time.

Magnuson et al. (2007) conducted a study using data from the Early Childhood Longitudinal Study–Kindergarten (ECLS-K) to determine whether later school quality moderated preschool fadeout effects. Results from multivariate ordinary least squares regressions first showed that consistent, nonparental preschool attendance was linked to higher third-grade math and reading test scores. However, when the authors adjusted their model for subsequent classroom experiences (i.e., large versus small class sizes and high versus low reading instruction), students who did not attend preschool but later attended schools of high quality caught up to their peers who did attend preschool (i.e., fadeout for students who attended high-quality elementary schools). This pattern is consistent with what is shown in Panel A of Figure 2, but only when students were subsequently enrolled in smaller classrooms with teachers who had at least a bachelor's degree and engaged in higher levels of reading instruction throughout the day.

Zhai et al. (2012), utilizing data from the Chicago School Readiness Project, showed significant effects for children who subsequently attended high-performing schools (no fadeout, Figure 2, Panel A) but not for children who subsequently attended low-performing schools (fadeout, Figure 1, Panel A). These results contrast with those of Magnuson et al. (2007), likely due to different counterfactuals and comparisons made. Most recently, Ansari and Pianta (2018) used data from the ECLS-K to determine whether academic benefits from preschool were sustained in fifth grade. Children were considered to have attended preschool if parents indicated that their child had attended a "day care center, nursery school, preschool, or prekindergarten program" for five or more hours per week. Children who attended those programs for less than five hours per week, in addition to children who were cared for by a relative, nonrelative, family child care provider, or parent were considered as not having attended preschool. When children later attended schools of high quality, preschool effects were sustained. On the other hand, when children later attended low-quality schools, there was fadeout/convergence (Ansari & Pianta, 2018).

Recent work from our own research group (Mumma et al., 2020) confirms that the counterfactual matters in examining the effects of elementary school quality on fadeout effects. Using data from the Miami School Readiness Project, we compared third-grade academic outcomes (GPA and math and reading test scores) of children who had attended public school pre-K, center-based care (CBC), or family child care (FCC) by means of child care subsidies for low-income families, and we examined the degree to which the quality of the later elementary school moderated pre-K effects. Elementary school quality was determined by a grade (A–F), given to each school by its school district. As in Zhai et al. (2012), school quality was based on the school's performance on high-stakes standardized tests and how it improved from one year to the next. Results showed that third-grade performance depended both on the comparison being made (children who attended public school pre-K versus children who attended CBC, or children who attended CBC versus children who attended FCC), *and* the quality of elementary school later attended (see Figure 4). For example, when comparing children who attended public school pre-K (the dotted diamond gray) to children who attended CBC (the black square line), those who attended public school pre-K consistently out-performed children who attended CBC; however, the margin was the smallest at the lower-quality schools and increased as the quality of elementary school increased (i.e., no fadeout, and persistence of pre-K effects largest at highest-quality schools). On the other hand, when comparing children who attended CBC (the black square line) to those who attended FCC (gray triangle line), results showed the opposite pattern. Children who attended CBC out-performed children who attended FCC by the largest margin at the poorest schools, but as elementary school quality increased, children who attended FCC caught up to their CBC peers, until there was no difference in third-grade performance when both groups attended the highest-quality schools (i.e., no fadeout at poorer schools, complete convergence at the highest quality schools; Figure 4).

These results provide insight into the mixed results of the previously mentioned studies, as the amount of fadeout observed depends on the contrast being made. Clearly, what is going on in the elementary school matters for all children's progress and will affect differences between groups with different pre-K experiences at later times. A huge problem with current discussions about fadeout is that they assume that the results are true regardless

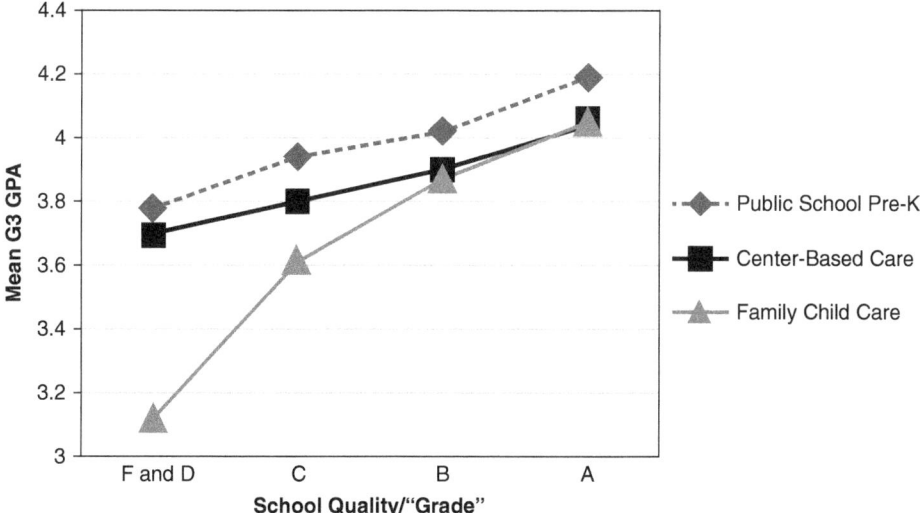

Figure 4. Mean third-grade grade point average by level of school quality, adjusted for FRL and school-entry level cognitive skills. FRL = free or reduced-price lunch. (Mumma et al., 2020.)

of the type and quality of elementary school the children end up attending. Another clear implication for research in this area is that we need to see whether pre-K and comparison groups end up going to the same quality schools or whether there are systematic differences in the later educational environments children experience, and we need to see how those later school and classroom environments moderate long-term pre-K effects.

Lack of Alignment/Continuity

Another critical issue known to affect the degree to which fadeout or convergence is observed for pre-K programs that has little to do with the pre-K program itself is the degree to which there is alignment or continuity between the child's pre-K experiences and the early years of elementary school. Indeed, several groups of researchers, foundations, funders, and policy makers have been part of a PK–3 movement (Graves, 2006; Kauerz, 2006; Stipek, Clements, Coburn, Franke, & Farran, 2017; Takanishi, 2016), which attempts to increase communication and coordination between the pre-K system and the public school K–3 system to aim for a seamless and systematic progression through the early years of school. The problem observed is that children in high-quality pre-K programs arrive at kindergarten with various kinds of academic knowledge, say, in literacy and math, and then the kindergarten teaches the same skills and content again rather than building on the skills already acquired. A variety of solutions are thought to be good, including having pre-K take place in the same building as the elementary school, using the same and appropriately sequenced curriculum across the grades including pre-K, using formative child assessments to inform instructional curriculum, integrating student data systems, aligning standards and learning goals, and getting elementary school teachers to talk and collaborate more with pre-K teachers. However, there has not been much research yet on whether these approaches work for improving outcomes for students and for reducing pre-K fadeout effects (Stipek et al., 2017; Whyte, McMahon, Coburn, Stein, & Jou, 2016). Also, we do not know whether fadeout effects are larger or smaller at schools that do a better job at PK–3 alignment. Presumably, effective PK–3 alignment would increase sustained long-term pre-K effects, since all children would be met at their own level when they come in. However, this remains an empirical question for now.

Broekhuizen, Mokrova, Burchinal, Garrett-Peters, and Family Life Project Key Investigators (2016) examined one aspect of the PK–3 alignment issue, finding that consistently maintaining a high-quality environment from pre-K to kindergarten is beneficial for children. Data were collected from nearly 1,200 children in rural North Carolina and central Pennsylvania, and 83% of the sample attended private or state/federal center-based care or preschool. Preschool and kindergarten quality were assessed using the Classroom Assessment Scoring System (CLASS; Pianta, LaParo, & Hamre, 2008), and teachers reported on children's social skills and behavior problems in both kindergarten and first grade. Children who attended higher quality pre-K *and* kindergarten classrooms had higher social skills and fewer behavior problems in first grade than their peers who had experienced the high-quality pre-K environments only. Clearly, stability in the provision of high-quality environments for children is important. The quality of the elementary school experience is going to influence sustained effects of pre-K programs, and one year of being in a high-quality pre-K intervention is not enough to inoculate children from a low-quality elementary school education.

Another example of the importance of follow-on alignment in elementary school for sustained pre-K effects comes from the Building Blocks (BB) early childhood math curriculum (Clements & Sarama, 2007; Duncan et al., 2015), where a "fadeout with resurrection" pattern (Figure 3 panel A) was recently observed in children's mathematics achievement. Duncan and colleagues (2015) built on the original study (Clements & Sarama, 2007) by investigating the moderating effect of having some kindergarten and first-grade teachers enroll in pedagogical development courses that focused on what their children had learned in their pre-K programs and how to align the curriculum and expectations. Other teachers whose children had received the pre-K math intervention did not receive such professional development. At the end of the preschool year, those participating in the BB program (compared to those who did not) had significantly higher math skills. While these effects disappear overall in kindergarten, children who were in classrooms where the teacher participated in the program showed much stronger maintenance of math skills in first grade than children whose later teachers did not receive the training. These findings suggested that additional professional development for kindergarten and first-grade teachers may be needed in order to ensure that the early gains made by children attending high-quality pre-K are built upon and maintained in elementary school. Continuity in social-emotional, classroom-organization, curriculum, and parent involvement approaches are also likely to be important (Stipek et al., 2017)

Other studies have found that kindergarten instruction that did not build upon skills already learned by children in pre-K did not produce sustained learning (Engel, Claessens, & Finch, 2013; Stipek et al., 2017). Although the majority of children entering school already knew how to count and how to recognize shapes, teachers spent the most time teaching this material (Engel et al., 2013). Such content redundancy was associated with later math achievement. Importantly, the lowest achieving math students *did* benefit from basic mathematics coverage, while higher-achieving math students benefited from more advanced mathematics instruction. Stipek and colleagues urged schools to adopt curricula that encompass continuous, connected content to allow students to build on their previously learned skills (Stipek et al., 2017).

Classic ECE intervention studies that implemented a follow-on elementary school component have also shown that fadeout can be reduced when one continues to work with teachers through third grade. Reynolds (1994) examined the reading and math test scores of children in Chicago who had attended a preschool intervention program, those who had attended the preschool intervention together with a follow-on intervention that lasted through third grade, and those who were not involved in any intervention but attended other preschool programs. When assessed in fifth grade, the children who were involved in the intervention program for their entire P–3 experience had significantly higher reading and math test scores, more positive teacher ratings, higher parental involvement in the school, and less grade retention and special education placement compared to the control group (Reynolds, 1994). The children who did not receive the additional follow-on intervention and attended just the preschool intervention showed fadeout on their third-grade reading and math scores, which were not significantly higher than those of their peers in the control group (Reynolds, 1994). Similarly, the Abecedarian Project implemented a school-age intervention to take place after its preschool intervention (Horacek, Ramey, Campbell, Hoffman, & Fletcher, 1987). Results showed that at age 15, the school-age intervention had the most positive results when paired with the preschool intervention (lower retention and higher math and reading scores), but that it did not provide a significant treatment effect on its own. Clearly, longer-term effects of early intervention depend largely on what happens later in elementary school.

Related to the issue of kindergartens reteaching content for children from high-quality pre-K programs is the *constraining content hypothesis*, as described by Bailey et al. (2016b) and visually represented in Figure 3, Panel C. Using the example of a high-quality, successful math intervention in pre-K (BB), the authors show that the early elementary school outcomes for children who attended the pre-K math intervention and arrived at school with strong math skills were constrained by the curriculum in kindergarten being at ceiling both for pre-K intervention attendees (the gray line in Figure 3 Panel C) and for high-functioning children who did not attend the intervention program and presumably learned emergent math skills at home or elsewhere (the black line). The argument is made that there is wide variability in children's school entry skills and what is plotted in black is comparison children who were at the same level in terms of math skills at the end of the pre-K intervention as those who experienced the intervention. Before the pre-K intervention, the treatment children (because most public pre-K programs are targeted to low-income children) were lower functioning in math and reached the level of high functioning children by the end of their high-quality pre-K intervention. The dotted line in Figure 3, Panel C, represents a hypothetical ceiling for math attainment based on where the kindergarten teacher is placing her instruction. The higher functioning comparison children and the pre-K treatment group are constrained and performing at ceiling because they already know the material covered, with presumably the only group benefitting from the kindergarten math instruction being the disadvantaged children who did not get exposed to the pre-K program and entered school with limited math skills (Bailey et al., 2016b).

Preexisting Child Differences

Bailey and colleagues (2016b) suggest yet another possible explanation for fadeout which has nothing to do with the pre-K program itself. They refer to it as the *preexisting differences hypothesis*, which is represented in Figure 3, Panel D. This theory postulates that fadeout may be due not to the quality of the preschool program or the elementary school but instead to preexisting (before pre-K entry) individual differences between the children themselves (be they due to genetics, cognitive/language skills, early family environment, SES, or a combination thereof) that cause their trajectories to return later to what they would have been without the intervention (the dashed line in Figure 3, Panel D; Bailey et al., 2016b). Note in Figure 3, Panel D, that the black line represents high-functioning comparison children who did not experience the pre-K program and show a strong linear trajectory of improvement and gains due to their preexisting differences in life circumstances (the same circumstances that put them ahead of the others at age 3). The at-risk children who went to the pre-K program (the gray line) showed improvements in pre-K but, after that was over, returned to their likely suboptimal learning environments in poverty at home and in low-resourced elementary schools; and those risk factors continued to depress their trajectories. Bailey and colleagues used data from the TRIAD intervention evaluation (Clements et al., 2013) to test this hypothesis on children's mathematical trajectories. In that study, child preexisting differences explained 70% of the observed fadeout effect in first grade—more than was explained by school environmental factors. Clearly, preschool intervention programs for children in poverty cannot magically get rid of all of the other risk factors that come with being in poverty. Some factors are going to continue to affect academic trajectories in school after the intervention. The fact that fadeout exists does not mean that the pre-K program did not work.

Peer Effects

The final factor in our discussion that is likely to influence long-term effects of pre-K programs but has nothing to do with the quality of the pre-K programs themselves is called *peer effects*. A child's peers in kindergarten and elementary school classrooms matter, as well, for early learning and likely for the appearance of pre-K fadeout effects (Hanushek, Kain, Markman, & Rivkin, 2003; Mashburn, Justice, Downer, & Pianta, 2009; Zimmer & Toma, 2000). The composition of the classroom in terms of its students is a separate aspect of school quality. Even after controlling for neighborhood demographics, teacher characteristics and quality, and individual differences across students, peer effects uniquely predict math and reading scores in third grade (Gottfried, 2012). Early expressive and receptive language abilities for children are positively associated with being in a classroom with other children that have relatively high levels of expressive language skills (Mashburn et al., 2009). If children in high-quality pre-K programs attend schools with competent peers, they are more likely to maintain and enhance the skills with which they left the program. Importantly, children from lower-income families with fewer skills do not seem to harm overall levels of classroom achievement (Hanushek et al., 2003), which is a comfort for parents of high-achievers who may be worried that lower functioning children will "bring down" the class (Jones & Glass, 2015).

Nowhere else in public education do we expect that a particularly great year/teacher in school is going to forever ensure that students exposed to that teacher will excel for the rest of their schooling. Yet we expect that students who went to a high-quality pre-K program at age 4 are always going to do better than those who did not? This is akin to saying that all the students who happened to have been assigned to Ms. Williams, a fabulous third-grade teacher, are going to have higher academic achievement on multiple measures throughout the rest of their schooling through 12th grade compared to other students who happened to have a different teacher in third grade. No one expects this kind of sustained effect for a single-grade school teacher or year in K–12 education. Why do we expect it from pre-K?

Conclusions and Implications

In summary, we feel that a number of problematic assumptions and instances of magical thinking have crept back into research on early childhood interventions and pre-K evaluations that are not serving the field well. We propose the following central concluding points:

1. *It is not at all clear that "sustained effects" or "no fadeout" is the right goal.* As described above, if "sustained effects" continue to be defined simply in terms of mean differences in much later performance between students who did and did not experience a particular pre-K program at age 4, we wonder if it is morally, theoretically, and ethically reasonable from an equity perspective to expect this—to expect that the early gaps in achievement should remain the same after many years of both groups being educated in the same public school system designed to bring up the rear and remove inequalities. Policy makers, funders, and researchers need to be careful about what they ask for. We are not sure that this is really what we want to see: that the same academic performance differences present at the kindergarten door remain throughout students' educational trajectories. This is what "sustained effects" and "no fadeout" mean. We need to think about long-term effects of pre-K programs in different ways.

2. *The occurrence of fadeout years later does not mean that your pre-K program has failed, is ineffective, or is not worthwhile.* The false and very dangerous assumption in the field is that the presence of fadeout years down the road is a sign that the pre-K program in question does not work (i.e., is not good, intense, or long enough) and perhaps should no longer be funded. This is not the case. Fadeout is practically guaranteed. Policy makers and funders need to understand that it is really quite something when you stop to think about it, and indeed an incredible achievement, that we have figured out how to make high-quality pre-K programs at scale that are able to seriously move the dial and spur excellent developmental and academic progress for preschool children in poverty and get them to arrive at the kindergarten door fully ready to go. We have done this. We should be celebrating. Mission accomplished! That is no small task. Now it is the job for us all to ensure that the K–12 education system and other child and family service agencies do their best at ensuring that all children continue to make excellent progress and have a chance to succeed. As discussed above, we need to get the pre-K system aligned, talking with, and coordinating with the K–12 education system to take the good things that are working well in pre-K and move them forward throughout education. Yes, the quality, intensity, and comprehensiveness, developmental appropriateness, and professional development/coaching involved in pre-K programs are critical for child outcomes, and we certainly need to measure and increase those things. Doing so does increase the chance that larger and more sustainable effects are found (Ramey & Ramey, 1998). But it is wrong to conclude that those things must not have been present if fadeout or convergence is found later.

3. *It is wrong to think that fadeout can be avoided if only we, as researchers, do our jobs better.* The dilemma for researchers and program evaluators is that we still hold ourselves to an untenable ideal: that we can prevent convergence if only our measures are good enough, our counterfactuals are pure enough, our samples are homogenous enough, our fidelity is strong enough, our analyses are clever enough, our selection effects are controlled enough, or our samples are big enough. Rather than falling into the trap of promising to funders that we will design a study that shows sustained effects, we need to be creative

and do something different. We need to educate policy makers and the public about fadeout/convergence. We need to build in follow-on alignment programs and work more with public schools. We need to follow samples for long enough to see sleeper effects and measure a diversity of outcomes, including perhaps skills that are not rapidly developing for all students, given minimal curriculum (Bailey et al., 2016a, Bailey et al., 2016b). We need to look longitudinally within children to see what experiences change individual academic trajectories. We need to determine the sustaining environments and conditions in elementary school that best support students who have attended pre-K and those who have not (Bailey et al., 2016b). We need to theorize better about what outcomes are and are not to be expected, and test more specific developmental cascade models and cumulative snowball effects (Cataldo & Ellis, 1988) to see how one skill at entrance to kindergarten transforms another skill or educational process, which then leads to another over time. Finally, we need to look at within-child change and trajectories rather than focusing on differences between a pre-K group and a comparison group at one point in time. And, as mentioned earlier, we need to be careful in our use of the terms "gains" and "losses."

4. *One year of a good pre-K program is not going to inoculate children living in poverty from all the evils yet to come later in schools, in the neighborhood, and in society.* As Brooks-Gunn (2003) reminded us 17 years ago, it is magical thinking to expect that even a very high-quality pre-K or Head Start program is going to place children living in the swamping conditions of poverty (Horowitz, 2003), forever on a trajectory that will be impervious to the threats of poorly resourced homes, schools, and neighborhoods. This is particularly important given that many public pre-K programs offered at scale are targeted explicitly for children in poverty, and universal pre-K programs are more likely to be taken up by families with fewer resources (Barnett, Lamy, & Jung, 2005; Duncan, Ludwig, & Magnuson, 2007). It is important to recall that that family SES (parental education, income, and social capital) and neighborhood/school quality are much stronger predictors of children's long-term academic and social outcomes than pre-K attendance (Brooks-Gunn & Duncan, 1997). These factors are not typically included in research on ECE interventions.

In conclusion, now is a critical time for researchers, educators, policy makers, and funding agencies to work together and take a critical look at the idea of preschool fadeout or convergence effects. Yes, we want our high-quality ECE programs to work, and we will continue to make that happen, but we do not want to set them up to fail by adopting an unrealistic, potentially false, and perhaps unethical goal. Consistent with the recommendations of the recent consensus statement on the state of knowledge about pre-K effects (Phillips et al., 2017), we need to move to a model of continuous and cumulative learning that starts in pre-K and continues through elementary school and beyond with continual recharging and alignment. This will require research-practice partnerships to design and evaluate effective, high-quality pre-K programs delivered at scale and close collaboration with elementary school teachers and principals to ensure continuity through many of the early years of schooling.

Acknowledgments

Our own empirical research discussed in this chapter was supported by the Early Learning Coalition of Miami-Dade/Monroe and by The Children's Trust.

References

Ackerman, D., & Coley, R. (2012). *State pre-K assessment policies: Issues and status* (Policy Information Report). Retrieved from Educational Testing Service website: https://www.ets.org/Media/Research/pdf/PIC-PRE-K.pdf

Allen, J., Gregory, A., Mikami, A., Lun, J., Hamre, B., & Pianta, R. (2013). Observations of effective teacher-student interactions in secondary school classrooms: Predicting student achievement with the Classroom Assessment Scoring System—Secondary. *School Psychology Review, 42*, 76–98.

Anderson, S., Kitchens, K., & Phillips, D. (2016, October). *School-based mechanisms of differential long-term pre-K effects among Black and White youth.* Paper presented at the Society for Research on Child Development conference "Babies, Boys, and Men of Color," Tampa, FL.

Ansari, A., Lopez, M., Manfra, L., Bleiker, C., Dinehart, L. H. B., Hartman, S.C., et al. (2016). Differential preschool effects in third grade. *Child Development, 88*(5), 1743–1756. doi:10.1111/cdev.12663

Ansari, A., & Pianta, R. (2018). The role of elementary school quality in the persistence of preschool effects. *Child and Youth Services Review, 86*, 120–127. doi:10.1016/j.childyouth.2018.01.025

Ansari, A., & Winsler, A. (2016). Kindergarten readiness for low-income and ethnically diverse children attending publicly funded preschool programs in Miami. *Early Childhood Research Quarterly, 37*, 69–80. doi:10.1016/j.ecresq.2015.06.002

Attar, B. K., Guerra, N. G., & Tolan, P. H. (1994). Neighborhood disadvantage, stressful life events and adjustments in urban elementary-school children. *Journal of Clinical Child Psychology, 23*(4), 391–400.

Austin, M. J., Tang, T., & Howard, L. (2015). Teaching critical thinking skills: Ability, motivation, intervention, and the Pygmalion effect. *Journal of Business Ethics, 128*(1). 133–143.

Bailey, D.H., Duncan, G., Odgers, C., & Yu, W. (2016a). Persistence and fadeout in the impacts of child and adolescent interventions. *Journal of Research on Educational Effectiveness, 10*(1), 7–39.

Bailey, D. H., Nguyen, T., Jenkins, J. M., Domina, T., Clements, D. H., Sarama, J. S. (2016b). Fadeout in an early mathematics intervention: Constraining content or preexisting differences? *Developmental Psychology, 52*(9), 1457–1469. doi:10.1037.dev0000188

Baker, C. N., Tichovolsky, M. H., Kupersmidt, J. B., Voegler-Lee, M. E., & Arnold, D. H. (2015). Teacher (mis)perceptions of preschoolers' academic skills: Predictors and associations with longitudinal outcomes. *Journal of Educational Psychology, 107*(3), 805–820.

Barnett, W. S. (2011). Effectiveness of early educational intervention. *Science, 333*, 975–978.

Barnett, W. S., Friedman-Krauss, A. H., Gomez, R. E., Horowitz, M., Weisenfeld, G. G., Clarke Brown, K., et al. (2016). *The state of preschool 2015: State preschool yearbook.* New Brunswick, NJ: National Institute for Early Education Research.

Barnett, W. S., Friedman-Krauss, A. H., & Jung, K. (2016, March). *New Jersey Abbott Preschool program longitudinal effects through eighth grade.* Paper presented at the spring 2016 conference "Lost in Translation: Building Pathways From Knowledge to Action" of the Society for Research on Educational Effectiveness, Washington, DC.

Barnett, W. S., Lamy, C., & Jung, K. (2005). *The effects of state prekindergarten programs on young children's school readiness in five states.* New Brunswick, NJ: National Institute for Early Education Research.

Bassok, D. (2010). Do Black and Hispanic children benefit more from preschool? Understanding differences in preschool effects across racial groups. *Child Development, 81*(6), 1828–1845.

Bernardi, F., & Ballarino, G. (2016). Introduction: Education as the great equalizer: A theoretical framework. In F. Bernardi & G. Ballarino (Eds.), *Education, occupation and social origin: A comparative analysis of the transmission of socio-economic inequalities* (pp. 1–19). Cheltenham, UK: Edward Elgar.

Broekhuizen, M. L., Mokrova, I. L., Burchinal, M. R., Garrett-Peters, P. T., & Family Life Project Key Investigators. (2016). Classroom quality at pre-kindergarten and kindergarten and children's social skills and behavior problems. *Early Childhood Research Quarterly, 36,* 212–222.

Brooks-Gunn, J. (2003). Do you believe in magic? What we can expect from early childhood intervention programs. *Social Policy Report, 17*(1), 3–15.

Brooks-Gunn, J., & Duncan, G. J. (1997). The effects of poverty on children. *The Future of Children, 7*(2), 55–71.

Cataldo, S., & Ellis, N. (1988). Interactions in the development of spelling, reading and phonological skills. *Journal of Research in Reading, 11*(2), 86–109. doi:10.1111/j.1467-9817.1988.tb00153.x

Clements, D. H., & Sarama, J. (2007). Effects of a preschool mathematics curriculum: Summative research on the Building Blocks project. *Journal for Research in Mathematics Education, 38*(2), 136–163.

Clements, D. H., Sarama, J., Wolfe, C. B., & Spitler, M. E. (2013). Longitudinal evaluation of a scale-up model for teaching mathematics with trajectories and technologies. *American Educational Research Journal, 50,* 812–850. doi:10.3102/0002831212469270

Currie, J., & Thomas, D. (2000). School quality and the longer-term effects of Head Start. *Journal of Human Resources, 35*(4), 755–74.

Duff, D., Tomblin, J. B., & Catts, H. (2015). The influence of reading on vocabulary growth: A case for a Matthew effect. *Journal of Speech, Language, and Hearing Research, 58*(3), 853–864. doi:10.1044/2015_JSLHR-L-13-0310

Duncan, G. J., Jenkins, J. M., Watts, T. W., Magnuson, K., Clements, D., Sarama, J., et al. (2015, March). *Preventing preschool fadeout through instructional intervention in kindergarten and first grade.* Paper presented at the spring 2015 conference "Learning Curves: Creating and Sustaining Gains from Early Childhood through Adulthood" of the Society for Research on Educational Effectiveness, Washington, DC.

Duncan, G. J., Ludwig, J., & Magnuson, K. A. (2007). Reducing poverty through preschool interventions. *The Future of Children, 17*(2), 143–160.

Duncan, G. J., & Magnuson, K. (2013). Investing in preschool programs. *Journal of Economic Perspectives, 27*(2), 109–132. doi:10.1257/jep.27.2.109

Engel, M., Claessens, A., & Finch, M. (2013). Teaching students what they already know? The (mis)alignment between mathematics instructional content and student knowledge in kindergarten. *Educational Evaluation and Policy Analysis, 35*(2), 157–178. doi:10.3102/0162373712461850

Every Student Succeeds Act of 2015, Pub. L. No . 114-95 § 114 Stat. 1177 (2015–2016).

Feller, A., Grindal, T., Miratrix, L. W., & Page, L. C. (2016). Compared to what? Variation in the impacts of early childhood education by alternative care-type settings. *The Annals of Applied Statistics, 10*(3), 1245–1285. doi:10.2139/ssrn.2534811

Fergus, E., Noguera, P., & Martin, M. (2014). *Schooling for resilience: Improving the life trajectory of Black and Latino boys.* Cambridge, MA: Harvard Education Press.

Garcia, E., & Weiss, E. (2015). *Early education gaps by social class and race start U.S. children out on unequal footing: A summary of the major findings in inequalities at the starting gate.* Washington, DC: Economic Policy Institute.

Garcia, J. L., Heckman, J. J., Leaf, D. E., & Prados, M. J. (2016). *The life-cycle benefits of an influential early childhood program* (NBER Working Paper Series No. 22993). Cambridge, MA: National Bureau of Economic Research.

Gottfried, M. A. (2012). Peer effects in urban schools: Assessing the impact of classroom composition on student achievement. *Educational Policy, 28*(5), 607–647. doi:10.1177/0895904812467082

Graves, B. (2006). *PK–3: What is it and how do we know it works?* (FCD Policy Brief Advancing PK–3 No. 4). New York, NY: Foundation for Child Development.

Growe, R., & Montgomery, P. S. (2003). Educational equity in America: Is education the great equalizer? *Professional Educator, 25*(2), 23–29.

Hanushek, E. A., Kain, J. F., Markman, J. M., & Rivkin, S. G. (2003). Does peer ability affect student achievement? *Journal of Applied Econometrics, 18*(5), 527–544. doi:10.3386/w8502

Harper, S. R., & Davis, C. H. F, III. (2012). They (don't) care about education: A counternarrative on Black male students' responses to inequitable schooling. *Journal of Educational Foundations, 26*(1), 103–120.

Hauser-Cram, P., Sirin, S. R., & Stipek, D. (2003). When teachers' and parents' values differ: Teachers' ratings of academic competence in children from low-income families. *Journal of Educational Psychology, 95*(4), 813–820. doi:10.1037/0022-0663.95.4.813

Hill, C. J., Gormley, W. T., & Adelstein, S. (2015). Do the short-term effects of a high-quality preschool program persist? *Early Childhood Research Quarterly, 32*, 60–79. doi:10.1016/j.ecresq.2014.12.005

Horacek, H. J., Ramey, C. T., Campbell, F. A., Hoffman, K. P., & Fletcher, R. H. (1987). Predicting school failure and assessing early intervention with high-risk children. *Journal of the American Academy of Child and Adolescent Psychiatry, 26*, 758–763.

Horowitz, F. D. (2003). Child development and the PITS: Simple questions, complex answers, and developmental theory. In M. E. Hertzig, & E. A. Farber (Eds.), *Annual progress in child psychiatry and child development: 2000–2001* (pp. 3–19). New York, NY: Brunner-Routledge.

Hudstedt, J. T., Barnett, W. S., Jung, K., & Goetze, L. D. (2009). *The New Mexico pre-K evaluation: Results from the initial four years of a new state preschool initiative.* New Brunswick, NJ: National Institute for Early Education Research, Rutgers University. Retrieved from https://www.newmexicoprek.org/Docs/NIEER%20Reports/NIEER_PreK_Evaluation_Results_From_The_Initial_Four_Years_Final_Report.pdf

Jones, N. H. (Host), Glass, I. (Host), Joffe-Walt, C. (Producer), & Menjivar, J. (Producer). (2015). The problem we all live with [Radio program episode]. In I. Glass (Host), *This American Life.* Chicago, IL: National Public Radio.

Kauerz, K. (2006). *Ladders of learning: Fighting fade-out by advancing PK–3 alignment* (Issue Brief No. 2). Washington, DC: New America Foundation.

Lee, V., & Loeb, S. (1995) Where do Head Start attendees end up? One reason why preschool effects fade out. *Educational Evaluation and Policy Analysis, 17*(1), 62–82.

Lipsey, M. W., Farran, D. C., & Hofer, K. G. (2015). *A randomized control trial of a statewide voluntary prekindergarten program on children's skills and behaviors through third grade.* Nashville TN: Peabody Research Institute, Vanderbilt University.

Lipsey, M. W., Hofer, K. G., Dong, N., Farran, D. C., & Bilbrey, C. (2013). Evaluation of the Tennessee Voluntary Prekindergarten Program: Kindergarten and first grade follow-up results from the randomized control design (Research Report). Nashville, TN: Peabody Research Institute, Vanderbilt University.

Love, J. M., Chazan-Cohen, R., Raikes, H., & Brooks-Gunn, J. (2013). What makes a difference: Early Head Start evaluation findings in a developmental context. *Monographs of the Society for Research in Child Development, 78*(1), vi–viii. doi:10.1111/j.1540-5834.2012.00699.x

Love, J. M., Kisker, E. E., Ross, C. M., Schochet, P. Z., Brooks-Gunn, J., Paulsell, D., et al. (2002). *Making a difference in the lives of infants and toddlers and their families: The impacts of Early Head*

Start. Washington, DC: U.S. Department of Health and Human Services. Retrieved from http://www.mathematica-mpr.com/3rdLevel/EHSTOC.HTM

Magnuson, K. A., Ruhm, C., & Waldfogel, J. (2007). The persistence of preschool effects: Do subsequent classroom experiences matter? *Early Childhood Research Quarterly, 22*(1), 18–38. doi:10.1016/j.ecresq.2006.10.002

Mashburn, A. J., Justice, L. M., Downer, J. T., & Pianta, R. C. (2009). Peer effects on children's language achievement during pre-kindergarten. *Child Development, 80*(3), 686–702. doi:10.1111/j.1467-8624.2009.01291.x

Mather, M., & Jarosz, B. (2014). The demography of inequality in the United States. *Population Bulletin, 69*(2), 2–16.

Mizala, A., Martínez, F., & Martínez, S. (2015). Pre-service elementary school teachers' expectations about student performance: How their beliefs are affected by their mathematics anxiety and student's gender. *Teaching and Teacher Education, 50,* 70–78. doi:10.1016/j.tate.2015.04.006

Morgan, P. L., Farkas, G., & Hibel, J. (2008). Matthew effects for whom? *Learning Disability Quarterly, 31*(4), 187–198. doi:10.2307/25474651

Mumma, K., Manfra, L., Bleiker, C., Dinehart, L. H. B., Hartman, S. C., & Winsler, A. (2020). *The influence of elementary school quality on differential effects of preschool programs in third grade.* Manuscript submitted for publication.

Ou, S. R., & Reynolds, A. J. (2006). Early childhood intervention and educational attainment: Age 22 findings from the Chicago Longitudinal Study. *Journal of Education for Students Placed at Risk, 11*(2), 175–198. doi:10.1207/s15327671espr1102_4

Ou, S. R., Reynolds, A. J., & Topitzes, J. W. (2004). Paths of effects of early childhood intervention on educational attainment and delinquency: A confirmatory analysis of the Chicago child-parent centers. *Child Development, 75*(5), 1299–1328. Retrieved from http://search.proquest.com/assia/docview/57113550/A53105B2CF034941PQ/76

Peisner-Feinberg, E., & Burchinal, M. (2016, March). *Effects of pre-K participation on children's third-grade assessments: Results from the NC Pre-Kindergarten Program.* Paper presented at the spring 2016 conference "Expanding the Toolkit: Maximizing Relevance, Effectiveness and Rigor in Education Research" of the Society for Research on Educational Effectiveness, Washington, DC.

Phillips, D.A., Gormley, W., & Anderson, S. (2016). The effects of Tulsa's CAP Head Start program on middle-school academic outcomes and progress. *Developmental Psychology, 52*(8), 1247–1261. doi:10.1037/dev0000151

Phillips, D. A., Lipsey, M. W., Dodge, K. A., Haskins, R., Bassok, D., Burchinal, M. R., et al. (2017). *Puzzling it out: The current state of scientific knowledge on pre-kindergarten effects. A consensus statement.* Washington, DC: Brookings Institution Press.

Pianta, R. C., LaParo, K. M., & Hamre, B. K. (2008). *Classroom Assessment Scoring System manual: Pre-K.* Baltimore, MD: Brookes.

Pressler, E., Raver, C. C., & Friedman-Krauss, A. R. (2016). The roles of school readiness and poverty-related risk for 6th grade outcomes. *Journal of Educational and Developmental Psychology, 6*(1), 140–156. doi:10.5539/jedp.v6n1p140

Ramey, C. T., & Campbell, F. A. (1991). Poverty, early childhood education and academic competence: The Abecedarian experiment. In A. Houston (Ed.), *Children in poverty: Child development and public policy* (pp. 190–221). New York, NY: Cambridge University Press.

Ramey, C. T., Collier, A. M., Sparling, J. J., Loda, F. A., Campbell, F. A., Ingran, D. L., et al. (1976). The Carolina Abecedarian Project: A longitudinal and multidisciplinary approach to the prevention of developmental retardation. In T. Tjossem (Ed.), *Intervention strategies for high-risk infants and young children* (pp. 629–665). Baltimore, MD: University Park Press.

Ramey, C. T., & Ramey, S. L. (1998). Prevention of intellectual disabilities: Early interventions to improve cognitive development. *Preventive Medicine, 27,* 224–232.

Reynolds, A. J. (1994). Effects of a preschool plus follow-on intervention for children at risk. *Developmental Psychology, 30*(6), 787–804. doi:10.1037/0012-1649.30.6.787

Reynolds, A. J., Richardson, B. A., Hayakawa, M., Lease, E. M., Warner-Richter, M., Englund, M, et al. (2014). Association of a full-day vs part-day preschool intervention with school readiness, attendance, and parent involvement. *Journal for the American Medical Association, 312*(20), 2126–2134. doi:10.1001/jama.2014.15376

Rosenthal, R., & Jacobson, L. (1968). Pygmalion in the classroom. *The Urban Review, 3,* 16–20. doi:10.1007/BF02322211

Rowley, S. J., Ross, L., Lozada, F. T., Williams, A., Gale, A., & Kurtz-Costes, B. (2014). Framing Black boys: Parent, teacher, and student narratives of the academic lives of Black boys. *Advances in Child Development and Behavior, 47,* 301–332. doi:10.1016/bs.acdb.2014.05.003

Scarborough, H. S., & Parker, J. D. (2003). Matthew effects in children with learning disabilities: Development of reading, IQ, and psychosocial problems from Grade 2 to Grade 8. *Annals of Dyslexia, 47–71.*

Schweinhart, L. J., Berruta-Clement, J. R., Barnett, W. S., Epstein, A. S., & Weikart, D. P. (1985). Effects of the Perry Preschool Program on youths through age 19. *Topics in Early Childhood Special Education, 5*(2), 26–35. doi:10.1177/027112148500500204

Shaywitz, B. A., Holford, T. R., Holahan, J. M., Fletcher, J. M., Stuebing, K. K., Francis, D. J., et al. (1995). A Matthew effect for IQ but not for reading: Results from a longitudinal study. *Reading Research Quarterly, 30*(4), 894–906. doi:10.2307/748203

SRI Education. (2016). *Virginia Preschool Initiative-Plus formative evaluation report.* Menlo Park, CA: SRI International.

Stipek, D., Clements, D., Coburn, C., Franke, M., & Farran, D. (2017). PK–3: What does it mean for instruction? *Social Policy Report, 30*(2), 3–22.

Sunderman, G. L., & Titan, C. (2014). *Can Maryland benefit from universal preschool? A review of the research on the efficacy of early education* (Policy Brief). College Park, MD: Maryland Equity Project, University of Maryland.

Takanishi, R. (2016). *First things first! Creating the new American primary school.* New York, NY: Teachers College Press.

Van Aar, J., Leijten, P., de Castro, B. O., & Overbeek, G. (2016). Sustained, fade-out or sleeper effects? A systematic review and meta-analysis of parenting interventions for disruptive child behavior. *Clinical Psychology Review, 51,* 153–163. doi:10.1016/j.cpr.2016.11.006

Weiland, C., Unterman, R., Martin, E., Rochester, S., Shapiro, A., Staszak, S., et al. (2017, February). *Impacts of Boston pre-K on children's academic outcomes, special education placement, and grade retention through third grade.* Paper presented at the spring 2017 conference "Expanding the Toolkit: Maximizing Relevance, Effectiveness and Rigor in Education Research" of the Society for Research on Educational Effectiveness, Washington, DC.

Weiland, C., & Yoshikawa, H. (2013). Impacts of a prekindergarten program on children's mathematics, language, literacy, executive function, and emotional skills. *Child Development, 84*(6), 2112–2130. doi:10.1111/cdev.12099

Whitehurst, G. J. (2016). Family support or school readiness? Contrasting models of public spending on children's early care and learning. *Evidence Speaks Reports, 1*(16), 2–8.

Whyte, K., McMahon, K., Coburn, C. E., Stein, A., & Jou, N. (2016). *PreK–3 alignment: A review of the evidence.* Stanford, CA: DREME Network.

Zhai, F., Raver, C. C., & Jones, S. M. (2012). Academic performance of subsequent schools and impacts of early interventions: Evidence from a randomized controlled trial in Head Start settings. *Children and Youth Services Review, 34*(5), 946–954. doi:10.1016/j.childyouth.2012.01.026

Zimmer, R. W., & Toma, E. F. (2000). Peer effects in private and public schools across countries. *Journal of Policy Analysis and Management, 19*(1), 75–92. doi:10.1002/(SICI)1520-6688(200024)19:1<75::AID-PAM5>3.0.CO;2-W

Chapter 9

Early Care and Education Quality

MARGARET R. BURCHINAL
University of North Carolina, Chapel Hill

Early care and education (ECE) now play an integral role in early development, so it is important to understand how ECE experiences impact children's learning and development. This chapter first describes the extensive literature relating ECE quality and programs to both short-term and long-term development. The chapter then discusses professional development designed to improve quality of ECE. It concludes by contrasting findings across these various research literatures in the context of the promise of ECE to promote both short- and long-term outcomes for all children.

Over three-fourths of young children in the United States experience nonparental care prior to kindergarten (Organisation for Economic Co-operation and Development, 2018), typically because reliable care is needed when parents are employed or because government provides ECE programs designed to address achievement gaps (Burchinal, Magnuson, Powell, & Hong, 2015). Both developmental theory and research emphasize that responsive and sensitive caregivers and stimulating experiences play a crucial role in children's early development. These theories and research literatures provide the framework for defining high-quality ECE.

High-quality early care and education (ECE) has been shown to be one of the most effective means for promoting opportunity for all children and for addressing gaps in educational achievement and even adult outcomes (Heckman, 2011), so policy makers have invested heavily in programs to increase access to high-quality ECE. Evaluations of programs and studies that relate observed ECE quality to child outcomes provide a mixed picture of the extent to which ECE is achieving this goal. To describe the extensive research literature, this chapter discusses the conceptualization and measurement of ECE quality, publicly funded ECE programs and initiatives, and the extent to which ECE quality and ECE programs appear to improve children's early learning and development.

ECE Quality

Developmental theories define ECE quality, and theory-derived definitions of ECE quality are reflected in ECE research. Attachment theory (Ainsworth, Blehar, Waters, & Wall, 1978) argues that children's early emotional adjustment depends on having frequent, warm, and sensitive interactions with parents and ECE care providers, which allow them to form a secure base. This secure base is thought to allow the children to engage meaningfully with objects and other people in their environment that promote social and cognitive development (Howes & Spieker, 2008). Vygotsky's sociocultural theory focuses on the kinds of interactions that facilitate learning (Vygotsky, 2001). The theory posits that children's development is optimized when a more skilled partner engages with a child to help the child complete a task that is slightly above the child's skill level, therefore enabling the child to accomplish tasks the child could not otherwise complete (Bodrova & Leong, 2007; Vygotsky, 2001). According to this theory, young children learn optimally when they are challenged by tasks and guided in resolving these tasks by caregivers who extend the children's understanding (e.g., Berk & Winsler, 1995). Piaget's constructivist theory describes cognitive development as a dynamic process in which children learn through actively engaging with objects and people to develop and test hypotheses as they learn new concepts (Gopnik, Meltzoff, & Kuhl, 1999). Bronfenbrenner's bioecological model describes how children's early development depends on the family and other primary caregiving settings, such as ECE, as the primary contexts for the young child, and on connections between family and ECE caregivers and contexts (Bronfenbrenner & Morris, 2006).

Early ECE Intervention Programs

Between 1970 and 1990, several ECE intervention programs were developed using these developmental theoretical frameworks. For example, the Perry Preschool/High Scope program (Cunha & Heckman, 2007) and Chicago Parent-Child Centers (Reynolds, Magnuson, & Ou, 2010) combined child care and parenting programs for preschoolers and their mothers; the Abecedarian Project (Campbell et al., 2012) provided full-time child care from infancy to kindergarten and onsite medical care. All of the programs focused on ensuring that children received sensitive, responsive care from their caregivers in accordance with all developmental theories, especially attachment theory. Perry Preschool and Chicago Parent-Child Centers emphasized connections between ECE and families as advocated by Bronfrenbenner's model and focused on providing children with hands-on experiential learning opportunities in accordance with Piaget's theory. Abecedarian focused on promoting language development through scaffolded interactions with caregivers, as recommended by Vygotsky. In randomized clinical trials, the treated participants obtained higher levels of education and employment, lower levels of crime and welfare, and fewer risk factors for cardiac and metabolic disease than did control participants (Campbell et al., 2012; Campbell et al., 2014; Cunha & Heckman, 2007). An evaluation of the earliest 10 intervention studies demonstrated that treated participants were more likely to graduate from high school and less likely to receive special education (Lazar, Darlington, Murray, Royce, & Snipper, 1982). These programs demonstrated that ECE could improve the lives of participants but did not document how the programs produced their impacts. They were assumed to be high quality, and the findings led to a focus on providing access to high-quality ECE to address achievement gaps (Heckman, 2011).

ECE Quality

Definitions of high-quality ECE were based on the aforementioned developmental theories (Burchinal, Magnuson, Powell, & Hong, 2015). Quality became a focus in ECE because of the large impacts of the ECE intervention projects on early development (Heckman, 2011). The National Association for the Education of Young Children (NAEYC, 2009) provides the professional guidelines regarding high ECE quality. Its guidelines include frequent, sensitive responsive interactions between the young child and the adult caregivers (as advocated by all theories); frequent opportunities to engage actively with age-appropriate toys, books, and objects and intentional learning opportunities (as promoted by Piaget's theory); intentional teaching in which adult caregivers structure activities to promote learning, and scaffold those activities for the child to extend learning opportunities through extended conversations (as promoted by Vygotsky's theory); and close reciprocal relationships between parents and ECE providers (as advocated by Bronfenbrenner's model) (NAEYC, 2009).

Measures of ECE quality reflect these conceptual frameworks for defining ECE quality. There are two widely used ECE quality measures, the Environmental Rating Scales (ERS; Harms, Clifford, & Cryer, 2014) and the Classroom Assessment Scoring System (CLASS; Pianta, La Paro, & Hamre, 2008).

The ERS focus on the child's access to age-appropriate toys and books, as promoted by Piaget, and on supportiveness of the caregivers, as recommended by Vygotsky (Burchinal et al., 2015). The ERS scales include the following: for measuring the quality of preschool classrooms, Early Childhood Environment Rating Scale, Third Edition (ECERS-3; Harms, Clifford, & Cryer, 2014); for infant-toddler classrooms, Infant-Toddler Environment Rating Scale, Third Edition (ITERS-3; Harms, Cryer, Clifford, & Yazejian, 2017); and for home-based ECE settings, Family Child Care Environment Rating Scale Revised Edition (FCCERS-R Harms, Cryer, & Clifford, 2007). ERS emphasize frequent access to a variety of activities in which the child actively engages. The ERS also measure caregiver sensitivity and responsiveness, health-related practices and the safety of the setting, and classroom management practices. According to the ERS, high-quality ECE settings have: five or more free play centers; conversations between caregivers and children during meals and snack time; access to a wide selection of books that are read to children in formal class activities and in informal interactions with the caregiver; and activities that encourage children to think, talk about, and reason about their experiences (Harms et al., 2014).

The CLASS focuses on the quality of teacher–child interactions and positive classroom management in accordance with attachment theory. The CLASS is an extension of a scale, the Observational Rating of the Childcare Environment (ORCE), developed by the NICHD Study of Early Child Care and Youth Development (NICHD Early Child Care Research Network [ECCRN], 1997). CLASS rates the teachers' sensitivity and instructional support with their children, the degree to which management of the classroom is positive and effective. According to Hamre (2014), this measure describes high-quality classrooms as having teachers who engage in frequent warm and responsive interactions with children; understand the developmental learning sequence (i.e., the sequence of skills that need to be learned in a given order for children to master a content area) to ensure that children understand prerequisite skills before being introduced to higher order skills; and attend to each child, individualizing the feedback to match his or her skill level. In addition, teachers and children engage in frequent conversations in which the adult elaborates on the students' responses by asking open-ended questions (Hamre, 2014).

The current ECE model also suggests that characteristics of the ECE teachers, classrooms, and programs, labeled *structural quality,* influence early development indirectly through their impact on process quality. These characteristics are thought to promote higher process quality (Build Initiative & Child Trends, 2014; NICHD ECCRN, 1999, 2002). They include factors such as caregivers' education and training, ratio of children to caregivers, number of children in the setting, leadership and administration of the ECE setting, parental involvement, inclusion of children with special needs, and inclusion of the home language and culture in the setting (Build Initiative & Child Trends, 2014; Burchinal, Zaslow, & Tarullo, 2016). Simplistically represented, this ECE model suggests these causal links: Structural Quality —> Process Quality —> Child Outcomes.

Many studies have documented the extent to which children show higher levels of cognitive or social outcomes when they attend ECE programs with higher structural and process quality. An extensive literature has examined associations between process quality and child outcomes, associations between structural and process quality, and associations between structural quality and child outcomes.

Child Outcomes and ECE Process Quality. The degree to which ECE quality ratings relate to early learning and development has been examined for over 30 years, with increasing attention to potential confounds over time. The earliest studies reported moderate-sized associations, typically between the ECERS and child outcomes, but they did not include many covariates to account for potential differences in the families that selected different quality ECE for their children (e.g., Burchinal et al., 2000; Clarke-Stewart, 1998; Howes, Rodning, Galluzzo, & Myers, 1988; Peisner-Feinberg & Burchinal, 1997; McCartney, 1984; Vandell & Corasaniti, 1988). The next set of studies addressed concerns about potential selection bias by including extensive child and family characteristics as covariates, often including baseline assessments on the outcome. Most of these studies yielded statistically significant, but quite modest, associations between some child outcomes and ECE quality as measured by the ECERS, CLASS, and ORCE (e.g., Augur, Farkas, Burchinal, Duncan, & Lowe 2015; Howes et al., 2008; Mashburn et al., 2008; NICHD ECCRN, 2002; Votruba-Drzal, Coley, & Chase-Lansdale, 2004). Some of these studies asked whether the modest associations were due to threshold effects such that a certain level of quality was necessary for quality to improve child outcomes. Somewhat inconsistent evidence indicated quality thresholds for the CLASS domain scores, but the associations between quality and outcomes remained modest even above the threshold (Burchinal, Vandergrift, Pianta, & Mashburn, 2010; Burchinal, Vernon-Feagans, Vitiello, & Greenberg, 2014; Burchinal et al., 2016; Hatfield, Burchinal, Pianta, & Sideris, 2016; Weiland, Ulvestad, Sachs, & Yoshikawa, 2013). Most recently, meta-analyses of large ECE studies that included extensive covariates and involved multiple ECE quality measures also indicated reliable but very small associations with child outcomes (i.e., effect sizes that averaged around .05 when statistically significant associations were detected) (Hong et al., 2019; Keys et al., 2013).

Some aspects of ECE quality appear to enhance specific skills among preschoolers, albeit modestly in the most recent studies. The degree to which caregivers engage in warm, responsive interactions with children modestly relate to gains in academic and social skills (Mashburn et al., 2008; Raver et al., 2008). The extent to which teachers provide detailed feedback and sequenced and elaborated support for learning modestly relates to gains in academic skills (Howes et al., 2008; Mashburn et al., 2008). Gains in language and academic skills were larger when caregivers engaged in more frequent multi-turn conversations, especially when those conversations involved elaborating on a given topic (Justice, Mashburn, Pence, & Wiggins, 2008; Wasik, Bond, & Hindeman, 2006). Finally, more opportunities to engage in age-appropriate activities with a range of varied materials, such as books, blocks, and water, relate to preschooler's language, math, and social skills (Peisner-Feinberg & Burchinal, 1997; Sylva, Melhuish, Sammons, Siraj-Blatchford, & Taggart, 2012).

Child Outcomes and Structural Quality. Structural quality indicators also have been extensively evaluated, in part because they are viewed as factors that improve process quality and are easier to regulate than process quality (Burchinal et al., 2015). Some studies relate structural quality indicators to process quality ratings, while other studies relate them to child outcomes. A few studies have examined the indirect pathway from structural quality through process quality to child outcomes. This literature is discussed below.

The degree to which individual structural quality indicators relate to process quality varies from large to no associations. Earlier research documented moderate to strong associations between teacher education, teacher training, ratio of children to adults, group size, caregiver wages, and administrator experience and communication style with global environmental quality (Burchinal et al., 2000; Phillipsen, Burchinal, Howes, & Cryer, 1997) and ratings of teacher-child relationships sensitivity (NICHD ECCRN, 1999). In contrast, the first large study of state pre-kindergarten (pre-K) programs did not find associations between process quality scores on the ECERS or CLASS with teacher education, training, class size, or child-adult ratios (Mashburn et al., 2008; Pianta et al., 2005).

Structural quality has been related to child outcomes in individual studies and in meta-analyses. Modestly higher preschool outcomes were observed in individual studies when their teachers had more education (Burchinal et al., 2000; NICHD ECCRN, 2002; Phillipsen et al., 1997) and classrooms had fewer children per teacher (NICHD ECCRN, 2002). More frequent behavior problems were reported in larger classrooms (McCartney et al., 2010). A comprehensive meta-analysis suggested that children's skill levels were higher when caregivers either had relatively intensive training or training to implement an evidence-based curriculum (Fukkink & Lont, 2007). Other meta-analyses combined results across parallel secondary data analysis of at least five large ECE studies. One meta-analysis reported slightly higher language and academic outcomes when teachers or administrators had more education, but did not find that class sizes or ratios were related to any outcome (Burchinal et al., 2016).[1] In contrast, an earlier meta-analysis did not find teacher education was related to either observed quality or child outcomes (Early et al., 2007). In summary, some, albeit mixed, evidence suggests that at least some of the structural quality relates very modestly to at least some child outcomes.

Child Outcomes and ECE Programs and Initiatives

Publicly funded ECE programs designed to improve access to higher quality ECE were initiated in 1967 with Head Start, and now include child care vouchers, state pre-K programs, and state and local quality rating and improvement systems.

Child Outcomes and Head Start

Head Start was initiated in 1967 as the first federally funded ECE program. It was quickly expanded from a summer program for low-income children to a program for 9–12 months per year providing center care for low-income preschoolers (Office of Head Start [OHS], 2018). From the beginning, Head Start was a community program with a focus on both parents and children, and it focused on the whole child, not just academic skills (OHS, 2018). Performance standards were introduced to ensure that programs provided moderately high to high-quality care, provided services to families and children, and involved families in the local program (OHS, 2018). Early Head Start was introduced about 20 years ago to provide both home-based and center care to infants and toddlers (OHS, 2018).

The quality of Head Start has been documented by the Family and Child Experiences Survey (FACES), Head Start Impact Study(HSIS), and many observational studies. FACES began in 1997 and has been conducted approximately every three years since then as a representative sample of Head Start programs (Office of Planning, Research, and Evaluation [OPRE], 2018). HSIS was a nationally representative study in which 3- and 4-year-old children were randomly assigned to attend Head Start or to a control group. Both the 2000 FACES and HSIS indicate that the global environmental quality of Head Start preschool classrooms is moderately high according to the ECERS (Aikens, Bush, Gleason, Malone, & Tarullo, 2016; Puma, Bell, Cook, Heid, & Lopez, 2005). More recent FACES data suggest that, both environmental quality and quality of teacher-child interactions have improved between 20006 and 2014. In 2014, the average ECERS score was about 4.5 (i.e., moderately high quality), and average CLASS domains ranged from 2.4 (i.e., moderately low quality) on Instructional Support to 5.4 (i.e., high quality) on Emotional Support (Aikens et al., 2016). The structural quality also improved between 2006 and 2014, with more training, especially mentoring and more teachers with a B.A. (mean of 70%), in part due to a mandate that 50% of lead teachers must have a college degree (Aikens et al., 2016).

The HSIS and other studies examined the extent to which Head Start improved child outcomes. After a year in Head Start, children showed modestly higher language and reading skills compared to the control children, with larger impacts for children whose families did not speak English at home (Puma et al., 2005). Children were followed through third grade, but the findings did not detect differences between treated and control children in elementary school (Puma et al., 2012). In contrast, a long-term quasi-experimental study of early Head Start participants suggests positive impacts of Head Start in adulthood (Ludwig & Miller, 2007).

Child Outcomes and Vouchers. Support for the employment of low-income families is provided by means-tested child care subsidies that are funded with both federal and state dollars. Child care subsidies lower the cost of private, market-based nonparental care for low-income families in which parents work or participate in education or other training activities (Magnuson, Ruhm, & Waldfogel, 2007). Currently, child-care subsidy programs are funded by a combination of three federal block grants that provide vouchers and a small set-aside for ECE quality improvement (Magnuson et al., 2007). The largest federal block grant, the Child Care and Development Fund, is designed to allow families with incomes below 85% of the state median to use the funds for their choice of type of care. Therefore, vouchers are used for any eligible child care provider, including informal care by friends, relatives, or babysitters. The recommended reimbursement rate is 75% of current market rates (Schulman & Blank, 2008), but states have substantial flexibility to establish income eligibility requirements, parental copayment fees, and provider reimbursement rates (Greenberg, 2007).

Use of child care subsidies appears to increase the use of slightly higher-quality care but does not appear to improve child outcomes. Children with these subsidies attended higher quality care than comparable children without subsidies because they were more likely to use center care, which is higher quality on average than home-based care—especially for families eligible for subsides (Johnson, Martin, & Brooks-Gunn, 2013). However, school readiness skills were not higher with subsidy receipt, and indeed, some evidence suggests that skill levels may be slightly lower (Herbst & Tekin, 2010; Johnson et al., 2013).

Child Outcomes and State Pre-Kindergarten Programs

Public pre-K programs are funded by states or local school districts. Most pre-K programs only enroll low-income children and children with special needs related to disabilities or home language, but some are available to all preschoolers (Friedman-Krauss et al., 2019). Unlike Head Start, these programs tend to focus on promoting children's academic and classroom behaviors rather than the whole child and family (Friedman-Krauss et al., 2019). Enrollment in these programs increased dramatically between 1990 and 2017, with 64 state and local programs by 2017 serving approximately 32% of 4-year-olds and 5% of 3-year-olds in their states (Friedman-Krauss et al., 2019).

As state and local initiatives, the pre-K programs vary widely in funding, program design, and quality (Friedman-Kraus et al., 2019). In 2017, pre-K programs are available in 44 states and the District of Columbia. These programs serve about 1.5 million children, with most programs serving 4-year-olds and a growing number of programs also serving 3-year-olds. The programs vary in their program day, with part-day care in about half of the programs, school-day care in about 25% of the programs and other combinations in the other 25%. Some programs are exclusively located in schools (or classrooms funded by schools in districts where room in schools is limited), whereas others use a mix of locations, including schools, Head Starts, and community-based ECE centers. In 2017, about two-thirds of the classrooms were in schools. Support services such transportation and health screenings and referrals are offered in some programs.

Not surprisingly, the structural and process quality of pre-K programs also varies widely (Friedman-Kraus et al., 2019). The structural quality is easier to describe because each program has performance standards that must be met for a classroom to receive pre-K funds. Of the 10 structural quality measures monitored by the National Institute for Early

Education Research, 3 of 45 programs studied met all 10 standards, 5 met 9 of the 10 standards, and 9 met less than half of the standards (Friedman-Kraus et al., 2019). Slightly over half the programs require teachers to have a college degree, but almost all mandated a minimum class size of 20 children and a 10:1 child/adult ratio. In addition, slightly over half mandated screening and referrals for health and special needs. About half the programs requiredmonitoring for process quality at least once every 5 years.

Some programs have funded evaluations that monitor process quality and child outcomes. The pre-K programs that have been evaluated tend to have the most rigorous performance standards, and the results indicate moderately high global environmental quality and quality of teacher-child interactions (Minervino, 2014). The four programs that had the most rigorous evaluations, all of which met most professional guidelines, yielded moderate-to-large impacts on academic skills, with effect sizes ranging from .40 to .62 (Minervino, 2014). A review of all the pre-K evaluations indicated that attending pre-K led to gains in academic skills and sometimes in language, executive functioning, and social skills (Phillips et al., 2017). Dual language learners and children from low-income families showed the largest gains (Phillips et al., 2017). Earlier studies that involved a wider range of pre-K programs indicated that, compared to children without ECE center experience, children who attended pre-K programs entered school with higher levels of math and literacy skills (Magnuson, Meyers, Ruhm, & Waldfogel, 2004; Phillips & Adams, 2001). Children in pre-K classrooms with higher process quality tended to have modestly larger gains in language and academic skills (Howes et al., 2008; Mashburn et al., 2008).

A few evaluations of pre-K programs have followed the children through third to fifth grade. Most show that children who attended pre-K have higher reading and math skills in elementary school compared to children from families with similar demographic characteristics who did not attend, although the magnitude of the pre-K impact declined over time (Phillips et al., 2017). However, one of the most rigorous studies found lower academic scores among children who attended the Tennessee pre-K program than among children who did not (Farran & Lipsey, 2015).

Child Outcomes and Quality Rating and Improvement Systems. Starting about 20 years ago, states created market-based incentive systems, termed Quality Rating and Improvement Systems (QRIS), designed to improve access to higher quality ECE for all children. Now, in 38 states these programs rate the quality of participating programs and report those ratings to help inform parental ECE decisions; they also provide assistance in quality improvement to participating ECE programs (Build Initiative & Child Trends, 2014). The quality ratings provide a standard approach based on multiple structural and process quality indicators that are made publicly available so parents can make informed decisions when they choose ECE settings for their children. Nearly all state QRIS systems assess staff training and education, classroom group size and adult-child ratios, inclusion of children with special needs, culturally and linguistically responsive practices, and the environmental quality or quality of teacher-child interactions. For some states, process quality is monitored only when the ECE program is deemed higher quality based on structural quality indicators (Build Initiative & Child Trends, 2014). States differ on whether and to what extent they include parent-involvement activities, business practices, or national accreditation status. The QRIS ratings are categorized into quality tiers, and the quality tier for participating programs is published, typically online. The assumption underlying this QRIS function is that parents often lack good information about program quality and, if they had it, they would be more likely to choose highly rated settings. As a result, lower quality providers would face an incentive either to improve the quality of their programs or to leave the market (Zellman & Perlman, 2008).

The quality improvements in QRIS involve incentives and technical assistance (Build Initiative & Child Trends, 2014). ECE programs that meet higher standards of quality can receive larger subsidy payments. Technical assistance is available, especially to programs at lower quality tiers. Many states provide extensive assistance with self-assessment as part of QRIS.

Validation studies of state QRIS have examined the extent to which QRIS tiers and ratings relate to process quality and child outcomes. Almost all validation studies indicate that ECE programs at higher quality tiers have higher ERS or CLASS scores, providing reassuring validation for the rating systems (e.g., Lipscomb, Weber, Green, & Patterson, 2016; Quick et al., 2016; Tout et al., 2016; Yazejian, Franco, Morgan, & Simpson, 2016). These validation studies, however, yield little to no evidence of higher skill levels among children who attend programs at higher quality tiers (Hestenes et al., 2014; Karoly, Schwartz, Setodji, Haas, 2016; Sabol & Pianta, 2015; Soliday Hong, Howes, Marcella, Zucker, & Huang, 2014; Thornburg, Mayfield, Hawks, & Fuger, 2009; Yazejian et al., 2016; Zellman, Perlman, Le, & Setodji, 2008).

Two studies used extant data to dig deeper into associations between QRIS and child outcomes. The first study used the data from the 11-state National Center for Early Development and Learning pre-K study, applied the QRIS criteria from 10 states to those data, and related them to gains in child outcomes during the pre-K year (Sabol, Soliday Hong, Pianta, & Burchinal, 2013). The researchers reported almost no reliable associations between the structural quality indicators and child outcomes, but significant associations with the process quality indicator. The second study used data from six other large ECE studies, including a national representative survey, Head Start surveys, state pre-K evaluations, and a professional development study (Hong et al., 2019). This study tried to optimize the development of a QRIS rating system by examining the dimensionality of the scale, the extent to which the research literature indicated each quality indicator was related to child outcomes, and the extent to which quality indicators related to child outcomes before and after being categorized based on professional guidelines. Unlike the Sabol study, this study found significant associations between child outcomes and some of the structural quality indicators (i.e., teacher and director education and use of curriculum), but not others (i.e., group size and ratio), and some of the process quality indicators (i.e., ratings of instructional quality but not ratings of emotional support or overall environmental quality). Perhaps most surprisingly, the researchers found that their QRIS rating based only on the structural indicators provided slightly better prediction of academic child outcomes than did their rating based on both structural and process indicators.

Professional Development to Improve ECE Quality

Professional development for child care teachers and providers is a major focus of programs and policy makers because of the wide-scale use of ECE for infants, toddlers, and preschoolers, the large public investment in ECE, and the belief that high-quality ECE is critical for promoting early development. Programs such as Head Start have generously funded quality improvement systems. State pre-K programs vary widely in terms of the level of monitoring and professional development (Friedman-Kraus et al., 2019). State and local initiatives such as Quality Rating and Improvement Systems rate the quality of participating child care settings and offer opportunities for quality improvement (Build Initiative & Child Trends, 2014). The directors of many centers and some child care homes encourage professional development (PD) among their staff (Datta, 2013).

The focus on improving ECE quality within Head Start, public pre-K, and community child care has resulted in large expenditures within these programs. While there are many PD programs for improving ECE quality, relatively few have been evaluated and even fewer have evidence that they improve ECE quality or child outcomes. It is not clear why some PD programs are more effective than others, but there are several likely explanations. First, the extent to which the PD successfully implements the intended changes in teaching practices is always a question. Second, many PD programs focus on improving aspects of quality that are only modestly related to child outcomes (Pianta, Barnett, Burchinal, & Thornburg, 2009).

Professional development for ECE teachers is increasingly a central focus of efforts to increase the magnitude of ECE program impacts (Martinez-Beck & Zaslow, 2006). PD is often used to help child care providers improve the overall quality of their settings. Most PD for improving ECE quality postulates that adults learn new knowledge and skills through reflections on their own practice and interactions with content experts over extended periods of time (Bransford, Brown, & Cocking, 1999), and most such training emphasizes active learning and collaborations with PD staff and/or other teachers (e.g., Wayne, Yoon, Zhu, Cronen, & Garet, 2008).

The focus of the most effective PD involves improving process quality scores, teaching specific teaching practices, or teaching a pedagogical framework (Burchinal et al., 2015). Many PD programs attempt to improve ECE quality through training with ECE quality measures such as the ECERS or CLASS. The focus is on improving quality to improve child outcomes. For example, MyTeachingPartner provides online consultation and coaching aligned with the CLASS (Pianta, Mashburn, Downer, Hamre, & Justice, 2008). Other PD programs use workshops and/or coaches to support teachers' use of specific curricula. These programs seek to promote the implementation of a curriculum already in use, a new curriculum, or adaptations to ongoing practice or curricula. Their focus is on improving teaching practices that have been shown to improve child outcomes. For example, PD for Head Start teachers was developed to improve literacy instruction through teaching and coaching practices that had been shown to be effective in prior research (Powell, Diamond, Burchinal, & Koehler, 2010). Finally, a third type of PD seeks to help teachers improve the quality of their teaching in terms of their lessons or practices within a common pedagogical or content framework. Here, the focus is on improving practices advocated by that framework in the belief they will improve child outcomes. For example, it is widely believed that support for the home language is important for dual language learners so PD for Head Start teachers was developed to incorporate Spanish literacy and Latino culture in the classroom where teachers did not speak Spanish (Buysse, Castro, & Peisner-Feinberg, 2010).

Although each of these three broad approaches embraces the emerging conceptualization of PD briefly described above (e.g., active participation of teachers for a semester or longer), the three approaches tend to have different theories of teacher change (see Burchinal et al., 2015, for details). Coaching is thought to improve ECE quality through experts' feedback on teachers' use of new instructional practices. Professional learning communities presumably improve ECE quality through collaborations with colleagues on lesson development and the collective discussion of reflections on the use of new lessons (Powell, Diamond, & Cockburn, 2012). Curricula should improve ECE quality through providing teachers and care providers with a set of organized activities organized around a pedagogical or content framework.

All of these types of PD are widely used, but evaluation of many PD programs has been limited (Desimone, 2009). Several studies have explicitly examined PD models for improving ECE quality, demonstrating success for PD models designed to improve ECE quality as measured by the ECERS (e.g., Bryant et al., 2009) and CLASS (e.g., Hamre et al., 2012; Pianta, Mashburn, Downer, Hamre, & Justice, 2008; Pianta et al., 2017), but not necessarily child outcomes. Other studies have demonstrated success in the extent to which programs explicitly designed to improve specific children's outcomes have changed both ECE quality and those outcomes in terms of literacy skills (e.g., Lonigan, Farver, Phillips, & Clancy-Menchetti, 2011; Powell et al., 2010), language skills (e.g., Wasik et al., 2006), and social skills (e.g., Raver et al., 2008). These studies demonstrated moderate to large gains in child outcomes within the content area that was the focus of instruction and sometimes in other areas. Finally, programs to change outcomes through implementation of a pedagogical framework have demonstrated some successes when applied to dual language learners (Espinosa, 2013). Most evaluations, however, do not systematically vary the PD and curriculum components, making it impossible to distinguish the effects of the PD and the curriculum components on child outcomes (Burchinal et al., 2015).

Attending workshops or courses is the most frequent form of PD (Datta, 2013) but typically does not change ECE quality and practices or child outcomes. A recent survey, the National Survey of Early Care and Education (NSECE), indicated that 84% of ECE teachers and 76% of home-based care providers reported attending workshops, and 32% of ECE teachers and 30% of home-based care providers reported attending classes (Datta, 2013) While most studies indicate that workshops are not effective in improving ECE quality, a few studies provide evidence that courses can be effective (Burchinal et al., 2015). A 14-week class based on the CLASS improved emotional and instructional interactions with students, levels of intentional teaching beliefs, and knowledge and skills in detecting effective interactions (effect sizes of .35 to .77) based on a randomized clinical trial (Hamre et al., 2012). ECE teachers' language and literacy practices were improved in a 15-week course plus coaching (effect size was .77) in a quasi-experimental study (Neuman & Cunningham, 2009) and in a six-day course on early literacy development (effect sizes of .48 to .60) in an experimental study (Dickinson & Caswell, 2007).

Coaching entails individualized support to a teacher or a teaching team by a content expert (e.g., early literacy specialist). The NSECE survey of care providers indicated that 29% of center teachers and 34% of home-based care providers had reported coaching during the past year (Datta, 2013). Coaching is also known as "consultation" or "mentoring." The coach observes teaching practices and provides tailored feedback on a teacher's efforts to implement recommended practices (Powell & Diamond, 2011). Coaching is often one component of a PD program that also includes introductory (e.g., Powell et al., 2010) or concurrent (e.g., Raver et al., 2008) workshops, an ongoing course (e.g., Neuman & Wright, 2010), and/or web resources that provide information and examples of recommended practices (Pianta, Mashburn, et al., 2008; Powell et al., 2010). Whereas few studies have examined each component in these multicomponent PD programs, two studies that contrasted the effects of coursework and coaching indicated that coaching was more effective than coursework in two ways, respectively: (a) changing the quality of literacy activities (Neuman & Wright, 2010) and (b) changing the quality of teacher-child interactions (LoCasale-Crouch et al., 2011).

Implementation of curricula designed to promote a pedagogical approach or learning within specific content areas has successfully improved ECE quality and child outcomes. Curricula designed to promote child development through self- and teacher-directed activities can improve ECE quality without associate gains in child outcomes (Preschool Curriculum Evaluation Research Consortium, 2008). Use of evidence-based curricula focused on scope and sequence of instruction within content areas has been related to substantial gains in children's literacy skills (e.g., Bierman et al., 2008; Neuman & Cunningham, 2009; Powell et al., 2010), math skills (e.g., Clements & Sarama, 2008), and social skills (Bierman et al., 2008; Raver et al., 2008). Some evidence indicates that use of more focused, sequenced curricula can produce large gains in child outcomes even within a large, publicly administered program, but most PD programs have limited evaluation and use practices with limited impacts on ECE quality and child outcomes (Weiland & Yoshikawa, 2013).

In summary, rigorous evaluation studies demonstrate that courses, coaching, and curricula can improve ECE quality and sometimes improve child outcomes, but most PD programs have limited evaluation (Burchinal et al., 2015).

Conclusion

The vast literature relating ECE experiences to child outcomes suggests that early development and learning are enhanced when children experience higher quality ECE, but that the magnitude of the associations between indicators of ECE quality and child outcomes vary widely. Overall, the literature indicates modest associations between gains in some child outcomes and some structural and process quality indicators (Burchinal, 2017). These associations tend to be quite small (e.g., effect sizes of .05 to .10) in statistically rigorous studies (e.g., Auger et al., 2015; Hong et al., 2019; Keys et al., 2013; Mashburn et al., 2008). Whereas findings from analyses of the National Center for Early Development and Learning pre-K study suggested that only process quality was related to child outcomes

(Mashburn et al., 2008; Sabol et al., 2013), findings from the most recent meta-analysis of six ECE projects found associations between some structural quality factors and child outcomes that were as large or larger than the associations between some process quality ratings and child outcomes (Hong et al., 2019). These findings raise questions about the current focus on improving process quality through professional development based on current ECE process quality measures. Increasing the focus on process quality in QRIS ratings is unlikely to produce substantial improvements in child outcomes.

Contrasting the ECE effect sizes on short-term child outcomes of widely used ECE process quality measures and of the most successful public ECE programs suggests that our current model of ECE quality may need to be adapted. The evaluations of publicly funded preschool programs report significant impacts on academic skills (with effect sizes of about .2 for Head Start and greater than .4 from the strongest pre-K programs). Associations between ECE process quality measures and child outcomes also were significant, but much smaller (with effect sizes of .1 and typically much smaller). The smaller associations for process quality than for publicly funded ECE programs challenge widely accepted views that ECE programs have their impact through providing children with high process quality. Similarly, the larger impacts of PD designed to improve instructional practices in specific content areas (e.g., Clements & Sarama, 2008; Powell et al., 2010; Raver et al., 2008) than of PD designed to improve process quality (e.g., Pianta et al., 2017) also indicate that improving process quality based on current measures is not sufficient. Overall, these findings suggest that ECE quality measures and professional development may need to place greater focus on instructional practices within content areas in order to increase the impact of ECE on child outcomes.

The findings also provide a much different image of the impacts of high-quality ECE when compared with the findings from the ECE early intervention studies such as Perry Preschool and Abecedarian Projects. There are many possible reasons. A major reason is likely that comparison groups in the early ECE intervention studies differ markedly from the comparison groups in today's studies (Duncan & Magnuson, 2013). The comparison groups in the earlier studies consisted primarily of low-income children who stayed home prior to kindergarten, whereas the comparison group in studies conducted in the past year consists of low-income children who attended other types of center care. Given that center care appears to be beneficial, especially for low-income children (Magnuson et al., 2007), this change in the "counterfactual" makes it more difficult to detect impacts now (Duncan & Magnuson, 2013). For example, Head Start impacts on children who attended the program appear to be much larger when those children are compared to children who attended center care, especially if they spoke Spanish at home (Bloom & Weiland, 2015).

Another reason might be the shift toward teaching academic skills to preschoolers. The earliest ECE studies and the early ECE intervention studies had their largest impacts on language skills, and promoting cognitive and language skills through frequent conversations was a major focus of the early ECE interventions (Campbell et al., 2012; Cunha & Heckman, 2007; McCartney, 1984; NICHD ECCRN & Duncan, 2003; Peisner-Feinberg & Burchinal, 1997). Teaching early literacy and numeracy skills in preschool became a focus about 20 years ago, and now ECE effect sizes for academic skills tend to be much larger than those for language and other cognitive skills such as executive functioning (e.g., Burchinal, 2017; Phillips et al., 2017; Puma et al., 2005). This is unfortunate because several studies suggest that cognitive skills, not academic skills, predict school-age academic and social skills. For example, recent studies found cognitive skills at entry to school such as vocabulary, general knowledge, and executive functioning related to the acquisition of academic skills in the elementary years, but academic skills at entry to school such as early reading and math skills did not[2] (Burchinal et al., 2020; Fuhs, Nesbitt, Farran, & Dong, 2014; Grissmer, Grimm, Aiyer, Murrah, & Steele, 2010; Pace, Alper, Burchinal, Golinkoff, & Hirsh-Pasek, 2017). Thus, it is likely that increased focus on academic skills and less focus on promoting language and other cognitive skills in ECE accounts for both part of the "fadeout" of ECE impacts on child outcomes and part of the discrepancy between the early ECE intervention studies and more recent ECE studies.

Finally, comparisons of the magnitude of the associations between child outcomes with both structural and process quality and with ECE program initiatives suggests we should extend our measurement of ECE quality. It appears that teaching programs that involve scope and sequence of instruction, a combination of hands-on learning and didactic instruction, and engaging age-appropriate content can have large impacts on children's early social and academic skills (e.g., Bierman et al., 2008; Clements & Sarama, 2008; Powell et al., 2010). Frequent warm and supportive interactions with caregivers that involve multi-turn conversations appear to provide children with the emotional base and cognitive stimulation to support early adjustment and development (Justice et al., 2008).

In conclusion, many children experience early care and education, often beginning in their first year, and the quality of those ECE experiences affects their early cognitive, academic, and social development. ECE quality tends to be moderately high for preschoolers, but varies depending on the child's age, ECE setting, and family background (Burchinal et al., 2015). Despite extensive efforts at professional development, we have remarkably little information about how successful many of those efforts are at quality improvement, and growing evidence that focusing on instructional practices is more effective at improving child outcomes than is focusing on ECE process quality. Improving the quality of ECE will likely involve thinking about effective ECE learning environments as a system and ensuring that all pieces—of curriculum and professional development—are integrated in a system. Ideally, this would entail using evidence-based developmentally appropriate curricula for which all teachers receive ongoing intensive professional development. Such an integrated, evidence-based system should provide teachers with the tools they need to be effective and all children with the opportunity to start elementary school with the skills to succeed.

Notes

1. It is important to note that almost all of the classrooms in these studies met the minimum guidelines for ratio and group size.

2. Note, all of these studies found academic skills at entry to school related positively to level of that skill during school years, but related negatively to gains over time in skill levels.

References

Aikens, N., Bush, C., Gleason, P., Malone, L., & Tarullo, L. (2016). Tracking quality in Head Start classrooms: FACES 2006 to FACES 2014 Technical Report (OPRE Report 2016-95). Washington, DC: Office of Planning, Research and Evaluation, Administration for Children and Families, U.S. Department of Health and Human Services. Retrieved from https://www.acf.hhs.gov/sites/default/files/opre/faces_cross_cohort_analysis_technical_report_final_b508.pdf

Ainsworth, M. D. S., Blehar, M., Waters, E., & Wall, S. (1978). *Patterns of attachment: A psychological study of the Strange Situation.* Hillsdale, NJ: Lawrence Erlbaum.

Auger, A., Farkas, G., Burchinal, M. R., Duncan, G. J., & Lowe, D. (2015). Preschool center care quality effects on academic achievement: An instrumental variables analysis. *Developmental Psychology, 50,* 2559–2571. doi:10.1037/a0037995

Berk, L. E., & Winsler, A. (1995). *Scaffolding children's learning: Vygotsky and early childhood education.* Washington, DC: National Association for the Education of Young Children.

Bierman, B. L., Domitrovich, C. E., Nix, R. L., Gest, S. D., Welsh, J. A., Greenberg, M. T., et al. (2008). Promoting academic and social-emotional school readiness: The Head Start REDI Program. *Child Development, 79,* 1802–1817. doi:10.1111/j.1467-8624.2008.01227.x

Bloom, H. S., & Weiland, C. (2015). Quantifying variation in Head Start effects on young children's cognitive and socio-emotional skills using data from the National Head Start Impact Study. Available at https://ssrn.com/abstract=2594430 or http://dx.doi.org/10.2139/ssrn.2594430

Bodrova, E., & Leong, D. J. (2007). *Tools of the mind: The Vygotskian approach to early childhood education.* Upper Saddle River, NJ: Pearson Education/Merrill.

Bransford, J. D., Brown, A. L., & Cocking, R. R. (Eds.). (1999). *How people learn: Brain, mind, experience and school.* Committee on Developments in the Science of Learning, National Research Council. Washington, DC: National Academies Press.

Bronfenbrenner, U., & Morris, P. A. (2006). The bioecological model of human development. In W. Damon & R. M. Lerner (Eds.), *Handbook of child psychology: Vol. 1. Theoretical models of human development* (6th ed., pp. 793–828). Hoboken, NJ: Wiley.

Bryant, D. M., Wesley, P. W., Burchinal, M., Sideris, J., Taylor, K., Fenson, C., et al. (2009). *The QUINCE-PFI study: An evaluation of a promising model for child care provider training: Final report.* Chapel Hill, NC: Frank Porter Graham Child Development Institute. Retrieved from http://www.researchconnections.org/childcare/resources/18531/pdf

Build Initiative & Child Trends. (2014). *A catalog and comparison of quality initiatives like quality rating and improvement systems* (QRIS) [Data system]. Retrieved from the QRIS Compendium website: http://qriscompendium.org

Burchinal, M. (2017) Measuring early care and education quality. *Child Development Perspectives, 12,* 3–9. doi:10.1111/cdep.12260

Burchinal, M., Foster, T. J., Bezdek, K. G., Bratsch-Hines, M., Blair, C., Vernon-Feagans, L., & Family Life Project Investigators. (2020). School-entry skills predicting school-age academic and social–emotional trajectories. *Early Childhood Research Quarterly, 51,* 67-80.

Burchinal, M., Magnuson, K., Powell, D., & Hong, S. (2015). Early childcare and education. In R. Lerner (Ed.), *Handbook of child psychology and developmental science* (7th ed., Vol. 4, pp. 1–45). Hoboken, NJ: Wiley.

Burchinal, M. R., Roberts, J. E., Riggins, R., Zeisel, S. A., Neebe, E., & Bryant, D. (2000). Relating quality of center-based child care to early cognitive and language development longitudinally. *Child Development, 71,* 339–357. doi:10.1111/1467-8624.00149

Burchinal, M., Vandergrift, N., Pianta, R., & Mashburn, A. (2010). Threshold analysis of association between child care quality and child outcomes for low-income children in pre-kindergarten programs. *Early Childhood Research Quarterly, 25,* 166–176. doi:10.1016/j.ecresq.2009.10.004

Burchinal, M., Vernon-Feagans, L., Vitiello, V., & Greenberg, M. T. (2014). Thresholds in the association between child care quality and child outcomes in rural preschool children. *Early Childhood Research Quarterly, 29*(1), 41–51. doi:10.1016/j.ecresq.2013.09.004

Burchinal, M., Zaslow, M., & Tarullo, L. (2016). Quality thresholds, features, and dosage in early care and education: Secondary data analyses of child outcomes. *Monographs of SRCD, 81*(2), doi:10.1111/mono.12236

Buysse, V., Castro, D. C., & Peisner-Feinberg, E. (2010). Effects of a professional development program on classroom practices and outcomes for Latino dual language learners. *Early Childhood Research Quarterly, 25*, 194–206. doi:10.1016/j.ecresq.2009.10.001

Campbell, F. A., Conti, G., Heckman, J. J., Moon, S. H., Pinto, R., Pungello, E., et al. (2014). Early childhood investments substantially boost adult health. *Science, 343*(6178), 1478–1485. doi:10.1126/science.1248429

Campbell, F. A., Pungello, E. P., Kainz, K., Burchinal, M., Pan, Y., Barbarin, O., et al. (2012). Adult outcomes as a function of an early childhood educational program: An Abecedarian project follow-up. *Developmental Psychology, 48*, 1033–1043. doi:10.1037/a0026644

Clarke-Stewart, K. A. (1998). Historical shifts and underlying themes in ideas about rearing young children in the United States: Where have we been? Where are we going? *Infant and Child Development, 7*(2), 101–117. doi:10.1002/(SICI)1099-0917(199806)

Clements, D. H., & Sarama, J. (2008). Experimental evaluation of the effects of a research-based preschool mathematics curriculum. *American Educational Research Journal, 45*, 443–494. doi:10.3102/0002831207312908

Cunha, F., & Heckman, J. (2007). The technology of skill formation. *American Economic Review, 97*(2), 31–47. doi:10.1257/aer.97.2.31

Datta, A. R. (2013*). Number and characteristics of early care and education (ECE) teachers and caregivers: Initial findings from the National Survey of Early Care and Education (NSECE)* (NSECE Research Brief/OPRE Report #2013-38). Retrieved from https://www.acf.hhs.gov/sites/default/files/opre/nsece_wf_brief_102913_0.pdf

Desimone, L. M. (2009). Improving impact studies of teachers' professional development: Toward better conceptualizations and measures. *Educational Researcher, 38*(3), 181–199.

Dickinson, D. K., & Caswell, L. (2007). Building support for language and early literacy in preschool classrooms through in-service professional development: Effects of the Literacy Environment Enrichment Program (LEEP). *Early Childhood Research Quarterly, 22*, 243–260. doi:10.1016/j.ecresq.2007.03.001

Duncan, G. J., & Magnuson, K. (2013). Investing in preschool programs. *Journal of Economic Perspectives, 27*(2), 109–132. doi:10.1257/jep.27.2.109

Early, D. M., Maxwell, K. L., Burchinal, M., Alva, S., Bender, R. H., Bryant, D., et al. (2007). Teachers' education, classroom quality, and young children's academic skills: Results from seven studies of preschool programs. *Child Development, 78*, 558–580. doi:10.1111/j.1467-8624.2007.01014.x

Espinosa, L. M. (2013). *Challenging common myths about dual language learners: An update to the seminal 2008 report.* New York, NY: Foundation for Child Development. Retrieved from https://www.fcd-us.org/prek-3rd-challenging-common-myths-about-dual-language-learners-an-update-to-the-seminal-2008-report/

Farran, D. C., & Lipsey, M. W. (2015). Expectations of sustained effects from scaled up pre-K: Challenges from the Tennessee study. *Evidence Speaks Reports, 1*(3). Retrieved from https://www.brookings.edu/research/expectations-of-sustained-effects-from-scaled-up-pre-k-challenges-from-the-tennessee-study/

Friedman-Krauss, A. H., Barnett, W. S., Garver, K. A., Hodges, K. S., Weisenfeld, G. G., & DiCrecchio, N. (2019). The State of Preschool 2018: State Preschool Yearbook. *National Institute for Early Education Research.*

Fuhs, M. W., Nesbitt, K. T., Farran, D. C., & Dong, N. (2014). Longitudinal associations between executive functioning and academic skills across content areas. *Developmental Psychology, 50*(6), 1698–709. http://doi.org/10.1037/a0036633

Fukkink, F., & Lont, A. (2007). Does training matter? A meta-analysis and review of caregiver training studies. *Early Childhood Research Quarterly, 22,* 294–311. doi:10.1016/j.ecresq.2007.04.005

Gopnik, A., Meltzoff, A. N., & Kuhl, P. (1999*). The scientist in the crib: What early learning tells us about the mind.* New York, NY: HarperCollins.

Greenberg, M. T. (2007). Next steps for federal child care policy. *The Future of Children, 17*(2), 73–96. doi:10.1353/foc.2007.0016

Grissmer, D., Grimm, K. J., Aiyer, S. M., Murrah, W. M., & Steele, J. S. (2010). Fine motor skills and early comprehension of the world: Two new school readiness indicators. *Developmental Psychology, 46*(5), 1008-1018. 10.3389/fpsyg.2014.00469

Hamre, B. K. (2014). Teachers' daily interactions with children: An essential ingredient in effective early childhood programs. *Child Development Perspectives, 8,* 223–230. doi:10.1111/cdep.12090

Hamre, B. K., Pianta, R. C., Burchinal, M., Field, S., LoCasale-Crouch, J., Downer, J. T., et al. (2012). A course on effective teacher-child interactions: Effects on teacher beliefs, knowledge, and observed practice. *American Educational Research Journal, 49,* 88–123. doi:10.3102/0002831211434596

Harms, T., Clifford, R. M., & Cryer, D. (2014). Early Childhood Environment Rating Scale, third edition (ECERS-3). New York, NY: Teachers College. 1234 Amsterdam Avenue, New York, NY 10027.

Harms, T., Cryer, D., & Clifford, R. M. (2007). *Family Child Care Environment Rating Scale Revised Edition (FCCERS-R).* Teachers College Press. 1234 Amsterdam Avenue, New York, NY 10027

Harms, T., Cryer, D., Clifford, R. M., & Yazejian, N. (2017). *Infant/Toddler Environment Rating Scale (ITERS-3).* Teachers College Press. 1234 Amsterdam Avenue, New York, NY 10027.

Hatfield, B. E., Burchinal, M. R., Pianta, R. C., & Sideris, J. (2016). Thresholds in the association between quality of teacher–child interactions and preschool children's school readiness skills. *Early Childhood Research Quarterly, 36,* 561–571. doi:10.1016/j.ecresq. 2015.09.005

Heckman, J. J. (2011). The economics of inequality: The value of early childhood education. *American Educator, 35*(1), 31–35.

Herbst, C. M., & Tekin, E. (2010). Child care subsidies and child development. *Economics of Education Review, 29,* 618–638. doi:10.1016/j.econedurev.2010.01.002

Hestenes, L. L., Kintner-Duffy, V., Wang, Y. C., LaParo, K., Mims, S. U., Crosby, D., et al. (2014). Comparisons among quality measures in child care settings: Understanding the use of multiple measures in North Carolina's QRIS and their links to social-emotional development in preschool children. *Early Childhood Research Quarterly, 30,* 199–214. doi:10.1016/j.ecresq.2014.06.003

Hong, S. L. S., Sabol, T. J., Burchinal, M. R., Tarullo, L., Zaslow, M., & Peisner-Feinberg, E. S. (2019). ECE quality indicators and child outcomes: Analyses of six large child care studies. *Early Childhood Research Quarterly, 49,* 202-217.

Howes, C., Burchinal, M., Pianta, R., Bryant, D., Early D. M., & Clifford, R. (2008). Ready to learn? Children's pre-academic achievement in pre-kindergarten programs. *Early Childhood Research Quarterly, 23,* 27–50.

Howes, C., Rodning, C., Galluzzo, D. C., & Myers, L. (1988). Attachment and child care: Relationships with mother and caregiver. *Early Childhood Research Quarterly, 3,* 403–416. doi:10.1016/0885-2006(88)90037-3

Howes, C., & Spieker, S. (2008). Attachment relationships in the context of multiple caregivers. In J. Cassidy & P. R. Shaver (Eds.) *Handbook of attachment: Theory, research, and clinical applications* (pp. 317–332). New York, NY: Guilford Press.

Johnson, A. D., Martin, A., & Brooks-Gunn, J. (2013). Child care subsidies and school readiness in kindergarten. *Child Development, 84,* 1806–1822. doi:10.1111/cdev.12073

Justice, L. M., Mashburn, A., Pence, K. L., & Wiggins, A. (2008). Experimental evaluation of a preschool language curriculum: Influence on children's expressive language skills. *Journal of Speech, Language, and Hearing Research, 51,* 983–1001. doi:10.1044/1092-4388(2008/072)

Karoly, L. A., Schwartz, H. L., Setodji, C. M., & Haas, A. C. (2016). Evaluation of Delaware Stars for Early Success. Rand Corporation. Santa Monica, CA

Keys, T. D., Farkas, G., Burchinal, M. R., Duncan, G. J., Vand Snaell, D. L., Li, W., et al. (2013). Preschool center quality and school readiness: Quality effects and variation by demographic and child characteristics. *Child Development, 84,* 1171–1190. doi:10.1111/cdev.12048

Lazar, I., Darlington, R., Murray, H., Royce, J., & Snipper, A. (1982). Lasting effects of early education: A report from the Consortium for Longitudinal Studies. *Monographs of the Society for Research in Child Development, 47*(2–3 Serial No. 195), 55–66.

Lipscomb, S. T., Weber, R. B., Green, B. L., & Patterson, L. B. (2016). Oregon's Quality Rating Improvement System (QRIS) Validation Study One: Associations with observed program quality. Corvallis, OR: Oregon State University.

LoCasale-Crouch, J., Kraft-Sayre, M., Pianta, R. C., Hamre, B. K., Downer, J. T., Leach, A., et al. (2011). Implementing an early childhood professional development course across 10 sites and 15 sections: Lessons learned. *NHSA Dialog, 14*(4), 275–292.

Lonigan, C. J., Farver, J. M., Phillips, B. M., & Clancy-Menchetti, J. (2011). Promoting the development of preschool children's emergent literacy skills: A randomized evaluation of a literacy-focused curriculum and two professional development models. *Reading and Writing, 24,* 305–337. doi:10.1007/s11145-009-9214-6

Ludwig, J., & Miller, D. L. (2007). Does Head Start improve children's life chances? Evidence from a regression discontinuity design. *Quarterly Journal of Economics, 122*(1), 159–208. doi.org/10.1162/qjec.122.1.159

Magnuson, K. A., Meyers, M. K., Ruhm, C. J., & Waldfogel, J. (2004). Inequality in preschool education and school readiness. *American Educational Research Journal, 41*(1), 115–157. doi:10.3102/00028312041001115

Magnuson, K. A., Ruhm, C., & Waldfogel, J. (2007). Does prekindergarten improve school preparation and performance? *Economics of Education Review, 26*(1), 33–51. doi:10.1016/j.econedurev.2005.09.008

Martinez-Beck, I., & Zaslow, M. (2006). Introduction: The context for critical issues in early childhood professional development. In M. Zaslow & I. Martinez-Beck (Eds.), *Critical issues in early childhood professional development* (pp. 1–16). Baltimore, MD: Brookes.

Mashburn, A. J., Pianta, R. C., Barbarin, O. A., Bryant, D., Hamre, B. K., Downer, J., et al. (2008). Measures of classroom quality in prekindergarten and children's development of academic, language, and social skills. *Child Development, 79,* 732–749. doi:10.1111/j.1467-8624.2008.01154.x

McCartney, K. (1984). Effect of quality of day care environment on children's language development. *Developmental Psychology, 20*(2), 244.260 doi.org/10.1037/0012-1649.20.2.244-2

McCartney, K., Burchinal, M., Clarke-Stewart, A., Bub, K. L., Owen, M. T., & Belsky, J. (2010). Testing a series of causal propositions relating time in child care to children's externalizing behavior. *Developmental Psychology, 46,* 1–17. doi:10.1037/a0017886

Minervino, J. (2014). *Lessons from research and the classroom.* Retrieved from https://docs.gatesfoundation.org/documents/Lessons%20from%20Research%20and%20the%20Classroom_September%202014.pdf

National Association for the Education of Young Children. (2009). *Developmentally appropriate practice in early childhood programs serving children from birth through age 8* [Position statement]. Retrieved from https://www.naeyc.org/files/naeyc/file/positions/PSDAP.pdf

Neuman, S. B., & Cunningham, L. (2009). The impact of professional development and coaching on early language and literacy instructional practices. *American Educational Research Journal*, *46*(2), 532–566.

Neuman, S. B., & Wright, T. S. (2010). Promoting language and literacy development for early childhood educations: A mixed-methods study of coursework and coaching. *Elementary School Journal*, *111*, 63–86. doi:10.1086/653470

NICHD Early Child Care Research Networkk. (1997). Familial factors associated with characteristics of nonmaternal care for infants. *Journal of Marriage and the Family*, *59*, 389–408. doi:10.2307/353478

NICHD Early Child Care Research Network. (1999). Child Outcomes when child-care center classes meet recommended standards for quality. *American Journal of Public Health*, *89*(7), 1072–1077

NICHD Early Child Care Research Network. (2002). Child-care structure → process → outcome: Direct and indirect effects of child-care quality on young children's development. *Psychological Science*, *13(3)*, 199–206. doi:10.1111/1467-9280.00438

NICHD Early Child Care Research Network, & Duncan, G. J. (2003). Modeling the impacts of child care quality on children's preschool cognitive development. *Child development*, *74*(5), 1454-1475.

Office of Head Start. (2018). *History of Head Start*. Retrieved from https://www.acf.hhs.gov/ohs/about/history-of-head-start

Office of Planning, Research, and Evaluation. (2018). *Head start family and child experiences survey (FACES), 1997–2022*. Retrieved from https://www.acf.hhs.gov/opre/research/project/head-start-family-and-child-experiences-survey-faces

Organisation for Economic Co-operation and Development. (2018). *Early childhood education and care*. Retrieved from http://www.oecd.org/els/family/database.htm

Pace, A., Alper, R., Burchinal, M., Golinkoff, R., & Hirsh-Pasek, K. (2017). *Measuring success: Within- and cross-domain predictors of academic and social trajectories in elementary school*. Paper presented at the biennial meeting of the Society for Research in Child Development, Austin, TX.

Peisner-Feinberg, E. S., & Burchinal, M. R. (1997). Relations between preschool children's child-care experiences and concurrent development: The cost, quality, and outcomes study. *Merrill-Palmer Quarterly*, *43*, 451–477.

Phillips, D., A, & Adams, G. (2001). Child care and our youngest children. *The Future of Children*, *11*(1), 35–51. doi:10.2307/1602808

Phillips, D. A., Lipsey, M. W., Dodge, K. A., Haskins, R., Bassok, D., Burchinal, M. R., et al. (2017). *Puzzling it out: The current state of scientific knowledge on pre-kindergarten effects*. Retrieved from https://www.brookings.edu/wp-content/uploads/2017/04/consensus-statement_final.pdf

Phillipsen, L., Burchinal, M., Howes, C., & Cryer, D. (1997). The prediction of process quality from structural features of child care. *Early Childhood Research Quarterly*, *12*(3), 281–303. doi:10.1016/S0885-2006(97)90004-1

Pianta, R., Barnett, W. S., Burchinal, M., & Thornburg, K. R. (2009). The effects of preschool education: What we know, how public policy is or is not aligned with the evidence base, and what we need to know. *Psychological Science in the Public Interest*, *10*, 49–88. doi:10.1177/1529100610381908

Pianta, R., Hamre, B., Downer, J., Burchinal, M., Williford, A., LoCasale-Crouch, J., et al. (2017). Early childhood professional development: Coaching and coursework effects on indicators of children's school readiness. *Early Education and Development*, *28*, 956–975. Retrieved from https://doi.org/10.1080/10409289.2017.1319783

Pianta, R., Howes, C., Burchinal, M., Bryant, D., Clifford, R. M., Early, D. M., et al. (2005). Features of pre-kindergarten programs, classrooms, and teachers: Prediction of observed classroom quality and teacher-child interactions. *Applied Developmental Science*, *9*(3), 144–159.

Pianta, R., La Paro, K. M., & Hamre, B. K. (2008). *Classroom assessment scoring system (Pre-K)*. Baltimore, MD: Brookes.

Pianta, R., Mashburn, A., Downer, J., Hamre, B., & Justice, L. (2008). Effects of web-mediated professional development resources on teacher-child interactions in pre-kindergarten classrooms. *Early Childhood Research Quarterly, 23*, 431–451. doi:10.1016/j.ecresq.2008.02.001

Powell, D. R., & Diamond, K. E. (2011). Improving the outcomes of coaching-based PD interventions. In S. B. Neuman & D. K. Dickinson (Eds.), *Handbook of early literacy research* (Vol. 3, pp. 295–307). New York, NY: Guilford.

Powell, D. R., Diamond, K. E., Burchinal, M. R., & Koehler, M. J. (2010). Effects of an early literacy professional development intervention on Head Start teachers and children. *Journal of Educational Psychology, 102*, 299–312. doi:10.1037/a0017763

Powell, D. R., Diamond, K. E., & Cockburn, M. K. (2012). Promising approaches to professional development for early childhood educators. In O. N. Saracho & B. Spodek (Eds.), *Handbook of research on the education of young children* (3rd ed., pp. 385–392). New York, NY: Routledge.

Preschool Curriculum Evaluation Research Consortium. (2008). *Effects of preschool curriculum programs on school readiness: Report from the Preschool Curriculum Evaluation Research Initiative* (NCER 2008–2009). Washington, DC: National Center for Education Research. Retrieved from https://ies.ed.gov/pubsearch/pubsinfo.asp?pubid=NCER20082009rev

Puma, M., Bell, S., Cook, R., Heid, C., Broene, P., Jenkins, F., et al. (2012). *Third grade follow-up to the head start impact study: Final report* (OPRE Report 2012-45). Washington, DC: U.S. Department of Health and Human Services, Administration for Children and Families. Retrieved from https://www.acf.hhs.gov/sites/default/files/opre/head_start_report.pdf

Puma, M., Bell, S., Cook, R., Heid, C., & Lopez, M. (2005). *Head Start impact study: First year findings*. Washington, DC: U.S. Department of Health and Human Services, Administration for Children and Families. Retrieved from http://www.acf.hhs.gov/sites/default/files/opre/first_yr_finds.pdf

Quick, H. E., Hawkinson, L. E., Holod, A., Anthony, J., Muenchow, S., Cannon, J. S., et al. (2016). Independent Evaluation of California's Race to the Top–Early Learning Challenge Quality Rating and Improvement System: Cumulative Technical Report. San Mateo, CA: American Institutes for Research.

Raver, C. C., Jones, S. M., Li-Grining, C. P., Metzger, M., Smallwood, K., & Sardin, L. (2008). Improving preschool classroom processes: Preliminary findings from a randomized trial implemented in Head Start settings. *Early Childhood Research Quarterly, 23*, 10–26. doi:10.1016/j.ecresq.2007.09.001

Reynolds, A. J., Magnuson, K. A., & Ou, S. R. (2010). Preschool-to-third grade programs and practices: A review of research. *Children and Youth Services Review, 3*, 1121–1131. doi:10.1016/j.childyouth.2009.10.017

Sabol, T. J. & Pianta, R. C. (2015). Validating Virginia's quality rating and improvement system among state-funded pre-kindergarten programs. *Early Childhood Research Quarterly*, 183–198. doi:10.1016/j.ecresq.2014.03.004

Sabol, T. J., Soliday Hong, S. L., Pianta, R. C., & Burchinal, M. R. (2013). Can ratings of pre-K programs predict children's learning? *Science, 341*, 845–846. doi:10.1126/science.1233517

Schulman, K., & Blank, H. (2008). *State child care assistance policies 2008: Too little progress for children and families*. Washington, DC: National Women's Law Center. Retrieved from http://www.nwlc.org/sites/default/files/pdfs/StateChildCareAssistancePoliciesReport08.pdf

Soliday Hong, S. L. S., Howes, C., Marcella, J., Zucker, E., & Huang, Y. (2014). Quality rating and improvement systems: Validation of a local implementation in LA County and children's school-readiness. *Early Childhood Research Quarterly, 30*, 227–240.

Sylva, K., Melhuish, E., Sammons, P., Siraj-Blatchford, I., & Taggart, B. (2012). Pre-school quality and educational outcomes at age 11: Low quality has little benefit. *Journal of Early Childhood Research, 9,* 109–124. doi:10.1177/1476718X10387900

Thornburg, K. R., Mayfield, W. A., Hawks, J. S., & Fuger, K. L. (2009, October). *The Missouri quality rating system school readiness study.* Columbia, MO: Center for Family Policy and Research.

Tout, K., Cleveland, J., Li, W., Starr, R., Soli, M., & Bultinck, E. (2016). Parent Aware: Minnesota's quality rating and improvement system: Initial validation report. Minneapolis, MN: Child Trends.

Vandell, D. L., & Corasaniti, M. A. (1988). The relation between third graders' after-school care and social, academic, and emotional functioning. *Child Development, 59,* 868–875. doi:10.1111/j.1467-8624.1988.tb03240.x

Votruba-Drzal, E., Coley, R. L., & Chase-Lansdale, P. L. (2004). Child care and low-income children's development: Direct and moderated effects. *Child Development, 75,* 296–312. doi:10.1111/j.1467-8624.2004.00670.x

Vygotsky, D. H. (2001). *Pedagogy.* London and New York: RoutledgeFalmer.

Wasik, B. A., Bond, M. A., & Hindeman, A. (2006). The effects of a language and literacy intervention on Head Start children and teachers. *Journal of Educational Psychology, 98,* 63–74. doi:10.1037/0022-0663.98.1.63

Wayne, A. J., Yoon, K. S., Zhu, P., Cronen, S., & Garet, M. S. (2008). Experimenting with teacher professional development: Motives and methods. *Educational Researcher, 37,* 469–479. doi:10.3102/0013189X08327154

Weiland, C., Ulvestad, K., Sachs, J., & Yoshikawa, H. (2013). Associations between classroom quality and children's vocabulary and executive function skills in an urban public prekindergarten program. *Early Childhood Research Quarterly, 28*(2), 199–209. doi:10.1016/j.ecresq.2012.12.002

Weiland, C., & Yoshikawa, H. (2013). Impacts of a prekindergarten program on children's mathematics, language, literacy, executive function, and emotional skills. *Child Development, 84,* 2112–2130. doi:10.1111/cdev.12099

Yazejian, N., Franco, X., Morgan, J., & Simpson, T. (2016). *North Carolina star rated license (QRIS) validation study.* Retrieved from https://files.nc.gov/ncelc/fpg_nc_qris_presentation_10-12-16_final.pdf

Zellman, G. L., & Perlman, M. (2008). *Child-care quality rating and improvement systems in five pioneer states: Implementation and lessons learned.* Santa Monica, CA: RAND. Retrieved from http://www.rand.org/content/dam/rand/pubs/monographs/2008/RAND_MG795.pdf

Zellman, G. L., Perlman, M., Le, V., & Setodji, C. M. (2008). *Assessing the validity of the Qualistar early learning quality rating improvement system as a tool for improving child-care quality.* Santa Monica, CA: RAND.

Chapter 10

Toward Deeper and More Policy-Relevant Evidence on Early Childhood Programs

Jacqueline Jones

Foundation for Child Development

Over the past 50 years, significant progress has been made in the United States to improve young children's learning and development. The federal government has supported a variety of early childhood initiatives such as Head Start and Early Head Start, the Child Care and Development Block Grant, Title I of the Elementary and Secondary Education Act, and the Individuals with Disabilities Education Act. In addition, under the Obama administration (2009–2017), the Department of Health and Human Services and the Education Department received significant resources through the American Recovery and Reinvestment Act of 2009. These funds supported systems-building initiatives such as the Race to the Top–Early Learning Challenge, incentives for innovative practices such as the Investing in Innovation Fund (i3), and placed-based strategies such as Promise Neighborhoods (Lombardi, Harding, Connors, & Friedman-Krauss, 2016).

Furthermore, increasing numbers of states have targeted resources to support early childhood programs. As reported in the 2017 *State of Preschool Yearbook* (published annually by the National Institute for Early Education Research; Friedman-Krauss, Barnett, Weisenfeld, Kasmin, DiCrecchio, & Horowitz, 2018), states invested more money than ever in preschool (though, with adjustments for inflation, per-child spending across states actually *fell* for the first time since 2014). In addition, cities across the country have made investments in early education (CityHealth & National Institute for Early Education Research, 2019). Promising child outcomes have been reported from Boston (Weiland & Yoshikawa, 2013) and Tulsa (Phillips, Gormley, & Anderson, 2016), and other municipalities are devoting public resources to support young children's learning and development prior to kindergarten.

This chapter will discuss what has been learned about the impact of early childhood programs, what remains to be understood, and how these research findings can inform public policy more effectively. While early childhood programs span the continuum of birth through age 8 and operate from multiple funding sources and in a variety of settings, the strongest body of empirical evidence comes from examinations of the effectiveness of publicly funded preschool programs. Given this robust body of research, this discussion will focus primarily on research from these programs. With substantial public funds devoted to early childhood programs and many cities and states looking to make these programs available to every child in residence, policy makers need empirical evidence that will help them better understand the essential components of program design and which components, or constellation of components, are most effective in achieving strong outcomes for specific subgroups of children. The chapter will also discuss the challenge of connecting research to policy in partnerships that are long term, respectful of the perspectives and expertise of researchers and policy makers, and mutually beneficial.

State of the Knowledge

Three landmark early intervention programs of the 1960s and 1970s, the Perry Preschool Program (Heckman, Moon, Pinto, Savelyev, & Yavitz, 2010b; Yoshikawa et al., 2013), the Chicago Parent Child Program (Reynolds, Ou, & Temple, 2018), and the Abecedarian Project in North Carolina (Campbell, Pungello, Miller-Johnson, Burchinal, & Ramey, 2001), were well-defined, small-scale, targeted interventions that were rigorously designed, implemented by highly trained staff, and subjected to long-term follow-up studies. Together these programs reported gains into adulthood which suggest that program participants are more likely to achieve higher reading and math scores, graduate from high school, delay childbearing, achieve higher rates of college enrollment, hold a job, and commit fewer crimes than non–program participants (Heckman, Moon, Pinto, Savelyev, & Yavitz, 2010a; Heckman et al., 2010b; Schweinhart et al., 2005). These studies and their longitudinal data provided the research base needed by early childhood advocates who sought support to increase access to early childhood intervention programs that would yield long-term positive outcomes.

However, the long-term gains have not always been realized in subsequent programs (Center on the Developing Child, Harvard University, 2016; Meloy, Gardner, & Darling-Hammond, 2019; U.S. Department of Health and Human Services, 2010). In addition, the opportunity/achievement gap continues to persist for poor and minoritized children (Bassok, Finch, Lee, Reardon, & Waldfogel, 2016; Magnuson & Waldfogel, 2016; Reardon & Portilla, 2016).

Typically, when public funds are used to support early childhood programs, there is an underlying assumption that the interventions will yield long-term positive results for young children. As program offerings have increased over time, researchers' attempts to gather empirical data on the long-term impact of early childhood education intervention on children, families and communities have met with mixed results. Brooks-Gunn (2003) argued that the expectations of preschool interventions may not be realistic and stated, "It is magical thinking to expect that if we intervene in the early years, no further help will be needed by children in the elementary school years and beyond" (p. 3).

Yoshikawa et al. (2013) looked beyond the 40-plus-year-old Perry and Abecedarian studies to more recent data from studies in Tulsa (Phillips et al., 2016) and Boston (Weiland & Yoshikawa, 2013) to advocate for the benefits of large-scale, locally funded preschool programs. They argued that more contemporary programs could also benefit social-emotional development, and they stressed the importance of "stimulating and supportive interactions between teachers and children and effective use of curricula" (p. 1).

Effective implementation of curricula focusing on specific domains such as language and literacy, math, and socio-emotional development also appeared important. However, Yoshikawa et al. (2013) acknowledged that few programs appeared to provide excellent quality and that coaching and mentoring for teachers was an important aspect to ensure a high level of instructional support. For children from low-income homes, the researchers concluded that a second year of preschool produced additional benefits, although the gains might be smaller than those of the first year. Although Yoshikawa et al. recognized that the evidence for long-term effects of preschool interventions is mixed, they argued that long-term benefits do occur.

The complexities of program implementation and evaluation were highlighted in a randomized control trial of the Tennessee Voluntary Prekindergarten (TN-VPK) program conducted by researchers from Vanderbilt University (Lipsey, Farran, & Durkin, 2018; Lipsey, Farran, & Hofer, 2015). The TN-VPK is a full-day prekindergarten program for 4-year-old children who will enter kindergarten the following school year. The Tennessee State Board of Education's standards required classroom teachers to hold a license in early childhood development and education; they also required a maximum class size of 20 and use of an approved age-appropriate curriculum. A randomized control trial was designed to determine whether the children who participated in the TN-VPK program made greater academic and behavioral gains in areas that prepared them for later schooling than comparable children who do not participate in the program. At the end of preschool, TN-VPK attendees had significantly higher achievement scores than those who did not attend, but this advantage disappeared by the end of kindergarten. By second grade, the TN-VPK children scored lower than the control group on most measures. The largest effects were seen with English learners regardless of mother's education status (Lipsey et al., 2015, p. 38). This negative trajectory is in contrast to other work on pre-K and has been subject to considerable conversation in the research community. For example, Meloy et al. (2019) have suggested that these results could be related to program quality and/or the methodological approach taken by the researchers.

Despite this negative finding, when researchers synthesize research across studies, there is still some level of agreement on what constitutes effective early childhood experiences. Researchers from Harvard's Center on the Developing Child (2016) have looked across a range of interventions and identified five key characteristics of programs that have been associated consistently with positive child outcomes. In these programs, there is a focus on supporting maternal and child health and nutrition before, during, and after pregnancy. The programs work to build caregiver skills, match interventions to sources of stress, improve the quality of the broader caregiving environment, and establish clear goals and appropriately target curriculum. Together, these characteristics highlight the importance of attending to multiple elements in early childhood programs, including health and well-being, program design, and caregiver quality.

In another synthesis, Philips et al. (2017) considered the variations in research findings across a variety of research studies and were able to define a set of six consensus points around what is known about the effectiveness of preschool programs (Phillips et al., 2017):

1. Preschoolers from economically disadvantaged circumstances and dual language learners often exhibit greater improvement in learning at the end of the preschool year than more advantaged and English-proficient young children.

2. Preschool programs vary in their effectiveness. An evidence-based curriculum, coaching for teachers, and classroom management may be factors contributing to program effectiveness.

3. The quality of early learning experiences before, during, and after preschool can contribute to the trajectory of children's learning. Early elementary school classrooms that provide individualization and differentiation in instructional content and strategies appear most effective.

4. Overall, children attending a diverse array of state and school district preschool programs are more ready for school at the end of their pre-K year than children who do not attend pre-K, with the most common improvements in literacy and numeracy.

5. There is little convincing evidence on the longer term impacts of scaled-up pre-K programs on academic outcomes and school progress. Existing evidence suggests that improvements in learning are detectable during elementary school, but studies also reveal zero or negative longer term impacts for some programs.

6. States should continue innovation and evaluation during and after preschool to monitor improvement in creating and maintaining children's learning gains. Research-practice partnerships are a promising strategy.

These points of consensus highlight the importance of understanding how certain contextual variables operate in early childhood programs. The demographics of the children served, the nature of the program's curriculum and the instructional practices, and the support for teachers can explain, and perhaps predict, short- and long-term gains for young children.

In an attempt to improve the quality of instruction for young children, Farran, Meador, Christopher, Nesbitt, and Bilbrey (2017) partnered with a school district to examine instructional practices in public school classrooms for 4-year-olds. They reported that eight instructional practices appeared to be consistently related to positive gain. The practices were labeled by the school staff as "the Magic 8":

1. Reducing transition time (routines and wait time for children)

2. Increasing the quality of instruction

3. Creating a more positive emotional climate

4. Teachers listening more to children

5. Providing more sequential activities

6. Fostering social learning (associative and cooperative) interactions

7. Fostering higher levels of child involvement

8. Creating more math opportunities. (Farran et al., 2017, p. 1474)

These types of efforts to work directly with schools and school districts are showing potential to generate more fine-tuned information that can be applied to policy and practice. More formal researcher-practitioner partnerships will be discussed later in this chapter.

Gaps in Our Knowledge

While much has been learned about early childhood programs, there is still much to be understood about the conditions under which certain program components, or constellations of components, may have a positive or negative impact on specific subgroups of young children. Typically, the evaluation of an early childhood program is designed to answer the question, *Does the program work?* Randomly assigning children to treatment and control groups to determine if the two groups demonstrate significant mean differences at various points in time allows causal inferences to be made regarding the differential impact of the program on the two groups of children. While such studies are considered the gold standard in program evaluation, they can leave researchers and policy makers with sparse understanding of the conditions within which the group differences did, or did not, occur and what program components were effective, or not, for certain children. In their review of the impact of a variety of preschool programs, Duncan and Magnuson (2013) raised a set of issues that should be considered if we are to engage in large-scale support of early childhood programs. They argued that more needs to be understood about how program components are connected to child outcomes, how program effects develop over time, and which skills (or constellation of skills) might produce improved outcomes in later life.

Reframing the Research Questions. As previously stated, early childhood program evaluations are often framed to answer the question, *Did it work?* However, the guiding question of the social sciences is not limited to "what works." Social scientists have long claimed to work toward answering the broader question of "what works, for whom, under what conditions" (Nielsen & Miraglia, 2017; Office of Planning, Research and Evaluation, 2016). Researchers from Harvard's Center on the Developing Child (2016) have argued that "the ultimate success of a child-centered or adult-focused program in achieving population-level impact depends upon the ability to learn what works (and doesn't) for whom, when, in what context(s)—and why" (p. 35).

What Works? What's the "It"? As Phillips et al. (2017) asserted, early childhood programs are not monolithic. They can vary widely in target population, the nature and scope of services, program dosage, and the expertise of the adults implementing the intervention. Examination of any given program's impacts would benefit greatly from a clear description of the program's components and the theory of change that underlies the intervention (Center on the Developing Child, Harvard University, 2016; Metz, Halle, Bartley, & Blasberg, 2013). Blase and Fixen (2013) argue that without greater specificity regarding the description and specification of core program components, it becomes difficult to assess a program's implementation, evaluation, improvement, and scale-up with certainty.

For Whom? In program evaluation, a clear description of the target population is essential; studies should indicate how the treatment group is similar, along a specific set of characteristics, to the population on whom the intervention was validated. Although age, socioeconomic level, eligibility for free- or reduced-price lunch, race, and ethnicity are traditional and useful descriptors of the target populations in early childhood programs, they may not portray the full range of contextual variables that have an impact on the effectiveness of the intervention. For example, are subsets of children in the target population experiencing the challenges of food insecurity, housing instability, exposure to domestic violence, drug abuse, or discrimination based on racial, ethnic, linguistic, or immigration status? These children may exhibit differential responses to various program components.

In addition, the control group warrants careful attention in early childhood education evaluations. As access to early childhood programs increases, there is an enhanced need to understand the potentially changing nature of the counterfactual. Few early childhood education opportunities were available during implementation of the Perry Preschool program, and the control group could be described as receiving no other formal early learning experiences. However, as state, local, and privately operated programs have developed, recent studies have reported control subjects who may have participated in other early childhood programs or, in some cases, participated in the intervention itself (Meloy et al., 2019; U.S. Department of Health and Human Services, 2010). The experiences of the control group can change the research question. Is the treatment group being compared to a control group that has experienced no other formal early childhood intervention? Or is the treatment group being compared to a control group that has experienced another (or the same) intervention? This distinction has significant policy implications for the inferences that can be made from the data and for effective allocation of resources.

Under What Conditions? An intervention occurs in a specific place and within the political, social, economic, racial, and linguistic context of that place. Descriptions of the conditions or context of the intervention include the program's financial, political, and cultural contexts; whether all treatment implementing professionals received comparable training; whether all participants received the same manner and dosage of the treatment, and whether, as a result, there were differential subgroup responses to the intervention. In addition, factors such as teacher competencies and turnover, program or school resources, and quality of school leadership may also interact with intervention efficacy. Considering these contextual factors will help clarify implementation influences, including local factors responsible for successful treatment enactment and different contexts, from treatment relationship to outcomes.

Some Challenges

Given the gaps in the research base on early childhood education, it may not be prudent to expect to fill the existing gaps in our knowledge of early childhood interventions by employing a *business as usual* approach. Precise definitions of the intervention and of the control and treatment groups, and a clearer understanding of the conditions within which the intervention was implemented, call for a move away from the status quo (Center on the Developing Child, Harvard University, 2016).

Methodological Issues

Moving research questions from *Does the program work?* to *Under what conditions do specific program components, or constellations of components, work best for certain children?* requires an openness to rigorous mixed-methods evaluation models. Methodological designs may need to be developed to answer a broader set of questions that are intended to tell the story of a specific program's implementation within a particular context. The gold-standard randomized controlled trials can be supplemented with high-quality qualitative studies that allow for a more complete understanding of the context in which the intervention was implemented. In addition, new tools may need to be developed to help identify and measure issues of equity, diversity, and inclusion, since these factors may interact with the early childhood intervention (Curenton et al., 2019)

Research to Policy Issues

Yet broadening the methodological design and enhancing the richness of the data are irrelevant unless the inferences and conclusions from empirical evidence resonate with the issues that policy makers face as they work to determine whether and how public funds should be allocated for early childhood programs. Ideally, policy makers would rely on the inferences and conclusions from empirical studies to inform their decisions. However, this is not always the case. Researchers express frustration with their perception that policy makers ignore research findings; policy makers claim to be unable to access the data they need, when they need it (Tseng, Easton, & Supplee, 2017). The researchers' meticulous attention to design, analysis, and interpretation of data may be undervalued in the policy makers' rapid-paced political context. Although frustrations exist on both sides, there is evidence that partnerships are emerging to bridge the research-policy gap (Boser & McDaniel, 2018; Foundation for Child Development, 2018; Roderick, Easton, & Bender Sebring, 2009; Tseng et al., 2017).

Promising Directions

The challenges of asking a more nuanced question than *Did the program work?* and of connecting research findings to policy are not new. However, they have become increasingly important as more programs are brought to scale and are supported by public funds. Fortunately, some approaches are developing that hold promise for each of these challenges.

Implementation Science

As early childhood researchers face the challenge of designing studies that provide empirical data on the effectiveness of interventions and the contexts in which they are delivered, the field of implementation science may help to create a framework for understanding and supporting early childhood interventions (Center on the Developing Child, Harvard University, 2016; Halle, Metz, & Martinez-Beck, 2013).

Martinez-Beck (2013) has defined implementation science as "the study of the process of implementing programs and practices that have research evidence suggesting they are worth replicating" (p. xix). An overarching framework for program implementation may facilitate an opportunity to define an intervention and highlight the local context in which the intervention might be implemented. Metz et al. (2013) outlined four iterative implementation stages: In *exploration*, researchers assess needs, examine fit and feasibility, operationalize a model, involve stakeholders, decide whether to move toward implementation. During *installation*, researchers acquire resources, make structural and instrumental changes, develop implementation supports, and prepare staff. During *initial implementation*, researchers initiate new services, manage change, and improve cycles. Finally, during *full implementation*, they focus on a full ramp-up through fine-tuned implementation and its outcomes, innovation, and development of standard practice. Building on this implementation framework, Franks and Schroeder (2013) outlined seven key areas that can fall within it, paraphrased here:

1. *Assessing readiness and capacity.* Assessing readiness to implement specific components and aspects of the identified model, before further investment is made in initiating a potentially costly implementation process.

2. *Structure of the implementation process.* Carefully articulating a methodology that is described up front so that the entities participating in the implementation process have a clear sense of the process and of what is expected of them.

3. *Engagement and buy-in.* Ensuring that participants in the implementation process have a clear sense of what is expected of them and are willing to actively participate in the implementation process.

4. *Program installation.* Transferring knowledge and new skills, which are acquired through a structured process of training, coaching, and technical assistance.

5. *Outcome evaluation and fidelity monitoring.* Monitoring model programs to ensure that they are being delivered with fidelity and are resulting in expected outcomes.

6. *Feedback and quality improvement.* Collecting data, not in isolation or for research purposes only, but for use in a systematic way for quality improvement and skill development.

7. *Innovation and adaptation.* Weighing the essential aspects of the intervention against a new local culture and context. It is necessary to ensure that the model is compatible with the local culture and context, and accommodations must often be made to ensure buy-in and successful implementation. However, care must be taken to ensure that innovations or adaptations do not compromise essential aspects of the model. (Franks & Schroeder, 2013, pp. 16–17)

The framework outlined above has potential to provide a systematic approach to bringing early childhood programs to scale. Defining the intervention and determining readiness for implementation, establishing a defined implementation structure, and ensuring stakeholder buy-in can frame the process so that program installation has an optimal chance for success. When evaluation, fidelity monitoring, and quality improvement are coordinated, it may be easier to understand what appears to be working, what seems problematic, and what is not getting the anticipated results. Through innovation and adaptation, the essential program components are tested against the new context to determine what can be scaled up in the specific setting and which groups of children can benefit from which program components.

Connecting Research to Policy Through Research-Policy-Practice Partnerships

As implementation science strategies can develop a better sense of the impact of specific program components on outcomes for young children, research-policy partnerships also have potential to connect research findings directly to public policy decisions. Regardless of the specific legislation or administrative issue, policy makers are typically attempting to answer a central question: *Should public funds be allocated to this program?* Researchers and policy makers can be at odds as researchers find their work unused and policy makers cannot find timely data to answer their questions. However, Research-Practice Partnerships (RPPs) may provide a bridge to meaningful linkages between research and policy. Such partnerships are developing across the country (Coburn & Penuel, 2016; Coburn, Penuel, & Geil, 2013; Roderick et al., 2009; Tseng et al., 2017; Vecchiotti, 2018). Coburn et al. (2013) define school district–level research-practice partnerships as "long-term, mutualistic collaborations between practitioners and researchers that are intentionally organized to investigate problems of practice and solutions for improving district outcomes" (p. 3). The RPPs described below are examples of attempts to bridge the research-policy divide.

Chicago. Founded in 1990, the UChicago Consortium on School Research, at the University of Chicago, was formed in an era of school decentralization. With more control given to local schools and principals, an awareness emerged of the need to create a stand-alone entity that would conduct independent, objective evaluations of the progress of reform and engage in research that would assist local schools in developing their own strategies. The consortium, therefore, was grounded from its inception in attention to practitioners' issues (Roderick et al., 2009). The consortium's work includes research related to the transition from preschool to kindergarten, preschool attendance, and organization practices that support high-quality programs.

Houston. The Houston Education Research Consortium (HERC) was designed specifically to develop a mutually beneficial partnership between the Houston Independent School District and Rice University (Lopez Turley & Stevens, 2015). The initiative was created to bring researchers and school district personnel together in a meaningful partnership that could develop a research agenda informed by the needs of local school district leaders and that could result in policy decisions informed by the research generated by the partnership (https://kinder.rice.edu/houston-education-research-consortium). The work of HERC includes research related to tracking postsecondary outcomes, predictors of school discipline, and the challenges of refugee settlement in Houston.

New York City. Another such partnership is developing in New York City. The NYC Early Childhood Research Network was formed as a partnership between a group of New York metropolitan area researchers and representatives of the city agencies involved in implementing New York's universal preschool initiative. However, the long-term goal was for researchers and policy makers to co-create a birth-to-third-grade research agenda that could inform policy decisions for the city. Initially, eight research studies were funded to provide city officials with a better understanding of the role of the early childhood workforce serving young children enrolled in preschool programs located in public and community-based settings (Foundation for Child Development, 2018).

Challenges for RPPs. While RPPs hold the promise of mutually beneficial partnerships, they face the challenges of funding, communication with multiple stakeholders, and building trust among the partners. In addition, researchers often find limited professional incentives for this type of applied research, which may not weight heavily, if at all, on the path toward tenure (Lopez Turley & Stevens, 2015; Vecchiotti, 2018).

Early childhood interventions are a complex interaction of many dynamic factors, including early learning and program standards, curriculum, data, comprehensive assessment systems, family and community engagement strategies, health promotion, early childhood workforce competencies, and so forth. The complexity of the work may call for greater collaboration across research, policy, and practice in an attempt to provide answers to the questions that are most relevant for policy and practice.

Conclusion

It is now generally accepted that high-quality early intervention programs can make a difference in the lives of young children and their families (Phillips et al., 2017; Yoshikawa et al., 2013). Yet, as more early childhood programs are offered to young children through federal, state, and municipal funding, the ability to achieve stronger positive outcomes for young children will require a more nuanced understanding of the critical components of effective early childhood programs for young children from birth through age 8. Meaningful program evaluation includes more than a design to answer the question, *Does the program work?* Methodologically, we need more precise definitions of the essential elements of interventions, more fine-tuned descriptions of target populations, including specific subgroups, and rigorous examinations of the contexts in which interventions are delivered. The field of implementation science offers a potential guiding framework within which early childhood research can capture the contexts of young children's lives as well as their performance on specific content.

Yet even the best designed study is only *policy-relevant* if it answers questions that are important to policy makers. If research is to inform the allocation of funds to support early childhood programs, stronger connections will need to be made between existing and emerging research and policy. Research-Practice Partnerships appear to be a promising strategy to bridge the research-policy gap. The innovative RPP models discussed above provide hope that the field of early childhood education can move beyond the successes of the past 50 years by asking new questions and forming new partnerships that expand and deepen the knowledge base and ultimately lead to substantial improvements in outcomes for young children and their families.

References

Bassok, D., Finch, J. E., Lee, R., Reardon, S. F., & Waldfogel, J. (2016). Socioeconomic gaps in early childhood experiences: 1998 to 2010. *AERA Open, 2*(3), 1–22.

Blase, K., & Fixen, D. (2013). *Core intervention components: Identifying and operationalizing what makes programs work* (ASPE Research Brief). Washington, DC: U.S. Department of Health and Human Services.

Boser, l., & McDaniel, A. (2018). *Addressing the gap between education research and practice.* Washington, DC: Center for American Progress.

Brooks-Gunn, J. (2003). Do you believe in magic? What we can expect from early childhood intervention programs. *Social Policy Report, 17*(1), 3–15.

Campbell, F. A., Pungello, E. P., Miller-Johnson, S., Burchinal, M., & Ramey, C. T. (2001). The development of cognitive and academic abilities: Growth curves from an early childhood educational experiment. *Developmental Psychology, 37*(2), 231–242.

Center on the Developing Child, Harvard University. (2016). *From best practices to breakthrough impacts: A science-based approach to building a more promising future for young children and families.* Cambridge, MA: Harvard University Press.

CityHealth & National Institute for Early Education Research. (2019). *Pre-K in American cities.* Retrieved from http://nieer.org/wp-content/uploads/2019/01/Pre-K-Report-Final.pdf

Coburn, C., & Penuel, W. R. (2016). Research-practice partnerships in education: Outcomes, dynamics, and open questions. *Educational Researcher, 45*(1), 48–54.

Coburn, C., Penuel, W. R., & Geil, K. E. (2013). *Research-practice partnerships: A strategy for leveraging research for educational improvement in school districts.* New York, NY: W.T. Grant Foundation.

Curenton, S. M., Iruka, I., Humphries, M., Jensen, B., Durden, T., Rochester, S, et al. (2019). Validity for the Assessing Classroom Sociocultural Equity Scale (ACSES) in early childhood classrooms. *Early Education and Development, 31*(2) 269–288.

Duncan, G., & Magnuson, K. (2013). Investing in preschool programs. *Journal of Economic Perspectives, 27*(2), 109–132. doi:10.1257/jep.27.2.109

Farran, D. C., Meador, D., Christopher, C., Nesbitt, K., & Bilbrey, L. E. (2017). Data-driven improvement in prekindergarten classrooms: Report from a partnership in an urban district. *Child Development, 88*(5), 1466–1479.

Foundation for Child Development. (2018, February). *The New York City Early Childhood Research Network: A model for integrating research policy, and practice.* New York, NY: Author.

Franks, R. P., & Schroeder, J. (2013). Implementation science. In T. Halle, A. Metz, & I. Martinez-Beck (Eds.), *Applying implementation science in early childhood programs and systems* (pp. 5–19). Baltimore, MD: Brookes.

Friedman-Krauss, A. H., Barnett, W. S., Weisenfeld, G. G., Kasmin, R., DiCrecchio, N., & Horowitz, M. (2018). *The state of preschool 2017.* New Brunswick, NJ: National Institute for Early Education Research.

Halle, T., Metz, A., & Martinez-Beck, I. (2013). *Applying implementation science in early childhood programs and systems.* Baltimore, MD: Brookes.

Heckman, J., Moon, S. H., Pinto, R., Savelyev, P., & Yavitz, A. (2010a). Analyzing social experiments as implemented: A reexamination of the evidence from the HighScope Perry Preschool Program. *Quantitative Economics, 1*(1), 1–46.

Heckman, J., Moon, S. H., Pinto, R., Savelyev, P., & Yavitz, A. (2010b). The rate of return to the HighScope Perry Preschool Program. *Journal of Public Economics, 94*(1–2), 114–128.

Lipsey, M., Farran, D. C., & Durkin, K. (2018). Effects of the Tennessee Prekindergarten Program on children's achievement and behavior through third grade. *Early Childhood Research Quarterly, 45*, 155–176.

Lipsey, M., Farran, D. C., & Hofer, K. G. (2015). *A randomized control trial of the effects of a state-wide voluntary prekindergarden program on children's skills and behaviors through third grade* (Research Report). Nashville, TN: Vanderbilt University Peabody Research Institute.

Lombardi, J., Harding, J. F., Connors, M. C., & Friedman-Krauss, A. H. (2016). Coming of age: A review of federal early childhood policy 2000–2015. In H. Dichter (Ed.) *Rising to the challenge: Building effective systems for young children and families: A BUILD e-book.* Retrieved from https://www.buildinitiative.org/Portals/0/Uploads/Documents/RisingtotheChallengePrologue.pdf

Lopez Turley, R., & Stevens, C. (2015). Lessons from a school-university research partnership: The Houston Education Research Consortium. *Educational Evaluation and Policy Analysis, 37*(1S), 6S–15S.

Magnuson, K., & Waldfogel, J. (2016). Trends in income-related gaps in enrollment in early childhood education: 1968 to 2013. *AERA Open, 2*(2), 1–13.

Martinez-Beck, I. (2013). Introduction: Where is the new frontier of implementation science in early care and education research and practice? In T. Halle, A. Metz, & I. Martinez-Beck (Eds.), *Applying implementation science in early childhood programs and systems* (pp. xix–xxx). Baltimore, MD: Brookes.

Meloy, B., Gardner, M., & Darling-Hammond, L. (2019). *Untangling the evidence on preschool effectiveness: Insights from policymakers.* Palo Alto, CA: Learning Policy Institute.

Metz, A., Halle, T., Bartley, L., & Blasberg, A. (2013). The key components of successful implementation. In T. Halle, A. Metz, & I. Martinez-Beck (Eds.), *Applying implementation science in early childhood programs and systems* (pp. 21–42). Baltimore, MD: Brookes.

Nielsen, K., & Miraglia, M. (2017). What works for whom in which circumstances? On the need to move beyond the "What works?" question in organizational intervention research. *Human Relations, 70*(1), 40–62.

Office of Planning, Research and Evaluation. (2016). *What works, under what circumstances, and how?* (2016-3). Washington, DC: U.S. Department of Health and Human Services.

Phillips, D., Gormley, W. T., & Anderson, S. (2016). The effects of Tulsa's CAP Head Start program on middle-school academic outcomes and progress. *Developmental Psychology, 52*(8), 1247–1261. doi:10.1037/dev0000151

Phillips, D., Lipsey, M., Dodge, K., Haskins, R., Bassok, D., Burchinal, M., et al. (2017). Puzzling it out: The current state of scientific knowledge on pre-K effects: A consensus statement. In *Issues in pre-kindergarten programs and policies.* Washington, DC, and Durham, NC: Brookings Institution Press & Duke Center for Child and Family Policy.

Reardon, S. F., & Portilla, X. A. (2016). Recent trends in income, racial, and ethnic school readiness gaps at kindergarten entry. *AERA Open, 2*(3), 1–18.

Reynolds, A. J., Ou, S.-R., & Temple, J. A. (2018). A multicomponent, preschool to third grade preventive intervention and educational attainment at 35 years of age. *JAMA Pediatrics, 172*(3), 247–256.

Roderick, M., Easton, J. Q., & Bender Sebring, P. (2009). *The Consortium on Chicago School Research: A new model for the role of research in supporting urban school reform.* Chicago, IL: University of Chicago.

Schweinhart, L. J., Montie, J., Xiang, Z., Barnett, W. S., Belfield, C. R., & Nores, M. (2005). *Lifetime effects: The High/Scope Perry Preschool study through age 40.* Ypsilanti, MI: HighScope Educational Research Foundation.

Tseng, V., Easton, J. Q., & Supplee, L. H. (2017). Research-practice partnerships: Building two-way streets of engagement. *Social Policy Report, 30*(4), 1–17. Washington, DC: Society for Research in Child Development.

U.S. Department of Health and Human Services. (2010). *Head Start impact study: Final report.* Washington, DC: Author.

Vecchiotti, S. (2018, January). Ins and outs of forming early childhood education research-to-practice and policy partnerships. *Philanthropy New York: Insights.* Retrieved from https://philanthropynewyork.org/news/ins-and-outs-forming-early-childhood-education-research-practice-and-policy-partnerships

Weiland, C., & Yoshikawa, H. (2013). Impacts of a prekindergarten program on children's mathematics, language, literacy, executive function, and emotional skills. *Child Development, 84*(6), 2112–2130. doi:10.1111/cdev.12099

Yoshikawa, H., Weiland, C., Brooks-Gunn, J., Burchinal, M., Espinosa, L., Gormley, W. T., et al. (2013). *Investing in our future: The evidence base on preschool education.* Washington, DC: Society for Research in Child Development.

Chapter 11

Early Childhood Systems for Birth Through Age 8: Conceptual Challenges and Research Needs

KRISTIE A. KAUERZ

University of Colorado Denver

In recent decades, many in the early childhood field have embraced systems approaches as a means to increase alignment, coherence, and continuity among and across programs and services. Systems hold promise to achieve more uniform high quality, increased access, reduced duplication, and improved effectiveness across disparate government agencies' efforts, as well as between and across public and private organizations. Although used frequently in the field, the term *system* often lacks conceptual clarity and analytic precision. This chapter addresses both, outlining key issues to inform research related to early childhood systems over the next decades.

At the outset, I distinguish among different "system" foci to anchor my perspective. The field of early childhood has deep roots in Uri Bronfenbrenner's *ecological systems theory*, which guides the understanding that children develop in a context of multiple relational environments, which include family, community, and society. A second use of "system" recognizes the nestedness of *organizational system* contexts and calls for the alignment of local, state, and federal agendas and policies in order to sustain practices that benefit young children (Cobb, Jackson, Henrick, Smith, & MIST Team, 2018; Stipek, Clements, Coburn, Franke, & Farran, 2017). For example, these systems reforms reflect the understanding that student learning is dependent on teacher learning, but teachers' opportunities to learn are dependent on school and district structures, which, in turn, are influenced by state and federal policies and priorities. A third use of the term "system," in *system thinking*, highlights the need for stakeholders to have the cognitive ability to understand interconnections and, importantly, the willingness to reflect on the difference between what they aspire to and what they actually produce (Stroh, 2015). This strand recognizes that stakeholders must possess specific ways of thinking that motivate them to change the way they work and with whom they work. Finally, a fourth use of "system" focuses on the necessity of a shared *system infrastructure* that supports programs (Kagan & Cohen, 1997). The elements of early childhood system infrastructure have been defined differently over time (Bruner, Stover Wright, Gebhard, & Hibbard, 2004; Cohen & Bhatt, 2012; Fixsen, Blase, Metz, & Van Dyke, 2013; Kagan & Cohen, 1997; Kagan & Kauerz, 2012) and include governance, finance, standards, quality improvement supports, workforce development, and accountability. In this

185

chapter, I unite these four foci, paying attention to relational and organizational contexts, as well as cognitive and structural aspects of systems-building approaches.

Further complexifying systems work in early childhood, there are two predominant system movements. Early care and education (ECE), or birth-to-five (0–5), systems-building approaches strive to bring greater coherence to the typically siloed programs that serve children prior to kindergarten, including child care; Head Start and Early Head Start; state-funded pre-K; special education services (Part C and Part B, Section 619); and more informal settings (Kagan & Kauerz, 2012). Preschool through third grade (P–3), or birth-through-eight (0–8), systems-building approaches strive to bring greater alignment across the array of ECE programs and K–12 public education (Bogard & Takanishi, 2005; Kauerz, 2006). These two systems-building movements (0–5 and 0–8) have distinct histories but share similar challenges. While a comprehensive review is beyond the scope of this chapter, I focus on systems-building approaches that address the intersection of ECE and K–12 systems.

First, I address three bodies of knowledge that are essential to understanding the importance of systems in early childhood. Next, I pose three persistent conceptual challenges that permeate early childhood systems building. To close, I propose some promising directions for future research that could provoke influential insights into systems-building efforts in early childhood.

Bodies of Knowledge: What We Know

The early childhood years, birth through age 8, are critical for learning and health into adulthood. High-quality programs and interventions during these years provide short- and long-term benefits to children and to society, but some children have more opportunities to reap the benefits than do other children. Three bodies of literature document these benefits and provide evidence of the need to build early childhood systems. Research in child development and learning (neuroscience, developmental psychology, and education), economics, and sociology all contribute fundamental understandings of how young children's experiences are influenced by early childhood systems.

Child Development and Learning

A growing conceptual base of child development and learning unites neuroscience, developmental psychology, and education (National Research Council & Institute of Medicine, 2000; National Scientific Council on the Developing Child, 2007) and has fueled attention from the public and policy makers. Neuroscience highlights the rapid and voluminous brain development that occurs during the first years of life and the important influence of children's early experiences in shaping the brain's circuitry. Developmental psychology and education emphasize that children's varied early experiences have a profound influence on subsequent learning and development. Access to high-quality interventions and programs can positively influence lifelong trajectories of health and well-being for children and families (National Research Council, 2001). The provision of these services relies on a combination of individual responsibility, informal social supports, and formalized structures in society. This body of research emphasizes the inseparable and highly interactive influences of nature and nurture, and the importance of the system of varied contexts and services that support children's learning and development.

Economics

The field of economics bolsters the importance of early childhood interventions, applying human capital theory and cost-benefit analyses to estimate the returns to society from investments in children's early experiences. Some of the best-known economic studies, those that include randomized control trials and longitudinal follow-up, include HighScope/Perry Preschool (Heckman, Moon, Pinto, Savelyev, & Yavitz, 2010), the Carolina Abecedarian Study (Barnett & Masse, 2007), and Chicago Child-Parent Centers (Reynolds, Temple, White, Ou, & Robertson, 2011). The HighScope/Perry Preschool project was a small-scale study that involved fewer than 60 children who experienced that intensive program as 3- and 4-year-olds. Both Abecedarian and Chicago Child-Parent Centers incorporated multiple types of intervention (e.g., high-quality preschool instruction plus intensive family support and/or health care services), providing them to children over an extended number of years. Economists estimate that the total benefit-cost ratios of these intensive interventions range from between 2.5 and 10.8 dollars for every dollar invested (Barnett & Nores, 2018).

Using these data, states, cities, and communities across the country have promoted and implemented large-scale early education programs. The program impacts have been mixed and predominantly much smaller than those described above. Scholars and practitioners alike concede that one reasonable explanation is that large-scale programs do not deliver services that are as intensive in quality or dosage as the smaller-scale, highly controlled studies (U.S. Department of Health and Human Services & Administration for Children and Families, 2010; Yoshikawa et al., 2013). The takeaway here is that the quality and mix of services provided to children has a strong influence on the magnitude of program impacts. As such, economic studies provide a critical foundation to systems research, documenting program designs that can produce long-lasting impacts, while also foregrounding questions related to the infrastructure needed to sustain and scale highly effective programs.

Sociology

The field of sociology elevates concerns about equity in early childhood programs and services, highlighting disparities in both opportunities and outcomes that exist for young children whose life course is threatened by socioeconomic disadvantage, family disruptions, and/or diagnosed disabilities (Duncan & Murnane, 2011). Achievement gaps exist by the time children enter kindergarten and do not change substantively between kindergarten and fourth grade (Reardon & Portilla, 2016). Children who grow up in families and communities with multiple risk factors often experience services delivered by federal, state, and local governments, independent nonprofit organizations, neighborhood associations, partnerships, and other administrative entities. The policies and practices of these institutions are highly fragmented, with complex points of entry that are especially problematic for underserved children and families (National Research Council & Institute of Medicine, 2000). The recognition that substantive disparities and inequities exist for subpopulations of children, and that a confusing web of programs and organizations mediates children's experiences, provides further grounding for the importance of systems-focused efforts.

Conceptual Issues That Lack Agreement

Despite the contributions of these fundamental bodies of knowledge, there are still major gaps in understanding early childhood systems, some of which I address in this section. Systems exist in numerous disciplines, in both physical and social sciences. Common to all of these is the understanding that systems span organizations, and boundaries define what organizations are responsible for doing and what powers and functions lie elsewhere. The field of public administration has focused on five elements—which in the field are often referred to as "boundaries"—and the conflicts that arise around them when organizations strive to work together as a system: mission, resources, capacity, responsibility, and accountability (Kettl, 2006). Considering the array of programs, organizations, and government agencies across ECE and K–12, these boundaries are relevant to early childhood systems building. Working effectively at and across the boundaries requires new strategies of collaboration, the contours of which are shaped by formal agreements (e.g., laws, rules/regulations, resources, funding structures) and by individual stakeholders (e.g., with values, perspectives, ideological presuppositions, actions) who influence organizations and the relationships between them. Put simply, systems building requires attention to both administrative and social capacities (Thomson & Perry, 2006), and to both structural/technical and adaptive change (Heifetz & Linsky, 2002).

In this section, I explore three conceptual issues related to boundaries in early childhood systems building: (a) How do traditionally distinct systems (i.e., ECE and K–12) negotiate and adopt a shared paradigm for young children's development and learning? (b) How do agencies and organizations overcome structural siloes and collaborate across sectors? And (c) How does the field support and encourage coherence and alignment without sacrificing a diverse delivery system that promotes the central role of families and communities in young children's lives?

Adopting a Shared Paradigm

How do traditionally distinct systems negotiate and adopt a shared paradigm for young children's development and learning?

If ECE and K–12 are to become more aligned and coherent, the two fields need to identify a common frame for children's learning and development. Yet the contrast between the underlying paradigms of ECE and K–12 is stark. The dichotomy has been characterized in various ways, including, but not limited to, the teaching of children versus the teaching of content, play versus rigor, private versus public, individualized versus standardized, targeted versus universal, home-based versus institutional. These perspectives reflect distinctly divergent assumptions about the purposes of services in ECE and K–12, about who is served, what is provided, how it is provided, and who is responsible for funding and governing those services.

The emergence and development of ECE programs in the United States has followed the general trajectory of social services, providing support to children whose families lack resources and/or children most at risk for poor developmental outcomes (Cahan, 1989; Kagan, Cohen, & Neuman, 1996). Inherent to most ECE programs is a dedication to developmentally appropriate practice, child-centered learning, and a core value of including and supporting children's families. ECE programs emphasize the uniqueness of each child and focus on teaching the whole child, ensuring that social, emotional, physical, and cognitive development are addressed.

In contrast, the development of the U.S. K–12 education system evolved from the Common School Movement of the early 19th century, in which public schools were viewed as a means to unify society by conveying norms for surviving in the new industrial culture (Kliebard, 1995). The late 19th century witnessed the professionalization of teachers, while accountability and standardized learning were emphasized in the 20th century (Spring, 2001). These values have been consistently reinforced by legal standards for "highly qualified teachers" and formalized methods of assessing student performance. The K–12 system focuses on teaching explicit academic skills and knowledge, delineated into specific content areas (e.g., literacy/reading, math, science, social studies). Content learning is evaluated with formal, summative assessments that measure mastery and are administered in controlled environments.

These paradigmatic contrasts have led many to question the desirability and feasibility of creating a shared paradigm. The challenges are rooted in deep, complex issues of individual cognition and social capacity. The creation of a shared paradigm requires more than recognizing and understanding a "new" perspective; it requires individuals to adapt not only their thinking, politics, and practices (Colaner, 2016) but also, and perhaps more importantly, their underlying values and worldview (Kuhn, 1996). The ability of ECE and K–12 to embrace shared values and speak with a common voice about children's learning and development is a critical ingredient for systems building. Theorists, policy makers, and practitioners alike need to grapple with how these different paradigms might unite or morph into a shared understanding about young children's learning and development.

Establishing Cross-Sector Governance

How do agencies and organizations overcome structural siloes and establish coherent governance approaches?

A shared paradigm is not a philosophical question only. An early childhood system requires coherent governance approaches. Yet paradigmatic differences in ECE and K–12 systems are reflected in the policy realm, where programs and services are organized and governed in separate siloes. The structures of ECE and K–12 are linked to different governing bodies and procedures, financing mechanisms, rules, regulations, and accountability structures. Coherent governance is further complicated by the fact that both ECE and K–12 are loosely coupled systems in and of themselves, meaning their internal elements share few and weak variables (Weick, 1976). For example, the ECE system—due to the many programs within it (e.g., Head Start, child care, state-funded pre-K, Special Education), each with its own different policy infrastructure—has been termed a "non-system" (Kagan & Kauerz, 2009). Similarly, the K–12 system is highly decentralized, with nearly 14,000 independently governed local school districts across the country, leading some to call it incoherent and virtually ungovernable (Cohen & Bhatt, 2012). Federal, state, and local governments play varying roles in ECE and K–12. Some programs are governed at the federal level (e.g., Head Start), and others at the local level (e.g., K–12 school districts). State governments provide primary leadership in some programs (e.g., state-funded pre-K and child care) and marginal, if any, leadership in others (e.g., Head Start). The fragmentation within ECE and K–12 further complicates governance *across* the two systems.

Structural and regulatory differences can affect access, quality, and equity (Ansari et al., 2017; Bassok, Greenberg, Fitzpatrick, & Loeb, 2016; Jenkins, Farkas, Duncan, Burchinal, & Vandell, 2016; Pianta, 2010; Whitebook, 2014). For example, different facilities standards may prohibit school districts from providing space for pre-school programs. State regulations for pre-K may require a specific square footage per child or a particular distance to access toilets. Elementary schools may have available space and the desire to house a pre-K classroom, but cannot adhere to the specific pre-K licensing requirements.

While there is growing attention to governance within ECE systems-building (Kagan & Gomez, 2015; Kagan & Kauerz, 2009), stakeholders who strive to create comprehensive approaches that span ECE and K–12 face considerable challenges. Given the fragmentation of ECE, the field lacks agreement on which parts of the ECE system need to become more tightly coupled with which parts of the K–12 system. Each vision demands a different governance solution. For example, some argue that 4-year-olds should become part of the K–12 system, and that the "new American primary school" should serve pre-K through fifth grade (Takanishi, 2016). However, if pre-K for 4-year-olds becomes an explicit part of the K–12 system, then it may become more disconnected from other programs within the ECE system, such as child care, Head Start, and infant/toddler services. From a policy and governance perspective, the coupling of pre-K with K–12 would engender universal access, formula-based funding, and increased professionalization of teachers. However, this decoupling within the ECE system belies what is known about the continuum of young children's learning and development (Markowitz, Bassok, & Hamre, 2018) and may lead to unwanted standardization of childhood experiences (Fuller, 2007). Greater alignment in one place creates misalignment in another place. To realize early childhood systems, cross-sector governance strategies will need to negotiate these either/or conundrums.

Navigating Alignment Without Sacrificing Differentiation

How is coherence built without sacrificing essential differentiation that matters to diverse children and families?

Another issue related to early childhood systems building is the paradox of isomorphism, in which actors make their organizations more and more similar (e.g., homogeneous in structure, culture, and output) without necessarily making them more efficient (DiMaggio & Powell, 1983). In early childhood systems, the tension arises between the competing areas of "education" and "care." Isomorphism may sometimes be desirable. For example, when different programs have different pay scales for the same work (Whitebook, 2014), making compensation for child care teachers more equitable in comparison to public school teachers is a preferred outcome. Similarly, as we learn more about the program variables that produce better outcomes for young children, it is sensible for more programs to adopt those policies and practices; Quality Rating and Improvement Systems (QRIS) are built on this premise of desired isomorphism (Schaack, Tarrant, Boller, & Tout, 2012). But isomorphism can also be undesirable. Some have argued that ECE's efforts to align with the standards movement in K–12, through the creation of early learning standards and increased attention to child assessments that measure school readiness, has led to an inappropriate pushdown of academics into kindergarten and pre-K programs (Bassok, Latham, & Rorem, 2016; Brown, Englehardt, Barry, & Ku, 2019), leading to the "educationalization" of early childhood (Kagan & Kauerz, 2007) and an unwanted isomorphism with the accountability culture of K–12 (Hatch, 2002).

Recent research posits the possibility of creating a hybrid logic that weds together care and education, in effect neutralizing any competition that one must prevail over the other (Colaner, 2016). The challenges of doing so are profound, as the relationship between isomorphism and power is an intimate one. Organizations that have more clout—socially, financially, politically—are most often those that prevail (Peters, 2001). Examples of this are abundant in early childhood. Across the world, most countries that have integrated ECE with public education have done so within the education system (Moss, 2018) rather than within a more care-focused system. In the United States, some argue that the school readiness movement emphasizes the needs of the politically powerful K–12 system over the fundamental rights of children (Bloch & Kim, 2015).

Isomorphism is further problematized because organizations can become more homogenized without simultaneously becoming more equitable. Within ECE, critical scholars question the isomorphic tendencies of Developmentally Appropriate Practice, highlighting how it defines differences in ways that sustain the centrality and superiority of Whiteness (Souto-Manning & Rabadi-Raol, 2018). Aligning ECE with a K–12 system that does little to address the diverse needs of children (Paris, 2012) or to ameliorate educational disadvantage (Brighouse & Schouten, 2011) poses serious concerns. The structural tidiness and isomorphism of "alignment and coherence" may have profound implications for which children are well served by the system and which are not. These issues demand greater deliberation.

Promising Directions for Future Research

Beyond the robust research agendas in neuroscience, developmental psychology, economics, and sociology, early childhood systems research can expand to include additional disciplinary foundations and methodological explorations. I propose increased attention to organizational and human cognition theories and related disciplines and methods. To this end, I introduce four overarching research questions that, explored empirically through organizational and cognitive perspectives, could contribute to the field's understanding and implementation of systems approaches.

Research Question 1: How do individual stakeholders make sense of and become compelled to engage meaningfully in systems change?

Systems-building is not merely a philosophical endeavor. It relies on individual stakeholders to imagine, design, engage with, and support changing the status quo. More work is needed to understand the cognitive and motivational factors that prompt practitioners and policy makers to view systems building as a worthwhile endeavor. Individual stakeholders can either frustrate or generate greater momentum for abandoning usual ways of thinking/doing and embracing fundamentally new, systems-focused approaches.

More work is needed to understand the motivational inputs that are needed for practitioners, policy makers, and other stakeholders to view systems building as a worthwhile endeavor. The field of human cognition explores how individuals make sense of change and how their prior knowledge, beliefs, and experiences influence their willingness to construct new understandings of their work (Spillane, Reiser, & Reimer, 2002). Research on leadership has distinguished between technical and adaptive challenges inherent in change (Heifetz & Linsky, 2002). *Technical challenges* are those with known solutions and accessible resources and procedures to address. *Adaptive challenges*, in contrast, lack clear solutions and require changed attitudes, values, and behaviors. Of particular relevance to the adaptive challenge of systems building, stakeholders often cannot see that the new result (an aligned system) will be any better than their current situation. Literature describes people's inherent unwillingness and limited capacity to change, especially when new activities and expectations appear inconsistent with pre-existing interests and agendas; new information is almost always interpreted in light of what is already understood (Spillane et al., 2002). Simply, change is hard for people, and current practice has built-in conservatism and inertia (Fullan, 2011). When considering competing paradigms, the challenge of shifting individuals' thinking and beliefs related to early childhood systems building is apparent. For example, the assumption that K–12 stakeholders need only to be told that young children learn best through play and that schools will then reframe the structure and interactions of elementary school classrooms is simplistic and ignores the complexity of human sense-making required for systems change.

Cognitive sense-making is largely unexplored in the literature on early childhood systems. Early childhood scholars should invest more effort to unpack and understand the social and psychological factors that inspire and support individuals to seek new alliances, to become "boundary spanners," and to manage and build interorganizational relationships and interdependency (Thomson & Perry, 2006). To fill this gap, scholars can use case study and grounded theory research. By interviewing system leaders at both practice and policy levels, scholars can discern beliefs, attitudes, skills, values, emotions, and other intrapersonal characteristics that propel and inhibit system-focused work. Research in this area could be incorporated into preservice, in-service, and leadership development programs within and across ECE and K–12.

Research Question 2: Under what conditions does shared, meaningful systems-building change occur?

Closely entwined with the intrapersonal variables just described, exogenous *inter*personal conditions influence system change. Cognitive change is shared and distributed among individuals in an interactive network (Spillane et al., 2002), and such networks operate in the context of professions, organizations, membership entities, and other thought communities. Systems building requires collective decision making where stakeholders engage in deliberative processes for designing and implementing policies and procedures that impact public and private entities, and straddle both ECE and K–12 agencies. A further gap is in understanding of the influence of collaborative processes—timing, sequence, and scope of engagement—on early childhood systems building.

Collaborative processes across ECE and K–12 need deeper qualitative and quantitative investigation. Research should be concerned with specific mechanisms by which meaningful changes to collaborative relationships, processes, and outcomes are accomplished, and should focus on understanding the differential influence of various contexts. To accomplish this, researchers anchored in cognitive sense-making theories and sociocultural and network studies can investigate the processes through which individuals learn from one another and the ways that networked interactions surface new perspectives related to shared paradigms and aligned effort. Emerging research examines how practices that include stakeholders during the early stages of collaboration affect outcomes such as higher levels of program success (Johnston, Hicks, Nan, & Auer, 2010). Similarly, other scholars have learned how specific communication structures fostered relationships that enabled positive change dynamics (Douglass, 2016).

Case study research could contribute to theory building about early childhood systems and provide analytical substance to tracing the temporal sequences of events and relationships that occur in various systems-building contexts. Investigating the efficacy of communities of practice, networked improvement communities, and other collaborative processes that intentionally bring together stakeholders from ECE and K–12 would contribute greatly to understanding early childhood systems building. Two quantitative methodologies that hold promise are *social network analysis*, in which communication and influence can be mapped and studied (Carolan, 2014), and *multiagent modeling*, which uses computational simulation to test simple social interaction theories generated from case studies (Epstein & Axtell, 1996).

Research Question 3: What institutional and organizational arrangements produce effective collaboration and coherence across and among ECE and K–12 programs?

A third area of inquiry for early childhood systems building centers on how disparate programs and services are organized, across ECE and K–12, to meet shared goals. Increasingly, collective decision making occurs inside new governance structures (Kagan & Gomez, 2015), shared backbone organizations in collective impact initiatives (Kania & Kramer, 2011; Kauerz, 2013), and other cross-sector entities (Geiser, Horwitz, & Gerstein, 2013; Regenstein & Lipper, 2013). What is not known is which structural arrangements engender the most perceived legitimacy and trust from partners, reflect shared paradigms and desirable isomorphism, and, as a consequence, lead to meaningful and positive systems change.

Some researchers are developing typologies and classifications for different forms of collaborative early childhood governance (Kagan & Gomez, 2015; Kauerz & Kagan, 2012; Selden, Sowa, & Sandfort, 2006) and identify a continuum of system efforts—from weaker networks to more stabilized/centralized agencies. Additional research is needed to theorize the taxonomy. For example, it would be fruitful to examine the nature of different cross-sector and interdependent structures to deepen understanding of the different functional approaches to accomplishing their missions. To date, most empirical research examining alignment between ECE and K–12 has been focused on understanding classroom practices (see, for example, Carr, Mokrova, Vernon-Feagans, & Burchinal, 2019; Franko, Zhang, & Hesbol, 2018; Stipek et al., 2017) and school/site-level implementation (Reynolds et al., 2017). Case studies document efforts to improve pre-K-to-third-grade school culture (Ritchie & Gutmann, 2014) and district-level implementation (Bardige, Baker, & Mardell, 2018; Marietta, 2010). The federal government recently funded the Early Learning Network, which will begin to produce additional research on alignment efforts around the country (see, for example, McCormick, Hsueh, Weiland, & Bangser, 2017).

However, more research is needed to investigate the organizational infrastructure and, importantly, the *cross*-organizational infrastructure needed to take these efforts to scale and to sustain them over time. Researchers can look to schools of thought such as *new institutionalism*, which focuses on ways in which action is structured and order made possible by shared systems of rules (Powell & DiMaggio, 1991), and *collaborative governance*, which emphasizes carefully structured arrangements that interweave public and private capabilities around shared goals (Donahue & Zeckhauser, 2011). These literatures focus on organization-level factors (e.g., dependence of one organization on another, centralization of resource supply) and field-level factors (e.g., degree of interactions/transactions among organizations) that may be influential in better understanding which structural arrangements are effective in achieving which goals related to early childhood systems.

Research Question 4: What are the relevant outputs and outcomes of early childhood systems-building efforts? How can they be measured?

A fourth area for research aims to deepen and broaden the definitions and metrics used to understand the outcomes of system work. Beyond single program evaluations and effects on child outcomes, how can the field discern what is an efficiently and equitably functioning system? While some scholars have proffered thinking about how to evaluate early childhood systems (Coffman, 2012; Coffman & Kauerz, 2012; Kagan, Gomez, & Roth, 2018), more conceptual and methodological work is needed. As outlined at the beginning of this chapter, systems work has multiple facets that include relational, organizational, cognitive, and structural dimensions. Each of these dimensions is important, and researchers and practitioners, as a first step, should consider how to define and measure their desired outcomes. For example, when considering nested organizations across local, state, and national contexts, is it "systems success" for there to be increased alignment at only the school/local level, with fragmentation still existing at the state and federal policy levels?

For the structural dimension, metrics might include the adequacy and sustainability of resources or the reduction of duplicative services and administrative functions. For the relational dimension, metrics might include stability of networks of organizations and programs, or the accomplishment of shared goals. For the cognitive dimension, metrics might include the prevalence of shared norms of trust or the breadth of routines and structures for collaboration among stakeholders. But how these variables can be reliably measured is a question ripe for deeper investigation.

While evaluations of systems must include outcomes such as those just outlined, they cannot entirely ignore child outcomes. I argue that the ultimate purpose in systems building is to improve the learning and development opportunities provided to children so that gaps close, inequities are addressed, and all children thrive and succeed. Ensuring that the development of new structures, bureaucracies, and processes produces meaningful change at the child level needs to be prioritized. These challenges are exemplified by current questions about whether the past decade's extraordinary investments in Quality Rating and Improvement Systems (QRIS) are producing the magnitude of change in program quality required to positively and significantly influence child outcomes (Goffin & Barnett, 2015; Tarrant & Huerta, 2015).

Because experimental designs (or other counterfactuals) are likely not possible, new methods for measuring system efficacy are needed. These investigations will need to integrate the principles of implementation science, wherein the fundamental questions are less about "Did it work?" and more about "What works, for whom, and under what circumstances?"

Inherent to these questions of evaluation and outcomes, systems building introduces new challenges of accountability. Because cross-sector coordination is complex and responsibility inevitably is shared—across organizations and levels of government, as well as across the public, private, and nonprofit sectors—accountability can be difficult to determine. As early childhood systems become more complex, with various governance structures, subsystems, and collaborative arrangements, ensuring that there is accountability for creating not just symbolic progress, but also significant change, is of utmost importance.

Conclusion

Systems work permeates the early childhood field. Systems theories, systems thinking, and systems building are commonly used by policy makers and practitioners alike. The focus on systems in early childhood is predicated on their potential to significantly increase both the scope and the scale of evidence-based supports provided to children and their families. However, many questions remain unanswered about early childhood systems, in particular those that serve to bridge ECE and K–12.

Conceptually, thorny issues related to what to align, how much can be aligned, and the desirability of such alignment, loom large. Alignment is not simply a technical challenge but also an adaptive one, which requires changing values, paradigms, and notions of accountability. Practically, new research approaches and methodologies will help researchers to discern the motivations of individual stakeholders to be systems builders, the processes that support productive collaboration, the structures that engender meaningful functions of governance, and the outcomes for which systems should be responsible. Addressing these issues provides rich opportunity for multidisciplinary, and *inter*disciplinary, scholars to expand their theoretical and empirical research to investigate early childhood systems.

References

Ansari, A., Manfra, L., Hartman, S. C., López, M., Bleiker, C., Dinehart, L. H. B., et al. (2017). Differential third-grade outcomes associated with attending publicly funded preschool programs for low-income Latino children. *Child Development, 88*(5), 1743–1756. doi:10.1111/cdev.12663

Bardige, B., Baker, M., & Mardell, B. (2018). *Children at the center: Transforming early childhood education in the Boston Public Schools.* Cambridge, MA: Harvard Education Press.

Barnett, W. S., & Masse, L. N. (2007). Comparative benefit-cost analysis of the Abecedarian program and its policy implications. *Economics of Education Review, 26*(1), 113–125.

Barnett, W. S., & Nores, M. (2018). Costs and benefits of early childhood education and care. In L. Miller, C. Cameron, C. Dalli, & N. Barbour (Eds.), *The SAGE handbook of early childhood policy* (pp. 485–503). Los Angeles, CA: SAGE.

Bassok, D., Greenberg, E., Fitzpatrick, M., & Loeb, S. (2016). Within- and between-sector quality differences in early childhood education and care. *Child Development, 87*(5), 1627–1645. doi:10.1111/cdev.12551

Bassok, D., Latham, S., & Rorem, A. (2016). Is kindergarten the new first grade? *AERA Open, 1*(4), 1–31. doi:10.1177/2332858415616358

Bloch, M. N., & Kim, K. (2015). A cultural history of "readiness" in early childhood care and education: Are there still culturally relevent, ethical, and imaginative spaces for learning open for young children and their families? In J. M. Iorio & W. Parnell (Eds.), *Rethinking readiness in early childhood education* (pp. 1–18). New York, NY: Palgrave Macmillan.

Bogard, K., & Takanishi, R. (2005). PK–3: An aligned and coordinated approach to education for children 3 to 8 years old. *Social policy report: A publication of the Society for Research in Child Development, 19*(3), 1–24.

Brighouse, H., & Schouten, G. (2011). Understanding the context for existing reform and research proposals. In G. J. Duncan & R. J. Murnane (Eds.), *Whither opportunity? Rising inequality, schools, and children's life chances* (pp. 507–522). New York, NY: Russell Sage Foundation.

Brown, C. P., Englehardt, J., Barry, D. P., & Ku, D. H. (2019). Examining how stakeholders at the local, state, and national levels made sense of the changed kindergarten. *American Educational Research Journal, 56*(3), 822–867. doi:10.3102/0002831218804152

Bruner, C., Stover Wright, M., Gebhard, B., & Hibbard, S. (2004). *Building an early learning system: The ABCs of planning and governance structures.* Des Moines, IA: State Early Childhood Policy Technical Assistance Network, Child & Family Policy Center.

Cahan, E. D. (1989). *Past caring: A history of U.S. preschool care and education for the poor, 1820–1965.* New York, NY: National Center for Children in Poverty.

Carolan, B. V. (2014). *Social network analysis and education.* Los Angeles, CA: SAGE.

Carr, R. C., Mokrova, I. L., Vernon-Feagans, L., & Burchinal, M. R. (2019). Cumulative classroom quality during pre-kindergarten and kindergarten and children's language, literacy, and mathematics skills. *Early Childhood Research Quarterly, 47,* 218–228. doi:10.1016/j.ecresq.2018.12.010

Cobb, P., Jackson, K., Henrick, E., Smith, T. M., & MIST Team (2018). *Systems for instructional improvement: Creating coherence from the classroom to the district office.* Cambridge, MA: Harvard Education Press.

Coffman, J. (2012). Evaluating system-building efforts. In S. L. Kagan & K. Kauerz (Eds.), *Early childhood systems: Transforming early learning* (pp. 199–215). New York, NY: Teachers College Press.

Coffman, J., & Kauerz, K. (2012). *Evaluating preK–3rd grade reforms.* Retrieved from the National P–3 Center website: https://nationalp-3center.org/wp-content/uploads/2019/10/Evaluating-P-3-Reforms.pdf

Cohen, D. K., & Bhatt, M. P. (2012). The importance of infrastructure development to high-quality literacy instruction. *Future of Children: Literacy Challenges for the Twenty-First Century, 22*(2), 117–138.

Colaner, A. C. (2016). Education versus family: Institutional logics in the early care and education field. *American Educational Research Journal, 53*(3), 673–707. doi:10.3102/0002831216646868

DiMaggio, P. J., & Powell, W. W. (1983). The Iron Cage revisited: Institutional isomorphism and collective rationality in organizational fields. *American Sociological Review, 48*(2), 147–160.

Donahue, J. D., & Zeckhauser, R. J. (2011). *Collaborative governance: Private roles for public goals in turbulent times.* Princeton, NJ: Princeton University Press.

Douglass, A. (2016). Resilience in change: Positive perspectives on the dynamics of change in early childhood systems. *Journal of Early Childhood Research, 14*(2), 211–225.

Duncan, G. J., & Murnane, R. J. (Eds.). (2011). *Whither opportunity: Rising inequality, schools, and children's life chances.* New York, NY: Russell Sage Foundation.

Epstein, J., & Axtell, R. (1996). *Growing artificial societies: Social science from the bottom up.* Washington, DC: Brookings Institution Press.

Fixsen, D., Blase, K., Metz, A., & Van Dyke, M. (2013). Statewide implementation of evidence-based programs. *Exceptional Children, 79*(2), 213–230.

Franko, M. D., Zhang, D., & Hesbol, K. (2018). Alignment of learning experiences from prekindergarten to kindergarten: Exploring group classifications using cluster analysis. *Journal of Early Childhood Research, 16*(3), 229–244. doi:10.1177/1476718X18775761

Fullan, M. (2011). *Change leader: Learning to do what matters most.* San Francisco, CA: Jossey-Bass.

Fuller, B. (2007). *Standardized childhood: The political and cultural struggle over early education.* Stanford, CA: Stanford University Press.

Geiser, K. E., Horwitz, I. M., & Gerstein, A. (2013). *Improving the quality and continuity of practices across early childhood education and elementary community school settings.* Stanford, CA: John W. Gardner Center for Youth and Their Communities.

Goffin, S. G., & Barnett, W. S. (2015). Assessing QRIS as a change agent. *Early Childhood Research Quarterly, 30*, 179–182.

Hatch, J. A. (2002). Accountability shovedown: Resisting the standards movement in early childhood education. *Phi Delta Kappan, 83*, 457–562.

Heckman, J. J., Moon, S. H., Pinto, R., Savelyev, P. A., & Yavitz, A. (2010). The rate of return to the HighScope Perry Preschool Program. *Journal of Public Economics, 94*(1–2), 114–128. doi:10.1016/j.jpubeco.2009.11.001

Heifetz, R. A., & Linsky, M. (2002). *Leadership on the line: Staying alive through the dangers of leading.* Cambridge, MA: Harvard Business Review Press.

Jenkins, J. M., Farkas, G., Duncan, G. J., Burchinal, M., & Vandell, D. L. (2016). Head Start at ages 3 and 4 versus Head Start followed by state pre-K: Which is more effective? *Educational Evaluation and Policy Analysis, 38*(1), 88–112. doi:10.3102/0162373715587965

Johnston, E. W., Hicks, D., Nan, N., & Auer, J. C. (2010). Managing the inclusion process in collaborative governance. *Journal of Public Administration Research and Theory, 21*, 699–721.

Kagan, S. L., & Cohen, N. E. (1997). *Not by chance: Creating an early care and education system for America's children.* New Haven, CT: Bush Center in Child Development and Social Policy, Yale University.

Kagan, S. L., Cohen, N. E., & Neuman, M. J. (1996). Introduction: The changing context of American early care and education. In S. L. Kagan & N. E. Cohen (Eds.), *Reinventing early care and education: A vision for a quality system* (pp. 1–18). San Francisco, CA: Jossey-Bass.

Kagan, S. L., & Gomez, R. E. (2015). *Early childhood governance: Choices and consequences.* New York, NY: Teachers College Press.

Kagan, S. L., Gomez, R. E., & Roth, J. L. (2018). Creating a new era of usable knowledge: Enhancing early childhood development through systems research. In L. Miller, C. Cameron, C. Dalli, & N. Barbour (Eds.), *SAGE handbook of early childhood policy* (pp. 566–583). Los Angeles, CA: SAGE.

Kagan, S. L., & Kauerz, K. (2007). Reaching for the whole: Integration and alignment in early education policy. In R. C. Pianta, M. J. Cox, & K. Snow (Eds.), *School readiness and the transition to kindergarten in the era of accountability* (pp. 11–30). Baltimore, MD: Brookes.

Kagan, S. L., & Kauerz, K. (2009). Governing American early care and education: Shifting from government to governance and from form to function. In S. Feeney, A. Galper, & C. Seefeldt (Eds.), *Continuing issues in early childhood education* (3rd ed., pp. 12–32). Upper Saddle River, NJ: Pearson.

Kagan, S. L., & Kauerz, K. (Eds.). (2012). *Early childhood systems: Transforming early learning.* New York, NY: Teachers College Press.

Kania, J., & Kramer, M. (2011). Collective impact. *Stanford Social Innovation Review* (Winter), 36–41.

Kauerz, K. (2006). *Ladders of learning: Fighting fadeout by advancing PK–3 alignment.* Washington, DC: New America Foundation.

Kauerz, K. (2013). *Financiers, engineers, and entrepreneurs for young children: Comprehensive birth-through-age-8 community strategies* [Work prepared for anonymous donor]. Retrieved from the National P–3 Center website: https://nationalp-3center.org/wp-content/uploads/2020/02/Financiers_Engineers_and_Entrepreneurs_2013.pdf

Kauerz, K., & Kagan, S. L. (2012). Governance and early childhood systems: Different forms, similar goals. In S. L. Kagan & K. Kauerz (Eds.), *Early childhood systems: Looking forward, looking backward.* New York, NY: Teachers College Press.

Kettl, D. F. (2006). Managing boundaries in American administration: The collaboration imperative. *Public Administration Review, 66*(s1), 10–19.

Kliebard, H. M. (1995). *The struggle for the American curriculum: 1893–1958* (2nd ed.). New York: Routledge.

Kuhn, T. S. (1996). *The structure of scientific revolutions* (3rd ed.). Chicago, IL: University of Chicago Press. (Original work published 1962)

Marietta, G. (2010). *Lessons for preK–3rd from Montgomery County Public Schools.* New York, NY: Foundation for Child Development.

Markowitz, A. J., Bassok, D., & Hamre, B. K. (2018). Leveraging developmental insights to improve early childhood education. *Child Development Perspectives, 12*(2), 87–92. doi:10.1111/cdep.12266

McCormick, M., Hsueh, J., Weiland, C., & Bangser, M. (2017). *The challenge of sustaining preschool impacts: Introducing ExCEL P–3, a study from the Expanding Children's Early Learning Network.* New York, NY: MDRC.

Moss, P. (2018). What place for "care" in early childhood policy? In L. Miller, C. Cameron, C. Dalli, & N. Barbour (Eds.), *The SAGE handbook of early childhood policy* (pp. 256–267). Los Angeles, CA: SAGE.

National Research Council. (2001). *Eager to learn: Educating our preschoolers* (B. T. Bowman, M. S. Donovan, & M. S. Burns, Eds.). Washington, DC: National Academy Press.

National Research Council & Institute of Medicine. (2000). *From neurons to neighborhoods: The science of early childhood development* (J. P. Shonkoff & D. A. Phillips, Eds.). Washington, DC: National Academy Press.

National Scientific Council on the Developing Child. (2007). *The science of early childhood development: Closing the gap between what we know and what we do.* Cambridge, MA: Center on the Developing Child.

Paris, D. (2012). Culturally sustaining pedagogy: A needed change in stance, terminology, and practice. *Educational Researcher, 41*(3), 93–97.

Peters, B. G. (2001). Administrative reform and political power in the United States. *Policy & Politics, 29*(2), 171–179.

Pianta, R. C. (2010). Going to school in the United States: The shifting ecology of transition. In S. L. Kagan & K. Tarrant (Eds.), *Transitions for young children: Creating connections across early childhood systems* (pp. 33–44). New York, NY: Teachers College Press.

Powell, W. W., & DiMaggio, P. J. (Eds.). (1991). *The new institutionalism in organizational analysis.* Chicago, IL: University of Chicago Press.

Reardon, S. F., & Portilla, X. A. (2016). Recent trends in income, racial, and ethnic school readiness gaps at kindergarten entry. *AERA Open, 2*(3), 1–18. doi:10.1177/2332858416657343

Regenstein, E., & Lipper, K. (2013). *A framework for choosing a state-level early childhood governance system.* Retrieved from BUILD Initiative website: http://www.buildinitiative.org/WhatsNew/ViewArticle/tabid/96/ArticleId/628/A-Framework-for-Choosing-a-State-Level-Early-Childhood-Governance-System.aspx

Reynolds, A. J., Hayakawa, M., Ou, S.-R., Mondi, C. F., Englund, M. M., Candee, A. J., et al. (2017). Scaling and sustaining effective early childhood programs through school-family-university collaboration. *Child Development, 88*(5), 1453–1465.

Reynolds, A. J., Temple, J. A., White, B. A. B., Ou, S.-R., & Robertson, D. L. (2011). Age 26 cost-benefit analysis of the Child-Parent Center early education program. *Child Development, 82*(1), 379–404.

Ritchie, S., & Gutmann, L. (Eds.). (2014). *FirstSchool: Transforming preK–3rd grade for African-American, Latino, and low-income children.* New York, NY: Teachers College Press.

Schaack, D., Tarrant, K., Boller, K., & Tout, K. (2012). Quality rating and improvement systems: Frameworks for early care and education systems change. In S. L. Kagan & K. Kauerz (Eds.), *Early childhood systems: Transforming early learning* (pp. 71–86). New York, NY: Teachers College Press.

Selden, S. C., Sowa, J. E., & Sandfort, J. (2006). The impact of nonprofit collaboration in early child care and education on management and program outcomes. *Public Administration Review* (May/June), 412–425.

Souto-Manning, M., & Rabadi-Raol, A. (2018). (Re)centering quality in early childhood education: Toward intersectional justice for minoritized children. *Review of Research in Education, 42*, 203–225. doi:10.3102/009173X18759550

Spillane, J. P., Reiser, B. J., & Reimer, T. (2002). Policy implementation and cognition: Reframing and refocusing implementation research. *Review of Educational Research, 72*(3), 387–431.

Spring, J. (2001). *The American school: 1642–2000* (5th ed.). Boston, MA: McGraw-Hill.

Stipek, D., Clements, D., Coburn, C., Franke, M., & Farran, D. (2017). PK–3: What does it mean for instruction? *Social Policy Report, 30*(2), 1–22.

Stroh, D. P. (2015). *Systems thinking for social change: A practical guide to solving complex problems, avoiding unintended consequences, and achieving lasting results.* White River Junction, VT: Chelsea Green.

Takanishi, R. (2016). *First things first! Creating the new American primary school.* New York, NY: Teachers College Press.

Tarrant, K., & Huerta, L. A. (2015). Substantive or symbolic stars: Quality rating and improvement systems through a New Institutional lens. *Early Childhood Research Quarterly, 30*, 327–338. doi:10.1016/j.ecresq.2014.04.002

Thomson, A. M., & Perry, J. L. (2006). Collaboration processes: Inside the black box. *Public Administration Review, 66*(s1), 20–32.

U.S. Department of Health and Human Services & Administration for Children and Families. (2010). *Head Start impact study: Final report.* Washington, DC: Author.

Weick, K. E. (1976). Educational organizations as loosely coupled systems. *Administrative Science Quarterly, 21*(1), 1–19.

Whitebook, M. (2014). *Building a skilled teacher workforce: Shared and divergent challenges in early care and education and in Grades K–12.* Seattle, WA: Bill & Melinda Gates Foundation.

Yoshikawa, H., Weiland, C., Brooks-Gunn, J., Burchinal, M., Espinosa, L. M., Gormley, W. T., et al. (2013). *Investing in our future: The evidence base on preschool education.* New York, NY: Society for Research in Child Development & Foundation for Child Development.

Chapter 12

Scaling Up Effective Preschool Education: New Directions for Research

W. STEVEN BARNETT

National Institute for Early Education Research, Rutgers University

ALLISON H. FRIEDMAN-KRAUSS

National Institute for Early Education Research, Rutgers University

CHRISTINA WEILAND

University of Michigan

With strong evidence that trajectories of educational success are well established by kindergarten (and change little thereafter), access to high-quality education in the first five years is seen as an important part of educational opportunity (Barnett & Lamy, 2013). Yet public programs in the United States have delivered less than what many have believed possible, particularly with respect to long-term gains in achievement (Phillips et al., 2017). In this chapter, we explore potential explanations and suggest directions for future research to increase our understanding and improve preschool program outcomes.

Public investments in early childhood have been greatly inspired by small-scale programs with impressive results in long-term term follow-up and benefit-cost analysis (Barnett, 2008; Yoshikawa et al., 2013). The most commonly cited studies are those of the Perry Preschool, Abecedarian program, and Chicago Child Parent Centers (CPC). The Perry Preschool and Abecedarian programs were found to produce immediate gains in children's general cognitive and language abilities of a full standard deviation. IQ gains were sustained into middle childhood for children who participated in Abecedarian, but not Perry Preschool, programs. The CPC program had somewhat smaller initial gains and did not measure IQ *per se.* For all three programs, initial gains were followed by substantial improvements in academic outcomes, including achievement, grade repetition, special education, and high school graduation. In addition, long-term positive impacts were found in other domains, including decreased delinquency and crime, increased employment and earnings, and improved indicators of adult health. Despite some variation in long-term outcomes (e.g., IQ increase, but no crime reductions from Abecedarian), there are strong similarities in findings from studies across all three programs. In economic analyses, estimated benefits greatly exceed the full cost for all three programs (Ramon, Chattopadhyay, Hahn, Barnett, & the Community Preventive Services Task Force, 2017).

Unfortunately, large-scale (and more recent) public preschool programs have not consistently replicated the results of the three programs discussed above. Typically, large-scale public programs have been found to produce much smaller initial and long-term impacts (Haskins & Brooks-Gunn, 2016; Phillips et al., 2017). In a recent meta-analysis, the average end-of-preschool effect size in studies conducted after 1980 was just 0.16 (Duncan & Magnuson, 2013), though some large-scale programs (e.g., in Boston, Tulsa, and New Jersey) have produced initial impacts that are considerably larger, ranging from .33 to .99 depending on the study and outcome (Barnett & Frede, 2017; Gormley, Gayer, Phillips, & Dawson, 2005; Weiland & Yoshikawa, 2013). Preschool non-attenders tend to catch up to attenders, with about half of the eventual convergence on cognitive outcomes during kindergarten and the remainder by the end of second grade (Li et al., 2017). In some recent studies, non-attenders catch up in full, while in others convergence is partial, with some achievement gains persisting (Barnett & Frede, 2017; Hill, Gormley, & Adelstein, 2015; Ladd, Muschkin, & Dodge, 2014; Malofeeva, Daniel-Echols, & Xiang, 2007). In one state-wide pre-K program in Tennessee, initial gains reversed, and pre-K appears to have had long-term negative effects (Lipsey, Farran, & Durkin, 2018). Multiple explanations for converging outcomes have been offered, including weak initial impacts, an anemic kindergarten curriculum, and teacher focus in the early primary grades on bringing up those at the bottom, but the Tennessee findings are more difficult to explain (Bailey, Duncan, Odgers, & Yu, 2017; Weiland, 2016).

These findings raise important questions that we address here. Based upon the full body of research, what kinds of results should be expected from large-scale public preschool programs? If better results can be expected at scale than have been achieved in the past, what do we know about what contributes to success and what barriers get in the way? To what extent does this depend on policy and practice in the primary grades? All of this leads to our final questions. In future research, what topics should be prioritized, and what approaches to those topics are likely to be most fruitful in supporting the greater success of large-scale public programs?

What Results Can We Expect to Reproduce at Scale?

The field should not expect public programs today to reproduce the results of the best-known small-scale programs from the past. Three major reasons for this are: (a) the widely relied upon older studies are outliers rather than representative in multiple respects, including their samples; (b) the counterfactual differs between older and newer studies; and (c) the population served has changed. These factors lead us to have lower expectations, but not low expectations, for the magnitude and persistence of effects from today's programs, as we explain below.

Generalizing From Outliers

Reproducibility—the production of similar results from similar programs using similar procedures with similar populations in similar circumstances—has become a hot topic in the sciences (Drummond, 2009). Medical science has found that carefully controlled studies have difficulty reproducing prior published findings (Ioannidis, 2005). The extent to which the same problem afflicts psychological and education research is debated, but at least some of the problems leading to irreproducibility in medical science seem likely to affect research on early childhood program impacts (Etz & Vandekerckhove, 2016; Gilbert, King, Pettigrew, & Wilson, 2016; Makel & Plucker, 2014; Patil, Peng, & Leek, 2016). In particular, much of the older research on long-term outcomes of preschool programs has characteristics identified as leading to overestimation of expected outcomes.

Beginning in the 1960s, there were many small, low-powered studies. Each study had large numbers of potential outcome measures that were analyzed without pre-selection of tested relationships, typically with no adjustments for the number of comparisons. Not all of these studies were published, and fewer were subject to long-term follow-up (Consortium for Longitudinal Studies, 1983). Bias in favor of positive findings on the part of researchers, journal reviewers, editors, and funders could be expected to skew the published (and now cited) literature toward those studies where chance favored stronger results (e.g., Pashler & Wagenmakers, 2012). Accordingly, the small-scale studies with long-term follow-up are more likely to be outliers in which chance led to larger estimated effects that are unlikely to be fully reproduced.

Change in the Counterfactual

The counterfactual to which a preschool program is compared has changed massively since the 1960s and 1970s and substantively even since the 1980s in ways that matter for program impacts (Chaudry & Datta, 2017). Control group children in the oldest studies were primarily in parent care, but over time, participation in some form of early care and education became much more common for the control group. Nearly half of control group children in the national Head Start Impact Study attended another preschool program (Bloom & Weiland, 2015). In a recent study of Boston's prekindergarten program, two-thirds of the control group was in non-parental care, with 57% in other preschool programs (Weiland & Yoshikawa, 2013). This change in the counterfactual can be expected to reduce estimated effects of public programs. For example, Feller and colleagues (2016) found that at the end of one year of Head Start and through the end of first grade, the effects of Head Start are larger (and more likely to be significant) for children who would have otherwise been home with their parents than for those who would have been in another preschool program. In most studies to date, with one exception being the Head Start Impact Study, information is not collected on the control group's experiences, including the quantity and quality of any preschool programs attended and of home learning activities, limiting our ability to understand what the differences are between the experiences of the treatment and control or comparison groups that might explain differences in outcomes (Weiland, 2018).

Over time, the broader contexts in which children and families live have improved as well, and while these changes benefit both groups equally in a comparative study, they also have changed the counterfactual. Access to health care has improved, as has health care itself, reducing the potential health benefits from preschool program participation. The air and water are cleaner, and children are less exposed to environmental toxins such as lead, even if some problems remain. Children and families are much more likely today to receive other services such as home visiting that can lead to improvements in home environments and, thereby, child development. Such changes in the counterfactual would tend to reduce the potential impacts of any public early care and education program compared to the potential impacts decades ago.

Change in the Population

The children and families served in public preschool programs today have changed in important ways. Parents are more educated, and parents of all income levels engage in more learning activities with their young children than in years past (Bassok, Finch, Lee, Reardon, & Waldfogel, 2016). More than 85% of the population graduate from high school (U.S. Department of Education, 2018), though some groups still lag (Murnane, 2013). The percentage of children born to teen mothers is much lower. Parents are less likely to smoke during and after pregnancy. These trends have likely improved child development and, thereby, reduced the potential size of preschool program impacts.

Additionally, in older studies, the children in the programs were almost all African American, and their parents often had unusually low educational levels and incomes. Today, 24% of Head Start enrollees and more than 40% of enrollees in some state prekindergarten programs are dual-language Spanish speakers (Barnett & Friedman-Krauss, 2016; Friedman-Krauss et al., 2019). Many participating families today have more personal and financial resources than those in the seminal studies. Overall, 28 out of 61 state prekindergarten programs are not income-targeted, meaning programs are much more income diverse than in the small studies, but also compared to public programs in decades past (Friedman-Krauss et al., 2019).

These changes in program composition potentially cut in both directions regarding preschool impact size. Dual language learners and children with special needs appear to benefit more than their peers from public preschool, at least in the short-term; children from higher-income and more educated families benefit less so (Bloom & Weiland, 2015; Yoshikawa, Weiland, & Brooks-Gunn, 2016). The expected impact of any given program depends in part on the demographics of those it serves. On balance, demographic changes are likely to have reduced the average impact of preschool programs and increased the variability in impacts among those served.

How Do Current Programs Compare to the "Models"?

Even if current large-scale programs *could* in theory reproduce the effects of earlier small-scale programs, they would have to replicate those small-scale programs with respect to *all* of their critical features. Yet, large-scale public programs have never been funded as generously as the two small-scale programs that produced the largest effects (Perry and Abecedarian) and have typically not been funded as well as the Child Parent Centers. Arguably this has led to both design failure and implementation failure, though both failures can also have other causes. Each type of failure to reproduce the successful programs is discussed below.

Design Failure

Most large-scale public programs *by design* have not had the structural features of the models that proved effective in small-scale studies. The Perry, Chicago, and Abecedarian programs, and other programs that demonstrated strong outcomes in small-scale studies, had six common elements. These were: (a) well-paid, well-educated teachers; (b) strong pedagogical leadership actively supporting reflective practice; (c) high teacher-to-child ratios in small classes; (d) duration over multiple years; (e) a well-developed, enriched curriculum that included some content and processes similar to those of the primary school; and (f) on-going child-focused communication between parents and the preschool (Frede; 1998; Hanushek, 2015). In contrast, most preschool teachers are poorly paid and have larger classes with little ongoing instructional support or time for reflection and study (Whitebook, McLean, Austin, & Edwards, 2018). Most state pre-K program enrollments are for one year at age four, and many provide only part-day services for as few as 10 hours per week (Barnett et al., 2017). Most children enrolled in Head Start attend for no more than one year (Barnett & Friedman-Krauss, 2016; Caronongan, Moiduddin, West, & Vogel, 2014).

A primary reason that large-scale public programs have not replicated the structural features of their small-scale counterparts is funding. While some public preschool budgets come close to the Chicago program's funding level, most are far below (Barnett et al., 2017; Barnett & Masse, 2007; Hanushek, 2015). Head Start and Early Head Start are two of the better-funded and most policy-transparent early childhood programs, but their broad goals for children and families greatly limit the amount of money that goes into the classroom (Barnett & Friedman-Krauss, 2016; Votruba-Drzal & Miller, 2016). Many state-funded pre-K programs receive less funding per child than Head Start, and, despite more circumscribed goals compared to Head Start, some fall even further short of the structural features of the small-scale models in the classroom (Barnett et al., 2017). Notably, the large-scale programs that have produced the strongest results in the recent literature have all had the same educational requirements for prekindergarten teachers (BA degrees or higher with certification) as for K–12 teachers and have paid their teachers on the same pay scale as K–12, as well (Barnett & Frede, 2017; Gormley, Gayer, Phillips, & Dawson, 2005; Weiland & Yoshikawa, 2013).

Implementation Failure

With much less funding and weaker structural features, large-scale public programs could not be expected to reproduce the same quality of services as the small-scale models. However, some public programs do receive funding comparable to that of the Chicago Parent Child Centers. It is worth asking how well those programs use those resources, if only for a single year in some cases. Research provides some examples of programs that offer fairly good observed educational quality at scale (e.g., Barnett & Frede, 2017; Weiland & Yoshikawa, 2013). Unfortunately, the quality of those aspects of preschool education most directly related to later achievement tends to be inadequate generally, and this cannot always be attributed to lack of resources (Barnett et al., 2017; Chaudry, Morrissey, Weiland, & Yoshikawa, 2017).

Implementation failure does seem to explain at least some of the limitations of today's programs, judging from the variation in observed quality among programs with similar resources and policies (e.g., Barnett & Friedman-Krauss, 2016). How much the experiences of children differ between the older small-scale models and today's large-scale public programs is difficult to discern. Researchers have not formally compared the detailed descriptive data regarding classroom practices, curriculum, and the supervision and other procedures that supported practice in the older programs to data from today's programs (Ramey et al., 1974; Reynolds, 2000; Weikart, 1967). However, typical practice in today's public programs has clear weaknesses and falls well short of best practice in public programs (Barnett & Frede, 2017; Valentino, 2018; Weiland, 2016). The fragmented governance of public education and limited capacity to support high-quality instruction generally present challenges (Cohen, Spillane, & Peurach, 2018; Payne, 2008). The even more complex public-private structures of mixed-delivery systems for publicly funded preschool education currently pose additional challenges in the early childhood sector, including standards that vary depending on the agency and even within agencies depending on whether the provider is a public school or privately owned (Friedman-Krauss et al., 2019). A study of a two-and-a-half year pilot of Boston's model in community-based (i.e., private) preschools, for example, found that implementation was undermined by structural barriers in private providers such as lack of common planning time for teachers, flexible start times for instruction to begin, and high turnover (Yudron, Weiland, & Sachs, 2018). However, successful implementation of public preschool in private preschools integrated into a single system of public education, with uniform standards and common curriculum (at the district level), in New Jersey provides hope and a model for mixed-delivery systems (Barnett & Frede, 2017).

What Is Known About Program Effectiveness?

Considerable research has been conducted about the relationships of structural and process quality to program effectiveness. In this section, we review what the field has learned since the older, small studies were initially conducted that would further illuminate the reasons large-scale public programs are less effective, and how they might be made more effective.

Impacts of Program Structure

Earlier, we identified six common features of the highly successful small-scale programs. With more specificity, Schweinhart (2007) suggested that large-scale public programs might replicate the small-scale programs well enough by serving children for two years at ages three and four with a certified teacher and assistant for no more than 16 children, a research-based curriculum in which staff have had substantial training, and weekly home visits focused on the children. Only one large-scale program comes close to meeting those structural criteria. New Jersey's Abbott preschool program meets these requirements except that family liaison staff members do not visit every family weekly (Barnett & Frede, 2017). However, other researchers have recommended against remodeling large-scale public programs to more closely replicate the structural features of the small-scale programs. The rationale is that research fails to find much association between structural features and program effectiveness (Hanushek, 2015; Pianta, Barnett, Burchinal, & Thornburg, 2009). In this section, we briefly review the research on the structural factors of program duration, teacher qualifications, professional development, class size and ratio, and curriculum. In so doing, we seek to both clarify what is known and how knowledge can be advanced by further research.

Program Duration. Do strong long-term gains from preschool require participation for more than one school year, and what are the gains from participating two years or beginning even earlier than age three? Head Start historically has enrolled both three- and four-year-olds, and some other prekindergarten programs now do so as well (Barnett et al., 2017). Among families with higher incomes (400%+ of the federal poverty line), 62% of children attend preschool at age three, versus just 32% of children from low-income families (0-200% FPL; Chaudry et al., 2017). In some studies, the gains children make at age three are quite similar to those made at age four, but research does not always investigate the extent to which these gains are cumulative (e.g., Puma et al., 2012). Yoshikawa and colleagues (2013) found that few studies have explicitly compared the impact of one versus two years of preschool education. Those that have did not randomly assign duration, and all focused on disadvantaged children. With these caveats, research generally finds that two years of preschool produce larger gains than one year, but that two years do not double the gains from one year (Yoshikawa et al., 2013). Researchers have suggested a number of explanations for unexpectedly small gains from additional years, including the possibility that four-year-olds make fewer gains in mixed-aged classrooms (Ansari, Purtell, & Gershoff, 2016).

Another duration question is how much may be gained educationally from increasing the hours of service. Three rigorous preschool studies have found larger effects for full-day than for part-day programs (Atteberry, Bassok, & Wong, 2019; Robin, Frede, & Barnett, 2006; Walters, 2015). There are many more studies of kindergarten, and full-day kindergarten often, but not always, has been found to be more effective than half-day (Gibbs, 2014; see Le, Kirby, Barney, Setodji, & Gershwin, 2006, for a review). Practically, full-day preschool may be necessary for some working families to take up a program. Relatively un-researched is the benefit of hours beyond the full school day schedule, or even the nature of the activities that take place outside the school day schedule, for preschool children.

Teacher Preparation, Professional Development, and Experience. Research on the associations between teacher characteristics and classroom process and child outcomes has produced mixed results, with the average estimated effects of teachers' having a four-year degree, specialized training in early childhood, and experience quite small (Early et al., 2007; Pianta et al., 2009). A recent meta-analysis examining the relationship between teacher degree level and Environmental Rating Scale scores found higher teacher qualifications to be associated with greater support for children's development (Manning, Garvis, Fleming, & Wong, 2017).

Moreover, there are no examples of programs producing large gains like those in the small-scale studies without highly qualified teachers (Kelley & Camilli, 2006), and some experts have concluded that as a practical matter, a four-year degree is necessary, but not sufficient, for teachers to acquire the knowledge and skills to be a highly effective teacher of young children (National Research Council, 2015). Research on how effectiveness of the B.A. degree might vary with the quality of preservice teacher preparation is notably lacking, yet likely an important factor.

In-service training of preschool educators might be thought to be a more effective approach to improving teacher quality, but this depends on successfully moving from small-scale experiments to large-scale public provision of such training. A meta-analysis on effects of in-service training on teachers' skills found larger, positive effects for training than for credentials. However, results were noticeably weaker for multi-site training in large-scale programs than in small-scale studies (Fukkink & Lont, 2007). Consistent with these findings, a recent randomized large-scale trial of state-provided intensive professional development focused on language and literacy failed to find significant impacts on teachers with or without substantial in-class coaching (Piasta et al., 2017), echoing the null findings of another multi-site professional development with respect to children's literacy and language (Pianta et al., 2017). Rigorous studies—including, but not limited to, randomized trials—of teacher preparation, experience, and in-service programs provided *on a large scale* are markedly scarce. Notably, in less successful examples, coaching was not tied to a specific curriculum, which may critically influence the effectiveness of coaching and in-service training (Weiland, 2016, 2018).

Although less widely studied, teacher well-being is also a crucial ingredient for supporting children's development (Jennings & Greenberg, 2009). Yet teaching preschool can be stressful, especially when exacerbated by poor working conditions and compensation, making it more challenging for teachers to provide supportive and engaging environments for young children (Friedman-Krauss, Raver, Morris, & Jones, 2014; Gerber, Whitebook, & Weinstein, 2007; Hamre & Pianta, 2004; Li-Grining et al., 2010). Rates of turnover within the ECE profession are also high. Nationally, 16% of Head Start teachers left over the course of one year (Barnett & Friedman-Krauss, 2016), and other estimates indicate that rates of turnover among ECE teachers can be as high as 29% (Rhodes & Huston, 2012; Whitebook & Sakai, 2003). Teacher turnover can have negative effects on children who benefit from experienced teachers and stability, and may also serve as an indicator of stress and lack of support for strong teaching.

Class Size and Ratio. Research findings have been mixed regarding the effects of class size and ratio on preschool program quality and outcomes, a result that is not unexpected given how variable the programs studied have been in terms of populations served, goals, funding, auspice, and other features. Some, but not all, studies have found smaller classes and lower ratios of students to teachers to be associated with modest improvements. However, findings are not fully consistent even across the studies reporting positive results (e.g., Abbott-Shim, Lambert & McCarty, 2000; Helburn, 1995; Howes, Phillips, & Whitebook, 1992; Mashburn et al., 2008; NICHD Early Child Care Research Network, 2002; Ruopp, Travers, Coelen, & Glantz, 1979).

Two recent reviews both concluded that evidence is lacking for important effects of class size on children's learning and development (Bowne, Magnuson, Schindler, Duncan &

Yoshikawa, 2017; Perlman et al., 2017). A meta-analysis by Bowne et al. (2017) finds some evidence for very modest positive effects of reduced class size (and improved ratio) below 15 (7.5:1), but not in the range above. In a qualitative review and meta-analysis, Perlman et al. (2017) concluded that little in the way of relationships between ratio and child outcomes was evident, but noted serious limitations of the research, including range restrictions on class size and ratio permitted by regulation, measurement problems with independent and dependent variables, and a lack of experimental studies.

The available experimental literature has other serious limitations. Only one of 29 studies reviewed by Perlman et al. (2017) was a randomized trial, and that study exposed children to different ratios for a relatively brief period. Another recent study randomized morning and afternoon class sessions of the same teacher to have either 15 or 20 students. Smaller classes had significantly larger gains in literacy skills but not in receptive vocabulary or math (Francis & Barnett, 2019). However, teachers could have been reluctant to create two very different plans for each of their sessions, limiting the benefits of class size reduction in this study.

Curriculum. The dominant view in the United States is that preschool education should be comprehensive, holistic, play-based, and intentional. Recently, some scholars have advocated for "domain specific" curricula that follow insights into children's developmental trajectories in a given domain and offer a specific scope and sequence individualized to each child (e.g., "Goldilocks" activities—not too hard, not too easy for their current skill level) over broad, "whole child" curricula (Phillips et al., 2017; Yoshikawa et al., 2016). By contrast, whole-child curricula are viewed as encompassing all domains of children's learning, offering activities that children tend to find engaging but leaving the scope and sequencing up to individual teachers. Domain-specific curricula have outperformed whole-child curricula on improving achievement test scores in rigorous trials, at least in the short-term (Chambers, Cheung, & Slavin, 2016; Nguyen et al., 2016; Phillips et al., 2017; Yoshikawa et al., 2016).

A more general finding that seems to have stood the test of time is that "programs with specific objectives and strategies to achieve them" are more effective in achieving their specific objectives (Bissell, 1972). Specificity with respect to objectives and strategies increases effectiveness not just for achievement, but for at least some aspects of social and emotional development, as well (Schindler et al., 2015). This still leaves the field with many unanswered questions about the short- and long-term impacts of curricular approaches. Despite recent advances, many of the domains prized by early childhood educators are rarely measured, including creativity, intrinsic motivation to learn, and a wide array of dispositions, habits, attitudes, and beliefs that make up the "whole child."

Impacts of Process Quality

Preschool program impacts most directly depend on the experiences (or process quality) they provide to children and families. A variety of measures have been developed to directly assess the quality of experiences preschools provide to children (Tout et al., 2010). While most large-scale public programs score fairly high on some of these measures—for example, on providing warm, sensitive interactions—their scores are particularly low on the scales most directly related to achievement (Barnett & Friedman-Krauss, 2016; Bassok & Galdo, 2016; Chaudry et al., 2017; Keys et al., 2013; Locasale-Crouch et al., 2007). However, a national study measuring process quality across publicly funded preschool programs has not been conducted in over a decade, and in addition to changes in preschool programs and populations, quality measures have also changed during this time. Precisely how the older, small-scale programs would have compared to large-scale public programs is unknown. These observational measures of preschool process quality had not been developed when the original Perry Preschool, Child-Parent Center and Abecedarian studies were conducted. Nevertheless, weak scores today on the aspects of measures relating most strongly to "instruction" and achievement are informative.

Although process quality measures do not capture all that we would wish to know about quality, scores on these are modestly related to children's learning and development in multiple domains (Broekhuizen, Mokrova, Burchinal, Garrett-Peters, and Family Life Project Key Investigators, 2016; Burchinal, Kainz, & Cai, 2011; Keys et al., 2013; Mashburn, et al., 2008; Zaslow, Anderson, et al., 2016; for long-term associations see, for example, Lehrl, Kluczniok, & Rossbach, 2016; Peisner Feinberg, et al., 2001). Some studies suggest thresholds for substantive gains at higher levels of quality (Burchinal et al., 2011). Other studies find no relationships with some commonly used measures, raising questions about both technical and practical problems with measures (Gordon, Fujimoto, Kaestner, Korenman, & Abner, 2013; Sabol & Pianta, 2014). Domain-specific measures of quality have been found to have higher correlations with domain-specific measures of child progress (Votruba-Drzal & Miller, 2016), and newer measures, currently under development, hold promise to better identify specific classroom practices tied to children's learning and development (Weiland, 2018). However, findings regarding which quality measures perform best vary with research methodology (Auger, Farkas, Burchinal, Duncan, & Vandell, 2014; for the primary grades, see Bacher-Hicks, Chin, Kane, & Staiger, 2017). It should be acknowledged that some general quality measures include aspects of quality (e.g., health and safety) not expected to affect measured child outcomes, and some important child outcomes go unmeasured in this literature. Despite these caveats, we conclude that inadequate process quality poses a serious challenge to producing large and persistent gains in learning and development with large-scale public preschool programs.

Future Research

The gap in results between today's large-scale public programs and the small-scale models has no single, simple explanation. For multiple reasons we have enumerated, it would be unreasonable to expect public programs to reproduce the strongest results from past small-scale studies. Yet, recent studies also suggest that public programs can be expected to perform much more strongly than has been typical, and new research can play an important role in making that happen. This new research can be broadly categorized as improved research on old questions and new research on new questions. We have suggested some avenues for this research in the prior sections, but we focus exclusively on recommendations for research in closing this chapter.

Improved Research on "Old" Questions

Although it has long been recognized that substantial variation may be masked by average treatment effects, research has continued to be quite limited in its capacity to illuminate the ways in which early education's effects vary based on interactions with (a) personal and family background characteristics and (b) broader contexts. The need to improve our research in these respects should not be neglected as we seek to better understand how to produce stronger, more persistent impacts on learning and development at scale. Larger samples in large-scale evaluations or entire programs designed with systematic variations in person and context are needed to rigorously investigate these interactions. This suggests more research looking at variations within classrooms and variations beyond classrooms.

How much inadequate funding constrains the effectiveness of large-scale preschool programs remains a largely unanswered question. Whether or not the high funding levels of the most intensive older models are practical (a question of political will), there is considerable room for increase before pre-K spending reaches even the level of current of K–12 expenditure per pupil (Barnett et al., 2017). The difficulty is how to conduct highly valid studies for drawing causal inferences regarding the effects of funding level. Multi-site, large-scale randomized trials of the impacts of additional funding seem impractical; long-term financial commitments are required to estimate the impacts of a permanent increase in funding. A short-term increase would not fully address the question. Methods applied to study the effects of K–12 funding on educational outcomes might be applied to preschool (e.g., Jackson, Johnson, & Persico, 2016; Lafortune, Rothstein, & Schanzenbach, 2018). Multi-site, small-scale randomized trials along the lines of the Educare studies also might prove fruitful (Yazejian et al., 2017). Large-scale studies randomized by site could be created within Head Start utilizing either federal funds or state supplements. Such studies could seek to better understand how funding matters by researching specific models in which multiple interdependent program features are enhanced simultaneously.

Even though the number of experimental studies of the impacts of structural features of programs is quite small, we do not think that an expansion of research focused on each feature in isolation would be very productive. If structural features matter much, they seem likely to do so interactively rather than individually and additively. Some features are so very highly interdependent—such as staff compensation and working conditions, qualifications, experience, and in-service professional development—that studying them as if they are independent could well produce misleading results. For example, most studies of teacher qualifications have ignored teacher compensation, which would be expected to affect teacher quality, morale, turnover, and other factors that may play a crucial role in program effectiveness. We suggest testing collections or systems of stronger features against weaker ones, particularly in combination with variations in program duration, to assess how much stronger features might matter if received consistently over longer days and a greater number of years.

It is difficult to see how studies of structural features can be conducted in isolation from the study of program funding more generally. Otherwise, improvements in some features are likely to be accompanied by the dilution of others, particularly those that tend to be measured (e.g., increased degree requirements accompanied by decreased degree quality). Researchers will have to confront the question of how randomized trials might be constructed with long-term commitments to the resources required to pay for more expensive sets of program features or examine what alternatives to randomized trials could be employed that are less artificial and allow for the estimation of the impacts of permanent changes in program features and funding.

We suggest new approaches to non-experimental research on structural features, as long-term, large-scale experiments are likely to be extremely expensive and to make only modest contributions to policy making (e.g., Widerquist, 2005). If the United States conducted birth cohort studies even once a decade that collected state-representative data on program structural and process quality as well as children's learning and development, these data might be used to compare the impacts of very different policy regimes across states and cities. This would be easier if data on preschool teacher qualifications and compensation, class size and ratio, curriculum and observational measures of teaching and the classroom environment were routinely collected for nationally representative samples at regular intervals. The United States has not collected a nationally representative sample of classroom observation data since 2005 (U.S. Department of Education, 2014).

The field has made progress through experimental research on curriculum and other changes in practice (process quality). However, a few improvements in methods could lead to greater gains. In particular, we recommend that studies create better-defined contrasts. A common practice in curriculum research has been to test a "model" or brand against an alternative that is characterized as "business as usual." However, neither curriculum brands nor "business as usual" can be expected to stay the same from one place or time to another. Branded curricula are revised with some frequency, which may be a necessity to maintain sales. "Business as usual" is no real definition at all. We will learn much more if studies measure the actual teacher practices and other educational experiences, including communication with parents, for both treatment and comparison groups. When the content and methods of alternative models are more clearly defined, it will be easier to draw useful general conclusions not just from individual studies, but across the literature.

We also suggest increased investment in qualitative and mixed-methods research that would go beyond measuring impacts by studying implementation to increase understanding of why variations in resources and features do or do not impact children's learning and development. Very few studies have examined how teachers, children, and families respond to changes in program features and practices, but those few have been highly illuminating. Even relatively "simple" changes such as class size reduction differ in the ways in which programs are allowed to implement the change, the time allotted for change, and technical assistance or professional development offered to promote the desired consequences (e.g., Graue, Hatch, Rao, & Oen, 2007; Sims, 2008; Stecher, Bohrnstedt, Kirst, McRobbie, & Williams, 2001). As part of this research, we recommend "postmortems," studies that focus on failures as well as successes, in order to understand what can go wrong and how the chances for success might be improved (Boruch & Ruby, 2013).

Improvements in measurement of both child outcomes and educational practice could contribute to more productive research. This will require substantial investment in measures development. Child outcome measures in most studies have tended to measure a relatively narrow set of outcomes, though studies have been improving in this regard (e.g., including measures of executive function). Research needs to move beyond basic measures of constrained skills to broader, deeper knowledge and skills that may better predict long-term achievement (Snow & Matthews, 2016). Moreover, the field's curriculum debates can only be addressed if we measure additional domains including creativity, motivation, and child well-being. Concerns that increased attention to academics has negative impacts on the well-being of young children, including their creativity, joy, and intrinsic desire to learn, can only be effectively addressed if substantial numbers of studies incorporate valid measures of these constructs. In addition, increased understanding of causal relationships between changes in early learning and development and persistent improvements in early learning and development can better inform the development of programs with more persistent impacts (Bailey, Duncan, Watts, Clements, & Sarama, 2018).

Finally, better measures of teaching practices and children's experiences might prove to be more strongly associated with measures of learning, development, and well-being, particularly if the child measures also were improved (Zaslow, Burchinal, Tarullo, & Martinez-Beck, 2016). For example, use of a new language and literacy measure, the Observation of Language and Literacy Instruction (OLLI) (Chiang et al., 2017), helped researchers to identify specific teaching practices such as focusing on higher-order thinking and defining new words during reading as promising practices in the early grades. Also, there is increasing recognition that the quality experienced varies among children within the same classroom (Vitiello, Booren, Downer, & Williford, 2012), and measures should capture such variation (e.g., Connor et al., 2009). Investments in new measures would benefit the entire field and ought to be supported with dedicated funding apart from specific research and evaluation studies on other topics.

New Research on New Questions

We propose a shift in emphasis for new research, as much (though certainly not all) of the past research on "what works" has focused on what happens within the classroom. One key prior question is why some children and not others participate. If children never show up in a classroom, it hardly matters for them what happens there. And, although of utmost importance to those who do attend, what happens inside the classroom is not exclusively determined at the classroom level. Not all elements of quality reside within the classroom or are measured by classroom observations (Coburn, 2003). Broader policies and practices of the educational system (e.g., teacher churn, teacher allocation to untested grades) that are not specific to early childhood education can be important determinants of young children's experiences within the classroom. Leadership is studied relatively little by those concerned with preschool program quality (Aubrey, Godfrey, & Harris, 2013). If research is to advance our understanding of how to produce stronger results at scale, it will have to place much greater emphasis outside the classroom on centers and schools, and on districts. As Fullan (2000, p. 581) has noted more generally: "We know a great deal about individual school success; we know far less about school system success." This includes understanding how context matters, including the other services available to children and families and the larger educational system in which they are embedded, and this will require large-scale studies in which context varies (e.g., Bassok, Gibbs, & Latham, 2019; Johnson & Jackson, 2017).

We recommend several new approaches to research focused on learning how to scale up effective programs. Broadly, one such approach can be characterized as developing large-scale demonstrations of coherent systems. Coburn (2003) has suggested such an approach that would lead to greater knowledge about four interrelated dimensions: depth of implementation, including adoption of pedagogical principles; sustainability over many years; spread of norms, beliefs, and principles; and ownership by teachers and administrators throughout a system. Reynolds and colleagues have followed such an approach in multiple studies replicating the child-parent centers in multiple sites with particular attention to factors that may contribute to larger and lasting gains (e.g., Reynolds et al., 2017; Reynolds, Ou, Mondi, & Hayakawa, 2017). They have laid out in detail how to conduct such a study and developed an array of tools for measuring implementation at scale. Their methods might usefully be applied to other models and truly at large scale—city- or state-wide. Researchers might also employ those methods and tools to "reverse engineer" high quality at scale, asking what it is that differentiates systems that produce high levels of success for disadvantaged students at scale over many years (e.g., Kirp, 2015).

More generally, the field could develop its own "implementation science" informed by K–12 research on school administration and reform that has been largely ignored in research on implementation failure in early childhood (e.g., Cohen & Hill, 2001; Cohen & Moffit, 2009; Halle, Metz, & Martinez-Beck, 2013; Leithwood, Harris, & Hopkins, 2008; McLaughlin, 1987). The early childhood field has devoted some attention to the problem of implementation, but most of this research has been confined to what goes on in an individual classroom as influenced by individual teachers, curriculum, and professional development (Dunst, Trivette, & Raab, 2013). The problem of producing fidelity system-wide and sustaining that fidelity over the long term is addressed by research on Quality Rating and Improvement Systems (QRIS) (Connors & Morris, 2015). Whether QRIS can be used to propel systems to high quality and effectiveness and, thereby, produce large gains that are sustained—particularly for disadvantaged children—will be an interesting question for the future.

In addition to broad studies of systems change, new research is needed on major components of systems. For example, QRIS is one commonly used approach to continuous improvement. Might other approaches be equally or more effective? Does that vary with program auspice? Policies often emphasize formative evaluation using a variety of measures. Do teachers actually use formative evaluation to individualize education for their students, and, if so, under what circumstances and to what effect? If not, what are the barriers to such practice? How well do the specific measures used actually work? Coaching is another common element of such systems, but we know relatively little about what makes coaching more or less effective.

Finally, we suggest that practice leaders, policy makers, and researchers collaborate in designing, launching, and studying the implementation and impacts of systemic efforts to produce large and persistent gains at scale. Program success depends on multiple interdependent factors, and scale-up with success requires attention to issues relating to governance, finance, preparation of the workforce, data systems, accountability and continuous improvement, and quality standards that depend as much on political as technical expertise.

References

Abbott-Shim, M., Lambert, R., & McCarty, F. (2000). Structural model of Head Start classroom quality. *Early Childhood Research Quarterly, 15*, 115–134.

Ansari, A., Purtell, K., & Gershoff, E. (2016). Classroom age composition and the school readiness of 3- and 4-year-olds in the Head Start program. *Psychological Science, 27*, 53–63.

Atteberry, A., Bassok, D., & Wong, V. C. (2019). The effects of full-day pre-kindergarten: Experimental evidence of impacts on children's school readiness. *Educational Evaluation and Policy Analysis, 41*(4), 537–562.

Aubrey, C., Godfrey, R., & Harris, A. (2013). How do they manage? An investigation of early childhood leadership. *Educational Management Administration & Leadership, 41*, 5–29.

Auger, A., Farkas, G., Burchinal, M. R., Duncan, G. J., & Vandell, D. L. (2014). Preschool center care quality effects on academic achievement: An instrumental variables analysis. *Developmental Psychology, 50*, 2559–2571.

Bacher-Hicks, A., Chin, M. J., Kane, T. J., & Staiger, D. O. (2017). *An evaluation of bias in three measures of teacher quality: Value-added, classroom observations, and student surveys* (No. w23478). Cambridge, MA: National Bureau of Economic Research.

Bailey, D. H., Duncan, G. J., Odgers, C. L., & Yu, W. (2017). Persistence and fadeout in the impacts of child and adolescent interventions. *Journal of Research on Educational Effectiveness, 10*(1), 7–39.

Bailey, D. H., Duncan, G. J., Watts, T., Clements, D. H., & Sarama, J. (2018). Risky business: Correlation and causation in longitudinal studies of skill development. *American Psychologist, 73*(1), 81–94.

Barnett, W. S. (2008). *Preschool education and its lasting effects: Research and policy implications* (EPRU Policy Brief). Boulder, CO and Tempe, AZ: Education and the Public Interest Center & Education and Policy Research Unit.

Barnett, W. S., & Frede, E.C. (2017). Long-term effects of a system of high-quality universal preschool education in the United States. In H. P. Blossfeld, N. Kulic, J. Skopek, & M. Triventi (Eds.), *Childcare, early education and social inequality: An international perspective* (pp. 152–171). Cheltenham, UK: Edward Elgar Publishing.

Barnett, W. S., & Friedman-Krauss, A. H. (2016). *The state(s) of Head Start*. New Brunswick, NJ: National Institute for Early Education Research.

Barnett, W. S., Friedman-Krauss, A. H., Weisenfeld, G. G., Horowitz, M., Kasmin, R., & Squires, J. H. (2017). *The state of preschool 2016: State preschool yearbook*. New Brunswick, NJ: National Institute for Early Education Research.

Barnett, W. S., & Lamy, C. (2013). Achievement gaps start early: Preschool can help. In P. L. Carter & K. G. Welner (Eds.), *Closing the opportunity gap: What America must do to give every child an even chance* (pp. 98–110). Oxford, UK: Oxford University Press.

Barnett, W. S., & Masse, L. N. (2007). Comparative benefit–cost analysis of the Abecedarian program and its policy implications. *Economics of Education Review, 26*, 113–125.

Bassok, D., Finch, J. E., Lee, R., Reardon, S. F., & Waldfogel, J. (2016). Socioeconomic gaps in early childhood experiences: 1998 to 2010. *AERA Open, 2*(3), 1–22.

Bassok, D., & Galdo, E. (2016). Inequality in preschool quality? Community-level disparities in access to high-quality learning environments. *Early Education and Development, 27,* 128–144.

Bassok, D., Gibbs, C. R., & Latham, S. (2019). Preschool and children's outcomes in elementary school: Have patterns changed nationwide between 1998 and 2010? *Child Development, 90*(6), 1875–1897. doi:10.1111/cdev.13067

Bissell, J. S. (1972). *Planned variation in Head Start and follow through.* Washington, DC: Department of Health, Education, and Welfare.

Bloom, H. S., & Weiland, C. (2015). *Quantifying variation in Head Start effects on young children's cognitive and socio-emotional skills using data from the national Head Start Impact Study.* Retrieved from https://www.mdrc.org/sites/default/files/quantifying_variation_in_head_start.pdf

Boruch, R., & Ruby, A. (2013). To flop is human: Inventing better scientific approaches to anticipating failure. *Emerging trends in the social and behavioral sciences: An interdisciplinary, searchable, and linkable resource* (pp. 1–16). Retrieved from https://onlinelibrary.wiley.com/doi/abs/10.1002/9781118900772.etrds0362

Bowne, J. B., Magnuson, K. A., Schindler, H. S., Duncan, G. J., & Yoshikawa, H. (2017). A meta-analysis of class sizes and ratios in early childhood education programs: Are thresholds of quality associated with greater impacts on cognitive, achievement, and socioemotional outcomes? *Educational Evaluation and Policy Analysis, 39*(3), 407–428.

Broekhuizen, M. L., Mokrova, I. L., Burchinal, M. R., Garrett-Peters, P. T., & Family Life Project Key Investigators. (2016). Classroom quality at pre-kindergarten and kindergarten and children's social skills and behavior problems. *Early Childhood Research Quarterly, 36,* 212–222.

Burchinal, M., Kainz, K., & Cai, Y. (2011). How well do our measures of quality predict child outcomes? A meta-analysis and coordinated analysis of data from large-scale studies of early childhood settings. In M. Zaslow, I. Martinez-Beck, K. Trout, & T. Halle (Eds.), *Measuring quality in early childhood settings* (pp. 11–32). Baltimore, MD: Brookes Publishing.

Caronongan, P., Moiduddin, E., West, J., & Vogel, C. A. (2014). *Children in Early Head Start and Head Start: A profile of early leavers* (Baby FACES and FACES 2009 Research Brief, OPRE Report 2014-54). Washington, DC: Office of Planning, Research, and Evaluation, Administration for Children and Families, U.S. Department of Health and Human Services.

Chambers, B., Cheung, A. C. K., & Slavin, R. E. (2016). Literacy and language outcomes of comprehensive and developmental-constructivist approaches to early childhood education: A systematic review. *Educational Research Review, 18,* 88–111.

Chaudry, A., & Datta, A. R. (2017). The current landscape for public pre-kindergarten programs. In K. Dodge & D. Phillips (Eds.), *The current state of scientific knowledge of pre-kindergarten effects* (pp. 5–18). Washington, DC: Brookings Institution Press.

Chaudry, A., Morrissey, T., Weiland, C., & Yoshikawa, H. (2017). *Cradle to kindergarten: A new plan to combat inequality.* New York, NY: The Russell Sage Foundation.

Chiang, H., Walsh, E., Shanahan, T., Gentile, C., Maccarone, A., Waits, T., et al. (2017). *An exploration of instructional practices that foster language development and comprehension: Evidence from prekindergarten through grade 3 in Title I schools* (NCEE 2017–4024). Washington, DC: National Center for Education Evaluation and Regional Assistance, Institute of Education Sciences, U.S. Department of Education.

Coburn, C.E. (2003). Rethinking scale: Moving beyond numbers to deep and lasting change. *Educational Researcher, 32*(6), 3–12.

Cohen, D. K., & Hill, H. C. (2001). *Learning policy.* New Haven, CT: Yale University Press.

Cohen, D. K., & Moffit, S. L. (2009). *The ordeal of equality: Can federal regulations fix the schools?* Cambridge, MA: Harvard University Press.

Cohen, D. K., Spillane, J. P., & Peurach, D. J. (2018). The dilemmas of educational reform. *Educational Researcher, 47*(3), 204–212.

Connor, C. M., Morrison, F. J., Fishman, B. J., Ponitz, C. C., Glasney, S., Underwood, P. S., & Schatschneider, C. (2009). The ISI classroom observation system: Examining the literacy instruction provided to individual students. *Educational Researcher, 38*(2), 85–99.

Connors, M. C., & Morris, P. A. (2015). Comparing state policy approaches to early care and education quality: A multidimensional assessment of quality rating and improvement systems and child care licensing regulations. *Early Childhood Research Quarterly, 30,* 266–279.

Consortium for Longitudinal Studies. (1983). *As the twig is bent—lasting effects of preschool programs.* Hillsdale, NJ: Lawrence Erlbaum.

Drummond, C. (2009). Replicability is not reproducibility: Nor is it good science. *Proceedings of the 26th Annual International Conference on Machine Learning.* Montreal, Quebec, Canada. Retrieved from http://cogprints.org/7691/7/ICMLws09.pdf

Duncan, G. J., & Magnuson, K. (2013). Investing in preschool programs. *The Journal of Economic Perspectives, 27,* 109–132.

Dunst, C. J., Trivette, C. M., & Raab, M. (2013). An implementation science framework for conceptualizing and operationalizing fidelity in early childhood intervention studies. *Journal of Early Intervention, 35,* 85–101.

Early, D. M., Maxwell, K. L., Burchinal, M., Alva, S., Bender, R. H., Bryant, D., et al. (2007). Teachers' education, classroom quality, and young children's academic skills: Results from seven studies of preschool programs. *Child Development, 78,* 558–580.

Etz, A., & Vandekerckhove, J. (2016). A Bayesian perspective on the reproducibility project: Psychology. *Plos One, 11*(2), 1–12.

Feller, A., Grindal, T., Miratrix, L., & Page, L. (2016). Compared to what? Variation in the impact of early childhood education by alternative care type. *Annals of Applied Statistics, 110,* 1245–1285.

Francis, J., & Barnett, W. S. (2019). Relating preschool class size to classroom quality and student achievement. *Early Childhood Research Quarterly, 49,* 49–58.

Frede, E. C. (1998). Preschool program quality in programs for children in poverty. In W. S. Barnett & S. S. Boocock (Eds.), *Early care and education for children in poverty: Promises, practices, and long-term results* (pp. 77–98). Albany: State University of New York Press.

Friedman-Krauss, A. H., Barnett, W. S., Garver, K. A., Hodges, K. S., Weisenfeld, G. G., &, DiCrecchio, N. (2019). *The state of preschool 2018: State preschool yearbook.* New Brunswick, NJ: National Institute for Early Education Research.

Friedman-Krauss, A. H., Raver, C. C., Morris, P., & Jones, S. M. (2014). The role of classroom-level child behavior problems in predicting preschool teacher stress and classroom emotional climate. *Early Education and Development, 25,* 530–552.

Fukkink, R. G., & Lont, A. (2007). Does training matter? A meta-analysis and review of caregiver training studies. *Early Childhood Research Quarterly, 22,* 294–311.

Fullan, M. (2000). The three stories of education reform. *Phi Delta Kappan, 81*(8), 581–584.

Gerber, E. B., Whitebook, M., & Weinstein, R. S. (2007). At the heart of child care: Predictors of teacher sensitivity in center-based child care. *Early Childhood Research Quarterly, 22*(3), 327–346.

Gibbs, C. (2014). *Experimental evidence on early intervention: The impact of full-day kindergarten* (EdPolicyWorks Working Paper No. 34). Retrieved from https://curry.virginia.edu/sites/default/files/files/EdPolicyWorks_files/34_Full_Day_KG_Impact.pdf

Gilbert, D. T., King, G., Pettigrew, S., & Wilson, T. D. (2016). Comment on "Estimating the reproducibility of psychological science." *Science, 351,* 1037.

Gordon, R. A., Fujimoto, K., Kaestner, R., Korenman, S., & Abner, K. (2013). An assessment of the validity of the ECERS-R with implications for measures of child care quality and relations to child development. *Developmental Psychology, 49,* 146–160.

Gormley, W., Gayer, T., Phillips, D., & Dawson, B. (2005). The effects of universal pre-K on cognitive development. *Developmental Psychology, 41*, 872–884.

Graue, E., Hatch, K., Rao, K., & Oen, D. (2007). The wisdom of class-size reduction. *American Educational Research Journal, 44*, 670–700.

Halle, T., Metz, A., & Martinez-Beck, I. (Eds.). (2013). *Applying implementation science in early childhood programs and systems.* Baltimore, MD: Paul H. Brookes Publishing Company.

Hamre, B. K., & Pianta, R. C. (2004). Self-reported depression in nonfamilial caregivers: Prevalence and associations with caregiver behavior in child-care settings. *Early Childhood Research Quarterly, 19*(2), 297–318.

Hanushek, E. A. (2015). The preschool debate: Translating research into policy. In I. G. Ellen, E. L. Glaeser, E. A. Hanushek, M. E. Kahn, & A. M. Renn (Eds.), *The next urban renaissance: How public-policy innovation and evaluation can improve life in America's cities* (pp. 25–40). New York, NY: Manhattan Institute for Policy Research.

Haskins, R., & Brooks-Gunn, J. (2016, Fall). Trouble in the land of early childhood education? *The future of children* (Policy Brief). Princeton, NJ: Princeton University. Retrieved from https://future-ofchildren.princeton.edu/sites/futureofchildren/files/media/starting_early_26_2_policy_brief.pdf

Helburn, S. W. (Ed.). (1995). *Cost, quality, and child outcomes in child care centers* (Technical Report). Denver: Department of Economics, Center for Research in Economics and Social Policy, University of Colorado at Denver.

Hill, C. J., Gormley Jr., W. T., & Adelstein, S. (2015). Do the short-term effects of a high-quality preschool program persist? *Early Childhood Research Quarterly, 32*, 60–79.

Howes, C., Phillips, D. A., & Whitebook, M. (1992). Thresholds of quality: Implications for the social development of children in center-based child care. *Child Development, 63*, 449–460.

Ioannidis, J. P. A. (2005). Why most published research findings are false. *PLOS Medicine 2*(8), e124.

Jackson, C. K., Johnson, R. C., & Persico, C. (2016). The effects of school spending on educational and economic outcomes: Evidence from school finance reforms. *The Quarterly Journal of Economics, 131*, 157–218.

Jennings, P. A., & Greenberg, M. T. (2009). The prosocial classroom: Teacher social and emotional competence in relation to student and classroom outcomes. *Review of Educational Research, 79*(1), 491–525.

Johnson, R. C., & Jackson, C. K. (2017). *Reducing inequality through dynamic complementarity: Evidence from Head Start and public school spending* (National Bureau of Economic Research Working Paper No. w23489). Retrieved from https://www.nber.org/papers/w23489

Kelley, P., & Camilli, G. (2006). *Effects of teacher qualifications in preschool education: A meta-analysis* (Working Paper). New Brunswick, NJ: National Institute for Early Education Research.

Keys, T. D., Farkas, G., Burchinal, M. R., Duncan, G. J., Vandell, D. L., Li, et al. (2013). Preschool center quality and school readiness: Quality effects and variation by demographic and child characteristics. *Child Development, 84*, 1171–1190.

Kirp, D. L. (2015). *Improbable scholars: The rebirth of a great American school system and a strategy for America's schools.* Oxford, UK: Oxford University Press.

Ladd, H. F., Muschkin, C. G., & Dodge, K. A. (2014). From birth to school: Early childhood initiatives and third-grade outcomes in North Carolina. *Journal of Policy Analysis Management, 33*, 162–187. doi: 10.1002/pam.21734

Lafortune, J., Rothstein, J., & Schanzenbach, D. W. (2018). School finance reform and the distribution of student achievement. *American Economic Journal: Applied Economics, 10*(2), 1–26.

Le, V. N., Kirby, S. N., Barney, H., Setodji, C. M., & Gershwin, D. (2006). *School readiness, full-day kindergarten, and student achievement: An empirical investigation.* Santa Monica, CA: RAND Corporation.

Lehrl, S., Kluczniok, K., & Rossbach, H. G. (2016). Longer-term associations of preschool education: The predictive role of preschool quality for the development of mathematical skills through elementary school. *Early Childhood Research Quarterly, 36*, 475–488.

Leithwood, K., Harris, A., & Hopkins, D. (2008). Seven strong claims about successful school leadership. *School Leadership and Management, 28*(1), 27–42.

Li, W., Duncan, G. J., Magnuson, K., Schindler, H. S., Yoshikawa, H., Leak, J., et al. (2017). *Timing in early childhood education: How cognitive and achievement program impacts vary by starting age, program duration, and time since the end of the program* (UCI SoE Working Paper). Irvine: University of California, Irvine.

Li-Grining, C. P., Raver, C. C., Champion, K. M., Sardin, L., Metzger, M. W., & Jones, S. M. (2010). Understanding and improving classroom emotional climate and behavioral management in the "real world": The role of Head Start teachers' psychosocial stressors. *Early Education and Development, 21*(1), 65–94.

Lipsey, M. W., Farran, D. C., & Durkin, K. (2018). Effects of the Tennessee Prekindergarten Program on children's achievement and behavior through third grade. *Early Childhood Research Quarterly, 45*, 155–176.

LoCasale-Crouch, J., Konold, T., Pianta, R., Howes, C., Burchinal, M., Bryant, D., et al. (2007). Observed classroom quality profiles in state-funded pre-kindergarten programs and associations with teacher, program, and classroom characteristics. *Early Childhood Research Quarterly, 22*, 3–17.

Makel, M. C., & Plucker, J. A. (2014). Facts are more important than novelty: Replication in the education sciences. *Educational Researcher, 43*(6), 304–316.

Malofeeva, E., Daniel-Echols, M., & Xiang, Z. (2007). *Findings from the Michigan School Readiness Program 6 to 8 follow up study.* Ypsilanti, MI: High/Scope Educational Research Foundation.

Manning, M., Garvis, S., Fleming, C., & Wong, G. T. (2017). *The relationship between teacher qualification and the quality of the early childhood care and learning environment: A systematic review.* Retrieved from https://www.campbellcollaboration.org/library/teacher-qualification-and-quality-of-early-childhood-care-and-learning.html

Mashburn, A. J., Pianta, R. C., Hamre, B. K., Downer, J. T., Barbarin, O. A., Bryant, D., et al. (2008). Measures of classroom quality in prekindergarten and children's development of academic, language, and social skills. *Child Development, 79*, 732–749.

McLaughlin, M. W. (1987). Learning from experience: Lessons from policy implementation. *Educational Evaluation and Policy Analysis, 9*(2), 171–178.

Murnane, R. J. (2013). U.S. high school graduation rates: Patterns and explanations. *Journal of Economic Literature, 51*, 370–422.

National Research Council. (2015). *Transforming the workforce for children birth through age 8: A unifying foundation.* Washington, DC: National Academies Press.

Nguyen, T., Watts, T. W., Duncan, G. J., Clements, D. H., Sarama, J. S., Wolfe, C., et al. (2016). Which preschool mathematics competencies are most predictive of fifth grade achievement? *Early Childhood Research Quarterly, 36*, 550–560.

NICHD Early Child Care Research Network. (2002). Child-care structure → process → outcome: Direct and indirect effects of child care quality on young children's development. *Psychological Science, 13*, 199–206.

Pashler, H., & Wagenmakers, E. J. (2012). Editors' introduction to the special section on replicability in psychological science: A crisis of confidence? *Perspectives on Psychological Science, 7*, 528–530.

Patil, P., Peng, R. D., & Leek, J. T. (2016). What should researchers expect when they replicate studies? A statistical view of replicability in psychological science. *Perspectives on Psychological Science, 11*, 539–544.

Payne, C. M. (2008). *So much reform, so little change: The persistence of failure in urban schools.* Cambridge, MA: Harvard Education Press.

Peisner-Feinberg, E. S., Burchinal, M. R., Clifford, R. M., Culkin, M. L., Howes, C., Kagan, S. L., et al. (2001). The relation of preschool child-care quality to children's cognitive and social developmental trajectories through second grade. *Child Development, 72*(5), 1534–1553.

Perlman, M., Fletcher, B., Falenchuk, O., Brunsek, A., McMullen, E., & Shah, P. S. (2017). Child-staff ratios in early childhood education and care settings and child outcomes: A systematic review and meta-analysis. *PloS one, 12*(1), e0170256.

Phillips, D. A., Lipsey, M. W., Dodge, K. A., Haskins, R., Bassok, D., Burchinal, M. R., et al. (2017). *Puzzling it out: The current state of scientific knowledge on pre-kindergarten effects, a consensus statement.* Washington, DC: Brookings Institution Press. Retrieved from https://www.brookings.edu/wp-content/uploads/2017/04/consensus-statement_final.pdf

Pianta, R. C., Barnett, W. S., Burchinal, M., & Thornburg, K. R. (2009). The effects of preschool education: What we know, how public policy is or is not aligned with the evidence base, and what we need to know. *Psychological Science in the Public Interest, 10*(2), 49–88.

Pianta, R., Hamre, B., Downer, J., Burchinal, M., Williford, A., LoCasale-Crouch, J., et al. (2017). Early childhood professional development: Coaching and coursework effects on indicators of children's school readiness. *Early Education and Development, 19,* 956–975.

Piasta, S. B., Justice, L. M., O'Connell, A. A., Mauck, S. A., Weber-Mayrer, M., Schachter, R. E., et al. (2017). Effectiveness of large-scale, state-sponsored language and literacy professional development on early childhood educator outcomes. *Journal of Research on Educational Effectiveness, 10,* 354–378.

Puma, M., Bell, S., Cook, R., Heid, C., Broene, P., Jenkins, F., et al. (2012). *Third grade follow-up to the Head Start Impact Study: Final report* (OPRE Report No. 2012-45). Washington, DC: Office of Planning, Research and Evaluation, Administration for Children and Families, U.S. Department of Health and Human Services.

Ramey, C. T., Collier, A. M., Sparling, J. J., Loda, F. A., Campbell, F. A., Ingram, D. L., et al. (1974). *The Carolina Abecedarian Project: A longitudinal and multidisciplinary approach to the prevention of developmental retardation.* Bethesda, MD: National Institute of Child Health and Human Development and National Heart and Lung Institute (DHEW/PHS).

Ramon, I., Chattopadhyay, S. K., Hahn, R., Barnett, W. S., & the Community Preventive Services Task Force. (2017). *Early childhood education to promote health equity: A community guide economic review.* Atlanta, GA: CDC, Community Guide Branch.

Reynolds, A. J. (2000). *Success in early intervention: The Chicago Child-Parent Centers.* Lincoln: University of Nebraska Press.

Reynolds, A. J., Hayakawa, M., Ou, S. R., Mondi, C. F., Englund, M. M., Candee, A. J., et al. (2017). Scaling and sustaining effective early childhood programs through school–family–university collaboration. *Child Development, 88,* 1453–1465.

Reynolds, A. J., Ou, S. R., Mondi, C. F., & Hayakawa, M. (2017). Processes of early childhood interventions to adult well-being. *Child Development, 88,* 378–387.

Rhodes, H., & Huston, A. (2012). Building the workforce our youngest children deserve. *Social Policy Report, 26*(1), 1–26.

Robin, K. B., Frede, E. C., & Barnett, W. S. (2006). *Is more better? The effects of full-day vs. half-day preschool on early school achievement* (NIIER Working Paper). New Brunswick, NJ: National Institute for Early Education Research.

Ruopp, R., Travers, J., Coelen, C., & Glantz, F. (1979). *Children at the center: Final report of the National Day Care Study* (Vol. 1). Cambridge, MA: Abt Books.

Sabol, T. J., & Pianta, R. C. (2014). Do standard measures of preschool quality used in statewide policy predict school readiness? *Education Finance and Policy, 9,* 116–164.

Schindler, H. S., Kholoptseva, J., Oh, S. S., Yoshikawa, H., Duncan, G. J., Magnuson, K. A., & Shonkoff, J. P. (2015). Maximizing the potential of early childhood education to prevent externalizing behavior problems: A meta-analysis. *Journal of School Psychology, 53,* 243–263.

Schweinhart, L. J. (2007, December). *How to take the High/Scope Perry Preschool to scale.* Paper presented at the National Invitational Conference of the Early Childhood Research Collaborative, Minneapolis, MN.

Sims, D. (2008). A strategic response to class size reduction: Combination classes and student achievement in California. *Journal of Policy Analysis and Management, 27,* 457–478.

Snow, C. E., & Matthews, T. J. (2016). Reading and language in the early grades. *Future of Children, 26,* 57–74.

Stecher, B., Bohrnstedt, G., Kirst, M., McRobbie, J., & Williams, T. (2001). Class-size reduction in California: A story of hope, promise, and unintended consequences. *Phi Delta Kappan, 82*(9), 670–674.

Tout, K., Starr, R., Soli, M., Moodie, S., Kirby, G., & Boller, K. (2010). *Compendium of quality rating systems and evaluations: The child care Quality Rating System (QRS) assessment.* Washington, DC: Administration for Children & Families.

U.S. Department of Education. (2014). *Digest of education statistics 2014.* Retrieved from National Center for Education Statistics website: https://nces.ed.gov/programs/digest/d14/tables/dt14_202.60.asp?current=yes

U.S. Department of Education. (2018). *The condition of education 2018* (NCES 2018-144). Retrieved from National Center for Education Statistics website: https://nces.ed.gov/programs/digest/d18/tables/dt18_219.10.asp

Valentino, R. (2018). Will public pre-K really close achievement gaps? Gaps in prekindergarten quality between students and across states. *American Educational Research Journal, 55*(1), 79–116.

Vitiello, V. E., Booren, L. M., Downer, J. T., & Williford, A. P. (2012). Variation in children's classroom engagement throughout a day in preschool: Relations to classroom and child factors. *Early Childhood Research Quarterly, 27*(2), 210–220.

Votruba-Drzal, E., & Miller, P. (2016). Reflections on quality and dosage of preschool and children's development. *Monographs of the Society for Research in Child Development, 81,* 100–113.

Walters, C. R. (2015). Inputs in the production of early childhood human capital: Evidence from Head Start. *American Economic Journal: Applied Economics, 7,* 76–102.

Weikart, D. P. (1967). *Preschool intervention: A preliminary report of the Perry Preschool Project.* Ann Arbor, MI: Campus Publishers.

Weiland, C. (2016). Launching Preschool 2.0: A road map to high-quality public programs at scale. *Behavioral Science & Policy, 2*(1), 37–46.

Weiland, C. (2018). Pivoting to the "how": Moving preschool policy, practice, and research forward. *Early Childhood Research Quarterly, 45,* 188–192.

Weiland, C., & Yoshikawa, H. (2013). Impacts of a prekindergarten program on children's mathematics, language, literacy, executive function, and emotional skills. *Child Development, 84,* 2112–2130.

Whitebook, M., McLean, C., Austin, L. J. E., & Edwards, B. (2018). *Early childhood workforce index – 2018.* Berkeley: Center for the Study of Child Care Employment, University of California, Berkeley. Retrieved from http://cscce.berkeley.edu/topic/early-childhood-workforce-index/2018/

Whitebook, M., & Sakai, L. (2003). Turnover begets turnover: An examination of job and occupational instability among child care center staff. *Early Childhood Research Quarterly, 18,* 273–293.

Widerquist, K. (2005). A failure to communicate: What (if anything) can we learn from the negative income tax experiments? *The Journal of Socio-Economics, 34,* 49–81.

Yazejian, N., Bryant, D. M., Hans, S., Horm, D., St. Clair, L., File, N., et al. (2017). Child and parenting outcomes after 1 year of Educare. *Child Development, 88,* 1671–1688.

Yoshikawa, H., Weiland, C., & Brooks-Gunn, J. (2016). When does preschool matter? *Future of Children, 26*(2), 21–36.

Yoshikawa, H., Weiland, C., Brooks-Gunn, J., Burchinal, M., Gormley, W., Ludwig, J., et al. (2013). *Investing in our future: The evidence base on preschool education.* Retrieved from http://srcd.org/sites/default/files/documents/washington/ mb_2013_10_16_investing_in_children.pdf

Yudron, M., Weiland, C., & Sachs, J. (2018). *The importance of adjusting for context: Learning from a pilot expansion of the Boston Public School Pre-K Model to community-based settings.* Manuscript under review. Boston, MA: Harvard Graduate School of Education.

Zaslow, M., Anderson, R., Redd, Z., Wessel, J., Daneri, P., Green, K., et al. (2016). I. Quality thresholds, features, and dosage in early care and education: Introduction and literature review. *Monographs of the Society for Research in Child Development, 81*(2), 7–26.

Zaslow, M., Burchinal, M., Tarullo, L., & Martinez-Beck, I. (2016). V. Quality thresholds, features, and dosage in early care and education: Discussion and conclusions. *Monographs of the Society for Research in Child Development, 81*(2), 75–87.

Chapter 13

Looking Internationally

Joseph Tobin

University of Georgia

Too little of the early childhood education research conducted by scholars in the United States engages with research conducted in other countries or by scholars from other countries. This parochialism makes not just for a limited view of what is possible in the practice of early childhood education and care, but also a weak discipline, one narrowly grounded in findings from one national context and constrained by North American conceptual orientations and preoccupations. I see this as primarily, but not only, a U.S. problem—such parochialism can be found among researchers, policy makers, and practitioners in other countries as well. In this chapter I argue that engagement with research conducted on early childhood education and care in other countries can reduce parochialism in two ways: by questioning taken-for-granted assumptions and by expanding the repertoire of the possible. Studies of early childhood education and care in other countries suggest that you can get good social and educational outcomes using approaches that differ significantly in many of the variables studied and considered causal in our domestic research.

In this essay I support this argument by presenting findings from studies on a Japanese pedagogical approach of low intervention in young children's fights and other struggles; high student-teacher ratios in East Asian preschools; and observational learning by children in Mexico. I also point out that countries known to have strong early childhood education, including Japan, Italy, and Finland, do much less assessing and testing of children than we do in North America.

My perspective on key issues and gaps in the research in this field reflects my background as a comparative educationalist, cultural anthropologist, and educational ethnographer who for many years has been studying preschools in other countries, most intensively in Japan and China. It is a dictum of anthropology that "Ethnography makes the exotic familiar and, in so doing, makes the familiar exotic." Educational anthropology makes the exotic familiar by showing how educational practices in other countries that to outsiders seem not just different but also counter-intuitive and even wrong-headed have meaning, sense, and functionality to cultural insiders. When, through ethnography, exotic educational practices are shown to make sense, familiar educational practices lose their taken-for-grantedness and new possibilities for research and practice arise. Such a comparative international approach can open up new research questions and unsettle the complacency and narrowness of our research agendas.

Teacher Interventions

In her (1984) article "Cooperation and Control in Japanese Nursery Schools," based on observations and interviews in 15 Japanese preschools, Catherine Lewis described a series of scenarios in which teachers intervened less often and less heavily than would their U.S. counterparts. These included situations in which children struggled with their shoes and clothing, misbehaved (as, for instance, by throwing stones at fish in a pond), and fought, verbally and physically. The most striking examples in her paper are quotes, like the following, from Japanese preschool teachers about how they routinely dealt with children's aggression: "We let them fight a bit, but not to the point of biting, etc. We have to let them experience pain to a small extent." . . . "I tell children to cry if they're being hurt, because the opponent will bite or pull until they cry" (p. 78). To make sense of this pedagogy of low intervention, Lewis combines Japanese emic explanations with references to Western theories of child development. She writes: "A growing research literature suggests that salient external control beyond that necessary to elicit compliance with a request tends to undermine children's internalization of the norm in question" (p. 71).

In conducting research for the Preschool in Three Cultures projects (Tobin, Wu, & Davidson, 1989; Tobin, Hsueh, & Karasawa, 2009), we learned that there is an emic term in Japanese for this low-intervention approach. *Mimamoru* refers to a pedagogy of holding back and watching, and waiting as long as possible before intervening as lightly as possible. Research conducted by Lewis, my research team, and other scholars has consistently documented the typicality of this practice in Japan (for example, Bamba & Walsh, 2013; Ben-Ari, 1997; Burke & Duncan, 2015; Hayashi & Tobin, 2012, 2015; Sato, 2004).

Video-cued interviews that my colleagues and I have conducted with Japanese preschool teachers and directors shed light on the thinking behind this low-intervention approach. In our 2015 book *Teaching Embodied: Cultural Practice in Japanese Preschools*, Akiko Hayashi and I suggest that such holding back is an implicit pedagogical practice that, while not explicitly covered in government guidelines or discussed in teacher education textbooks, nevertheless is characteristic of experienced Japanese early childhood education practitioners. For example, commenting on a scene we filmed in her classroom of a group of girls fighting verbally and physically over a teddy bear, Morita-sensei, a preschool teacher in Kyoto, commented:

> If I think a fight, such as this one in the video, is unlikely to result in anybody getting hurt, I stay back and wait and observe. I want the children to learn to be strong enough to handle such small quarrels. I want them to have the power to endure. If it's not dangerous, I welcome their fighting. (Hayashi & Tobin, 2015, pp. 24–25)

Another experienced teacher explained:

> Japanese teachers wait until children solve their problems on their own. Children know what they are capable of handling. So, we wait. You could say that it is because we believe in children that we can wait. Otherwise, children become people who can't

do things without permission. Of course, if they are in a situation where they don't know what to do, we talk it over with them, and then we wait and watch [*mimamoru*] to see what happens. (Hayashi & Tobin, 2015, p. 20)

I readily acknowledge that there are cultural, structural, and even legal reasons why it is not likely, or perhaps even desirable, for preschool teachers in the United States and other countries to adopt this Japanese pedagogical approach. However, from working for many years with preservice and in-service early childhood educators in the United States, I have seen how becoming aware of this Japanese low intervention approach to dealing with children's frustrations and misbehavior can impact practice. Confronted by children's misbehavior and hearing in their heads the voices of Japanese preschool teachers explaining why they are slow to intervene can lead U.S. practitioners to ask themselves a series of questions: "Am I so sure the children can't handle this dispute on their own?" "If I intervene, will the children conclude that all that is stopping them from hurting each other is an adult authority?" Learning about the Japanese logic behind the pedagogy of *mimamoru* can contribute to questioning of assumptions about the utility of quick intervention and can open up new ways of conceptualizing the role that preschools play in children's social-emotional development.

Class Size and Student-Teacher Ratios

The belief in the necessity of teachers' mediating young children's fights is connected with another largely unquestioned belief of U.S. early childhood education, namely that student-teacher ratios must be kept low in order to allow a teacher to give adequate attention to each child in her care. Most U.S. practitioners, policy makers, and scholars believe that a low student-teacher ratio is a key indicator of quality (e.g., S. Barnett, Schulman, & Shore, 2004; National Association for the Education of Young Children, 2005). How, then, do we reconcile this consensus with the fact that student-teacher ratios in Chinese, Japanese, and Korean preschools (and in many other countries) are much larger than in the United States, without obvious ill effects on child outcomes? Scholars, policy makers, and practitioners in these East Asian countries do not consider student-teacher ratios to be an important quality factor. Large (by U.S. standards) class sizes and high student-teacher ratios (for example, 25 four-year-old children with one teacher) are a given rather than a variable used to define program quality or explain student outcomes. In other words, student-teacher ratios seem to be correlated with quality in the North American, Anglophone, and European contexts, but not in many Asian countries with high educational achievement. If this is the case, we need to see assessments of teacher and program quality as highly contingent and contextual, and to reconceptualize research on this topic in ways that pay more attention to the relationship of student-teacher ratios to other factors (S. Barnett et al., 2004).

In fact, most of the well-designed studies on this topic in the United States suggest that class size and ratios make a statistically significant difference (though the effect size is small), but only when combined with other aspects considered essential to quality, including teacher experience and a faithfully implemented curriculum (W. S. Barnett, 2008; Burchinal, Roberts, Riggins, Zeisel, Neebe, & Bryant, 2010a; Burchinal, Vandergrift, Pianta, &

Mashburn, 2010b; Pianta et al., 2010). It is therefore difficult to disentangle the effects of class size and student-teacher ratios from other factors, absent a study that, for example, randomly assigns children in the same preschool to classrooms with different class sizes and student-teacher ratios.

There is also a black box problem here: Studies that correlate student outcomes with program features do not tell us what it is about smaller class size and lower student-teacher ratios that produces better outcomes. The implication, rarely made explicit, is that when children get more one-on-one interaction with teachers and when there are fewer children per teacher in a class, teachers can provide each child with more attention and more scaffolding of each child's linguistic, cognitive, and social-emotional development. For example, as Burchinal et al. wrote:

> We believe that, if our findings are causal, the goals of pre-kindergarten programs may only be achieved if programs ensure high-quality teacher-child interactions and at least moderate-quality instruction. These findings indicate that social outcomes were more strongly influenced by the quality of teacher-child interactions, but only when teachers are actively and positively engaged with children. (2010a, p. 174)

The notion of "high-quality teacher-child interactions" advanced here assumes that teachers must be "actively and positively engaged with children" in order to best support the development of children's social skills. The central assumption is that what is most helpful for children is teacher attention and scaffolded conversation. One-on-one interactions are assumed to be key, and these interactions between students and teachers are less common as the class size and child-adult ratio grows.

Here is where comparative and international research can be helpful. First of all, just knowing that there are preschools in East Asia that function with large classes provides a sort of existence proof that it is possible for classes of 25 four-year-olds and one adult to run well with no apparent ill effects on children's development. On a deeper level, ethnographic studies of these East Asian classes can lead to a questioning of the ethnocentrism and parochialism of assumptions in the literature about how children develop and the ways in which preschool teachers can foster children's development.

Japanese early childhood educators believe that Japanese children's social and cognitive development in preschool settings derives primarily not from interacting with teachers, but from non-adult-mediated interactions (Tobin, Wu, & Davidson, 1987; Walsh, 2002). Moreover, too much adult mediation is believed to hinder the quality and frequency of these peer interactions. As a Japanese child psychologist quoted in *Preschool in Three Cultures* argued: "When the class size falls below 20 children per teacher, it becomes a kind of danger zone, where there are still too many children for teachers to give one-on-one attention but too few to make it clear to children and the teacher that it is up to the children to handle their own problems" (Tobin et al., 1989, p. 120).

I am not arguing that lower class size is not beneficial for children in U.S. preschool classrooms. What I am suggesting is that we need more nuanced research and research conclusions on the interactions of student-teacher ratios and class size with other factors.

My hunch is that very low student-teacher ratios are beneficial only if teachers teach in a way that is focused on the frequency and intensity of their one-on-one interactions with individual students. Under such pedagogical approaches, more children per teacher means less instructional time for each.

There is an implication here for practice and policy: If it is the case that for preschool children in the United States having dyadic interaction with teachers is crucial, why not provide them with more time each day to work one-on-one with a teacher? This could be done without changing the overall student-teacher ratio in a preschool if, for example, in a class with two teachers and eighteen children, each teacher were to spend 15 minutes each day with each child in dyadic interaction while the other teacher worked with the rest of the class. I am not calling for this particular curricular innovation, but rather making the case that once we are aware of how ratios are handled and viewed differently in other countries, we can begin to consider more innovative approaches to class size and student-teacher ratios in our own early education settings.

Observational Learning

Until the last 50 years or so, in most of the world (including North America), most young children were cared for and supervised most of the day not by preschool teachers and not by their mothers, but by older children (Whiting & Edwards, 1988). When looked at from this perspective, preschools where young children spend the day in age-segregated groups with unrelated adults are the more exotic settings, the more radical experiments in child socialization. Settings like the Mayan Yucatan, where children spend much of the day in the company of mixed-age groups of children, under sporadic supervision and guidance from older relatives and neighbors, are the historical and global norm. In such settings, much of children's learning comes not from direct instruction from an adult, but instead from observing other children and adults engaging in practice. Research conducted on observational learning by young children in Mayan and other non-preschooled societies provide a significant challenge to many of our taken-for-granted assumptions about the care and education of young children and about our conceptions of how children learn. As Gaskins and Paradise (2009) argue in their overview of studies of observational learning in Mayan communities,

> While observational learning has long been recognized as a universal learning strategy used by children in their daily lives and has been reported in many ethnographic accounts, we argue that its unique potential as a primary learning strategy has been underestimated both because it is hard to see happening in children's everyday experience and because other learning strategies, especially verbal ones, are more central to Euro-American ethnographers' own ethnotheories of learning. (p. 103)

In their studies comparing learning in young children of different backgrounds, Barbara Rogoff and her research team have found that the observational learning and skills typical of Mayan children (Rogoff, Paradise, Arauz, Correa-Chávez, & Angelillo, 2003), and more generally of Mexican-heritage children, wane with increased exposure to the culture of U.S. schooling (Silva, Correa-Chávez, & Rogoff, 2010). The authors conclude this article with implications for practice:

> School could make use of a likely propensity for keen observation among children with familiarity with Indigenous practices, along with teaching them how to engage in the adult-directed attentional management common in schools. More broadly, observing ongoing interactions in which one is not involved may be beneficial to all children as a method of learning and being involved in community life. Indeed, schools could make greater use of children's observation of others as a pedagogical tool that may benefit all children's learning. (p. 910)

This conclusion has implications not just for early childhood educational practice but also for our conceptions of how children learn. As Rogoff et al. (2003) argue, observational learning and what they term "intent participation" provide a challenge and an alternative to "transmission" and "acquisition" models of learning:

> In both approaches learning is seen as accretion of information or skills, brought across a boundary from the external world to the mind of the learner. . . . Contrasting with transmission and acquisition models, in intent participation, learners engage collaboratively with others in the social world. Hence, there is no boundary dividing them into sides. There is also no separation of learning into an isolated assembly phase, with exercises for the immature, out of the context of the intended activity. (p. 182)

What could a U.S. preschool supportive of intent participation and observational learning look like? Perhaps there would be larger classes, with children of different ages. Children would learn from teachers less from direct instruction or mediation of their interactions than from observing adults engaged in meaningful activities and overhearing adult-adult talk. This happens a bit in U.S. preschools now, but not as much as it could. For meaningful observational learning and intent participation, the adults in the classroom need to be doing something in addition to minding and teaching the children. Children should be given opportunities to observe adults engaged in non-pedagogical work such as cooking and gardening, and they should be allowed to participate in this work according to their interest and ability. Preschool children and their teachers should be less cut off from life outside the school walls.

Preschool Teaching Expertise

Finding differences internationally where we might expect similarity (for example, in student-teacher ratios in preschools in Japan or in how Mayan children learn) is instructive. So, too, is finding similarity cross-nationally where we might expect difference. In *Preschool in Three Cultures* (Tobin et al., 1989) and *Preschool in Three Cultures Revisited* (Tobin et al., 2009), my colleagues and I found considerable differences in the pedagogical practices and beliefs of Japanese, Chinese, and U.S. teachers. In our research on preschool teaching expertise in China, Japan, and the United States, Akiko Hayashi and I therefore have been surprised to find a great deal of similarity in the ways that early childhood educational practitioners in these three countries describe the trajectories of teachers' acquisition of expertise (Hayashi & Tobin, 2018). In all three countries, experienced teachers describe how, after 10 or more years of experience, they become less in a rush; less driven by scripts; more able to quickly assess a situation and determine if it requires intervention and, therefore, more able to handle a class with a looser grip; and less inclined to intervene quickly or aggressively when children are struggling. After many years of experience, the teachers in these three countries do not become the same in their pedagogical practices. Chinese and U.S. teachers still describe themselves as intervening more quickly when children are struggling than do Japanese teachers. But even if the teachers do not end up in the same place, the direction of change described by our informants from all three countries is the same. This finding is an example of how looking internationally in our research can help us identify patterns in early childhood educational practices that transcend national boundaries.

Conclusions

In part because its focus is almost entirely domestic, much of the research in the field of early childhood education in the United States (as in many other countries) is comfortable and complacent. Too many studies show predictably positive effects of programs deemed, a priori, to be exemplary, or show predictably negative effects of programs defined, a priori, as low quality (e.g., programs with high staff turnover and poor facilities). Too many studies show statistically significant but modest effect-size findings on the contributions of various structural factors to children's learning outcomes. Too much of the research agenda asks smallish questions: What are the effects of having two fewer children per teacher? An additional year of training for teachers? Twenty more minutes per day of phonics?

More engagement with research conducted on early childhood education in other countries, as well as by scholars from other countries, is one way to question taken-for-granted assumptions about practice and policy, expand the repertoire of the possible, introduce new conceptual frameworks, and open up new lines of research. For example, research on observational learning conducted by Rogoff and others in the Yucatan can push us as researchers to pay more attention to variations in how young children from different cultural backgrounds learn best in U.S. preschool and elementary classrooms. This work can catalyze changes in policy and practice by providing a rationale for giving children of all backgrounds more opportunities to spend time in mixed-age groups and more opportunities for observational learning. Similarly, research conducted in East Asian countries that presents the logic behind their large (by U.S. standards) class sizes and student-teacher ratios can expand the ways that early childhood education researchers conceptualize the interplay of ratios and class size with pedagogical approaches.

A narrowness of vision and imagination in much of the domestic research on early childhood education means that this research can lead only to modest rearranging rather than to radical reimagining of approaches to educating and caring for young children. U.S. preschools and elementary schools are stuck in assumptions that are too rarely challenged, namely that in a classroom there must be 20 or so children of similar age, with two teachers, who watch continuously, intervene quickly, and scaffold enthusiastically. In contrast, if we paid more attention to how young children are cared for and educated in other countries and cultures, we could consider how preschool could be otherwise. For example, classrooms for young children could be home to children of mixed ages, with fluctuating arrangements of group size and structures throughout the day, with children having some one-on-one time with an adult, some time in small groups, and some with a large group, with varying amounts of adult attention, from short periods of didactic instruction to long periods of minimally supervised play and social interactions. Such changes could allow for more observational learning and intent participation, more child agency, and more collective problem solving.

On a macro level, I suggest that we can learn from other countries the value of not investing so much of the time and energy of children, teachers, and researchers in testing and assessing children. Countries such as Japan, Italy, and Finland that are known for having strong early childhood education and care systems and high educational outcomes do very little testing and assessing of young children and fund few studies designed to show the impacts of variations in program inputs (Sahlberg, 2015). The belief that such assessments and studies are crucial to improving the quality of early childhood education is itself a culture-bound assumption, unsupported by domestic evidence and contradicted by the experience of other countries.

I want to close by returning to where I began, with the problem of parochialism. The field of psychology has been faulted for studies of a sample of undergraduates in Ann Arbor, Mich., and then making claims from the data about the ways human beings think. Much of the research in early childhood education makes a similar category error, using studies of teachers and students in the United States to generate truths about teaching and learning in general. There is nothing wrong with U.S.-based researchers studying U.S. classrooms from a U.S. viewpoint, unless, that is, this research lacks awareness of its limitations. Even when U.S.-based researchers look beyond the United States, our attention is mostly directed to Anglophone publications and based on studies in other Anglophone countries (Canada, the UK, Australia, and New Zealand), countries that share much with the United States, not just linguistically but also culturally, politically, and socially. Therefore, when we read (or write) statements in scholarly literature such as, "Smaller student-teacher ratios are correlated with program quality and positive learning outcomes," or "Children benefit from one-on-one attention from teachers," a voice in our head should automatically add the qualification "in the United States."

References

Bamba, S., & Walsh, D. (2013). *Ibasho:* A place where one belongs. *Journal of Early Childhood Education, 19*(2), 15–27.

Barnett, S., Schulman, K., & Shore, R. (2004). Class size: What's the best fit? *Preschool Policy Matters, 9,* 1–12.

Barnett, W. S. (2008). *Preschool education and its lasting effects: Research and policy implications.* Boulder, CO, and Tempe, AZ: Education and Public Interest Center & Education Policy Research Unit. Retrieved from http://nieer.org/wp-content/uploads/2016/08/PreschoolLastingEffects.pdf

Ben-Ari, E. (1997). *Body projects in Japanese culture: Culture, organization and emotions in a preschool.* Richmond, UK: Curzon.

Burchinal, M., Roberts, J., Riggins, R., Zeisel, S., Neebe, E., & Bryant, D. (2010a). Relating quality of center-based child care to early cognitive and language development longitudinally. *Child Development, 71*(2), 339–357.

Burchinal, M., Vandergrift, N., Pianta, R., & Mashburn, A. (2010b). Threshold analysis of association between child care quality and child outcomes for low-income children in pre-kindergarten programs. *Early Childhood Research Quarterly, 25,* 166–176.

Burke, R., & Duncan, J. (2015). *Bodies as sites of cultural reflection in early childhood education.* New York, NY: Routledge.

Gaskins, S., & Paradise, R. (2009). Learning through observation in daily life. In D. F. Lancy, J. Bock, & S. Gaskins (Eds.), *The anthropology of learning in childhood* (pp. 85–117). Lanham, MD: AltaMira Press.

Hayashi, A., & Tobin, J. (2012). Reframing an ethnography of a Japanese preschool classroom. *Visual Anthropology Review, 28*(1), 13–31.

Hayashi, A., & Tobin, J. (2015). *Teaching embodied: Cultural practice in Japanese preschools.* Chicago, IL: University of Chicago Press.

Hayashi, A., & Tobin, J. (2018, March). *Conceptualizing similarities and differences in how teachers acquire expertise in three countries: Japan, China, and the United States.* Paper presented at the Comparative and International Education Society Conference, Mexico City, Mexico.

Lewis, C. (1984). Cooperation and control in Japanese nursery schools. *Comparative Education Review, 28*(1), 69–84.

National Association for the Education of Young Children. (2005). *Teacher-child ratios within group size.* Retrieved from https://www.naeyc.org/sites/default/files/globally-shared/downloads/PDFs/accreditation/early-learning/staff_child_ratio.pdf

Pianta, R., Howes, C., Burchinal, M., Bryant, D., Clifford, R., Early, D., et al. (2010). Features of pre-kindergarten programs, classrooms, and teachers: Do they predict observed classroom quality and child-teacher interactions? *Early Childhood Research Quarterly, 25,* 166–176.

Rogoff, B., Paradise, R., Arauz, M. R., Correa-Chávez, M., & Angelillo, C. (2003). Firsthand learning through intent participation. *Annual Review of Psychology, 54,* 175–203.

Sahlberg, P. (2015). *Finnish lessons 2.0: What the world can learn from educational change in Finland.* New York, NY: Teachers College Press.

Sato, N. E. (2004). *Inside Japanese classrooms.* New York, NY: RoutledgeFalmer.

Silva, K. G., Correa-Chávez, M., & Rogoff, B. (2010). Mexican-heritage children's attention and learning from interactions directed to others. *Child Development, 81*(3), 898–912.

Tobin, J., Hsueh, Y., & Karasawa, M. (2009). *Preschool in three cultures revisited: China, Japan, and the United States.* Chicago, IL: University of Chicago Press.

Tobin, J., Wu, D., & Davidson, D. (1987). Class size and student/teacher ratios. *Comparative Education Review, 31*(4), 533–549.

Tobin, J., Wu, D., & Davidson, D. (1989). *Preschool in three cultures: Japan, China and the United States.* New Haven, CT: Yale University Press.

Walsh, D. (2002). The development of self in Japanese preschools: Negotiating space. In L. Bresler & A. Ardichvili (Eds.), *Research in international education: Experience, theory, and practice* (pp. 213–246). New York, NY: Peter Lang.

Whiting, B., & Edwards, C. (1988). *Children of different worlds.* Cambridge, MA: Harvard University Press.

Chapter 14

Reflecting on and Repositioning Early Childhood Education Research

VIVIAN L. GADSDEN
University of Pennsylvania

FELICE J. LEVINE
American Educational Research Association

Reflecting on this volume and anchoring on future research directions are collaborative tasks for those involved in this project and those who are our readers. Whatever our cross-cutting ambitions at the outset, which were strongly shared by those who participated in our research conference, this book primarily captures the state of our knowledge in early childhood research that has evolved over decades from diverse vantages. In its totality, this work speaks to what is known in our field, identifies gaps, and addresses implications of that knowledge derived from arenas of specialization in early childhood development, education, and child care. In this concluding chapter, we offer some cross-cutting reflections centering on salient contributions and emerging issues and questions. We also briefly consider how a shift in research policies and investments could enable a next generation of integrative scholarship in early childhood education.

What Have We Learned?

In discussions on the well-being of young children, the research on early childhood care, child development, and early childhood education (all referred to here as early childhood research) is represented as separate yet inextricably linked areas of inquiry. The focus on topics such as neuroscience and the developing brain has renewed long-standing questions and sparked new interest in early childhood learning and development in general, as well as in the conditions and multiple contexts of early education. The current research on young children is steeped in debates about quality of care and nurturing, on the one hand, and strengthening learning contexts and supporting parents, on the other.

Despite over five decades of acknowledging the importance of early learning in pre-K, through programs such as Head Start and Early Head Start, and despite countless reports reinforcing the critical nature of children's cognitive and social-emotional development, we find that many young children and their families have little to no entry into high-quality programs, either prior to or during formal schooling. In too many cases, the problems of educational inequality and racial and class disparities are relatively unchanged. As the Introduction to this volume suggests, in early childhood education there have been tensions regarding where to focus attention (e.g., on learning or teaching) and how policy might respond to the needs across the different points of entry into the problem. Nonetheless, researchers and practitioners alike widely acknowledge that the responsibility for ensuring young children's care, education, and healthy development sits with multiple actors—from parents and families to teachers, programs and schools, and communities.

In conceptualizing this volume, we were interested in calling attention to the intersections among early education, child development, and child care. We aimed to examine the reciprocal relationships, rather than the tensions alone, between learning and teaching. In other words, we wanted to use the volume as a space for early childhood specialists, across areas of inquiry, to rethink how efforts in the field can reflect what we have learned and build upon that knowledge. We asked how we might reimagine the field as contributing to emerging and cutting-edge knowledge in the broader field of education and social science research while being beneficiaries of it. We took into account the ways in which the fields of early childhood care, child development, and early childhood education maintain their own identities, integrate knowledge from the three fields, and converge in the service of promoting young children's seamless and healthy growth, learning, and transitions. Rather than seeking a detailed approach, we were intentional in asking for work in which contributors would draw upon their considerable expertise to reflect on two questions: (a) What are the critical research issues in the burgeoning areas on young children? and (b) What research, practice, and policy questions and perspectives are needed to address them?

As is true in other fields, early childhood specialists seek consistency in order to make strong statements about the outcomes of interventions. They seek to respond to the question, What specific dimensions of an approach or intervention contribute to children's later knowledge and practices? Finding consistency in young children's early learning and school experiences is particularly difficult, given children's differential home and educational contexts and the differential availability of resources, quality of care, and exposure to early learning opportunities outside the home. Researchers (e.g., Chaudry & Waldfogel, 2016) have described the system of early childhood education as inadequate and fragmented, noting that most children do not receive high-quality opportunities unless their families have the means to provide them with benefits. Chaudry and Waldfogel note that market-based and privately financed services operate separately from publicly funded programs and serve different populations with different levels of quality. Even when programs' missions are deliberate in addressing poverty rather than race, the racial divide persists (Demma, 2018).

To add to the problem, we now know that countless children in low-resourced homes live in neighborhoods where no pre-K early childhood services exist (Malik, Hamm, Schochet, Novoa, Workman, & Jessen-Howard, 2018), making difficult both the transition to school and the opportunity for pre-K and K–3 efforts to be linked strategically. Municipalities such as Philadelphia have studied the question of access to early child care and learning resources and have initiated efforts (e.g., beverage taxes) to expand the limited number of programs available to children from these families. Although the problems reach into rural areas, the data for cities have been more readily available. Through evaluations such as the MacArthur network's Actionable Intelligence, cities such as Philadelphia have identified "early childhood deserts"—areas where there are no programs or services available to children within a large distance (LeBoeuf, Barghaus, Henderson, Coe, Fantuzzo, & Moore, 2017). In other cities, such as New York, private and public sources have joined together to identify potential pathways for change (Foundation for Child Development, 2018) and are tracking problems associated with poverty (for example, the long-term research and data tracking at the Research Alliance for New York City Schools at New York University).

As the contributors to this volume agree, the overarching goal of early childhood programs and instruction is to meet young children's needs. This goal is fueled by the idea that the playing field can, in fact, be leveled. At the same time, the authors recognize that such leveling will be unsustainable and is unlikely to respond to core issues associated with poverty, racial bias, and the economic and cultural levers that reduce access and opportunity. The intent to improve young children's lives and to provide them with the care, nurturing, and learning they need to achieve, academically and personally, must be matched by efforts to build the capacity of teachers, schools, parents, and families to leverage the resources within and outside their immediate contexts. However, commitments to enhancing early childhood care, child development, and early childhood education are not restricted to teaching and learning, but rely as well on a range of factors related to health and neighborhoods (Duncan & Murnane, 2011; Gadsden, 2014; Halle et al., 2009). Several other factors that bear mentioning have been proposed for creating the physical and social environments that young children need in order to thrive: paid parental leave, child care assistance for children with working parents, universal early education beginning at age 3, and a transformation of Head Start to address the needs of the most disadvantaged (see Chaudry & Waldfogel, 2016; Gadsden, Ford, & Breiner, 2016).

The chapters in this volume attend to an array of issues in early childhood research, practice, and policy. The authors highlight the potential for home and school to work in tandem to promote young children's learning and to support teachers. They identify options for policy at different levels to invoke new understandings of and responses to the needs of children and families. While the authors point to a range of issues and questions in the chapters, we focus here on five cross-cutting themes that examine past work in the field and are forward-looking foci for the field.

1. Curriculum, Teaching, and Classroom Practice

A fundamental assumption in the field is the relationship of early childhood care, child development, and early childhood education to school readiness. Several researchers, including contributors to this volume, have pointed to the reciprocity of expectations and preparation in early schooling for children and schools: That is, just as children must be prepared for school, schools must be prepared for the diversity of children who enter their doors (see Gadsden, 2014; McWayne, McDermott, Fantuzzo, & Culhane, 2007; Stipek, 2002). These researchers also make clear the importance of the transition to school and the content of K–3, reinforcing the point that the curriculum used in early childhood matters, in both substance and delivery. Several instruments have been developed and implemented to measure outcomes. Fewer have focused on the constituent features of curriculum building; children's responses to the different dimensions of a curriculum; and, as fitting, the impact of the curriculum on children's outcomes. The contributors to this volume challenge the assumption that a curriculum alone can effect change, and they shed light on the need to unpack what we mean by "outcomes"—that is, what counts as an outcome and how we know what contributes to it.

The contributors to this volume similarly argue for greater attention to teaching and classroom practices, including teachers' comfort with different curricula and the ethnic and class diversity of students. Without giving up on child-centered approaches, they also agree on the centrality of teachers in bringing the depth and meaning crucial to the curriculum and its potential long-term effects. However, they also point to the need for a teacher workforce that is diversified, consistent with demographic shifts in the United States, and paid at a level commensurate with their responsibilities for young children. In addition, while early childhood programs are ostensibly designed to address school readiness, they differ in how they define a rigorous academic program focused on children's cognitive development (e.g., in math, language, and literacy) and on their social-emotional learning (i.e., how practices around play and discovery are interpreted and addressed). Of equal concern are the practices that are a part of K–12 settings and whether and how they build upon pre-K experiences. Across chapters, the contributors lend support to the importance of curricula that stimulate children's thinking and that are responsive to their learning needs. The authors also underscore the significance of teaching and classroom practices and of inviting parents, families, and communities to be partners.

2. New and Differentially Centered Attention to Professional Development

This volume's focus on professional development includes the curriculum but also foregrounds who teachers are, how they engage in and support their students' inquiry, and what contributes to the formation of teacher identities. All are issues that have been part of the emerging data on teachers, teacher preparation, and teaching (see Introduction, this volume). From the 1987 statement of the National Association for the Education of Young Children to more recent work by Bredekamp (2014) and others, research on the role of teachers has focused on facilitating young children's learning through child-centered approaches, and more recently, on returning to a more directed role for teachers and teacher-child interactions, particularly in K–3 settings. However, the foundational question is not simply whether and when teachers are exposed to professional development activities but, equally important, what will constitute these activities. A mounting body of work has brought attention to professional development in early childhood care and education, particularly in relation to the diversity among young children and their families. Moving away from narrow conceptions of young children and families who are poor, minority, dual language learners, or immigrants as being at risk, to focusing on implicit bias and embedded social structural racism, the field has begun to acknowledge the problems of a one-size-fits-all approach to pedagogy and practice (Takanishi & Le Menestrel, 2017).

The contributors suggest that professional development, by necessity, must take different forms. It may be targeted to a specific type of engagement, such as classroom conversations. It may lean toward new understandings of what children already know and toward fusing what they know into pedagogy and research. It may require that we understand more about language, children's facility in two languages, and increased preparedness to promote language development for dual language learners. It may focus on increasing sensitivities and knowledge of difference and diversity—for example, ethnic, racial, cultural, special needs, gender, and religious diversity. It may be developed around the idea of humanizing both research and practice and creating policies that demonstrate the depth of understanding and the humanization of the field.

Throughout these chapters, the authors point to the possibilities inherent in sound professional development. However, the possibilities are unlikely to be realized in the absence of well-planned approaches and multi-tiered mechanisms aimed at addressing the needs of the whole child and whole family (Fantuzzo, Gadsden, & McDermott, 2011). At once, these approaches and mechanisms will require that researchers, practitioners, and policy makers consider the range of experiences that contribute to young children's vulnerabilities, among them poverty and trauma, while integrating their strengths and the resources of families and communities (Blair & Raver, 2016). In this way, efforts in the field will represent a systemic shift away from weighing the deficits in young children's experiences to crystalizing what children can achieve and what they know. As a result, we will learn more about how teachers engage children and families in meaningful interactions and committed relationships for change.

3. *Contexts for Learning: Home, School, Culture, and Difference*

Sociocultural theories, along with social ecological theory, have come to redefine much of early childhood care, child development, and early childhood education. They have been largely responsible for expanding the focus from the child as a single entity to the physical and emotional spaces where children grow and learn. By focusing on contexts such as home and school and on issues such as culture and difference, we have opportunities to move past superficial references to change. We are positioned to interrogate the meanings attached to these concepts and to determine how they factor into children's and families' "ways of doing and functioning" and their affordances in teaching and implementing curricula. Research studies focus heavily on families as the mediators of children's learning and academic experiences. Yet we appear still to have only modest data on how homes and families contribute to children's school experiences and how learning in school is extended to home. We have equally modest data on the cultural practices that determine families' relationships with schools and notably little knowledge about the cultural dimensions of who (e.g., mother, father, grandparent) in families takes on the responsibility of guiding, nurturing, teaching, and supporting young children's development.

In addition, there are questions about the school lives of children—for example, the component features and nature of the curricula used to teach them, classroom encounters, and the role of policy in shaping the experiences and destinies of children and those who teach them. Programs serving young children and schools have at their disposal information about factors that preclude parents and families from actively engaging with their children's schools and schooling. However, even with good intentions, teachers and schools can contribute to parents' and families' sense of alienation. While home-school partnerships are the hallmark of early childhood efforts, partnerships are laden with issues of authority and power that affect the flow of communication, as well as assumptions, differences in social histories, and stereotypes that influence choices, interactions, and decision making, and that exacerbate mistrust.

Although discussions of diversity have been largely limited to issues of race, class, and gender, diversity refers as well to a number of other factors, such as immigrant origins and status, language, special needs of children, parents' work situations, parents' identities and household configurations, poverty or class status, and literacy levels. Programs often find that they focus on one or two of these with considerable clarity and on others with little direction. In many settings, there may be similarities in the backgrounds and expectations of parents and teachers. However, in programs and schools serving socially marginalized communities, there is often a mismatch between parents' and teachers' socioeconomic experiences, racial and cultural histories, linguistic practices, and experiences with bias, discrimination, and access. Some mismatches may be minor to working with parents, while others may be fundamental to whether and how communication is created and sustained and whether parents feel honored and respected.

Recent discussions about undocumented families have been especially salient, complex, and disturbing, as the core tenets of early childhood development are violated in the treatment of many young children and families at U.S. national borders. The issues of race, class, gender, and difference more broadly are also enormously complicated, as neither teachers nor families represent a singular identity. There is a high likelihood that assumptions will be formed and that assumptions will influence these interactions even in the face of competing data. The question of how families, teachers, and administrators co-construct and communicate the goals for and expectations of their children is critical to teachers' understanding of the home context and parents' and families' ability to embrace the school context.

4. *Refining Conceptualizations and Methodologies Associated With Early Childhood Care, Development, and Education*

In the Introduction and the chapters in this volume, authors urge us to rethink and refine conceptualizations of early childhood care and education. One argument has focused on examining closely the ways in which each major term (*early childhood care, child development,* and *early childhood education*) has been defined and on seeking clarity around the constituent features of each. Such clarity is important to recalculating the possibilities for a more comprehensive approach that covers the multiple dimensions of cognitive and noncognitive factors, of context and the individual, of teachers and classroom practices, of assessment and pedagogy, and of greater understanding of different experiences and identities among young children and families. In particular, the conceptualizations must avoid an either/or paradigm that vacillates between placing children and families versus teachers at the center of the curriculum. Although developmentally appropriate practice continues to be a salient theme for the work done in schools, early childhood care and education, in particular, must consider more than academic learning. It is concerned with the continuum of experiences that children have and the examples of what they know and where they demonstrate what they know, while reconciling what children can do with what they do not know.

A reason to focus on expansive conceptualizations of early childhood care, child development, and early childhood education is to reconsider the methodologies used in practice and research. The U.S. early childhood agenda has been enhanced as a result of its relationship with international efforts (Organisation for Economic Co-operation and Development, 2017). Looking through international lenses—from practices in Japan to classrooms in Brazil and Ghana—allows the field to observe how teachers in other countries, similar to and different from the United States, conceptualize practice, expectations around children's classroom thinking and doing, relationships with parents, and fluid boundaries across school, home, and community. It has the potential to yield new insights. Given the shifts in the demography of the United States and shifts in the questions that will need to be addressed, the quantitative/qualitative divide becomes less prominent in the search for the right questions and the use of fine-tuned methods to uncover nuanced issues. While the focus on multiple methods sufficiently addresses the problem of rigor, the question that persists is what methodological framings serve the field best or the need to humanize our approaches (Gutiérrez, 2018).

5. Intervention Research and Policies Intended to Promote Early Learning Programs Serving Young Children and Their Families

Early childhood care, child development, and early childhood education have been focused heavily on intervention research. Yet there are multiple questions about whether and how intervention research yields the breadth and depth of information needed to effect change. In recently developed initiatives of organizations, municipalities, and foundations, such as the New York City Early Childhood Research Network, focused on young children and families, we find increasing questioning of our purposes and goals. The National Academy of Sciences consensus reports on the workforce (Allen & Kelly, 2015), parenting (Gadsden, Ford, & Breiner, 2016), and dual language learners (Takanishi & Le Menestrel, 2017) all point to the need for a more strategic analysis of issues related to the preparation of teachers and the role of parents. However, the issues facing early childhood care and education are not limited to these extremely important factors. As the authors suggest, questions related to the retention of learning and fadeout have significant practical implications for learning and teaching over the long term and enormous research merit. The issues facing dual language speakers are integrated into questions of immigration and current debates surrounding the poor treatment of young children and their families at U.S. borders and in places around the world.

There is wide agreement that the past 20 years have seen enormous shifts in public funding of early childhood education and early childhood development. From the implementation of the Quality Rating and Improvement System to efforts toward universal enrollment, the field is both vested in and reflecting change, though not necessarily at scale. The data are at best mixed but mostly unsupportive of the idea that these investments have had long-term effects. As Pianta, Downer, and Hamre (2016) wrote, "The evidence suggests that it's time to shift our attention to children's and teachers' everyday experiences in classrooms, and to put those experiences at the core of what we mean by quality in early education" (p. 131). The issues are both "in plain sight" and hidden. Whether transparent or nuanced, they must be teased apart not only in federal initiatives but also at the state and local levels and through multidisciplinary and cross-domain efforts engaging researchers and practitioners.

Research Support and Recommendations

Our aim in undertaking this initiative was to forge new connections in early childhood research across arenas of inquiry that have been largely freestanding in terms of communities of scholars, journals, research training programs, and mechanisms of funding. The conference that formed the backbone of this volume made vivid the benefits that would derive from more intentional integration of the frameworks, methods, and modes of inquiry that are core to research in child development, child care, and early childhood education. Several steps could help catalyze increased connectivity and convergence of research. We hope this volume invites researchers to move in that direction.

Throughout the volume, we explicitly encourage fostering greater cross-field integration. Low-hanging fruit that could immediately be pursued includes initiatives such as the Early Career Fellowship Program in Early Childhood Education and Development, jointly undertaken by AERA in collaboration with the Society for Research in Child Development. For this fellowship a cohort of 22 talented scholars within seven years of their doctoral degrees was selected to build bridges and engage in ongoing communication about their otherwise distinct research interests in child development or education. In addition to promising collaborations across research societies, other low-hanging fruit could include joint traineeships or other programming across departments or units within schools of education or between schools of education and the arts and sciences or professional schools. Also, initiatives could be launched among research institutions or universities to hold seminars or colloquia series to nurture interests, generate new ideas, and stimulate networks of potential collaboration. Some funding is necessary, of course, to allow for modest steps, create incentives, and enhance the legitimacy of moving in new directions. Nevertheless, as financial support is being developed, relevant stakeholders can pursue proactive steps.

Funding for research and research infrastructure can make a difference in each of the arenas that were topics of attention at our conference and led to chapters in this volume. Federal science agencies (e.g., the Institute of Education Sciences, the National Science Foundation, the National Institute of Child Health and Human Development) and private foundations could contribute to breaking down silos through funding initiatives, including seed money grants as well as standard awards. Several public and private agencies that fund education research are undertaking their own rethinking about new, cross-cutting topical areas. We encourage their giving serious thought to advancing multidisciplinary, multimethod convergence in early childhood research.

Designing such projects is beyond the scope of a closing commentary, but it should include attention to building teams with expertise in micro- and macro-contexts and in the diverse care and educative settings in which early childhood learning and development take place. Funding needs also to be of some duration, both to be longitudinal in scope and to address the various contexts and systems that shape the development, education, and care of children of diverse backgrounds and exposures.

Also, to move to the next generation of integrative research, training grants are essential to building a generation of research scholars with the foundational knowledge and methodological savvy to undertake this work. Such programs require a designed curriculum and sufficient fellowship funding to allow for cross-skill training and immersion without distraction from other priorities. Equally important is attention to the design of databases, the use of administrative data, the sharing of data consonant with human research protection, and the support of data archives with dedicated data collections in early childhood research (e.g., Inter-university Consortium for Political and Social Research, Databrary).

Emphasizing the need to invest in human resources, tools, and research facilities and platforms could be viewed as a mere "wish list" creation. However, it would be shortsighted for institutions, in particular research funding agencies, to be dismissive of such forms of support. Big research ideas require the infrastructural capacities and platforms to address them.

Conclusion

Re-envisioning the future of early childhood research builds on the premise that all of children's early experiences are educational—experiences at home, in early education and child care settings, and in other supportive contexts and settings. The chapters in this volume reflect the shifts in early childhood research and practice and the possibilities for deepening our understanding of the clear intersections. The volume comes at a time when several issues have been highlighted in national reports—for example, the workforce, implementation research, parents and parenting, the impact of economic, educational, and health disparities—and when there continues to be heightened interest in early childhood development and education.

Takanishi (2016), in noting the dramatic disparities in access and quality of young children's experiences in the United States, describes efforts around early childhood care, development, and education as "the civil and human rights challenge of our times" (p. 1). The chapters speak overwhelmingly to the issues of quality in children's direct classroom experiences, the nature of classroom interactions, the substance of curricula, the role and significance of teachers and their wherewithal to engage children, and the value of professional development in supporting teachers. However, much of this volume has focused, as intended, on children in low-resourced homes and historically disenfranchised communities.

Even with the breadth of this volume and with attention to disparities in access and support, we appreciate that many significant issues at the intersection of early childhood development and education received only limited mention. Assessing children with developmental delays, diverse abilities and disabilities, and physical and socioemotional limitations and providing educational supports and interventions for these children, their families, and their teachers constitute one such area. There are dedicated scholars specializing in early childhood special education, and their work along with that of other experts in child development creates an additional opportunity for even more integrative and interdisciplinary research of the type called for in this volume. We trust that what we have mapped here will be viewed more as paradigmatic of the possibilities than exhaustive of the topics.

This volume is being released at a precarious moment, when the United States and countries around the globe are experiencing a dual pandemic—Covid-19 and systemic racism reflected in policies and practices that adversely affect some populations disproportionately. The persistent inequalities that have threatened the education and well-being of millions of poor children and families of color over time could not be more visible and devastating. They are measurable with micro-level data over time and across geographic locations worldwide. At the same time, the intensity and intersections of the problems facing children, their families, and early childhood providers and teachers are especially poignant, with the options available to children and families being as fragile and unpredictable as those in the workforce (Whitebook, Phillips, & Howes, 2014). Research on the brain has brought much-needed attention to some of these issues and the tenuous nature of inequality by highlighting the often-masked reality that disproportionate numbers of children may be disadvantaged from the earliest points in their lives.

The perennial questions facing efforts designed to address the needs of low-income families, and low-income families of color in particular, are whether the hardest to reach will be reached, what constitutes positive change, and how to sustain positive change, recognizing the constancy of some institutions (e.g., schools and teachers) and the inconsistencies of social hierarchies and structural inequalities. The challenge and its response sit not only with policy makers but also with researchers, who can support new conceptualizations and the needed transformations in the field, and with teachers, who must try to reach more children and more families through a bounty of rich experiences.

References

Allen, L., & Kelly, B. B. (2015). *Transforming the workforce for children birth through age 8*. Consensus Study Report. Washington, DC: National Academies of Sciences, Engineering, and Medicine.

Blair, C., & Raver, C. C. (2016). Closing the achievement gap through modification of neurocognitive and neuroendocrine function: Results from a cluster randomized controlled trial of an innovative approach to the education of children in kindergarten. *PLOS ONE, 9*(11). Retrieved from https://doi.org/10.1371/journal.pone.0112393

Bredekamp, S. (2014). *Effective practices in early childhood education: Building a foundation* (2nd ed.). Boston, MA: Pearson.

Chaudry, A., & Waldfogel, J. (2016). A 10-year strategy of increased coordination and comprehensive investments in early child development. *Behavioral Science & Policy 2*(1), 47–55.

Demma, R. (2018). *Understanding how parent choice and program leadership foster socioeconomic diversity within high-quality early learning programs: A case study of two Baltimore City sites*. Unpublished doctoral dissertation, University of Pennsylvania.

Duncan, G., & Murnane, R. (Eds.). (2011). *Whither opportunity? Rising inequality, schools, and children's life chances.* New York, NY: Russell Sage Foundation.

Fantuzzo, J., Gadsden, V., & McDermott, P. (2011). An integrated curriculum to improve mathematics, language, and literacy for Head Start children. *American Educational Research Journal, 48*(3), 763–793.

Foundation for Child Development. (2018). *The New York City Early Childhood Research Network: A model for integrating research, policy, and practice.* New York, NY: Author.

Gadsden, V. L. (2014). *Evaluating family and neighborhood context for preK–3.* New York, NY: Foundation for Child Development.

Gadsden, V. L., Ford, M. A., & Breiner, H. (Eds.). (2016). *Parenting matters: Supporting parents of young children, 0–8.* Consensus Study Report. Washington, DC: National Academies of Sciences, Engineering, and Medicine.

Gutiérrez, K. D. (2018). Social design–based experiments: A proleptic approach to literacy. *Literacy Research: Theory, Method, and Practice, 67*(1), 86–108.

Halle, T., Forry, N., Hair, E., Perper, K., Wandner, L., Wessel, J., et al. (2009). *Disparities in early learning and development: Lessons from the Early Childhood Longitudinal Study–Birth Cohort (ECLS-B).* Bethesda, MD: Child Trends.

LeBoeuf, W., Barghaus, K., Henderson, C., Coe, K., Fantuzzo, J., & Moore, J. (2017). *The use of integrated data to inform quality pre-K expansion in Philadelphia.* Philadelphia, PA: Penn Child Research Center.

Malik, R., Hamm, K., Schochet, L., Novoa, C., Workman, S., & Jessen-Howard, S. (2018). *America's child care deserts in 2018.* Washington, DC: Center for American Progress.

McWayne, C., McDermott, P. M., Fantuzzo, J., & Culhane, D. (2007). Employing community data to investigate social and structural dimensions of urban neighborhoods: An early childhood education example. *American Journal of Community Psychology, 39,* 47–60.

National Association for the Education of Young Children. (1987). Position statement on quality, compensation, and affordability in early childhood programs. *Young Children, 43*(1), 31.

Organisation for Economic Co-operation and Development. (2017). *Starting strong 2017: Key OECD indicators on early childhood education and care.* Paris, France: Author. Retrieved from https://doi.org/10.1787/9789264276116-en

Pianta, R., Downer, J., & Hamre, B. (2016). Quality in early education classrooms: Definitions, gaps, and systems. *The Future of Children, 26*(2), 119–137.

Stipek, D. (2002). At what age should children enter kindergarten? A question for policy makers and parents. *Social Policy Report, 16*(2), 3–16.

Takanishi, R. (2016). *First things first! Creating the new American primary school.* New York, NY: Teachers College Press.

Takanishi, R., & Le Menestrel, S. (Eds.). (2017). *Promoting the educational success of children and youth learning English: Promising futures.* Consensus Study Report. Washington, DC: National Academies of Sciences, Engineering, and Medicine.

Whitebook, M., Phillips, D., & Howes, C. (2014). *Worthy work, STILL unlivable wages: The early childhood workforce 25 years after the National Child Care Staffing Study.* Berkeley, CA: Center for the Study of Child Care Employment, University of California, Berkeley.

Name Index

Subject Index

The letter f following a page number indicates a figure, the letter n indicates an endnote, and the letter t indicates a table.

About the Contributors

Editors

Sharon Ryan is professor of early childhood education at Rutgers, the State University of New Jersey. She uses a range of qualitative and mixed methods designs to research early childhood curriculum and policy, teacher education, and professional development. She has published a number of articles, book chapters, and reports in these areas.

M. Elizabeth Graue is Sorenson Professor of Curriculum & Instruction and Director of the Center for Research on Early Childhood Education at the University of Wisconsin, Madison. Her research focuses on early childhood policy and practice. Her recent work has been related to professional development for pre-K teachers on early math and instructional supports and the development of an observation tool for play-based instructional practice.

Vivian L. Gadsden is the William T. Carter Professor of Child Development and Professor of Education at the University of Pennsylvania Graduate School of Education. Her research examines learning across the life-course, with a focus on young children, parents, and families in racially and economically marginalized communities.

Felice J. Levine is executive director of the American Educational Research Association. Her early research emphasized the development of senses of justice and beliefs and behaviors in children and youth. More recently, her work focuses on science policy issues, research ethics, data access/sharing, the academic workforce, and higher education. She is collaborating on an education data resource hub to support discovery, collaboration, and capacity building.

Authors

W. Steven Barnett is Board of Governors Professor of Education and co-director of the National Institute for Early Education Research at Rutgers University. His research interests are in education policy and economics, particularly with respect to public investments in the learning and development of young children. This work includes benefit-cost analyses; studies of long-term impacts on cognitive, social, and economic outcomes; and research into the systemic determinants of classroom quality and effectiveness.

Margaret R. Burchinal is a senior scientist at the Frank Porter Graham Child Development Institute and a research professor in development psychology at the University of North Carolina, Chapel Hill. She was the lead statistician for many major child care studies, including the NICHD Study of Early Child Care and Youth Development. She currently leads one of the IES Early Childhood Network research studies and co-leads an adult follow-up of the Abecedarian Project.

Robert Crosnoe is the associate dean of liberal arts and Rapoport Professor of Sociology at the University of Texas at Austin, where he is also a research associate of the Population Research Center. His main field of interest is child and adolescent development, and he conducts mixed methods research on the connections among educational trajectories, social psychological functioning, and health and how these connections factor into socio-economic and immigration-related inequalities in the United States.

Stephanie M. Curenton is an associate professor at Boston University Wheelock College of Education and Human Development. Her research interests relate to promoting children's health and education using research to inform culturally responsive, anti-bias teaching practices and socially equitable public policies. Curenton studies the social, cognitive, and language development of children within various ecological contexts, such as parent-child interactions, early childhood education programs, early childhood workforce programs, and related state and federal policies.

Megan Franke is a professor of education at the University of California, Los Angeles. Her research focuses on the development of children's mathematical thinking and understanding teacher learning with attention to children's thinking and classroom practice.

Allison H. Friedman-Krauss is an assistant research professor at the National Institute for Early Education Research (NIEER) at Rutgers University. Her research focuses on (a) unpacking impacts of early education interventions, (b) early education quality, and (c) the cognitive and social-emotional development of low-income children. She also works on early childhood education policy issues, including leading work on NIEER's annual *State of Preschool* report.

Eugene E. García is professor emeritus at Arizona State University. He has published 16 books and over 200 articles and book chapters related to bilingual development and educational equity. His most recent book is *An Asset-Based Approach to Latino Education in the United States* (2018), co-authored with Mehmet (Dali) Öztürk (Routledge).

Shari L. Gardner is an education researcher at SRI International's Center for Education Research and Innovation. Her research involves using innovative teaching and learning approaches and digital tools to improve the quality and equity of STEM education for all students—especially early learners, students with disabilities, at-risk students, and students from groups underrepresented in STEM fields.

Bryant Jensen is an associate professor of teacher education at Brigham Young University. His research addresses equitable teaching and learning for Latina/os and other children from marginalized communities. He is especially interested in validating formative uses of measures of teaching to improve schooling and early education programs. Jensen is the lead developer of the Classroom Assessment of Sociocultural Interactions (CASI), an observation measure designed to capture cultural aspects of teacher-child interactions.

Nicholas C. Johnson is an assistant professor in the School of Teacher Education at San Diego State University. His research investigates how young children learn mathematics, and how teachers make sense of and leverage children's ideas in their instructional practice.

Jacqueline Jones is the president and CEO of the Foundation for Child Development. Her current research interests focus on the use of implementation science in providing broader context to the study of early childhood program effectiveness and the role of research-practice partnerships in the application of empirical data to public policy decision-making.

Kristie A. Kauerz is director of the National P–3 Center and associate clinical professor at the School of Education and Human Development at the University of Colorado Denver. Her work is anchored in collaborations with school districts, state agencies, and early learning stakeholders, through which she explores the paradigmatic, organizational, and policy divides that exist between the early care and education (ECE) and K–12 systems.

Brandon McMillan is an assistant professor at Brigham Young University. His research focuses on student mathematical thinking and how educators can leverage student thinking to facilitate development of mathematics understanding, as well as challenge deficit thinking.

Kaitlyn Mumma recently graduated from George Mason University. She is currently working as a senior analyst in early childhood education at Abt Associates. Her research interests focus on early childhood education, school quality, early literacy skills, and dual language learners.

Amy Noelle Parks is an associate professor of elementary and early childhood education at Michigan State University. Her research interests include understanding mathematics classrooms from the perspectives of young children, and she is the author of *Exploring Mathematics Through Play in the Early Childhood Classroom* (Teachers College Press.)

Shana E. Rochester is an inaugural American Association of Colleges for Teacher Education (AACTE)/Holmes Postdoctoral Fellow in Boston University's Wheelock College of Education and Human Development. Her research focuses on how educational contexts (e.g., early childhood classrooms, family-based programs in partnership with elementary schools, museums) affect school-aged children's development. She is particularly interested in the development of African American children, and her work considers the role of family members and/or trained educators in shaping children's academic, cognitive, and social development.

Deborah J. Stipek is the Judy Koch Professor of Education, the Peter E. Haas Faculty Director of the Haas Center for Public Service, and the former I. James Quillen Dean of the Graduate School of Education at Stanford University. Her scholarship concerns instructional effects on children's achievement motivation and early childhood education. She currently chairs the Heising-Simons Development and Research in Early Math Education Network.

Yusra M. Syed is a speech-language pathologist at Emory Healthcare in Atlanta, Georgia. Her research interests and professional endeavors lie in the realms of developmental and neurogenic communication disorders, swallowing and swallowing disorders, and health education and behavioral sciences. She is passionate about working with both pediatric and adult populations, particularly those of cultural and linguistic diversity.

Joseph Tobin is the Elizabeth Garrard Hall Professor of Early Childhood Education at the University of Georgia. His research interests include international comparative studies of early childhood education; immigration and education; children and the media; and video-based research methods. His books include *Preschool in Three Cultures Revisited* and *Children Crossing Borders: Immigrant Parent and Teacher Perspectives on Preschool for Children of Immigrants*.

Angela Chan Turrou is a senior researcher and teacher educator at the University of California, Los Angeles, Graduate School of Education and Information Studies. Her work lives at the intersection of children's mathematical thinking, classroom practice, and teacher learning across early childhood and elementary settings. Turrou seeks to transform school mathematics experiences for our youngest learners.

Anita A. Wager is a professor at Vanderbilt University's Peabody College. Her research focuses on teacher education that supports culturally relevant and socially just mathematics teaching in early childhood and elementary school. In her work with teachers to explore mathematics learning in play-based classrooms, Wager examines how teachers draw on children's resources in and out of schools to plan activities, prepare the environment, and notice mathematical practices that children engage with in play.

Christina Weiland is an associate professor at the University of Michigan. Her research focuses on the effects of early childhood interventions and public policies on children's development, especially on children from low-income families. She is particularly interested in the active ingredients that drive children's gains in successful, at-scale public preschool programs.

Adam Winsler is a professor of applied developmental psychology at George Mason University. His research interests and over 100 publications are on the topics of early childhood education, school readiness, private speech, self-regulation, bilingualism, immigrant student outcomes, the educational trajectories of ethnically diverse students in poverty, and the effect of the arts on child development.